CRUCIBLE OF POWER

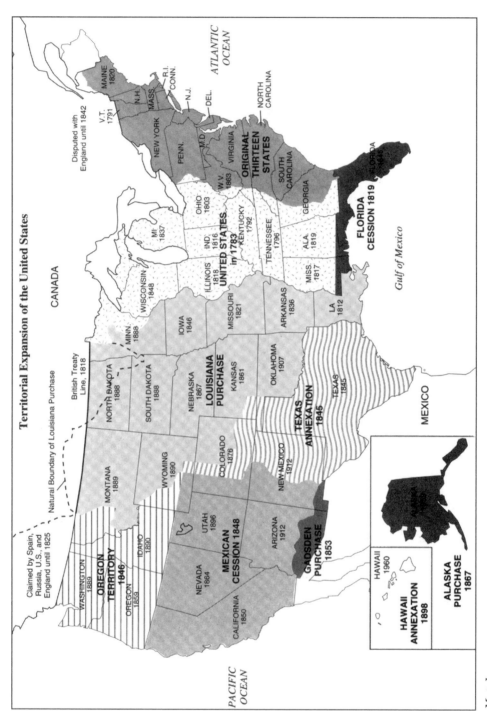

Territorial Expansion of the United States

PACIFIC OCEAN

CANADA

ATLANTIC OCEAN

Claimed by Spain, Russia, U.S. and England until 1825

British Treaty Line, 1818

Natural Boundary of Louisiana Purchase

Disputed with England until 1842

MAINE 1820

V.T. 1791

R.I. CONN.

N.H.

MASS.

N.Y. (NEW YORK)

N.J.

PENN.

DEL.

M.D

VIRGINIA

W.V. 1863

ORIGINAL THIRTEEN STATES

NORTH CAROLINA

SOUTH CAROLINA

GEORGIA

FLORIDA 1845

FLORIDA CESSION 1819

Gulf of Mexico

OHIO 1803

IND. 1816

UNITED STATES in 1783

KENTUCKY 1792

TENNESSEE 1796

ALA. 1819

MISS. 1817

ILLINOIS 1818

MI 1837

WISCONSIN 1848

MINN. 1888

IOWA 1846

MISSOURI 1821

ARKANSAS 1836

LA 1812

NORTH DAKOTA 1888

SOUTH DAKOTA 1888

NEBRASKA 1867

KANSAS 1861

LOUISIANA PURCHASE

OKLAHOMA 1907

TEXAS 1845

TEXAS ANNEXATION 1845

MEXICO

MONTANA 1889

WYOMING 1890

COLORADO 1876

NEW MEXICO 1912

IDAHO 1890

UTAH 1896

MEXICAN CESSION 1848

ARIZONA 1912

GADSDEN PURCHASE 1853

WASHINGTON 1889

OREGON TERRITORY 1846

OREGON 1859

NEVADA 1864

CALIFORNIA 1850

HAWAII 1960

HAWAII ANNEXATION 1898

ALASKA PURCHASE 1867

Map 1

CRUCIBLE OF POWER

A History of American Foreign Relations to 1913

HOWARD JONES

A Scholarly Resources Inc. Imprint
Wilmington, Delaware

Scholarly Resources Inc.
104 Greenhill Avenue
Wilmington, DE 19805-1897
www.scholarly.com

Library of Congress Cataloging-in-Publication Data

Jones, Howard, 1940–
    Crucible of power : a history of American foreign relations to 1913 /
Howard Jones.
      p.   cm.
    Includes bibliographical references and index.
    ISBN 0-8420-2916-8 (pbk.)
    1. United States—Foreign relations—To 1865.   2. United States—
Foreign relations—1865–1921. I. Title.

E183.7 .J743 2002
327.73–dc21

                                           2001054183

In Memory of Howie

ABOUT THE AUTHOR

Howard Jones received a Ph.D. from Indiana University and taught at the University of Nebraska before coming to the University of Alabama in 1974. He is now University Research Professor in the Department of History. A recipient of both the John F. Burnum Distinguished Faculty Award for teaching and research and the Blackmon-Moody Outstanding Professor Award, he teaches courses in American foreign relations and the U.S.-Vietnam War.

He is the author or editor of more than a dozen books, including *To the Webster-Ashburton Treaty: A Study in Anglo-American Relations, 1783–1843* (1977)—recipient of the Phi Alpha Theta Book Award and nominated for the Pulitzer Prize and the Stuart L. Bernath Book Award; *Mutiny on the Amistad: The Saga of a Slave Revolt and Its Impact on American Abolition, Law, and Diplomacy* (1987, revised 1997)—used in writing the screenplay for Steven Spielberg's movie "Amistad" and a selection of Book-of-the-Month Club, History Book Club, and Quality Paperbacks Book Club; *"A New Kind of War": America's Global Strategy and the Truman Doctrine in Greece* (1989)—nominated for the Harry S. Truman Book Award and for the Phi Alpha Theta Book Award; with Randall B. Woods, *Dawning of the Cold War: The United States' Quest for Order* (1991)—nominated for the Warren F. Kuehl Award and for the George Louis Beer Prize; *Union in Peril: The Crisis over British Intervention in the Civil War* (1992)—a History Book Club Selection and winner of the Phi Alpha Theta Book Award; with Donald A. Rakestraw, *Prologue to Manifest Destiny: Anglo-American Relations in the 1840s* (1997)—recognized by *Choice* magazine as one of the "Outstanding Academic Books" for 1997; and *Abraham Lincoln and a New Birth of Freedom: The Union and Slavery in the Diplomacy of the Civil War* (1999)—nominated for the Lincoln Prize and the Bancroft Prize. He has published articles in several journals, the most recent in the *Journal of American History* as the centerpiece of a forum and entitled "Cinqué of the *Amistad* a Slave Trader? Perpetuating a Myth." He is presently completing a book entitled *Death of a Generation: John F. Kennedy and Vietnam.*

CONTENTS

LIST OF MAPS

ACKNOWLEDGMENTS

This book, like most publications, has benefited from the contributions of others. Superb suggestions have come from both undergraduate and graduate students here at the University of Alabama, as well as from numerous friends in the profession along with the anonymous readers of the manuscript. In particular, I wish to thank Carol Jackson Adams, John Belohlavek, Kinley Brauer, Susan Brewer, Douglas Brinkley, Paul C. Clark, Robert A. Divine, Robert H. Ferrell, Mark Gilderhus, Paul Grass, Mary Ann Heiss, Peter Hill, Tim Johnson, Tim Maga, Pete Maslowski, Forrest and Ellen McDonald, Teresa Peebles, Donald A. Rakestraw, Guy Swanson, and Randall B. Woods for their encouragement along with many useful comments. For helping me through the countless trials and tribulations of securing the illustrations, I thank Scott Keller and Nancy Smelley. No one can write a book without the gift of time. For affording me that precious commodity, I express sincere gratitude to Kay Branyon, Loretta Colvin, Julie P. Moore, Nancy (again), and Fay Wheat.

On a more personal level, I wish to express appreciation to the most important people in my life—my family. Only these loved ones understand the time and solitude required in research and writing, and only they were willing to put up with my short temper and abrasive behavior as I attempted to make sense out of my many meaningless sentences and hopelessly tangled paragraphs. To my parents, to my spouse and closest confidante, Mary Ann, to my daughters Deborah and Shari, to Howie, whose brief life provided us with lasting memories, and to the lights of our lives—my grandchildren, Ashley and Timothy—I extend heartfelt gratitude for your patience and, most important, your love.

Howard Jones
Tuscaloosa, Alabama, Fall 2001

PREFACE

The central theme of America's foreign relations has been the long and steady rise of the republic to world power, followed by its gradual assumption of the position it occupies today: the first among several prominent nations. The history of U.S. foreign affairs comprises a fascinating account of a growing empire based on principles of self-government that made it unique from the Old World. In no way can a history of the United States stand as complete without the incorporation of its foreign policy. And yet, in too many instances this part of the nation's history has not received its due. In a finely crafted television documentary of the Civil War, for example, foreign affairs won barely a mention—despite all manner of documentation establishing the Lincoln administration's feverish concern about preventing a British intervention that could have profoundly affected the outcome of the war and impeded the growth of the United States to world power.

Washington's leaders have been fairly consistent in promoting the national interest as they perceived it. Whereas European diplomats talked almost exclusively of power relationships, strategic considerations, economic interests, and imperialist aims, Americans emphasized, along with those same realities, certain ideals that made their country exceptional: natural rights; the republican ideas of popular rule, free trade, neutral rights, and freedom of the seas; a missionary spirit that permeated its expansionist impulse; the separation of political and economic concerns in foreign policy; and freedom from Old World political and military entanglements. At the same time, however, they recognized that their major objective was to protect the nation's vital interests.

This work seeks to demonstrate the complexities involved in the decision-making process that led to the rise and decline of the United States (relative to the ascent of other nations) in world power status. It focuses on the personalities, security interests, and expansionist tendencies behind the formulation and implementation of U.S. foreign policy. It highlights the intimate relationship between foreign and domestic policy. It gives due attention to the historical antecedents of the nation's twentieth-century foreign policy. And it relies on the natural chronology of events to organize and narrate the story as the nation's leaders saw it. Policymaking cannot take place in a vacuum. Events occur concurrently and day after day, only at times appearing to be manageable. No one should expect contemporary leaders in Washington to grasp the intricate relationships among events and peoples world-wide that we as historians—with the advantage of hindsight—attempt to do.

Only a narrative approach can uncover the tangled and often confusing nature of foreign affairs. The compartmentalization of individual topics in thematic chapters tends to impose a design on these events that did not exist. A topical approach can create the illusion that history takes place in a well-ordered fashion, making policymakers vulnerable to unwarrantable criticisms for failing to discern "patterns" of behavior or "lessons" in history. Should readers recognize that events are largely uncontrollable, they will understand the plight of policymakers who daily encounter a kaleidoscopic array of problems rarely susceptible to simple analysis and ready solution. If readers come to realize that the outcome of events is not inevitable and that the complexity of history makes decision-making a difficult process, this book will have served its purpose.

Hopefully this work will stand on the strengths of readability, organization, accuracy, and fairness. My intention is to offer a straightforward, balanced, and comprehensive history of the major events in the nation's foreign affairs, from the American Revolution to the present. Readers wanting more detailed accounts should examine the many fine articles and monographic studies cited in the "Selected Readings" following each chapter. For citations (and summations) to these and numerous other historical works, they should consult the superb *Guide to American Foreign Relations since 1700,* edited by Richard Dean Burns and soon to be available in a revised, updated version. Also invaluable is the four-volume *Encyclopedia of U.S. Foreign Relations,* edited by Bruce W. Jentleson and Thomas G. Paterson. Finally, they should read the first-class journal of our profession, *Diplomatic History,* which features articles that often stand at the cutting edge of the field.

CHAPTER 1

The Revolutionary Beginnings of American Foreign Policy, 1775–1789

Colonial Background of the American Revolution

The diplomacy of the American Revolution focused on winning independence from England while warding off the imperial interests of France and Spain. To achieve these objectives, the American colonists often expressed idealistic convictions though recognizing the primacy of power politics. European leaders directed their craft toward the pursuit of power and profit; the Americans sought many of the same objectives but softened the language by propounding a God-given "law of nations" that governed—or ought to govern—international relations. One principle never changed. In the course of their first involvement in foreign affairs, the Americans set the pattern for succeeding generations by pursuing their own security above all else.

America's pronouncements were rooted in its colonial past. When the early Puritans proclaimed that they were building a new Zion, a "city on a hill" which would serve as a model for the corrupt Old World to follow, they established the basis for isolationism, the American goal of non-entanglement in European political affairs. From English political writers, mainly John Locke, they learned natural rights' theory; from the French and Scottish Enlight-

enments they learned to despise and distrust what they perceived to be the deceit and trickery of formal diplomacy. Americans also learned to believe in free trade, freedom of the seas, and peaceful intercourse among nations. These objectives were an integral part of American interests because adherence to them offered protection against the Old World. When America's early diplomats—particularly Benjamin Franklin but also John Jay and John Adams—dealt with the Old World, they recognized that any nation's prime goal was to protect self-interest through the use of power.

During the colonial and early national periods of American history the prime determinants of international relations derived not from the New World but from the Old. Between 1689 and 1815 the nations of Europe, especially Britain and France, were locked in almost continuous struggle, and in that struggle the Americans were little more than pawns. During that long and tumultuous period, Spain, Austria, Prussia, and other powers shifted sides, and America broke imperial ties and fought its first two wars as a nation; but through it all, the central antagonists remained England and France. These countries fought each other seven times in that era, and in so doing they engulfed much of the world in sixty years of warfare.

1

The last of the colonial wars—variously known as the French and Indian War, the Seven Years' War, and the Great War for the Empire—ended in 1763 with Britain in command of North America and, on paper at least, the most powerful country in the Western world. Outside North America the British preserved the European balance of power, maintained supremacy at sea, and gained a strong political base in India that stimulated business and territorial occupation. Inside North America their forces wrested Canada from France along with all its land claims east of the Mis-

sissippi River. On securing Florida from Spain (France's ally in the war), Britain held the entire eastern half of North America from the Hudson Bay to the Gulf of Mexico. In addition, Britain retained a number of West Indian islands captured during the war. Of its once vast empire, France managed to keep two islands in the West Indies—Guadeloupe and Martinique—and two small ones off Newfoundland—Miquelon and St. Pierre. The British restored Cuba to Spain in exchange for the latter's agreement to grant navigation rights on the Mississippi to the British, and, as compen-

Map 2
The most striking difference between Map 2 and Map 3 (opposite page) is the almost total absence of France from North America. This humiliation at the peace table helped encourage the French to join the Americans in the Revolutionary War against England.

sation for losing Florida, Spain received New Orleans and Louisiana from France.

The French had lost not only the war but also the peace, meaning that the Treaty of Paris of 1763 offered little prospect for ending Anglo-French hostilities. To those French people who could recall their nation's magnificence under King Louis XIV, it was mortifying to suffer such devastating losses on the battlefields; to incur humiliation at the peace table proved too much to bear. The elder William Pitt of England had stirred up a relentless drive for empire, and the diplomats at Paris responded by imposing severe peace terms. The French burned with the spirit of revenge, making another Anglo-French war predictable.

Meanwhile, France's removal from North America encouraged a feeling of commonality among Americans that served as the prelude to independence. The colonists believed they no longer needed the protection of the British Empire, whereas the London government desperately sought to rebuild its financial base and could no longer ignore the colonists' long-time pattern of flagrantly violating imperial regulations. Thus in a highly volatile coincidence in history, Englishmen at home sought to tighten the bonds of empire—and to require the colonists to share the burden of maintaining it—at precisely the time when the colonists no longer regarded those close ties as necessary. In the explosive pre-Revolutionary decade of the 1760s, colonial Americans tried

Map 3

to avoid paying taxes and obeying laws that they regarded as unjust. At stake, they claimed, were fundamental liberties stemming from natural law and therefore holding precedence over human law. They defended their position with ringing appeals to the "rights of Englishmen" and the "rights of man."

The path to revolution lay pockmarked by mutual misperceptions and misunderstandings. England's priority after 1763 was to tax the American colonies in an effort to pay for the French and Indian War as well as to meet the costs of the new North American empire. The colonists' priority was to enjoy a newly acquired right to autonomy within the empire. The London government indignantly believed that its North American colonies had fought only when their own interests were at stake. The colonists, however, regarded their role in the war as crucial to the empire's victory and expected a greater voice in its governance. British relations with France's former Indian allies presented an acute and double-edged problem. Not only must the crown placate those Native Americans most in danger of losing their homeland to a host of migrating colonists, but it must also satisfy those same land-hungry settlers who felt it their right to take such land.

The result was more trouble. Parliament drew a fiercely negative reaction from across the Atlantic when it issued the Proclamation of 1763 restricting Americans from moving west of the Appalachian Mountains. Although the British meant this proclamation as a temporary measure to help defuse an Indian uprising led by Pontiac of the Ottawas while allowing a survey of the land for orderly sale, they failed to make these objectives clear. Then, as the British passed a series of tax measures, the Americans complained about "no taxation without representation" and found a sympathetic audience among more than a few observers in England. Whig Edmund Burke in the House of Commons warned against such taxation and came to view the Americans as defenders of personal liberty against royal tyranny. The colonists soon believed that the

king had become the instrument of court conspirators who sought to destroy freedom through tyrannical rule. This heated atmosphere made revolution only a matter of time.

When the colonists rebelled and sought foreign assistance, they came face to face with a Western world that remained a group of predatory nation-states, monarchical in form and spirit while committed to mercantilism or commercial domination through the acquisition of colonies. Such possessions, according to theory, provided the mother country with the commerce that yielded the gold and silver so necessary to empire. Indeed, the only safeguard against war seemed to be a raw balance of power that had converted the interests of the European powers from nearby small nations to overseas colonies. The law of nations exercised only partial restraints. Despite the Enlightenment's call for natural rights, the Old World rigidly clung to the divine right of kings theory and continued its timeless preparations for war and empire. The resumption of the Anglo-French struggle drove home these fundamental truths during the formative era of the United States.

The French Alliance

The American colonists quickly became immersed in the realities of world politics during the turbulent aftermath of the French and Indian War. In the words of William Pitt, France took on the shadowy image of a "vulture hovering over the British empire, and hungrily watching the prey that she is only waiting for the right moment to pounce upon." The French foreign minister, Étienne-François, Duc de Choiseul, sent instructions to his agents that denounced England as evil and urged the American colonists to rebel against the crown. The expulsion of his beloved France from North America, he warned, had not satiated Britain's relentless drive for empire; it now craved the remainder of Spain's New World holdings as well. Choiseul complained to King Louis XV that England was a permanent enemy who sought to control the world's commercial lifelines. The fiery foreign minister fell from grace in 1770, in part because the king feared that his incessant scheming could lead to premature war with England.

From 1764 through the outbreak of their own revolution in 1789, the French engaged in numerous clandestine activities designed to avenge the humiliation of the Treaty of Paris. They disrupted English commercial and colonial policies, secretly supported the Americans in their protests against unpopular legislation, and led them to believe that a break with the mother country would guarantee French military assistance. French hopes rose with the furor over the Stamp Act of 1765, the Tea Act and Boston Tea Party of 1773, the Intolerable Acts of the following year, and the outburst of fighting at Lexington and Concord in

Comte de Vergennes
French foreign minister who hated England and secretly approved assistance to the Americans even before the Declaration of Independence. *Charles Gravier, Comte Vergennes. Engraved by Vangeliste after a portrait by A. F. Caller. Reproduced courtesy of the Franklin Collection, Yale University Library.*

1775. The French readied themselves to take advantage of the impending collapse of the British Empire.

Choiseul's removal had not stemmed France's official hatred for the English, because in 1774 the new foreign minister under King Louis XVI, Charles Gravier, Comte de Vergennes, made clear that the French quest for revenge remained the driving force behind their foreign policy. Although debonair in manner and outwardly calm, Vergennes inwardly seethed with anger. But no one had doubts about his position. At one point he declared that "England is the natural enemy of France; and she is a greedy enemy, ambitious, unjust and treacherous: The unalterable and cherished object of her policy is, if not the destruction of France, at least her degradation and ruin." France's duty, he insisted, was to destroy England.

Vergennes's opportunity for striking at England came through the machinations of a Frenchman of many talents, Pierre Augustin Caron de Beaumarchais. A master of intrigue, Beaumarchais was also a poet, musician, playwright author of the comedies *The Barber of Seville* and *The Marriage of Figaro,* and celebrated maker of a watch so small that Madame de Pompadour, the French king's mistress, could wear it in a ring on her finger. Beaumarchais, working as secret agent for the crown, had found an eager listener in Virginia businessman Arthur Lee in London about the massive unrest in the British colonies, and in early 1776 he suggested to his French government that it encourage the rebellion in America by extending secret military aid in the guise of a loan. His arguments were persuasive. Bolstered by a matching contribution from King Charles III of Spain, French aid to America began in May 1776 through Beaumarchais, who worked under the name of a fictitious front organization called Roderigue Hortalez and Company. Only French finance minister Baron Turgot opposed the arrangement, insisting that American independence would take place regardless of French actions and warning that England would gain the most from the resulting growth in Atlantic commerce. He resigned in futility ten days later, following his prophetic warning that such drains upon the French treasury would add to the heavy burden of a general French military and naval buildup and ultimately lead to bankruptcy. Thus, before the Declaration of Independence and even prior to the arrival of American emissaries in Paris, Hortalez and Company sent America muskets, cannons, cannon balls and powder, bombs, mortars, tents, and enough clothing for 30,000 men. It is no exaggeration to say that French (and Spanish) assistance kept American hopes alive during the crucial spring of 1776.

The growing rebellious mood in America during early 1776 had still needed a spokes-man who could mobilize the dissatisfied colonists into a concerted drive for independence; such a spokesman appeared in the form of Thomas Paine, who had only recently arrived in America from an England he had grown to hate. In his incendiary pamphlet *Common Sense,* the most widely read document of the American Revolution except the Declaration of Independence itself, Paine put his acerbic wit to work in arguing that independence was the only way for America to avoid entanglements in Old World affairs. He also recognized the value of breaking with British mercantile policies and moving toward free trade. "There is something absurd," he declared, "in supposing a continent to be perpetually governed by an island." The British monarchy was "the most prosperous invention the Devil ever set on foot for the promotion of idolatry." Reconciliation with the "royal brute" and his court conspirators was out of the question. "Any submission to, or dependence on, Great Britain," he wrote, "tends directly to involve this Continent in European wars and quarrels, and set[s] us at variance with nations who would otherwise seek our friendship, and against whom we have neither anger nor complaint." American foreign policy, he declared, should be independent of Old World political alliances and built on the doctrine of freedom of the seas. "Our plan is commerce, and that, well attended to, will secure us the peace and friendship of all Europe."

Thomas Paine
The author of *Common Sense,* he urged Americans to push for indepencence from England and refrain from political entanglements with the Old World. *A 1793 engraving by William Sharp; Library of Congress.*

Although Paine expressed what many Americans had already been saying in the months following Lexington, he made them realize the impossibility of returning to the empire of 1763. The central problem, as he and his thousands of readers saw it, lay so deeply engrained in the Anglo-American relationship that a total break with the monarchy and British constitution was unavoidable. "We have it in our power," Paine proclaimed, "to begin the world over again." Paine's writings bestowed a Christian cast on American events and challenged the colonists to seek nothing less than liberty. *Common Sense* dictated a push for independence.

The Congress Voting Independence
Signatories of this document attempted not only to justify the movement for
independence, but also to establish the credibility of the United States as a step
toward securing foreign alliances. *Painting by Robert Edge Pine (completed after his
death by Edward Savage) displayed in Independence Hall, Philadelphia; Independent
National Historical Park Collection.*

In June 1776, when Richard Henry Lee
introduced in the Continental Congress his
resolution for independence, he also proposed
the immediate negotiation of treaties of alliance with Britain's principal enemies. The
author of the ensuing Declaration of Independence, Thomas Jefferson, drew heavily
from John Locke's contract theory of government in providing a moral and intellectual
justification for a move toward independence
already achieved in the hearts and minds of
Americans. Jefferson rejected the divine right
of kings theory in attributing the major share
of the crisis to King George III, who had
allegedly violated the Americans' natural or
"inalienable rights" of "life, liberty, and the
pursuit of happiness." The revolution was a
respectable action that deserved worldwide
acclamation.

Americans recognized the necessity of proving their credibility to the world. Lee told fellow Virginian Patrick Henry that independence
was the only way to ensure a foreign alliance;
no European state would deal with the Americans as long as they remained Britain's colonists. On the face of things, the Americans'
eager courting of European monarchs seemed
to contradict their professed ideals and their
aversion to foreign entanglements. But some
Americans were realistic enough to know that
they could not win their independence from
Britain without French help, and yet idealistic
enough to believe that they could benefit from
such assistance without incurring long-lasting
obligations.

To secure outside assistance, the Continental Congress appointed John Adams as
head of a committee to draft a "model treaty"

(or "Plan of 1776") to guide formal negotiations with France and other interested nations. As principal architect of the model treaty in September 1776, Adams issued a warning similar to Paine's: Americans must avoid entangling political alliances. "I am not for soliciting any political connection, or military assistance, or indeed naval, from France," Adams wrote an acquaintance. "I wish for nothing but commerce, a mere marine treaty with them." His model treaty called for the separation of political and economic concerns and for recognition of the principles of "free [neutral] ships, free [neutral] goods," and freedom of the seas based on reciprocal commercial arrangements. Adams refused to offer France any political concessions for fear that Vergennes would ask for Canada and the fisheries of Newfoundland; he proposed instead to entice the French with the prospect of ending British commercial dominance of North America.

Like Paine, Adams wanted to draw all Europe into the American market, on the theory that by establishing commercial ties with several nations the fledgling republic could avoid the danger of dependence on any single nation. In the spirit of the Enlightenment, Adams sought to establish a peace based on world economic interdependence. Thus his treaty guide was idealistic in conception and realistic in purpose. To guarantee the new nation commercial advantages without political obligations, the guide offered France trading opportunities in the New World, which then belonged to England. The model treaty exemplified the finest form of foreign policy—idealism, balanced with realism.

Meanwhile, the Continental Congress in Philadelphia prepared to implement the model treaty by sending a three-member delegation to France. Some months earlier Congress had asked Arthur Lee, the same American who had talked with Beaumarchais, to submit reports on European attitudes toward the growing unrest in America. Congress, not aware of Beaumarchais's secret preparations for aid, had also dispatched Connecticut congressman Silas Deane to Paris to seek military assistance. It

Benjamin Franklin
Regarded by many in Europe at the Enlightenment personified, he was instrumental in negotiating the Franco-American Treaties of 1778 and the Treaty of Paris of 1783 ending the Revolutionary War. *Painting ca. 1789; Historical Society of Pennsylvania.*

now appointed Franklin, Jefferson, and Lee to join Deane in France. Only Franklin made the trip: Jefferson turned down the appointment because of his wife's ill health, and Lee was already with Deane in Paris.

Lee and Deane were as new to the world of diplomacy as the American militia was to war, but Franklin had long since become master of the trade. In addition to sixteen years as Pennsylvania's agent in London, he had earlier, in 1754, presented the Albany Plan of Union in a vain effort to unite the colonies for defensive reasons while establishing a closer bond with England. Franklin had learned to be shrewdly non-pretentious. Plainspoken, simply dressed, and deceptively humble, he was capable of arranging the truth as it suited him. He also realized the importance of American expansion to security. Besides representing the people who had taken the lead in resisting the hated British, he had one other distinct advantage when he arrived in Paris in December of 1776: The French regarded him as the embodiment of the Enlightenment in America. Inventor of the lightning rod, stove, harmonica, bifocals; author of the immensely popular and internationally read pieces of wisdom in *Poor Richard's Almanack;* natural philosopher who, like Jefferson, had won an honored place in the French Academy—these were only a few of the achievements credited to the seventy-year-old Franklin by the French "philosophes" who revered science and reason. The image as much as the reality of this wealthy, wily, colorful, and extraordinarily gifted man helped to convince the French court, intellectuals, and common people that aid to America would bring down the lofty British and further the cause of humanity.

Realistic considerations, however, governed French international behavior. Despite Franklin's highly favorable impact on the French, and despite the all-consuming French desire to humble the British, the Vergennes ministry held back on formal recognition of the United States and official extension of military aid. Such decisions could not be taken lightly, for they surely entailed war with England—and probably without Spain, France's closest ally. King Charles III of Spain certainly wanted England brought down: It had recently taken both Gibraltar (1704) and Florida (1763) from his beloved country. Yet the Spanish recognized the danger of example. Could the monarchy assist republicans engaged in revolution and not expect to encourage a similar eruption among its own colonies in New

Battle of Saratoga
British Gen. John Burgoyne's surrender to American forces in upper New York late in 1777 ultimately assured French recognition of the United States. *Henry Cabot Lodge,* The Story of the Revolution, *1898.*

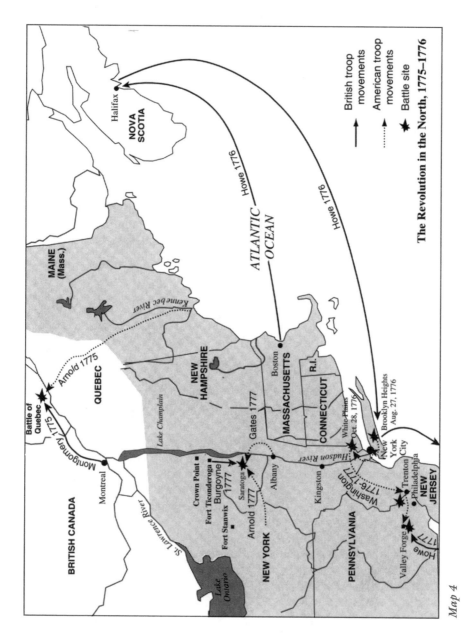

The Revolution in the North, 1775–1776

British troop movements

American troop movements

Battle site

ATLANTIC OCEAN

Halifax

NOVA SCOTIA

Howe 1776

Howe 1776

BRITISH CANADA

Montreal

Battle of Quebec

Montgomery 1775

Arnold 1775

QUEBEC

St. Lawrence River

Lake Ontario

Kennebec River

MAINE (Mass.)

Lake Champlain

NEW HAMPSHIRE

Crown Point

Fort Ticonderoga

Fort Stanwix

Burgoyne 1777

Saratoga 1777

Arnold 1777

Gates 1777

Albany

Kingston

Hudson River

NEW YORK

PENNSYLVANIA

Washington 1776–1777

Trenton

Philadelphia

Valley Forge

Howe 1777

NEW JERSEY

White Plains Oct. 28, 1776

New York City

Brooklyn Heights Aug. 27, 1776

Boston

MASSACHUSETTS

R.I.

CONNECTICUT

Map 4
The American Revolution in the North.

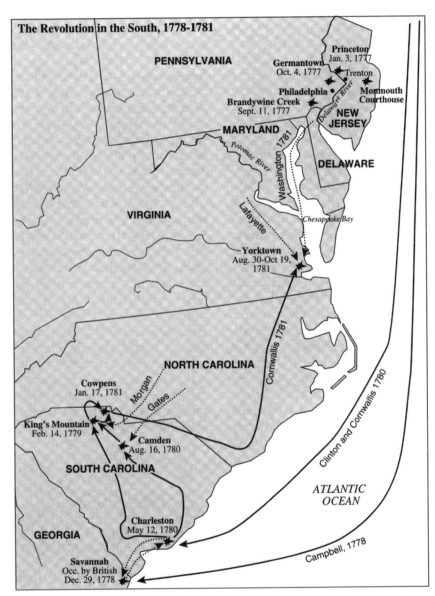

Map 5
The American Revolution in the South.

Spain? Would an independent United States confine itself east of the Appalachian Mountains, not daring to threaten Spain's interests in the Mississippi Valley? Another problem for the French was the Americans' unproven military ability. In a memorandum to the French king, Vergennes wrote that France should avoid a deeper involvement until the Americans established their credibility with a decisive battlefield victory. Such a victory was long in coming: In the dreary months following the brief exultation of July 1776, American prospects for success in the crucial Philadelphia area dimmed as the Continental Army under General George Washington lost to Sir William Howe's forces at Brandywine and Germantown in the autumn of 1777 and went on to suffer horrendous hardships during the ensuing winter at Valley Forge.

Yet the tide had already begun to turn in that same dismal autumn of 1777. The British continued their offensive from the north, intending to divide New England from the rest of the colonies and take Philadelphia. From New York City, Howe was to follow the Hudson River (then called the North River) northward to Albany, where he would join General John Burgoyne marching south out of Canada. Unaccountably, Howe did not follow these plans. He instead moved south by himself and took the capital of Philadelphia, while Burgoyne went on to defeat in upper New York near a little village called Saratoga, on October 17, 1777. Stunned by the loss, Burgoyne urged leaders in London to seek an immediate peace.

America's victory at Saratoga quickly took its place as an epoch in world history. The news arrived in France early in December and set off waves of enthusiasm for the Americans, whereas in England a distraught Lord North as prime minister immediately moved for conciliation. A secret agent, Paul Wentworth, made his way to the Americans in Paris to offer assurances of fair treatment if their people across the ocean would resume their rightful position within the empire. Finding his audience unreceptive during that early January of 1778, Wentworth impatiently sputtered that England would continue the war for another decade rather than grant independence. "America," Franklin crisply replied, "is ready to fight fifty years to win it." In the meantime he cunningly placed additional pressure on Vergennes by leaking news of the British offer to the French. The foreign minister may already have gathered this information from the spies following Wentworth; two days after Franklin's conversation with the British agent, a French official asked Franklin how to prevent America from settling with England on anything other than total independence. A commercial and military alliance, Franklin deftly responded. That same day, January 8, 1778, Franco-American negotiations began in Paris, and less than a month afterward, on February 6, the diplomats concluded two path-breaking treaties.

The Franco-American treaties adhered only in part to Adams's guidelines of 1776. The first, the Treaty of Amity and Commerce, closely followed the idealistic principles of the model treaty. It signified French recognition of the United States; called for a restricted list of contraband or illicit goods that did not include naval stores and foodstuffs; endorsed the rights of neutrals to trade with belligerent or war-making nations; recognized the principle of "free ships, free goods," in that no confiscation of nonmilitary materials could take place when a ship showed neutral colors; and included a "most favored-nation-clause," which declared that if either nation allowed commercial benefits to others, each signatory to the treaty would share in those same privileges.

The second agreement, the Treaty of Alliance, reflected the realities of the international situation. Colonial experience, Thomas Paine's influence, and model treaty notwithstanding, the American negotiators in Paris agreed to a military pact that would become effective in the event of a war between France and England. The United States and France promised not to make peace until American independence was definite and vowed that neither party would enter a separate peace with the British without the other's formal approval. Article XI of the Treaty of Alliance would have troublesome implications in the future, for in it the United States and France mutually guaranteed their claims to territory in North America, "from the present time and forever against all other powers."

The negotiations between France and America, though secret, became known to the British within two days of the treaties' signatures because Franklin's personal secretary, Dr. Edward Bancroft, was a spy. When Silas Deane first arrived in Paris in July 1776 as an agent of the Continental Congress, he had been delighted to find his old friend Bancroft working with the American delegation. Not knowing that Bancroft was also in the private employ of the British, Deane permitted him to serve as interpreter during the discussions with Beaumarchais concerning the delivery of French goods to the American armies. Indeed, Deane eventually shared so many official secrets with Bancroft that King George III moaned that the days were not long enough to read them all. During the treaty talks of 1778, Bancroft kept a steady stream of information flowing to London—including copies of the treaties themselves.

Bancroft's reports persuaded the British government to try to stop America's ratification of the French alliance by sending a mission to America, headed by Lord Carlisle, to offer local autonomy and restoration of the empire as it existed in 1763. Unfortunately for the British, the treaties reached Philadelphia before the Carlisle mission did, and on May 4, just two days after their arrival, Congress approved the twin pacts. A month later Carlisle's group arrived, only to find that Congress refused to meet with the men until they agreed to discuss British evacuation of America and recognition of American independence. After five months of arguments, threats, and attempted bribery, the mission returned home in failure.

The Treaty of Alliance filled Americans with such exhilaration that, for the moment, they forgot all talk of model treaties. Wash-ington happily declared from the bitter cold of Valley Forge that the alliance ensured independence, and even the usually staid John Adams hailed the pact as a major triumph for the United States. The exuberance over the French treaty temporarily clouded its inherent danger. Despite earlier pronouncements about the great attributes of isolationism, America's diplomats had taken an international course by enmeshing their people's future in European political affairs. Furthermore, they had done so on a permanent basis.

On June 17, 1778, the French and English navies clashed in the English Channel, and the strange military alliance of monarchy and republic went into effect. The Franco-American Treaty of 1778 became the first entangling alliance with Europe entered into by the United States, and it would be the last until the mid-twentieth century, when the nation signed the Declaration of the United Nations against the Axis powers in 1942 and seven years later became part of the North Atlantic Treaty Organization.

Diplomacy of War

Encouraged by its success with France, the United States tried to build alliances with Spain, Russia, and the Netherlands as well. Although French desire for vengeance had overcome French dictates of caution, other countries were uncomfortable with America's revolutionary principles, fearful of British retaliation if the Franco-American effort failed, and more concerned with commercial and territorial goals than with the independence and integrity of the United States. These nations found it safer to stand behind the shield of neutrality—at least until the verdict of the war became clear.

Americans first tried to persuade the Spanish to increase their secret aid, but the Madrid government perceived the fledgling nation as a new danger in North America and became even more hesitant about helping the rebels. The truth is that Spain's decision to help the Americans was attributable to its desire to see the English and their former colonists exhaust each other in battle. A Spanish diplomat best expressed his country's fears: [The American] "republic has been born as it were a pigmy. But a day will come when it will be a great, a veritable awe-inspiring colossus in these regions." After the battle of Saratoga, the Spanish actually cut back assistance to the young nation.

After the signing of the treaties of 1778, France exerted enormous pressure on Spain to help the Americans, for Vergennes was convinced that success against Britain depended on Spanish naval support. In truth, Vergennes was negotiating from a tenuous position because, in his zeal to defeat the British, he had severely strained relations with Spain by supporting Beaumarchais's secret aid plan in 1776 without first getting Spain's approval. Nonetheless, on April 12, 1779, Vergennes secured the secret Treaty of Aranjuez, whereby Spain agreed to join French military operations against the British. To obtain this pact he engaged in double-dealing that violated the spirit of the French treaties with the United States. Vergennes accepted Spain's refusal to extend the alliance to include the United States, or even to recognize its independence. More important, he gave in to Spain's demand that France refrain from signing a separate peace with the British until the Spanish had won back Gibraltar. U.S. fortunes had become irrevocably attached to a European political matter.

Unaware of the intricacies of the Franco-Spanish Treaty, the Americans were elated when Spain declared war on England on June 21, 1779, and they immediately moved toward securing a formal alliance and financial assistance from the Madrid government. In September 1779 Congress sent thirty-four-year-old John Jay of New York to Spain to seek recognition of U.S. independence and a $5 million loan. Jay came from a long line of wealthy French-Dutch merchants and had gone to King's College (later Columbia) before becoming involved in revolutionary politics; such experience could not have prepared him for the shabby treatment he received in

Spain. Things began to go awry from the moment he entered that country in January 1780. He and his wife battled fleas, bugs, terrible roads, and high-priced innkeepers on their inland trip to the Spanish court. Soon after arriving in Madrid their infant daughter suddenly took ill and died. To make matters worse, Jay found the king too preoccupied with hunting to bother with affairs of state, and the foreign minister, Don José Moniño, Conde de Floridablanca, refused to see him. Jay suffered further indignities: Spanish officials intercepted and read his correspondence; spies eavesdropped on his conversations; and his money ran out because Congress, confident that he would secure a financial agreement in Madrid, had incurred other monetary obligations impossible to meet.

By the summer of 1781, Congress so desperately felt the need for Spanish aid that it authorized Jay to give up claims to the Mississippi River. Although British military fortunes in the south were on the rise, the congressional decision to drop demands for the river was short on wisdom. Not only did Jay's offer sacrifice the only bargaining position the United States had, but if accepted it would have undercut the new nation's potential for expansion. For this overly generous concession the Spanish were to help the Americans preserve territories now held—which did *not* include land west of the Alleghenies. Floridablanca turned down this attractive deal, probably in hope that his soldiers would solidify their hold on the Floridas and, without American ties, move on to acquire the vast region between the mountains and river. In light of the Americans' relentless western push, he doubtless questioned any assurances of their remaining east of the mountains.

After more than two years of frustration and embarrassment, Jay had secured from Floridablanca only sufficient funds to cover daily expenses, but he had developed enough hostility toward European diplomacy to last him the rest of his life. The host government had never officially received him. After one stormy session with Spanish officials, Jay angrily declared to the French ambassador that he had come to Madrid "to make *propositions,* not *supplications.*" Furthermore, he suspected the French of undermining America's expansionist aims by privately assuring Spain of territories west of the Appalachian Mountains. The Spanish foreign minister eventually agreed to give Jay about $175,000, a paltry sum that placed the United States in the uncomfortable position of receiving just enough assistance to instill a flickering hope that more was forthcoming, but not enough to call the mission a success. Jay's humiliating experience left him embittered and wary about Old World craftiness.

While Jay underwent his trials in Spain, Americans turned for assistance to the new League of Armed Neutrality, organized in 1780 by Catherine the Great of Russia to defend freedom of the seas. The empress had opposed Britain's restrictions on Russian trade in the Baltic Sea and had invited Sweden and Denmark-Norway to ally in defense of neutral rights. Although the League later expanded to include Prussia, the Holy Roman Empire, the Kingdom of the Two Sicilies, and Portugal (normally a British ally), it was, Catherine admitted, an "armed nullity" of small-navy nations too weak to challenge British supremacy at sea. Yet it managed to close the Baltic to belligerents and to cut off Britain's chances for European allies. More important to Americans, its idealistic goals were similar to those contained in the model treaty.

The Continental Congress resolved to support the League's objectives and dispatched Francis Dana of Massachusetts to the Court of St. Petersburg in a futile attempt to negotiate a treaty permitting America's participation. Despite two years of effort, Dana never persuaded Catherine to welcome him officially. How could a belligerent ally with a neutral? Would the United States remain independent? The Russian empress had to ponder the costs of recognizing America. War with Britain was out of the question.

American hopes for foreign aid again rose in 1780 when British relations with the Netherlands seriously deteriorated and resulted in war. Dutch merchants had been engaged in a prosperous carrying trade to Europe and America that relied on their small West Indies island of St. Eustatius as a way station; during one year in the war over 3000 ships, including some from the bogus Hortalez and Company, had operated out of the island and thus threatened Britain's effort to put down the American revolt. An Anglo-Dutch treaty of 1678 had stipulated that each power would come to the assistance of the other if threatened by a third party. Instead, the Dutch had allied with the League of Armed Neutrality. England proposed a deal: If the Dutch halted the trade in naval materials to the French, it would not invoke the treaty of 1678. The Dutch refused the offer and sent armed escorts for their commercial vessels. The anticipated exchange of fire took place, and the English declared war on the Netherlands in late 1780.

Earlier in the summer of 1780, when it appeared that England and the Netherlands would soon be at war, the Continental Congress had transferred John Adams from Paris to Amsterdam to secure a treaty of assistance. He met stubborn resistance, for the Dutch preferred the guaranteed profit of the carrying trade to a nearly certain war with England caused by their extending aid to the Americans. It was like negotiating with a "school of sharks," the straitlaced Adams bitterly complained. Finally, in April 1782, he won Dutch recognition of American independence, and in June he secured a large loan from bankers in Amsterdam. The following October he negotiated a treaty of amity and commerce. Adams's mission was a success.

Throughout much of the war's diplomacy, Americans felt secure with France, yet several factors suggest that their European ally was more dangerous than Mother England. Americans had insisted from the beginning of the war that their independence was to be final and unequivocal: The fighting would continue until the British troops had pulled out of the United States all the way to the Mississippi River and until the crown admitted to

America's independence. And yet in 1780 and 1781, Vergennes supported an Austro-Russian attempt to mediate the war, which, if successful, would have come too early to ensure America's independence and would have left large parts of the country in British hands. Vergennes then managed to reconstitute the U.S. peace delegation in Paris. Fearing that the headstrong John Adams was not subject to manipulation, Vergennes used the talents of his minister in the United States (including bribery of congressional members) to secure four additional members to the commission: two Francophiles—Franklin and Jefferson (who again declined to serve for personal reasons)—and two Americans of French descent—Jay and Henry Laurens of South Carolina. In the meantime Vergennes arranged a revision of the U.S. peace demands. The new directives of 1781 stipulated that the commissioners were to take no initiatives in the negotiations without France's approval. As fate would have it, the war would have to save the Americans from their ally as well as from their enemy.

Diplomacy of Peace

At a Virginia hamlet called Yorktown on October 19, 1781, a band struck the tune "The World Turned Upside Down" while British soldiers, resplendent in bright red uniforms, stacked their weapons before the American Revolutionary Army. Earlier that day General Lord Charles Cornwallis had surrendered his 7000 regulars to a combined force of 9000 Americans under General Washington and 8000 French soldiers under General Comte de Rochambeau. The Marquis de Lafayette, who was also at Yorktown, ordered the band to play "Yankee Doodle" to remind the British that they had surrendered to the Americans as well as to the French. On hearing the news, Franklin shrewdly proclaimed: "The infant Hercules has now strangled his second serpent that attacked him in his cradle." In England Lord North repeatedly stammered, "Oh God! It is all over!"

England's dramatic defeat at Yorktown intensified its people's widespread desire to end the fighting. The American war, never popular in Britain, was steadily depleting the nation's resources, steering it into conflict with most of the Western world, eroding its maritime supremacy in the English Channel, and threatening to expose the country itself to invasion. Would it not be wiser to trade with the Americans than to fight them? Although British forces would go on to later victories, popular attention focused instead on recent reverses in the Caribbean and on the mounting national debt. By early March 1782 Parliament resolved to bring a close to the war, and shortly afterward the Marquis of Rockingham, a leader of the Whig opposition who had pledged to end the fighting, replaced North as prime minister. In early April Richard Oswald, a wealthy, elderly Scottish merchant, former slave trader, friend of Franklin's, and onetime resident of Virginia, embarked for Paris to discuss peace with the Americans. Before the talks could begin, Rockingham died, and Lord Shelburne, a long-time advocate of Anglo-American peace, free trade, and commercial ties between the Atlantic peoples, became head of the British government. Although he had hoped to keep the colonies, for the first time peace seemed conceivable.

In the initial discussion of mid-April, Franklin moved to take advantage of Britain's troubles. Oswald was inexperienced in diplomacy and indiscreetly admitted that his country's involvement in this war had been unwise and that peace was necessary. Franklin saw the opening and slyly suggested that the cession of Canada would smooth Anglo-American relations. He then called for British recognition of U.S. independence and favorable national boundaries and, according to some accounts, suggested the feasibility of a separate peace. Franklin had learned much from his long service abroad. Although Vergennes was aware of Oswald's mission, of course, he never heard about either Franklin's Canada proposal or his hint of a separate peace.

The need for political adjustments in England delayed the attempted negotiations for a few weeks and gave Franklin a chance to invite Adams and Jay to join him in Paris. While the London government debated the direction of foreign affairs, Franklin was stricken with a serious attack of the gout and a disabling kidney disease that kept him in bed for more than three months. He needed help in the long hours ahead. Although Laurens, a long-time business associate and friend of Oswald's, would not arrive until the last stages of the negotiations, Adams returned to Paris in late October and found Jay already there; the disgruntled emissary to Spain had arrived in Paris the previous June after a welcome departure from Madrid.

Jay was deeply suspicious of European diplomacy after his insulting experiences in Spain, and he immediately agreed with Franklin's refusal in August to enter formal talks until Oswald got official permission to recognize the former colonies as the United States. The Shelburne ministry refused to recognize U.S. independence before signing a peace treaty, however, and directed Oswald to negotiate with the Americans as "colonies or plantations." Continued protests from Franklin and Jay persuaded the British cabinet in late August to agree in principle to preliminary recognition of the United States if the Americans first insisted that the king recommend that Parliament pass such a resolution. After this face-saving measure, Shelburne offered a type of compromise, authorizing Oswald to meet with representatives of the "thirteen United States."

The irony is that, despite the ongoing war with England, Jay reserved his worst fears for the French. Shortly after his arrival in Paris, he had discussions with the Spanish ambassador and a representative of Vergennes, both meetings confirming his suspicions that the French intended to help the Spanish keep the Americans out of the Mississippi Valley. He was already indignant over Vergennes's attempt to dismiss the wording of Oswald's August instructions as a technicality, and he was not assured by the French foreign minister's declaration that the important point was British recognition of U.S. independence in the final treaty. Jay's anxiety deepened when he received a copy of a communication sent from the French chargé d'affaires in the United States to Vergennes, which called on the foreign minister to oppose the U.S. request for fishing rights off Canada. If this was not convincing evidence of French duplicity, Vergennes's private secretary, Joseph de Rayneval, clinched the case in early September by informally proposing to Jay that Britain receive the area above the Ohio River, with Spain and the United States dividing the region below.

These developments fitted Jay's direst apprehensions about France. Its interest in keeping Spain in the war, he thought, had caused Vergennes to offer America's western claims; Jay could not have known that the real reason was the French foreign minister's failure to deliver Gibraltar to his ally. While mutual Spanish and U.S. distrust kept them occupied, only the British would stand in the way of France's control of North America. Jay realized these were high stakes, but he also knew that empires had been won and lost at the peace table as well as on the battlefield.

Jay's apprehensions seemed substantiated when he learned that in early September Vergennes sent Rayneval to London on a secret mission—probably, Jay thought, to satisfy Spanish demands in North America. The French foreign minister, indeed, had instructed his secretary to inform the British that generous concessions to the Americans were inadvisable and unnecessary. It is impossible to be sure, but Vergennes had apparently left the door ajar for a separate Franco-British peace that would provide concessions to Spain at the expense of the United States. Shelburne gathered from Rayneval's statements that the French supported U.S. claims to independence but preferred limited national boundaries and no American fishing rights off Newfoundland. To the king, Shelburne perceptively noted that the French appeared "more jealous than partial to America."

Jay believed that his most trying task was to persuade Franklin to set aside French sentiments and act in the American interest. "Let us be grateful to the French for what they have done for us," he advised Franklin, "but let us think for ourselves. And, if need be, let us act for ourselves." This was wise counsel. Although Franklin had initially downplayed Jay's alarm, Adams (who had just arrived in Paris) likewise recognized the French danger and worked to bring Franklin to their side. Vergennes, Adams snidely remarked, meant "to keep his hand under our chin to prevent us from drowning, but not to lift our heads out of water." Perhaps Franklin's sickness kept him from arguing the issue with his younger colleagues; more likely, he privately agreed with them and only reluctantly turned on France, the country he loved.

In any case Jay had already taken the initiative toward a separate peace. Without telling either Franklin or Adams, he sent a confidant of Shelburne's then assigned to Paris, Benjamin Vaughan, to inform the London ministry that it must deal separately with the Americans. Vaughan would give the Americans a good hearing. He was pro-American, a friend of Franklin's, and related to Laurens by marriage. England, Jay insisted, would secure better terms from France if an Anglo-American peace were already in existence. He also argued that such a treaty was not possible without Oswald's authorization to speak with the Americans as Commissioners of the United States of America; that England could not defeat the United States and should work out a conciliation; and that France sought to conspire with England in limiting U.S. territorial growth and therefore found it advantageous to delay recognition of American independence until the final treaty. Oswald's arguments, combined with Vaughan's calls for ending the war with the United States and establishing commercial relations, convinced Shelburne to make the changes in instructions. By October the shift was under way toward separate peace negotiations.

The military aspects of the war worked with the ongoing diplomatic maneuvers to shape the preliminary peace talks in Paris. Oswald's instructions in early September 1782 had been to accept U.S. demands for a boundary north to the Nipissing line (the southwestern tip of Quebec prior to the Quebec Act of 1774), and *not* to seek the return of prewar debts or confiscated Loyalist property. But soon after the delegates in Paris initialed this draft treaty on October 5 and sent it to London, news arrived that the three-year siege of Gibraltar was over and that the massive rock fortress still belonged to England. Shelburne tightened his stipulations. He now required restitution for English creditors and Loyalists, and he even made an eleventh-hour attempt to salvage the Old Northwest. Although the prime minister may have made this last proposal only to achieve satisfaction on the other two points, Franklin considered it too much. The British, he complained, "wanted to bring their boundary down to the Ohio and to settle the Loyalists in the Illinois country. We did not choose such neighbors."

The Americans eventually made concessions on their boundary expectations. On the northeast boundary they retreated from the St. John River to the St. Croix. In the west they gave up the Nipissing line and consented to a border following the St. Lawrence River and Great Lakes and then stretching to the northwestern point on the Lake of the Woods before moving due west to the Mississippi River. Britain and the United States signed the preliminary peace treaty on November 30, 1782, with the understanding that it would not go into effect until the French and English had settled their differences.

Vergennes complained about the United States's separate peace talks with England, but in reality he knew they had saved him from a weblike situation with Spain. Strictly speaking, the discussions did not constitute a violation of the Franco-American Treaty of 1778 because the resulting preliminary pact was not to take effect until Britain and its other antagonists had also signed peace treaties. Yet Vergennes was caught in a dilemma. Although freed from his secret Gibraltar obligation to

Map 6
That America survived as a nation against the French, English, and Spanish was a tribute to the abilities of the Founding Fathers.

Spain, he would now have to deal with bitter Spanish criticism for the United States's independent course. After considerable thought he decided to explain to the Madrid government that the United States had violated the Treaty of Alliance and left the war, and that the French had no choice but to bow out.

Franklin applied the coup de grâce to the separate peace controversy when he secretly implied to Vergennes that further French protests could drive the Americans into an alliance with England. The foreign minister had first congratulated the Americans on their successful negotiations, but two weeks afterward he sent a face-saving note to Franklin which was surprisingly mild in tone:

> I am at a loss, sir, to explain your conduct and that of your colleagues on this occasion. You have concluded your preliminary articles without any communication between us. . . . You are about to hold out a certain hope of peace to America without even informing yourself on the state of the negotiation on our part.
>
> You are wise and discreet, sir; you perfectly understand what is due to propriety; you have all your life performed your duties. I pray you to consider how you propose to fulfill those which are due to the King?

Franklin explained that the agreements were only preliminary to the final treaty and apologized for failing to notify the French government before entering the talks, but he assured Vergennes that his lapse was not due to "want of respect to the King, whom we all love and honor." Franklin then salved Vergennes with a master stroke: "*The English, I just now learn, flatter themselves they have already divided us.* I hope this little misunderstanding will therefore be kept secret, and that they will find themselves totally mistaken."

In the same letter Franklin had the audacity to ask for another French loan; even more amazing, the financially strained French government, probably fearing America's collapse, approved the request.

Franklin's private exchange with Vergennes did not remain secret from the British for long. Bancroft had become secretary to the full American peace delegation and had already smuggled considerable information about the negotiations to the British. Their knowledge of the Franco-American rift helps to explain the transparent effort by British agents in Paris to establish an amicable relationship with the Americans. The London government intended to undercut French interests in the New World.

On September 3, 1783, England and the United States signed the "Definitive Treaty of Peace," the Treaty of Paris officially ending the American Revolutionary War. The general settlement incorporated a British pact made with France and Spain the previous January, along with a treaty with the Netherlands. Except for Spain's receiving the Floridas, the terms were identical to those in the preliminary treaty of 1782. The British promised to withdraw military and naval holdings "with all convenient speed," and they agreed that use of the Mississippi River was to be forever "free and open to the subjects of Great Britain, and the citizens of the United States." On paper, U.S. independence seemed final and complete.

On learning the provisions of the Anglo-American pact, Vergennes cynically remarked that "the English buy the peace more than they make it." The treaty terms, in fact, were more liberal than America's military victories had earned, and they undoubtedly contributed to Shelburne's fall from power. Some Britons accused him of abandoning both the Loyalists and the Indians of the Northwest; others denounced him for virtually relinquishing Britain's navigation rights on the Mississippi by allowing the northern U.S. boundary to stretch above the source of the river. The British prime minister, however, was an advocate of the free trade gospel espoused by his friend Adam Smith and desired above all to replace the Franco-American alliance with Anglo-American commercial ties. Indeed, he had widened the gap between France and the United States by recognizing U.S. independence and agreeing to its boundary demands. Even so, one parliamentary member declared that Shelburne had "certainly proved himself a great Christian, for he had not only parted with his cloak to America, but he had given his coat likewise."

But all was not harmonious among the peace delegates in Paris, because disagreements developed over other matters soon after settlement of the larger questions of independence and national boundaries. The British wanted exclusive fishing rights off Newfoundland's Grand Banks as well as sole use of the Canadian coastal areas for drying and curing their catch. John Adams staunchly defended the interests of fellow New Englanders. A compromise of sorts was the result, by which the Americans won the "liberty" but not the "right" to fish in waters off both Newfoundland and Canada. Decades of controversy followed during which one Adams descendant after the other attempted to resolve the matter.

Heated exchanges also took place over two other issues—treatment of the Loyalists (called Tories by those who joined the revolution) and private debts owed by Americans to Britons. Although Franklin's son had remained loyal to the British after serving as royal governor of New Jersey, the elderly diplomat in Paris vehemently resisted appeals for light treatment. "Your ministers," he blurted out to the British delegates, "require that we should receive again into our bosom those who have been our bitterest enemies, and restore their properties who have destroyed ours; and this while the wounds they have given us are still bleeding." On the debt problem, the crown sought reparations for property losses sustained by the perhaps 80,000 colonists who had left their homeland rather than join the rebellion. The British were incredulous when the Americans, who had incurred heavy financial obligations before 1775, argued that the war had wiped them from the record.

Adams eventually emerged with a settlement. The U.S. delegates agreed to "earnestly recommend" that the states return properties taken from "real British subjects" during the war, and they assured British business leaders

that they would "meet with no lawful impediment" in attempting to collect money from Americans. Little hope for satisfaction existed on either count. On the first issue, most Loyalists were born in America and did not fit the treaty's classification. On the second, the debt issue remained a source of argument, and the central government established under the Articles of Confederation in 1781 lacked the power to tell the states what to do.

Despite some discontent, the treaty was a good peace for both the United States and Britain. The Americans in Paris had handled themselves well in an experienced and hardened European world, and they had stayed clear of a dangerous political involvement in continental affairs while using Europe's problems to advantage. Furthermore, they had seen the right moment to violate instructions and break French ties; Shelburne had likewise discerned the time to accept the demise of mercantilism and release the American colonies. Both Atlantic nations understood that the promotion of their own economic ties could shut out the French from North America.

Ironically, France emerged as the major casualty of its victory over the British. Vergennes's shifting diplomatic efforts had cost his country an American ally, the loyalty of Spain, and, most serious, the world's recognition of Britain's defeat. He had failed to reverse the outcome of the French and Indian War in 1763, for the British had not been humbled and France still had no foothold on the North American continent. On paper, France stood victorious in 1783, much as Britain had reigned triumphant twenty years earlier. Yet in both instances outward appearances obscured the reality. As in 1763, the defeated parties in Paris walked away with fewer obligations and prepared to maneuver for a stronger position in both North America and other places. The major difference in the latter war was that the French had no rich colonies to share the financial burden. The revolution that followed in France in 1789 was profoundly more critical than the one faced by the British in 1776: It tore down the nation from within and ultimately wrapped the succeeding Napoleonic empire in a series of disastrous world wars that culminated in still another French humiliation—this one at Waterloo in 1815.

Problems in Governance

The establishment of independence did not automatically guarantee the United States automatic membership in the international community of nations. In ridding itself of the mother country, the new nation also threw off imperial protection and now lay exposed to Old World powers whose avowed intention was to promote their own interests. Jefferson, Washington, and other Americans believed, for example, that British subversion lay behind the rebellion in Massachusetts over monetary issues led by Daniel Shays in 1786–1787. And more than a few Americans discerned a connection between Shays and Vermont's Green Mountain Boys, a group led by Ethan and Ira Allen, who sought union with Canada. Even though both of these allegations remain unproved, Americans recognized that their infant republic was powerless to do anything about such dangers. Their constitution, the Articles of Confederation, loosely encompassed thirteen sovereign states held together only by the demands of a war that was now over. The national government lacked the coercive power to resolve either the domestic or foreign problems left by the war.

If Confederation leaders could have enforced the powers granted them, the Founding Fathers might not have met in Philadelphia as early as 1787. But Congress could not pass laws that bound individuals and found it nearly impossible to deal with states that retained their sovereignty and sense of independence. Reverence for states' rights was understandable after years of royal rule, but adherence to these same principles now threatened to undermine the new nation from within and without. When Congress formulated domestic and foreign policies, the states often ignored them. The result was a notori-

ously weak national defense structure that invited encroachments from alien powers. U.S. foreign policy lacked the all-important quality of leverage, not only because of the nation's domestic social, political, and economic problems, but also because John Jay, as the new secretary of foreign affairs, lacked the means of enforcing the powers he did possess.

Events since the shots first fired at Lexington and Concord had not brought economic liberation from England: By 1790 nearly half of America's exports and 90 percent of its imports were with the mother country. Furthermore, the diffused nature of the Articles of Confederation assured each state of its own tariff and customs regulations, and the result was competition among Americans themselves. The United States's prime avenue into the British commercial system had been through Shelburne, but his generous peace terms had already driven him from office. A widely read pamphlet written by Lord Sheffield in 1783 better expressed the British attitude toward trade with the Americans. No need existed for commercial reciprocity, he declared, because the new government under the Articles lacked the power to halt the deluge of cheaper British goods that would hit U.S. markets after the war. To tighten the vise, the British closed their West Indies ports to U.S. shipping. The long tradition of mercantilism did not terminate with either the writings of Adam Smith or the knell rung at Yorktown.

The British posed another obstacle to the American nation when they refused to evacuate the northwest territory immediately after the war. The day before formal ratification of the Treaty of Paris, April 8, 1784, the London government secretly decided to instruct its governor general in Canada to maintain control over a series of forts strung from Lake Champlain to Lake Michigan. When pressed later, the English insisted that U.S. failures to fulfill treaty obligations relating to British creditors and Loyalists had brought on the refusal to leave the posts. Yet the treaty only required that the Congress *recommend* that states open the courts to Loyalists. Besides, the decision to keep the forts came *before* the Americans had had an opportunity to deny a hearing to the Loyalists. The Americans were convinced that the British government wanted to preserve the fur trade and was arming the Indians in an effort to stop U.S. migration into the area.

Soon other problems developed with England. The physical characteristics of the North American hinterland did not correspond with the descriptions contained in the Treaty of Paris, and this fact mystified representatives from both sides who attempted to mark the Canadian-American boundary. Southerners complained about having received no compensation for slaves taken by British soldiers leaving America after the war. Stories spread along the North American frontier that the British had bribed the people of Vermont (not yet part of the United States) with the offer of commercial use of the St. Lawrence River if they pursued their separatist plans. In the meantime Virginia and Maryland violated the Paris Treaty by prohibiting their courts from helping British subjects collect debts. When John Adams, the first U.S. minister to London, inquired in 1785 why the British had not reciprocated with a representative to the United States, they scoffed and wondered whether *thirteen* would be necessary.

The postwar situation with Spain was little better. By the end of 1784 nearly 50,000 Americans had moved into the trans-Appalachian west and endangered Spanish claims to the area. Perhaps part of the confusion was due to British manipulations in the Paris negotiations of 1783. The settlement allowed Americans free use of the Mississippi River "from its source to the ocean," whereas Britain's pact with the Spanish did not mention this guarantee. A similar problem existed with the northern boundary of Florida. Americans understood it to be the thirty-first parallel, whereas the British gave Spain the right to keep West Florida—without specifying its boundaries. The Spanish claimed the same border established by England in 1764—the junction of the Mississippi with the Yazoo

River, or the line of 32°28′. Then, in 1784, the Spanish closed the Mississippi River at New Orleans, forcing Americans into the hard decision of giving up their commerce or switching their allegiance to Spain. Combined with ongoing Indian problems and growing separatist sentiment stirred up by British agents, Spanish-American relations approached crisis intensity.

The Spanish, however, had only a few hundred soldiers in Louisiana and found it prudent to negotiate a settlement with the United States. In 1785 they sent Don Diego de Gardoqui to talk with Secretary John Jay in New York about the possibility of conceding the Mississippi River to Spain in exchange for a commercial treaty and favorable boundary adjustments. Gardoqui spoke excellent English; he had been in charge of shipping Spanish munitions to America during the war; and he was one of the few Spaniards who had made a favorable impression on Jay during the latter's nightmarish stay at the court in Madrid. Armed with a ready smile and a sack of money used for social occasions as well as to bribe members of Congress, Gardoqui offered lavish compliments to both the secretary and his wife that they thankfully received, while he played on the northeast's apprehensions over the west's rapid commercial development. Although the Spanish emissary's motives were transparent, he almost succeeded.

A year of painful discussions led only to frustration. In early August 1786, fellow New Yorkers and other northeastern merchants exerted pressure on Jay to consider a trade agreement that permitted U.S. access to Spain's home ports and those in the Canary Islands if he persuaded Congress to waive use of the Mississippi River for perhaps twenty-five years. A fiery debate followed in Congress, during which sectional alliances within that body barely forestalled the concession. Late in August a majority in Congress—seven northern states (Delaware had no delegate in Congress)—voted in favor of the suggestion, but five southern states did not. Some westerners bitterly muttered threats of secession followed by an alliance with either Spain or England; others vowed to *take* New Orleans. Land speculators, along with southerners holding territorial claims in the southwest, joined the growing number of citizens with commercial interests and other dissatisfied Americans who accused Jay of attempting to sell out their country. Jay dropped the issue when he realized the impossibility of lining up the nine states necessary to ratify an agreement.

France also presented serious difficulties to the postwar United States. Although the treaty of 1778 bound both nations to protect each other's possessions forever, the Paris government did not offer support when England and Spain threatened America's claims in the trans-Appalachian west. Jefferson, new minister to France when Franklin returned home in 1784, secured only limited commercial access to its holdings in the West Indies because, the French complained, the United States first had to repay war debts. The French, hurting from within and stung by Britain's refusal to act the part of the vanquished, angrily waited for another renewal of the long-time struggle for North America.

The new republic's relations with Native Americans in the territories raised issues that lasted for generations. U.S. commissioners signed treaties at Fort Stanwix in New York in 1784 and at Hopewell, South Carolina, in 1785–1786 with emissaries from the Cherokee, Chickasaw, Choctaw, and Iroquois nations, all of which permitted Americans to move into the lands west of the Allegheny Mountains. The Creeks from the Georgia area, however, did not sign the Hopewell pacts and resisted the American migrations through the end of the decade. Indeed, Native Americans later denounced the agreements, alleging that their so-called signatories had lacked the authority to give away the territories.

Another foreign problem involved the Barbary Coast pirates of northern Africa. While the Americans were colonists, the British Empire had provided protection against piracy in the Mediterranean—primarily by buying off the pirates. With the restraints of mercantilism

lifted, the advantages of the system likewise came to a close. Americans found it difficult to fill the monetary demands of Morocco, Algiers, Tunis, and Tripoli, mainly because of embarrassing financial shortages. Finally, in 1787, the United States negotiated a treaty with Morocco, but it still lacked means for halting the raids by the other Barbary states. Such was the Mediterranean situation in May 1787 as fifty-five delegates gathered in Convention Hall in Philadelphia.

U.S. foreign and domestic difficulties provided an atmosphere conducive to constitutional reform. Using the Articles of Confederation as foil, the delegates emerged four months later with a new document that seemingly strengthened the central government while safeguarding the rights of the states and American people. Human beings had a natural propensity toward evil, the founders of the new nation believed, and the remedy lay in spreading governmental powers and establishing a system of checks and balances. In addition to correcting numerous domestic flaws, the U.S. Constitution placed the executive branch of the national government in charge of foreign policy and made the Constitution and treaties "the Supreme Law of the land." The president had the power to oversee diplomatic negotiations, grant recognition to new states, make appointments, welcome foreign dignitaries, and ratify treaties with other nations, provided that two-thirds of the senators present gave their "advice and consent." Although the two-thirds provision probably reflected southern and western distrust for the east caused by the Jay-Gardoqui negotiations, Americans overlooked these signs of sectional discontent to exalt the unity afforded by the new Constitution. They could now agree with the forecast made by the American geographer Jedidiah Morse in 1789: "We cannot but anticipate the period, as not far distant, when the AMERICAN EMPIRE will comprehend millions of souls, west of the Mississippi."

The Constitution, ratified in 1788 and put into operation the year afterward, established the nation on a firm domestic and foreign policy base and set the machinery in motion for George Washington to become the first president of the United States in 1789. The embarrassments thrust on the country by foreign hostilities during the Confederation period had provided a vital impetus to the creation of a constitution that drew on idealistic principles but rested primarily on a realistic foundation.

The New Nation and Foreign Policy

Despite the ideals expressed in the model treaty, the success of the young nation's first foreign policy was largely attributable to French military assistance in the Revolutionary War. After the jubilation of victory had culminated in the Constitution, Americans realized that the war's demands had altered their original foreign policy based on Enlightenment ideals to accommodate the compromises necessitated by the realities of world politics. The repercussions of the French Treaty of Alliance, the outbreak of France's own revolution in 1789, U.S. commercial needs abroad, and the onset of still another round of Anglo-French wars made both an American defense network and involvement in European political affairs virtually inescapable. The timing of the new nation's completion was fortunate in view of the French Revolution and the rise of Napoleon. The last chapter of the long Anglo-French struggle for world control was about to unfold. And in the course of this unfolding, the Americans would confront another serious challenge to their security: Rather than win national independence, this time they had to hold on to it.

Selected Readings

Adams, William H. *The Paris Years of Thomas Jefferson*. 1997.

Alden, John R. *The American Revolution, 1775–1783*. 1954.

Bailyn, Bernard. *The Ideological Origins of the American Revolution*. 1967.

Bemis, Samuel F. *The Diplomacy of the American Revolution*. 1935.

Brands, H. W. *The First American: The Life and Times of Benjamin Franklin*. 2000.

Brecher, Frank W. *Losing a Continent: France's North American Policy, 1753–1763*. 1998.

Calloway, Colin G. *The American Revolution in Indian Country: Crisis and Diversity in Native American Communities*. 1995.

Christie, Ian R., and Labaree, Benjamin W. *Empire or Independence, 1760–1776: A British-American Dialogue on the Coming of the American Revolution*. 1976.

Clark, Ronald W. *Benjamin Franklin: A Biography*. 1983.

Colbourn, H. Trevor. *The Lamp of Experience: Whig History and the Intellectual Origins of the American Revolution*. 1965.

Crowley, John E. *The Privileges of Independence: Neomercantilism and the American Revolution*. 1993.

Cunningham, Noble E., Jr. *In Pursuit of Reason: The Life of Thomas Jefferson*. 1987.

Darling, Arthur B. *Our Rising Empire, 1763–1803*. 1940.

Dowd, Gregory E. *A Spirited Resistance: The North American Indian Struggle for Unity, 1745–1815*. 1992.

Dull, Jonathan R. *A Diplomatic History of the American Revolution*. 1985.

———. *Franklin the Diplomat: The French Mission*. 1982.

———. *The French Navy and American Independence: A Study of Arms and Diplomacy, 1774–1787*. 1975.

Egnal, Marc. *A Mighty Empire: The Origins of the American Revolution*. 1988.

Ferling, John E. *John Adams: A Life*. 1992.

Fitzsimons, David M. "Tom Paine's New World Order," *Diplomatic History* 19 (1995): 569–82.

Foner, Eric. *Tom Paine and Revolutionary America*. 1976.

Gilbert, Felix. *To the Farewell Address: Ideas of Early American Foreign Policy*. 1961.

Hagan, Kenneth J. *This People's Navy: The Making of American Sea Power*. 1991.

Henkin, Louis. *Foreign Affairs and the Constitution*. 1972.

Higginbotham, Don. *George Washington and the American Military Tradition*. 1985.

Hoffman, Ronald, and Albert, Peter J., eds. *Diplomacy and Revolution: The Franco-American Alliance of 1778*. 1981.

Horsman, Reginald. *The Diplomacy of the New Republic, 1776–1815.* 1985.

Hutson, James H. "Intellectual Foundations of Early American Diplomacy," *Diplomatic History* 1 (1977): 1–19.

———. *John Adams and the Diplomacy of the American Revolution.* 1980.

———. "The Partition Treaty and the Declaration of American Independence," *Journal of American History* 58 (1972): 877–96.

Jensen, Merrill. *The Articles of Confederation: An Interpretation of the Social-Constitutional History of the American Revolution, 1774–1781.* 1963.

———. *The Founding of a Nation: A History of the American Revolution, 1763–1776.* 1968.

Jones, Dorothy V. *License for Empire: Colonialism by Treaty in Early America.* 1982.

Kaplan, Lawrence S., ed. *The American Revolution and "A Candid World."* 1977.

———. *Colonies into Nation: American Diplomacy, 1763–1801.* 1972.

Keane, John. *Tom Paine: A Political Life.* 1995.

Lang, Daniel G. *Foreign Policy in the Early Republic: The Law of Nations and the Balance of Power.* 1985.

Lofgren, Charles A. *"Government from Reflection and Choice": Constitutional Essays on War, Foreign Relations, and Federalism.* 1986.

Lopez, Claude Anne. *Mon cher Papa: Franklin and the Ladies of Paris.* 1966.

McDonald, Forrest. *Novus Ordo Seclorum: The Intellectual Origins of the Constitution.* 1985.

———. *States' Rights and the Union: Imperium in Imperio, 1776–1876.* 2000.

Mackesy, Piers. *The War for America, 1775–1783.* 1964.

Maier, Pauline. *American Scripture: Making the Declaration of Independence.* 1997.

Marks, Frederick W., III. "Foreign Affairs: A Winning Issue in the Campaign for Ratification of the Constitution," *Political Science Quarterly* 86 (1971): 444–69.

———. *Independence on Trial: Foreign Affairs and the Making of the Constitution.* 1973.

———. "Power, Pride, and Purse: Diplomatic Origins of the Constitution," *Diplomatic History* 11 (1987): 303–19.

Middlekauff, Robert. *Benjamin Franklin and His Enemies.* 1996.

———. *The Glorious Cause: The American Revolution, 1763–1789.* 1982.

Miller, John C. *Triumph of Freedom: 1775–1783.* 1948.

Monaghan, Frank. *John Jay: Defender of Liberty.* 1935.

Morgan, Edmund S. *The Birth of the Republic, 1763–1789.* 1956.

———. *The Genius of George Washington.* 1980.

Morris, Richard B. *The Forging of the Union, 1781–1789.* 1987.

———. *The Peacemakers: The Great Powers and American Independence.* 1965.

Murphy, Orville T. *Charles Gravier, Comte de Vergennes: French Diplomacy in the Age of Revolution, 1719–1787.* 1982.

Nobles, Gregory H. *American Frontiers: Cultural Encounters and Continental Conquest.* 1997.

Nordholt, Jan Willem Schulte. *The Dutch Republic and American Independence.* 1982. Originally published in the Netherlands in 1979. Translated by Herbert H. Rowen.

Onuf, Peter. *Statehood and Union: A History of the Northwest Ordinance.* 1987.

———, and Onuf, Nicholas. *Federal Union, Modern World: The Law of Nations in an Age of Revolutions, 1776–1814.* 1993.

Palmer, Robert R. *The Age of the Democratic Revolution: A Political History of Europe and America, 1760–1790.* 1959.

Pancake, John S. *1777: The Year of the Hangman.* 1977.

Perkins, Bradford. *The Creation of a Republican Empire, 1776–1865.* 1993. The Cambridge History of American Foreign Relations, vol. 1. Cohen, Warren I., ed.

Rakove, Jack N. *The Beginnings of National Politics: An Interpretive History of the Continental Congress.* 1979.

———. *Original Meanings: Politics and Ideas in the Making of the Constitution.* 1996.

Ritcheson, Charles R. *Aftermath of Revolution: British Policy Toward the United States, 1783–1795.* 1969.

Robbins, Caroline. *The Eighteenth-Century Commonwealthman: Studies in the Transmission, Development and Circumstance of English Liberal Thought from the Restoration of Charles II until the War with the Thirteen Colonies.* 1968.

Rosenberg, Emily S. "A Call to Revolution: A Roundtable on Early U.S. Foreign Relations," *Diplomatic History* 22 (1998): 63–70.

Saul, Norman E. *Distant Friends: The United States and Russia, 1763–1867.* 1991.

Savelle, Max. *The Origins of American Diplomacy: The International History of Anglo-America, 1492–1763.* 1967.

Scott, H. M. *British Foreign Policy in the Age of the American Revolution.* 1990.

Shackelford, George G. *Thomas Jefferson's Travels in Europe, 1784–1789.* 1995.

Smelser, Marshall. *The Winning of Independence.* 1972.

Smith-Rosenberg, Caroll. "Dis-Covering the Subject of the 'Great Constitutional Discussion, 1786–1789," *Journal of American History* 79 (1992): 841–73.

Sofka, James R. "The Jeffersonian Idea of National Security: Commerce, the Atlantic Balance of Power, and the Barbary War, 1786–1805," *Diplomatic History* 21 (1997): 519–44.

Stephanson, Anders. *Manifest Destiny: American Expansionism and the Empire of Right.* 1995.

Stinchcombe, William C. *The American Revolution and the French Alliance.* 1969.

Stourzh, Gerald. *Benjamin Franklin and American Foreign Policy.* 1954.

Stuart, Reginald C. *United States Expansionism and British North America, 1775–1871.* 1988.

Tucker, Robert W., and Hendrickson, David C. *The Fall of the First British Empire: Origins of the War of American Independence.* 1982.

Van Alstyne, Richard W. *Empire and Independence: The International History of the American Revolution.* 1965.

———. *The Rising American Empire.* 1960.

Varg, Paul A. *Foreign Policies of the Founding Fathers.* 1963.

Weber, David J. *The Spanish Frontier in North America.* 1992.

Weeks, William E. *Building the Continental Empire: American Expansion from the Revolution to the Civil War.* 1996.

Whitaker, Arthur P. *The Spanish-American Frontier, 1783–1795: The Westward Movement and the Spanish Retreat in the Mississippi Valley.* 1927.

Whiteley, Peter. *Lord North: The Prime Minister Who Lost America.* 1996.

Williams, William A. "The Age of Mercantilism: An Interpretation of the American Political Economy, 1763–1828," *William and Mary Quarterly* 15 (1958): 419–37.

Wood, Gordon S. *The Creation of the American Republic, 1776–1787.* 1969.

———. *The Radicalism of the American Revolution.* 1992.

Wright, Esmond. *Franklin of Philadelphia.* 1986.

Wright, J. Leitch. *Britain and the American Frontier, 1783–1815.* 1975.

CHAPTER 2

The Federalist Era and the
Wars of the French Revolution,
1789–1801

Washington the President

As the tall, august, and stern-faced Virginian walked out onto the balcony of Federal Hall in New York City, he probably took for granted the pomp accorded a U.S. president. Perhaps on this day, April 30, 1789, George Washington wished he had declined the honor in favor of quiet retirement at Mount Vernon. Yet the American people demanded his services again and, charismatic and public-minded statesman that he was, Washington agreed to become the nation's first chief executive. He would set precedents in domestic and foreign affairs, and he would direct the United States toward political and economic stability, the latter a double-edged feat that required wisdom, patience, and tact. Washington realized that in foreign policy no clear lines existed between external and internal affairs. He also recognized the overwhelming importance of making decisions that protected the nation's security.

The Constitution only vaguely outlined the machinery of foreign policy. It did not establish an office for the purpose, although Congress filled that void in July 1789 by creating the Department of Foreign Affairs, which in two months became known as the Department of State and was comprised of five members.

The Department of War oversaw Indian affairs, a move that suggested the likelihood of force over diplomacy in dealing with Native Americans. Ambiguity clouded the relations among the branches of government, especially in regard to the treaty process. The Constitution stipulated that the executive was to seek the "advice and consent" of the Senate in making treaties, and President Washington and Secretary of War Henry Knox dutifully arrived in that body's chambers on a Saturday morning in 1789 to ask its advice and consent on seven points in a proposed treaty with the Creek Indians. The clatter of wagons outside the building drowned out Washington's first attempt to be heard. Trying two more times to speak above the racket he became so irritated that Vice President John Adams asked for the president's papers, read the proposals, and on each point asked the senators: "Do you advise and consent?" Only a few at first gathered what was going on. Then, as more understood, they thought Washington wanted them to discuss and argue each point at length. This drove the president to anger. Already upset because he regarded senators as mere subordinates, he had now wasted precious time in listening to their senseless bickering. He sprang to his feet with a reddened face to exclaim that "this defeats every purpose of my coming here."

Storming out, he muttered that he would "be damned if he ever went there again!" Eventually an understanding developed that the president should seek both the advice and consent of the Senate *after* he had already taken action.

Washington's appointments of Alexander Hamilton as secretary of the treasury and Thomas Jefferson as secretary of state did not lessen the problems of determining a foreign policy. The personal and professional rivalry between the men led to a bitter struggle that deeply divided the country and promoted the formation of America's first political party system. Their differences in background, philosophy, personality, and temperament would soon split the administration over foreign as well as domestic matters.

The president's two central advisers were a classic study in contrasts. Hamilton, born into a financially troubled family in the British West Indies, was five feet and seven inches in height but deceptively taller because of the erect, soldierlike dignity with which he carried himself. Outgoing, brash, charming, elitist, conservative, and staunchly pro-English, he rigidly advocated a strong central government based on implied powers. Jefferson, reared by his wealthy Virginia plantation family, was over six feet tall but appeared shorter because of his stooped walk. Reserved in manner, philosophical in demeanor, humble in spirit, liberal in thought, and avowedly pro-French, he firmly supported a decentralized government and the protection of states' rights. Although Jefferson was in charge of foreign affairs, Hamilton conceived his role as similar to that of England's prime minister: Control of the treasury entitled him to delve into foreign matters. When at one point Jefferson wrote a 17,000-word protest against England's violations of the Treaty of 1783, Hamilton put all that work to naught by privately assuring the British minister to the United States that this view did not represent that of the Washington administration. Hamilton's financial plan of 1790–1791 further encouraged political division because, among other issues, it urged commercial ties with England and an increased role for the na-

George Washington
As commander of the Continental Army and later president of the United States, Washington became both man and monument in American history. *Charles Wilson Peale; Library of Congress.*

tional government. Jefferson countered with warnings against British encroachments in the New World and calls for decentralized government. After considerable infighting, those who followed Hamilton became known as Federalists, while supporters of Jefferson allied with fellow Virginian James Madison and called themselves anti-Federalists, or Republicans.

The Washington administration's first foreign policy test came in 1789 when an Anglo-Spanish dispute over Nootka Sound in the far northwest threatened to affect the United States. Spain had earlier proclaimed exclusive control over the entire Pacific coast. But this claim ran counter to British interests. During the summer of 1789, Spanish soldiers seized British traders who had tried to establish a post in Nootka Sound. Both countries prepared for war, which caused a serious problem for the

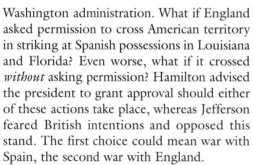

Alexander Hamilton and Thomas Jefferson
The differences between Alexander Hamilton
(left) as secretary of the treasury and Thomas
Jefferson (right) as secretary of state led to
division over foreign policy as well as to the
formation of the nation's first political party
system: Hamiltonian Federalists and Jeffersonian
Republicans. Hamilton: *Charles Wilson Peale;
Library of Congress.* Jefferson: *Jean Antoine
Handon; Collection of the New York Historical
Society.*

Washington administration. What if England
asked permission to cross American territory
in striking at Spanish possessions in Louisiana
and Florida? Even worse, what if it crossed
without asking permission? Hamilton advised
the president to grant approval should either
of these actions take place, whereas Jefferson
feared British intentions and opposed this
stand. The first choice could mean war with
Spain, the second war with England.

Fortunately for the United States, Spain
capitulated to Britain before the crisis spread
into Louisiana and Florida. Spain had called
on its French ally for help, but revolution had
broken out in France and precluded any possibility of assistance. The ensuing Nootka Sound
Convention of 1790 required Spain to return

property taken from Britain and permitted its
traders and settlers to enter these territories,
no longer exclusively Spanish.

The Nootka crisis had several notable repercussions. It showed the administration that the
long-standing struggle among the European
powers over the New World had not ended
with American independence and that the republic would remain an integral part of that
struggle. It demonstrated that self-interest was
the prime consideration in foreign affairs and
that the British therefore remained the country's chief threat in North America. For the
moment at least, France was preoccupied with
internal problems, and Spain by itself posed no
serious challenge to the United States. The
Anglo-Spanish war scare also caused a debate

among Washington's advisers that suggested the strong role Hamilton intended to play in foreign affairs. Finally, it had the unforeseen effect of improving Anglo-American relations by awakening the British to the possibility that the United States could take advantage of their troubles elsewhere to seek concessions. The London government had already expressed concern about congressional threats to impose discriminatory tariff and tonnage duties on British goods. That problem, combined with the Nootka crisis, made it no coincidence that England in 1791 sent its first minister, George Hammond, to the United States.

The second and greatest foreign policy challenge faced by Washington's presidency related to the French Revolution of 1789, for that domestic struggle grew into a world war that again affected North America and threatened to pull in the United States. Relations with France were uneasy before Washington became president. The first minister from Paris to the United States in 1787, Comte de Moustier, lasted only a year because of personal difficulties, compounded by his indiscreet expressions of French interest in Spanish Louisiana. Then war broke out in Europe in 1793, pitting England and France against each other again. The U.S. desire to trade with both belligerents encouraged a neutral stance, but the Washington administration feared that France might invoke the Treaty of Alliance of 1778 by requesting American military aid. The ensuing crisis raised profound questions relating to treaties and the nature of isolationism that proved timeless in scope and vital to America's well-being.

The French Revolution

In July 1789 French mobs stormed the Bastille in Paris, setting off a revolution that many Americans quickly identified with their own. Observers in the United States rejoiced that the insurgents' ideals coincided with theirs of the previous decade, because the French renamed streets after their cry of "Liberty, equality, and fraternity" and called for a Declaration of the Rights of Man similar to the Declaration of Independence. Jeffersonians raised liberty poles, wore liberty caps, called each other "citizen" and "citizeness" to correspond with new titles in France denoting equality, and praised the Girondin political party for its republicanism. But after France declared itself a republic in September 1792, the romance of the revolution suddenly gave way to an ugly phase when European monarchs joined the exiled French nobility in an attempt to restore King Louis XVI to the throne. In response, the National Convention in Paris voted 361 to 360 in January 1793 to behead the king, and a long string of similar executions followed that included Queen Marie Antoinette and up to 20,000 others. Concerned Americans asked whether a reign of terror and the abolition of godly worship were legitimate costs for the establishment of republicanism. Most thought not. Many agreed with Jefferson, however, who wrote, "My own affections have been deeply wounded by some of the martyrs to this cause, but rather than it should have failed I would have seen half the earth desolated; were there but an Adam and an Eve left in every country, and left free, it would be better than it now is."

The French Revolution suddenly became no longer a matter of mere spectator interest in February 1793, when France declared war on England, Spain, and the Netherlands and thereby raised the question of what U.S. policy should be if the Paris government invoked the treaties of 1778. Differences between Federalists and Republicans hardened, the former accusing the Republicans of planning to drag the United States into the war on the side of anarchy, the latter charging the Federalists with opposing French revolutionary ideals and conspiring to end liberty at home.

During the ensuing debates among the president's advisers, Hamilton declared that because the collapse of the monarchy changed the form of government in France and because treaties were between governments and not between peoples, America's obligations under the pacts of 1778 had been suspended. Not until France had established a legitimate government should these treaties be reenacted. The treaties were "defensive" in nature and *France* had declared war on England. Should the United States support the revolution and end up on the wrong side, Hamilton warned, a new king would come to power, the United States would have alienated all monarchies in Europe, and France would have renewed its hope of reestablishing its empire in North America. Jefferson countered with an argument for *de facto* recognition—that King Louis XVI had acted only as a representative of the French nation and that a mere change in the form of government did not abrogate treaties. The nation and its government *in fact* remained—and so did the treaties. Yet Jefferson did not favor U.S. aid to France. If the French asked for help under the treaties of 1778, the United States could decline on the ground that the French had not offered assistance when the British refused to evacuate the northwest fur posts.

The discussions soon focused on whether the president should issue a proclamation of neutrality. Jefferson, supported by Attorney General Edmund Randolph, stood in opposition on the constitutional ground that only Congress could declare war and therefore only it could declare neutrality. The secretary of state also argued against a declaration of neutrality without first securing trading privileges from the belligerents. Hamilton, backed by Secretary of War Knox, warned that the use of neutrality to wrest concessions from England could thrust the United States into the war. Congress had not declared war, Hamilton concluded, and the president's duty was to keep the peace. He could proclaim neutrality and continue trade.

On April 22, 1793, President Washington accepted Hamilton's argument and proclaimed neutrality. Out of deference to Jefferson, he did not mention the word *neutrality* in the proclamation, but he urged Americans to follow a "friendly and impartial" policy toward the warring nations. Refusal to obey would lead to prosecution in U.S. courts for any transgression of international law. Congress eventually followed with the Neutrality Act of June 1794, which defined the duties of Americans as neutrals.

Trouble had already developed around a young French emissary sent to the United States, Citizen Edmond Charles Genet. Brash, charming, multitalented, and an idealistic advocate of worldwide revolution for human freedom, he unleashed a popular storm that threatened to draw the United States into France's war with England. Genet's letter of accreditation forecast the problems he would face in America. His superiors addressed it to Congress, not to the president, because of their erroneous belief that the legislature, like the National Convention in Paris, embodied the sovereignty of the country. Genet's instructions were clear: Negotiate a pact with the United States to spread republicanism to all humanity; instigate a liberation movement in Louisiana, Florida, and Canada; secure advance payments on the Revolutionary War debt; request free passage of privateers (privately owned ships licensed by the government to raid enemy vessels) and prizes (captured ships and cargo, which France alleged was implicit in the provision of the Treaty of Amity and Commerce of 1778, because it forbade such privileges to France's enemies). Genet did not invoke the Treaty of Alliance, but he intended to use the United States as a base of operations against England and Spain.

Genet arrived in the United States on April 8, 1793, not in Philadelphia (the new capital since 1790) but in Charleston, South Carolina. The reason was simple: Charleston was a hotbed of republican sentiment, which Genet intended to kindle into a crisis that would force the Washington administration to comply with French wishes. The state's governor, William Moultrie, was openly favorable to France and dramatically reminded Americans of its help during the Revolutionary War. But Moultrie had other motives that were not necessarily patriotic in nature: He (along with many South Carolinians) held frontier land claims that would rise in value if Spain were removed from Florida and the Mississippi Valley.

Edmond Charles Genet
"Citizen" Genet from France became the focal point of domestic and foreign policy in the United States when he attempted to seek help from Americans during the country's war with England and Spain. *Library of Congress.*

Genet immediately went to work in Charleston and elsewhere in securing assistance against England. He persuaded the governor to permit the commissioning of more than a dozen privateers, which eventually captured more than eighty prizes in the war. French consuls in the United States, following Genet's instructions, set up admiralty courts that condemned and sold the prizes. Although the U.S. Supreme Court declared these actions illegal a year later, that was no help in 1793. Meanwhile, Americans served on the privateers in violation of the neutrality proclamation, but when several of them were arrested, pro-French juries found them innocent. Some captures occurred in U.S. territorial waters, eliciting vigorous protests from British Minister Hammond. When Genet was unsuccessful in securing advance payments on the debt the United States owed France, he prepared to

wrest New Orleans from the Spanish by commissioning an expedition of Americans led by the aged and habitually inebriated Revolutionary War hero George Rogers Clark. This scheme failed, but Genet was undaunted. The envoy began an anti-administration propaganda campaign, arranging the publication of pro-French editorials in Philadelphia's newspapers that urged Americans to disregard the president's posture of neutrality.

The United States's greatest concern—that Genet might call for its intervention on the side of France in the European war—did not materialize, because he knew that the United States had no navy and that it was more advantageous to seek help for France's trade in the Caribbean. Numerous times British naval commanders seized American ships with French goods aboard and escorted them into prize courts that condemned the cargoes. The British argued that the absence of an Anglo-American treaty guaranteeing the rights of neutrals permitted Royal Navy officers to confiscate goods on board these ships. To counter these losses, Genet offered liberal trade concessions to American merchants willing to carry food and naval stores from the French West Indies to Europe.

Genet angered the Washington administration by his actions and by his purposefully delayed arrival in the nation's capital. The president's decision in March to receive the French envoy, although he stipulated a reception with no cordial welcome, actually constituted a tacit recognition of the French treaties and acceptance of Jefferson's arguments for *de facto* recognition. But the neutrality proclamation had upset Genet, and he retaliated by taking twenty-eight days to make the weeklong journey through Republican backcountry from Charleston to Philadelphia. Finally at his destination, he encountered a president visibly angered by this affront to the Executive Office. The president's icy reception caused Genet to charge that "old Washington" envied his fame. Francophilic Americans joined in criticizing the president, and Genet attended a banquet in the capital during which 200 guests toasted the guillotine while an artillery battery outside fired rounds of approval. Woodcuts soon appeared, attributed by some to Genet, which pictured Washington as victim of the blade.

Jefferson agreed with the president that Genet had gone too far. He informed the emissary that granting military commissions in U.S. territory was an insult to the nation, and he cited various authorities on international law in declaring that a belligerent's fitting of privateers was a violation of neutrality. Genet nonetheless licensed a recently seized British ship as privateer and ordered it, with Americans aboard and under French colors, down the Delaware River to take Louisiana from Spain. To protests from Jefferson and the governor of Pennsylvania, Genet indignantly replied that he would appeal to Congress and to the American people for a popular ruling on U.S. obligations to France under the treaties of 1778. Genet believed that the division in the United States afforded an opportunity to liberate it from aristocratic control, and he refused to listen to Jefferson's protests. Nor would he accept Jefferson's arguments that the president had a constitutional right to interpret treaties. Genet's intentions to defy the president led Jefferson to term his actions "disrespectful and even indecent." Washington lashed out, "Is the minister of the French Republic to set the acts of this Government at defiance *with impunity*? What must the World think of such conduct, and of the Government of the United States submitting to it?"

Genet had a legitimate basis for several of his claims, but he misread the situation in the United States. Because the Treaty of Amity and Commerce of 1778 denied certain privileges to France's enemies in war, it left the implication that France should enjoy these same privileges. Furthermore, before France intervened in the Revolutionary War, it had permitted privileges to Americans that President Washington now refused to the French. Moreover, the cold nature of the neutrality proclamation constituted a break with standard European practice: The United States, as

France's ally, could have declared a "friendly" neutrality instead of a "strict" neutrality. But the Frenchman failed to understand that President Washington followed a course of neutrality not to hurt France but to protect the United States.

Providential intervention, as some have called it, saved the United States from internal upheaval and a likely war with France. Vice President John Adams, for one, was worried that the "terrorism" caused by Genet would lead to anarchy in the United States, as it had done in France. But during the height of the Genet crisis in late summer of 1793, yellow fever swept the nation's capital and scattered Philadelphians into the countryside. At the cost of more than 4000 lives among a population of 55,000, the epidemic dispersed the mobs and, Adams believed, saved the city and nation from revolution.

Washington ended the episode in August by securing unanimous support from his advisers for Genet's recall. In the meantime the French arranged the departure of the U.S. minister in Paris, Gouverneur Morris, for interfering in French affairs on behalf of the king and his supporters. Genet's Girondin party, however, had lost power to Maximilien Robespierre and the radical Jacobins, and the ensuing consignment of republicans to the gallows moved Genet to ask Washington if he could remain in the United States. The president gave in, with the stipulation that Genet retire from public life. His successor, Jean Fauchet, arrived in February 1794 with orders to restore amicable relations with the United States and to arrest Genet and send him home for trial and probable execution. Genet discreetly chose a longer life over a martyred death. He married the daughter of Governor George Clinton of New York, became a naturalized U.S. citizen, and lived a quiet, prosperous life until his death in the 1830s. But he never came to understand either Washington's constitutional role in foreign policy or the adulation Americans felt for him after the Revolutionary War. Genet remained under the delusion that he had failed because *Jefferson* had betrayed France by blocking all efforts to secure American help in the war with Britain.

Jay's Treaty

As U.S. relations with France improved, those with Britain deteriorated in almost direct proportion. The Definitive Treaty of Peace of 1783 had become a mockery by the spring of 1794. British soldiers remained in the northwest fur posts. Indians were armed with British weapons and angry with continued U.S. encroachments onto their land. The United States had rejected British efforts to mediate the growing conflict between the Indians and the U.S. citizens in the Ohio Valley; the British then sought to carve a "neutral, Indian barrier state" from American territory that would protect their fur trading interests. At sea the problems were equally serious. The English had already captured more than 250 American merchant vessels in the French West Indies. James Madison and others in Congress believed that American products were vital to England's war effort and pushed through a sixty-day embargo on goods bound for foreign ports. Only the tie-breaking vote of Vice President Adams prevented the Senate from passing a nonintercourse bill against Britain, but Congress called out 80,000 militia and authorized the defense of U.S. harbors. Danger awaited those who opposed this wave of Anglophobia; in Baltimore and Norfolk, mobs tarred and feathered Americans who spoke favorably of the mother country.

At the outset of the French wars in 1793, the British introduced maritime restrictions that curtailed U.S. freedom of the seas and insulted national honor. Within a year the privy council, the advisory body to the king, had announced three Orders-in-Council that ignored the principle of "free ships, free goods," by prohibiting neutrals from carrying contraband or illegal war materiel to France and its islands in the Caribbean. One justification, the British explained, was the Rule of 1756, which they had arbitrarily proclaimed during the French and Indian War. The rule held that

ports not open in peacetime remained closed in war. Another justification was the doctrine of "continuous voyage," which permitted British cruisers to seize American vessels moving from the French West Indies, even if en route home, on the ground that their ultimate destination was the enemy—France. In 1793, to stop desertions, the British asserted the right to search U.S. ships and "impress" or force runaways back into the Royal Navy. This practice of impressment, according to Americans, violated their nation's rights at sea—a charge that intensified when British naval officers ultimately removed Americans as well as Britons. The United States was in a precarious position. To insist on neutral rights could mean war with Britain; failure to do so permitted affronts to U.S. honor and violated the treaties of 1778 with France.

Federalists feared war and, in mid-April, Hamilton and a few allies persuaded the president to appoint John Jay, then chief justice of the Supreme Court, as special emissary to England to resolve problems between the nations. Experienced in European diplomacy after his time in Madrid and Paris during the Revolution, veteran of the abortive negotiations with Gardoqui, and secretary of foreign affairs under the Articles of Confederation, Jay nonetheless had two distinct disadvantages: He was a Federalist and he was openly pro-English. Jeffersonians were unable to block Jay's approval by the Senate. The battle became so bitter that President Washington departed from the established procedure of discussing a diplomat's instructions with the Senate. He instead asked Edmund Randolph as secretary of state to draft secret instructions (Jefferson had tired of the continual political battles and resigned at the end of 1793). Jay himself had misgivings about the appointment: "No man could frame a treaty with Great Britain without making himself unpopular and odious."

Under these circumstances, it is doubtful that anyone could have negotiated a favorable treaty with the British. Somehow Jay was to exact concessions from a nation that could not grant them because of their potential negative

John Jay
Jay became one of the nation's most vilified
diplomats after negotiating a treaty with England
in 1795 that did not achieve what America
expected. *Begun by Gilbert Stuart ca. 1783 and
completed by John Trumbull ca. 1804–1808;
National Portrait Gallery.*

impact on its war effort. Furthermore, he had
no leverage because 90 percent of U.S. imports
came from England, and his general instructions were to avoid war at nearly any cost.
Specifically, he was to seek reparations for
British violations of American shipping, negotiate an agreement whereby neither nation
would furnish arms to the Indians for use
against the other nation, settle all Anglo-
American problems since the Treaty of 1783,
and negotiate a commercial agreement. Randolph overcame Hamilton's objection and included a warning to England that failure to
comply with their government's requests could
cause the United States to join the League of
Armed Neutrality, the alliance of small-navy
nations formed in 1780. Hamilton feared that
such a threat would lead to war and took care

of that problem privately. Before Jay arrived in
London in June, Hamilton secretly informed
British Minister Hammond that the isolationist tenets of the Washington administration precluded the country from joining the
alliance. Hamilton's action was of questionable propriety, but it had no effect on the negotiations. The British considered the League
too weak to challenge their supremacy at sea.
Moreover, Hamilton had not told Hammond
anything new. The London government had
secured a copy of Jay's correspondence with
the Department of State and realized that a
U.S. alliance posed no danger. And yet, even
with all these odds against him, Americans expected Jay to hold fast to the French treaties
of 1778, win commercial rights in the British
West Indies, bring an end to impressment, establish the rights of neutrals at sea, and gain
recognition of national honor.

Jay surprisingly received a warm welcome
in London, one quite different from his customary treatment during his dark days in Madrid. In fact, the British were so cordial that he
decided against informing people back home
for fear that they might think he had sold out
to England. This was sound reasoning: When
Americans learned that he had followed English custom by kissing the queen's hand, they
accused him of prostrating America before the
English—and probably for gold. The London
government played on Jay's well-known van-
ities. A private report in the hands of Lord
Grenville, the British foreign secretary, outlined the procedure he intended to follow during the negotiations:

> [Jay] can bear any opposition to what he advo-
> cates provided regard is shown to his ability. He
> may be attacked by good treatment but will be
> unforgiving if he thinks himself neglected. . . .
> He certainly has good sense and judgement. . . .
> But almost every man has a weak and assailable
> quarter, and Mr. Jay's weak side is *Mr. Jay.*

Jay's overriding concern for peace prevented him from exploiting the biggest advantage he had: England's realization that war
would hurt its campaign against France and

close its largest commercial outlet—the United States.

Jay and Grenville signed the Treaty of Amity, Commerce, and Navigation on November 19, 1794, which offered measured satisfaction on issues affecting North America but did not contain the maritime concessions that Americans had expected. The British agreed to evacuate the northwest fur posts by June 1, 1796, but with the stipulation that traders and citizens of either nation, with the exception of the hated British Hudson's Bay Company, could use the land and waters of the continental interior to pursue their business. Such provisions, Jay and Grenville hoped, would calm people along the border. The Mississippi River remained open to England, although Jay resisted Grenville's effort to expand control south to present-day Minneapolis. The United States won most-favored-nation status in the British Isles and economic privileges in the British West Indies, but the latter remained closed to American ships more than seventy tons in size. In exchange for this limited concession, Jay agreed that American vessels would not export cotton, sugar, and other staples from the islands to any port other than in the United States. The remaining problems—reparations for maritime violations, pre–Revolutionary War debts, the northeast boundary of present Maine—would later go before joint Anglo-American arbitration commissions for settlement.

Jay did not achieve anything close to what Americans had demanded. His treaty contained no mention of impressment, no guarantee of neutral rights, no end to paper or non-enforceable blockades, and no indemnification for slaves taken from the United States by departing British soldiers in 1783. Jay recognized that under certain conditions the British could confiscate American food shipments headed for France, with compensation, and agreed that French goods on U.S. vessels were subject to seizure and that the British could treat naval stores as contraband. Thus, he violated the treaties of 1778 with France. In a transparent effort to conceal these mutually exclusive treaty provisions, the signatories in

London attached an innocuous assurance that no part of their pact would violate existing treaties with other countries.

President Washington received the treaty shortly after Congress adjourned in March 1795, leading him to call the Senate into special session the following June. Meanwhile, he kept its terms secret, which further fanned the fears of Republicans and Francophiles, who mounted an intense propaganda campaign against a treaty they had not seen. The Senate debated the agreement in secret session (a standard procedure that then looked mysterious), in which the Federalists managed to save it by the minimum two-thirds vote of 20 to 10. The verdict took on a sectional cast, with all but two New Englanders voting in favor and the entire south standing in opposition. The Senate consented to the pact only after rejecting the restrictive terms relating to America's trade with the British West Indies.

During the debate a Republican senator surreptitiously informed the newspapers of the treaty's contents, and that set off a raging public battle. Republicans hanged and burned Jay in effigy for failing to gain a renunciation of impressment, reciprocal commercial privileges with the British, and recognition of America's freedom of the seas. Southerners, less concerned with principles than with economic interests, denounced Jay for failing to secure compensation for their confiscated slaves, as well as relief from debt obligations incurred before the Revolution. An angry crowd in Charleston toppled the statue of William Pitt, once hailed by pre–Revolutionary era Americans as their chief spokesman in Parliament. In New York City a heckler stoned Hamilton when he spoke for ratification of the treaty, and someone snidely remarked that Jay could have crossed the country at night by the light of his burning effigies. The author of *An Emetic for Aristocrats* described the negotiations in Biblical style, complete with the devil:

> One John, surnamed Jay, journeyed into a far country, even unto Great Britain. 2. And the word of Satan came unto him saying, Make thou a covenant with this people, whereby they

may be enabled to bring the *Americans* into bondage, as heretofore: 3. And John answered unto Satan, of a truth . . . let me find grace in thy sight, that I may secretly betray my country and the place of my nativity.

The bitter exchanges seemed to drum on endlessly. An anonymous writer scrawled his wrath on a fence: "Damn John Jay! Damn every one that won't damn John Jay!! Damn every one that won't put lights in his windows and sit up all night damning John Jay!!!" On the Federalist side, the ablest defense of the treaty came from a series of twenty-eight articles signed "Camillus" but written by Hamilton. So persuasive were these pieces that Jefferson complained to Madison, "Hamilton is really a Colossus to the anti-Republican party. Without numbers, he is an host within himself."

President Washington considered Jay's most important achievement the maintenance of peace, yet when he signed and thereby ratified the treaty on August 18, 1795, he too had serious reservations. He had objected to the restrictive West Indian clause, which the Senate deleted, and he had doubts about other commercial provisions. A feature that might have made the treaty attractive—British removal from the northwest fur posts—had become a matter of small consequence because of General Anthony Wayne's recent victory over the Indians at the battle of Fallen Timbers. Britain's ability to hold the posts had depended on Indian support, but in August 1794 the Indians had failed to resist Wayne's forces and had become disillusioned with their so-called allies. In the ensuing Treaty of Greenville of 1795, the Indians agreed to leave Ohio country, making it impossible for the British to remain there, irrespective of Jay's Treaty.

But Jay's handiwork had maintained a tenuous Anglo-American peace. He emphasized to the president that Britain, as a nation at war, could not make concessions injurious to its cause. The president had no alternative but to ratify the treaty. He could not take a sharply divided country, having almost no army and under a limited and still experimental government, into a war that would expose it to both Indians and Spanish along the western frontier and the powerful British navy on the seas. War with England was out of the question.

The partisan and sectional nature of the treaty fight became even more pronounced when Madison led Republicans in the House of Representatives in one last attempt to block the pact by refusing to appropriate money for its implementation. The debate reached a fiery climax in the spring of 1796, when the president turned down a House request to hand over official materials relating to the treaty on the ground that such a move would violate the constitutional provision stipulating that the treaty power rested only with the Executive Office and the Senate. The atmosphere became so heated that one Republican Anglophobe stabbed his brother-in-law, another Republican, for speaking in favor of the appropriation. In April the House voted 51 to 48 to approve the funds. Most yeas came from Federalist New England and New Jersey; the nays came from the Republican south.

Jay's Treaty was important for several reasons. Britain's signature on the document and the territorial concessions contained within it reconfirmed U.S. sovereignty. The treaty marked the beginning of a ten-year Anglo-American rapprochement, or harmonious relationship, that permitted U.S. trade with Britain to triple and allowed the young nation to solidify its status. The joint commission approach to international disputes encouraged the use of arbitration in diplomacy, which itself marked a major breakthrough in international relations. And, by putting English and U.S. relations on a more friendly footing, the treaty necessarily changed U.S. relations with Spain and France.

In regard to Spain, the changes effected by Jay's Treaty were highly advantageous to the United States. The Spanish foreign minister, Don Manuel de Godoy, had initiated a move toward negotiations when he learned in July 1794 that Jay was preparing to depart for England. Godoy suggested to the Washington administration that Spain was amenable to an agreement pertaining to the Florida boundary and use of the Mississippi River. After some delay the president directed South Carolina Federalist Thomas Pinckney, then minister to London, to leave for Madrid as special envoy.

By the time Pinckney arrived in Spain in June 1795, conditions were highly favorable to a settlement. Spain had pulled out of the European war, on the way to switching sides from England and allying with France. Spanish leaders did not know the terms Jay had negotiated with England, but the mere existence of an Anglo-American pact was alarming. In July, Spain deserted England by signing the Treaty of Basel with France, a pact that made peace between the European nations and turned over Spain's eastern half of Santo Domingo to France. Fearful of British retaliation, Godoy assumed the worst when he heard of Jay's negotiations.

Godoy was concerned about areas west of the Appalachians, because Jay's Treaty, as far as he knew, might have authorized an Anglo-American force to seize Spain's possessions in North America. Moreover, the Spanish had failed in their efforts to foment separatism and Indian uprisings in the west, and the steadily growing westward movement in the United States seriously threatened their holdings on the continent. Perhaps western concessions along with his own treaty with France would delay U.S. migration west. Knowing that the French hoped to reestablish their imperial interests in North America, Godoy calculated that a clash between the United States and France could preserve the declining Spanish empire and restore his popularity to the point that he could again appear in public. Pinckney's Treaty resulted from Godoy's effort to win American favor and stave off an Atlantic alliance against his country.

Pinckney sensed his advantages. In the palace monastery at San Lorenzo, he asked for and received the following concessions: free navigation of the Mississippi River; the "right of deposit" (storage of goods while awaiting shipment) at New Orleans for three years, renewable there or at some other port; a northern boundary of Florida at the thirty-first par-

allel, which constituted a considerable retreat from Spain's previous demands for a line almost a hundred miles north at 32°28'; a mutual pledge not to stir up an Indian rebellion against either Spain or the United States; Spain's approval of the U.S. definition of neutral rights; and the establishment of mixed commissions to resolve U.S. damage claims for depredations committed by the Spanish navy during the European conflict. Godoy convinced the Spanish Council of State that the possibility of war with Britain prevented a refusal of Pinckney's requests.

In October 1795 Pinckney's Treaty was signed, securing everything the U.S. minister had sought, although in fact Spanish forces did not pull out of the disputed area above Florida for three years. The treaty caused a surge of nationalism in the United States by opening the river, restraining the Indians, and ending Spain's separatist efforts in the southwest. It also had a reciprocal effect on Jay's Treaty. Southerners and westerners in the House of Representatives cast their support for the treaty with England in hope of drawing a northern endorsement of the agreement with Spain. In March 1796 the Senate unanimously approved Pinckney's Treaty.

In regard to France, news of Jay's negotiations likewise had an unsettling effect. U.S. relations with France had improved since James Monroe, Virginia Republican and an ardent Francophile, had arrived in Paris as minister in 1794. Before the National Convention Monroe passionately supported the ideals of the French Revolution and, amid wild cheers, received the traditional fraternal kiss signifying the bonds between the countries. Despite Washington's proclamation of neutrality, Monroe implied that U.S. sympathies lay with the French. During the uproar over Jay's mission, he promised that his country would not violate the Treaty of Alliance. President Washington, Monroe assured the French, would *not* ratify the treaty.

But Washington *did* sign the treaty, and all of Monroe's best efforts could not arrest the rapid decline in Franco-American relations. In the summer of 1796 the Paris government renounced the rights of neutrals defined in the treaties of 1778, and in late August the president became exasperated with Monroe's blatant supplications and called him home. When Washington sent Charles Cotesworth Pinckney of South Carolina (brother of Thomas Pinckney) to succeed Monroe, the French Directory refused to receive him and warned that failure to leave the country would lead to his arrest. Pinckney prudently left for the Netherlands. The French minister in Philadelphia, Pierre Adet, who had brought pressure on members of Congress to vote against the House appropriations bill for Jay's Treaty, cast support for Thomas Jefferson in the presidential election of 1796, hinting darkly that only Jefferson's election would prevent France from making war on the United States. By the end of the year war with France seemed imminent.

Relations with France and England had a direct impact on Washington's Farewell Address, published in the Federalist newspaper *American Daily Advertiser* of Philadelphia in September 1796. The president had decided against a third term (setting another precedent that lasted until the election of Franklin D. Roosevelt in 1940), and with Hamilton as coauthor of his last public declaration, he recommended that the nation avoid "permanent alliances" with any country. Ideas expressed earlier by Thomas Paine and John Adams permeated the document. The Atlantic Ocean, Washington asserted, separated the United States from the Old World, allowing Americans to stand clear of its peculiar political troubles. Americans should permit only "temporary alliances for extraordinary emergencies." The president also warned that party division at home invites "foreign influence and corruption." In a statement reflecting America's recent encounters with France and England, he concluded that such foreign influence poses one of the most dangerous threats to a republic. Washington's Farewell Address did not constitute a call for pure isolationism; rather, it was a plea for a realistic foreign policy that protected the national interest by adhering to the principle of noninvolvement, keeping Europe and the United States out of each other's political affairs.

Even though war seemed to be on the horizon when Washington left office, his achievements in foreign relations had been outstanding. Perhaps during his two terms as president circumstance deserves more credit than the man, but Washington had dignified the Executive Office without following the tempting paths toward monarchy. He had held the nation together and in so doing had set precedents for a restrained and flexible policy that safeguarded the U.S. interest. Under Washington's leadership, the United States had finally realized the assurances contained in the Treaty of 1783. The administration had placed the nation on sound economic footing, established credibility at home by putting down the small-scale but greatly publicized Whiskey Rebellion of 1794 in western Pennsylvania, met debt obligations to French and Dutch creditors by implementing Hamilton's financial program, maintained neutrality during the French wars and thereby won a measure of respect in international affairs, secured control of the Mississippi River along with the beginnings of a commercial inroad into New Orleans, and opened the way to U.S. settlement of the areas north of Spanish Florida.

Adams the President

By an electoral vote of 71 to 68, John Adams narrowly defeated Thomas Jefferson for the presidency in 1796. The closeness of his victory, combined with the strange circumstance making Jefferson, as runner-up, his vice president, boded ill for the Adams administration. (The provision for separate ballots for president and vice president did not go into effect until passage of the twelfth amendment in 1804.) Hamilton's political manipulations largely accounted for the unusual outcome. He had tried to prevent the election of Adams by maneuvering Thomas Pinckney into the presidency. But Hamilton was convincing only on an open stage. He was anything but Machiavellian, making his attempts at political intrigue as devious as a falling boulder.

Adams had barely emerged as president, determined to avenge this insult but continually hampered by a Federalist party almost fatally divided between his followers and those of Hamilton. Washington's popularity had meanwhile declined largely because of Jay's Treaty, and, even though he denied any party affiliation, with his decline had gone the central strength of the Federalist party that had claimed him as its own. His legacy to Adams included troubles with Hamiltonians in the thoroughly factionalized party as well as the growing strain with France. The popular base of the Federalist party had stagnated while that of the Republicans had flourished, because their democratic ideals had attracted immigrants and other nonelites of U.S. society.

Adams's personal traits added to his tribulations, for he was a veritable anachronism in a nation moving toward greater popular participation in government. Sixty-two years of age and vice president for eight years, he was vain, humorless, cold, and puritanical—personal flaws that mitigated his better traits of fervent nationalism, strong will, and deep intellect. Finally, he faced bitter dissension within the administration that he had helped bring on himself. Partly because he did not wish to seem presumptuous, but mainly because he could not find able men willing to serve in the existing political climate, Adams retained Washington's entire cabinet. That move was ill-advised: These men were friends and admirers of Hamilton's, and Hamilton and Adams were far from friends and admirers of each other. With this situation and the French problem, the overriding question confronting the new administration was which realm of U.S. affairs would explode first—domestic or foreign.

While the breach in the Federalist party threatened to wreck the administration, Adams faced more pressing problems with France that forced him into negotiations. In 1797 the French declared that U.S. vessels carrying enemy cargo of any kind were subject to capture and warned that French officers would

John Adams
President of the United States during the Quasi-War with France, he earlier headed the committee to draft the model treaty in 1776 and helped negotiate the Treaty of Paris of 1783. *Library of Congress.*

treat everyone aboard as pirates. By June France had seized more than 300 U.S. ships in the West Indies. In one instance the commander of a French privateer had an American tortured in a vain effort to convince him to say the cargo he carried was English and subject to confiscation. Adams followed the example of his predecessor and dispatched a special mission to France that was composed of South Carolina Federalist Charles Cotesworth Pinckney, still in the Netherlands; John Marshall, a Federalist from Virginia, a distant cousin of Jefferson's, and later the chief justice of the Supreme Court; and Republican Elbridge Gerry of Massachusetts, the president's longtime friend who accepted after Jefferson and Madison turned down the invitation.

In October the delegation was introduced to the Byzantine nature of European diplomacy by Charles Maurice de Talleyrand-Périgord, former bishop of the Roman Catholic Church during the *ancien régime* and now foreign minister. Talleyrand had lived in exile in the United States during the early stages of the French Revolution and had become convinced that the new American nation was so weak that the mere threat of commercial restrictions would force it into compliance with the treaties of 1778. He hoped that protracted negotiations would hurt Adams's chances for reelection and bring in a Republican administration favorable to France. Talleyrand would then work toward the acquisition of Louisiana from Spain and the reestablishment of the French empire in North America.

The timing of the American mission was unfortunate, because the European war had tipped in France's favor and its leaders showed no inclination to defer to their visitors. The young Corsican, General Napoleon Bonaparte, had secured the Treaty of Campo Formio with Austria in mid-October and had won several battles in Italy. Talleyrand was in no mood for concessions and displayed a haughtiness insulting to the U.S. representatives. He and Napoleon hoped to destroy the United States by pulling it into the war with England.

The episode took a mysterious and ominous twist when three Frenchmen entered the anteroom where the U.S. delegation waited. Claiming to speak for Talleyrand, they demanded an apology for disparaging remarks Adams had made about France in his recent message to Congress and called for a payment of $250,000 and a loan of $12 million as prerequisites to negotiations. To sweeten the proposal, Talleyrand sent a woman to persuade the three to submit to French requests. Although she had a memorable impact on Marshall, the Americans were not swayed by either her charms or Talleyrand's heavy-handed intimidation: "No; no; not a sixpence," Pinckney fervently replied to the suggested bribe.

Many would like to think that the U.S. diplomats turned down the French demands for money because they believed such action morally wrong, but the truth was that Pinckney, Marshall, and Gerry knew that the use of bribes—in the form of money and women— was standard procedure in European diplomacy. Besides, the United States had sent large amounts of money to the Barbary states of North Africa to prevent piracy of American commercial vessels in the Mediterranean. The problem was that the three diplomats' instructions did not authorize payment of such a huge sum, because any major exchange of money would have taken the appearance of a loan that would have violated neutrality and caused war with England. The risks were too great, especially when the delegation would gain only the right to negotiate. After months of frustration, Pinckney and Marshall demanded their passports. Talleyrand, who believed that continued negotiations would prevent a U.S. war he did not want, urged Gerry to remain; but soon afterward the Adams government called him home.

News of the sharp diplomatic exchanges in Paris arrived in the United States in early 1798 and stirred up popular demand for war. President Adams appeared before Congress in May to report that peace attempts had failed and that he was preparing U.S. defenses against France. Frantic, disbelieving Republicans in the House denounced the president for pushing unnecessarily for war and demanded to see the official correspondence from the delegation to France. Adams broke Washington's precedent and complied, after changing the names of Talleyrand's three agents to X, Y, and Z. On reading the dispatches, the Republicans realized that the president's allegations about French insults were true and tried to block the release of the papers to the public. Adams, however, ordered the printing of 10,000 copies of the XYZ dispatches and whipped emotions to such a fever pitch that many people called for war. Newspapers claimed that when X, Y, and Z demanded the bribes, Pinckney roared: "Millions for defense but not one cent for tribute!" Although he repeatedly denied having made such a statement, those words became permanently attached to him during his lifetime and followed him to his grave, to be emblazoned on a tablet over his tombstone in Charleston. Americans chanted the phrase to inspire the fainthearted into joining a war for honor. The song "Hail Columbia" was written to heighten the feelings of nationalism. President Adams, torn between his predecessor's advice to avoid war and the popularity that was his for the first time, solemnly assured Americans that he would not send another minister to France until that government promised to receive him as "the representative of a great, free, powerful, and independent nation."

By the summer of 1798, the United States had taken several steps toward a formal declaration of war. Congress approved a war loan, authorized a "Provisional Army" of 10,000 men to supplement 3500 regulars stationed along the frontier, created a marine corps, and established a navy department (formerly an adjunct of the war department) that increased the number of ships from three to twenty-seven. In addition, Congress authorized the arming of merchant vessels and commissioning of privateers, and it abrogated the treaties of 1778 on the ground that French maritime seizures had already violated their provisions.

Adams attempted to persuade Washington to become general of the army, but the Virginian adamantly refused the offer until Hamilton, Adams's archenemy, became his second in command and took charge of field operations. Adams was unable to contain his wrath. Hamilton dreamed of leading his soldiers into Louisiana and Florida, and he favored Anglo-American cooperation in removing Spain and France from the Caribbean and South America, in line with the aims of Francisco de Miranda and other contemporary Latin American revolutionaries.

The combination of patriotism and distrust of French sympathizers in the United States set off a national frenzy in 1798. Suspicion of fellow Americans as well as French and Irish aliens in the country became so rife that leading Republicans, including Vice President Jefferson, were watched for treasonous behavior.

One of the milder Federalist comments about waffling Republicans was that they reminded him of the "weak dupe who finds himself compelled to turn an unfaithful wench out of doors, stopping her at the threshold to whine over their former loves, and to remind her of past joys." From their pulpits ministers denounced godless France, and other Americans warned that anarchy was about to sweep the United States—perhaps set off by slave uprisings. Adams's supporters proudly wore black badges, and fights broke out over the XYZ Affair. The president rode the wave of xenophobia by dramatically declaring, "The finger of destiny writes on the wall the word: War."

Federalists in Congress responded that same year with a series of laws aimed more at the Jeffersonians than at subversion. Justifying them as wartime measures, Congress passed the Alien Act, which permitted the president to crack down on dissent by arresting and deporting "dangerous" aliens; the Alien Enemies Act, which authorized the deportation of enemy aliens in time of war; and the Sedition Act, which forbade "any false, scandalous and malicious writing" against the government and led to the indictment of twenty-five Republican newspaper editors, ten of whom were tried and convicted by Federalist-dominated juries. The Federalists revealed their real purpose when they included in their legislative package the Naturalization Act. It raised residency requirements for citizenship from five to fourteen years in an ill-disguised effort to slow the growth of the Republican party, which had already attracted great numbers of naturalized citizens. But the Federalists were not through. That summer George Logan, a Philadelphia Quaker, traveled to Paris as an unauthorized peace emissary and received a warm welcome from the Directory. This episode enraged the secretary of state, Timothy Pickering. At his urging, the Federalists in Congress rammed through the Logan Act, which prohibited diplomatic involvement by private citizens under penalty of a $5000 fine, a year in prison, or both.

These congressional measures confirmed the Republicans' worst fears. More than party strife was involved, Jefferson warned: The republic itself was at stake because the Federalists were conspiring to establish monarchical rule.

The Republicans attacked these acts with the Kentucky and Virginia Resolutions. Secretly written by Jefferson and Madison in 1798 and 1799, the resolutions appealed to the Tenth Amendment to the Constitution in arguing that the states must mediate between the people and the central government to protect liberty. They also employed the "compact theory" of government to call the Alien and Sedition Acts violations of freedom of speech guaranteed by the First Amendment. Both writers appeared to advocate interposition as remedy, but their solution was a Republican victory at the polls in 1800.

President Adams meanwhile recalled his predecessor's sage advice and resisted the popular clamor for war. Admittedly, Adams had reversed himself upon learning that Hamilton was to be second in command, but his decision for peace was prudent for other than personal reasons. War with any European power, as Washington had argued, would be disastrous to the United States. But Adams shocked fellow Federalists by refusing to ask Congress for a declaration of war, and he soon faced a rebellion within his party by leaving it in the politically vulnerable position of having to justify wartime laws during peacetime. Maritime incidents continued for more than two years, during which time the U.S. Navy seized nearly one hundred armed French ships in what became known as the Quasi-War. But neither nation formally declared war.

President Adams finally decided to send another mission to France to resolve the countries' differences. He had learned from three sources—William Vans Murray, U.S. minister to the Netherlands; John Quincy Adams, representing his father in Berlin; and Talleyrand himself—that France wanted to settle its disputes with the United States. Adams seized the moment and appointed an all-Federalist delegation comprising Murray; Oliver Ellsworth,

chief justice of the Supreme Court; and William R. Davie, former governor of North Carolina. The Senate approved Adams's plan, and the men left for Paris in March 1800.

By autumn of that year the delegation had taken advantage of a changed situation in the European conflict to negotiate an end to the Quasi-War. Napoleon, now in control of the French government, needed a break in the war with England to enable him to solidify his position at home and abroad, and he worked with Talleyrand to offer acceptable terms to the Americans. The two Frenchmen had devised a scheme to avenge the humiliations of the 1763 Treaty of Paris by consummating their country's long-time designs on North America. They were well aware of the enthusiastic reports of the economic and military value of the Ohio and Mississippi valleys, and now thought that a settlement with the United States would put pressure on Spain to cede Louisiana to France. The vast province, Napoleon and Talleyrand believed, might become a granary to feed Santo Domingo, and the island, in turn, could provide critical sugar supplies for France. Restoration of the French empire in North America necessitated a truce in the war with England and a resolution of difficulties with the United States. Although the possibility of a French return to the continent posed a threat to U.S. interests, the more immediate objective was to prevent war with France. The time was right for Americans to profit again from Europe's troubles.

Negotiations with France stretched over seven months, because Talleyrand fell ill and Napoleon was often gone during the war in Italy, but the two countries finally signed the Convention of 1800 in September. The pact upheld the maritime principles sought by the United States in the model treaty. Both nations recognized the most-favored-nation principle in trading with one another, and they agreed to return ships taken during the Quasi-War. When the U.S. delegation sought indemnification for violations of the treaties of 1778, however, the spokesman for the French, Napoleon's brother Joseph, countered that the United States had abrogated the treaties and could not seek reparations under them. Further discussions postponed the matter to "a convenient time." After more complications, the French agreed to cancel the treaties if the Americans gave up their damage claims stemming from recent maritime seizures. The United States assumed the claims and eventually settled $20 million in damages to its citizens (not until the early 1900s). But this was a small price for gaining release from the French Alliance of 1778.

At Joseph Bonaparte's country estate at Mortefontaine, Napoleon held a huge party to celebrate the treaty-signing ceremony. Unknown to the Americans, the first consul and Talleyrand had already moved toward planting a new French empire in North America. That same day (though dated the following day, October 1), the French secretly concluded the Treaty of San Ildefonso with the Spanish, which awarded territory in Italy to Spain in exchange for Louisiana.

The Convention of 1800 marked an end to America's first era in foreign policy. It substantiated the neutrality principles found in the model treaty of 1776, confirmed the wisdom of Washington's Farewell Address in warning against permanent alliances, and sealed the fate of the rapidly declining Federalist party. Most important, it freed the republic of its entangling alliance of 1778. Washington and Adams had preserved the national interest by keeping the country out of war. Trade was increasing because of the rapprochement with Britain brought by Jay's Treaty and U.S. problems with France; settlers were pushing westward because of the treaties with Spain and the Indians; and Eli Whitney's invention of the cotton gin in 1793 had pointed the way to a thriving industry that would, however, bring a host of problems relating to slavery and the African slave trade. But the nation had an independent foreign policy that rested on realistic principles. Adams asked that posterity remember his success in preventing war with France, yet one has mixed feelings about the epitaph he arranged to have inscribed on his tombstone: "Here lies John Adams, who took upon himself the responsibility of the peace with France in the year 1800." Adams had taken a courageous and politically unpopular stand against war. But his initial policies had recklessly and needlessly taken the nation to the edge of conflict, while administering a near lethal dose to his staggering political party. Adams had helped to ensure the Republicans' victory in 1800.

Achievements of the Federalist Era

During the Federalist era the United States formulated a realistic foreign policy that effectively safeguarded the new nation's political and economic interests. Hamilton's financial plan brought economic order, and Jefferson's persuasive arguments during the Genet crisis established a precedent for *de facto* recognition of foreign governments that prevailed until Woodrow Wilson's presidency during the early twentieth century. Washington's policies were sometimes unpopular, but they were always in line with the national interest. The controversies between Hamilton and Jefferson, although divisive and bitter, facilitated the president's desire to make balanced decisions based on widely diverse points of view. The Neutrality Proclamation, Jay's Treaty, Pinckney's Treaty, the Treaty of Greenville, and the Convention of 1800 were all monuments to a realistic brand of diplomacy that helped the United States secure the guarantees contained in the Treaty of 1783 ending the Revolutionary War.

The Federalists' successes were tempered by the realization that Adams's French policies had combined with the aristocratic, vindictive, and warlike nature of many of his colleagues to wreck the party. A proud people proclaimed vindication of independence, republican principles, and national integrity in 1800 by electing Jefferson over Adams as president. Labeled idealist and pacifist, Jefferson and his successor eight years later, friend and ally James Madison, would belie their images by venturing into diplomatic paths skillfully avoided by Washington and Adams and taking the nation into war with England.

Selected Readings

Adams, William H. *The Paris Years of Thomas Jefferson.* 1997.

Allison, Robert J. *The Crescent Obscured: The United States and the Muslim World, 1776–1815.* 1995.

Ammon, Harry. *The Genet Mission.* 1973.

Bemis, Samuel F. *Jay's Treaty: A Study in Commerce and Diplomacy.* 1923; 1962.

———. "Washington's Farewell Address: A Foreign Policy of Independence," *American Historical Review 39* (1934): 250–68.

———. *Pinckney's Treaty: America's Advantage from Europe's Distress, 1783–1800.* 1926; 1960.

Bowman, Albert H. *The Struggle for Neutrality: Franco-American Diplomacy during the Federalist Era.* 1974.

Boyd, Julian P. *Number 7: Alexander Hamilton's Secret Attempts to Control American Foreign Policy.* 1964.

Burt, Alfred L. *The United States, Great Britain and British North America.* 1940.

Charles, Joseph. *The Origins of the American Party System.* 1956.

Chinard, Gilbert. *Honest John Adams.* 1933.

Combs, Jerald A. *The Jay Treaty: Political Battleground of the Founding Fathers.* 1970.

Crowley, John E. *The Privileges of Independence: Neomercantilism and the American Revolution.* 1993.

Darling, Arthur B. *Our Rising Empire, 1763–1803.* 1940.

DeConde, Alexander. *Entangling Alliance: Politics and Diplomacy under George Washington.* 1958.

———. *The Quasi-War: Politics and Diplomacy of the Undeclared War with France, 1797–1801.* 1966.

Dowd, Gregory E. *A Spirited Resistance: The North American Indian Struggle for Unity, 1745–1815.* 1992.

Elkins, Stanley M., and McKitrick, Eric. *The Age of Federalism.* 1993.

Ellis, Joseph J. *Passionate Sage: The Character and Legacy of John Adams.* 1993.

Gilbert, Felix. *The Beginnings of American Foreign Policy.* 1961. Originally published as *To the Farewell Address: Ideas of Early American Foreign Policy.* 1961.

Hagan, Kenneth J. *This People's Navy: The Making of American Sea Power.* 1991.

Horsman, Reginald. *The Diplomacy of the New Republic, 1776–1815.* 1985.

Hutson, James H. "Intellectual Foundations of Early American Diplomacy," *Diplomatic History 1* (1977): 1–19.

Jensen, Merrill. *The New Nation: A History of the United States during the Confederation, 1781–1789.* 1950.

Kaplan, Lawrence S. *Colonies into Nation: American Diplomacy, 1763–1801.* 1972.

———. *Jefferson and France.* 1967.

Ketcham, Ralph L. *Presidents Above Party: The First American Presidency, 1789–1829.* 1984.

Kurtz, Stephen G. *The Presidency of John Adams: The Collapse of Federalism, 1795–1800.* 1957.

Lang, Daniel G. *Foreign Policy in the Early Republic: The Law of Nations and the Balance of Power.* 1985.

Levin, Phyllis L. *Abigail Adams: A Biography.* 1987.

Lewis, James E., Jr. *The American Union and the Problem of Neighborhood: The United States and the Collapse of the Spanish Empire, 1783–1829.* 1998.

Liss, Peggy K. *Atlantic Empires: The Network of Trade and Revolution, 1713–1826.* 1983.

Lycan, Gilbert L. *Alexander Hamilton and American Foreign Policy, A Design for Greatness.* 1970.

McCoy, Drew R. *The Elusive Republic: Political Economy in Jeffersonian America.* 1980.

McDonald, Forrest. *Alexander Hamilton: A Biography.* 1979.

———. *The Presidency of George Washington.* 1974.

———. *States' Rights and the Union: Imperium in Imperio, 1776–1876.* 2000.

Marks, Frederick W. *Independence on Trial: Foreign Affairs and the Making of the Constitution.* 1973.

Miller, John C. *Alexander Hamilton: Portrait in Paradox.* 1959.

———. *The Federalist Era, 1789–1801.* 1960.

O'Brien, Conor C. *The Long Affair: Thomas Jefferson and the French Revolution, 1785–1800.* 1996.

Perkins, Bradford. *The Creation of a Republican Empire, 1776–1865.* 1993. *The Cambridge History of American Foreign Relations*, vol. 1. Cohen, Warren I., ed.

———. *The First Rapprochement: England and the United States, 1795–1805.* 1955.

Phelps, Glenn A. *George Washington and American Constitutionalism.* 1993.

Ritcheson, Charles R. *Aftermath of Revolution: British Policy toward the United States, 1783–1795.* 1969.

Schom, Alan. *Napoleon Bonaparte.* 1997.

Sharp, James R. *American Politics in the Early Republic: The New Nation in Crisis.* 1993.

Spalding, Matthew, and Garrity, Patrick J. *A Sacred Union of Citizens: George Washington's Farewell Address and the American Character.* 1996.

Stinchcombe, William C. "Talleyrand and the American Negotiations of 1797–1798," *Journal of American History* 62 (1975): 575–90.

———. *The XYZ Affair.* 1980.

Stuart, Reginald C. *United States Expansionism and British North America, 1775–1871.* 1988.

Varg, Paul A. *Foreign Policies of the Founding Fathers.* 1963.

———. *New England and Foreign Relations, 1789–1850.* 1983.

Watts, Steven. *The Republic Reborn: War and the Making of a Liberal America, 1790–1820.* 1987.

Weber, David J. *The Spanish Frontier in North America.* 1992.

Whitaker, Arthur P. *The Mississippi Question, 1795–1803.* 1934.

———. *The Spanish-American Frontier, 1783–1795.* 1927.

White, Leonard D. *The Federalists: A Study in Administrative History.* 1948.

Wright, J. Leitch. *Britain and the American Frontier, 1783–1815.* 1975.

CHAPTER 3

Jeffersonian Diplomacy, 1801–1809

Prospects of a Republican Foreign Policy

International conditions were not auspicious when Thomas Jefferson took the presidential oath of office in March 1801. The new Republican administration confronted so many problems with England, France, and Spain that he and Secretary of State James Madison would soon become deeply involved in the Napoleonic Wars in Europe. During the election campaign the Federalists castigated Jefferson for his long-time pro-French sentiment and his earlier collaboration with Madison in the Kentucky and Virginia Resolutions, which contained a governmental theory built on the premise that the demise of the state was preferable to the sacrifice of individual liberty. Many Americans feared that Jefferson, author of religious freedom in Virginia, sought to abolish godly worship; others assailed the writer of the Declaration of Independence as a dangerous radical who would destroy the nation before seeing his ambitions deterred. Many Americans wondered whether the new president could handle the continuing challenges from abroad. Would not Jefferson, a product of the Enlightenment's emphasis on idealistic principles and rational behavior,

rigidly oppose a strong military establishment as conducive to war and soon fall prey to hardened, realistic European diplomats and warriors striving only to achieve their national interests?

Jefferson immediately tried to dispel fears about his foreign policy. In his inaugural address he asserted that "we are all Republicans, we are all Federalists," and, in accordance with the precepts of Paine's *Common Sense,* Adams's model treaty, and Washington's Farewell Address, called for "peace, commerce, and honest friendship with all nations, entangling alliances with none." Jefferson agreed with Franklin and many other contemporaries that the number of Americans would escalate rapidly and that westward expansion would relieve the threat of overpopulation and ensure the new republic's continued growth and security. In the distant future, Jefferson assured fellow Virginian James Monroe in 1801, Americans would inhabit both continents in the hemisphere, building a safe world based on republican principles. Thus, a strong sense of mission and a deep concern about individual liberty, combined with realistic commercial and national security interests, guided Jefferson's expansionist foreign policy.

The Barbary Wars

President Jefferson's international problems did not concern only England, France, and Spain, because as mentioned in the previous chapter, independence also brought difficulties with the Barbary Coast pirates of North Africa. Since 1776 America's merchant marine had no longer enjoyed British imperial protection and had found its passage into the Mediterranean blocked by the pirate vessels of Algiers, Morocco, Tripoli, and Tunis. Jefferson came to realize that U.S. commercial freedom in this part of the world rested on his willingness to use military force.

In the earlier days of the republic, however, the Washington and Adams administrations found bribery less costly than war and joined Britain and other European nations in simply paying tribute to the Barbary states that totaled nearly $10 million. The United States bought its first treaty in the mid-1780s from Morocco, but the other three coastal states continued to raid American shipping and enslave seamen. In the following decade Congress authorized the construction of six frigates to escort commercial vessels through the Mediterranean; but before they were ready for action, the dey (pasha or ruler) of Algiers negotiated a treaty with the United States, by which his country received money plus yearly naval stores. The U.S. government soon purchased similar treaties with Tripoli and Tunis, but the raids went on. The most insulting incident came in October 1800, when the dey of Algiers forced the captain of the warship *George Washington* to lower the Stars and Stripes, raise Algerian colors, and transport that country's ambassador and gifts to the sultan in Constantinople. While Americans were praising Charles Cotesworth Pinckney for allegedly declaring to the French "Millions for defense, but not one cent for tribute," the United States was plying pirates with extortion money.

The situation continued to worsen until just two months after Jefferson's inauguration, when the pasha of Tripoli declared war

Thomas Jefferson
Before becoming president in 1801, Jefferson wrote the Declaration of Independence and, while secretary of state under Washington, advocated a decentralized form of government that became a basic principle of anti-Federalists. *Charles Wilson Peale; Library of Congress.*

on the United States. The president did not ask Congress for a declaration of war but acted on the constitutional provision making him commander-in-chief of the country's armed forces. He sent a squadron to the Mediterranean and sought a buildup of the navy. In June 1805, after some minor skirmishes, the United States claimed victory over Tripoli and signed a treaty that only temporarily eased problems in the Mediterranean. The United States bought peace with humiliating terms that included a ransom payment for imprisoned American sailors and an agreement that new consuls would bear gifts for the pasha.

If U.S. problems with the Barbary states demonstrated that Jefferson was not a pacifist, they also showed that he preferred buying a peace over having to win it through war. His idealistic aversion to war and strong navies gave way to the realities of protecting the nation's commerce and honor. But when it became possible to reopen the sea lanes by signing a treaty that gained only a semblance of honor, he did so. In a real sense, he had returned to the methods of both the Federalists and the British before him. It was cheaper to pay tribute than go to war.

But the purchased peace did not last, leading the United States again to use force. In 1807 the maritime crisis with England forced President Jefferson to order the navy home from the Mediterranean, and for nearly a decade that included the War of 1812, America's commercial vessels fended for themselves against pirates. Finally, in March 1815, Congress approved military action against Algiers, whose dey had declared war on the United States. During the summer the U.S. Navy repeatedly battered the Barbary states of Algiers, Tripoli, and Tunis. Help from European warships finally ended the tributes and the piracy.

Louisiana Purchase

Jefferson's first major decision in foreign affairs concerned the Louisiana Territory, the vast area stretching west of the Mississippi River to the Rocky Mountains, which involved the competing interests of France, Spain, and England. Jefferson had always advocated American migration west. As governor of Virginia during the Revolution, he had urged General George Rogers Clark to deal humanely with the inhabitants of areas he seized; in that way, Jefferson surmised, they would accept American control and benefit from its republican liberties. While secretary of state, he favored intervention in the Anglo-French war rather than risk the danger of England's acquiring Louisiana and the Floridas. Thus, when he spoke to Monroe of Americans peopling the entire continent, the president's expansionist aims were well in place. Scientific curiosity, commercial interests, the spread of individual freedom, continental expansion intended to safeguard a growing U.S. empire from Eu-

ropean encroachment—all drew him to this sprawling and unknown wilderness lying west of the Mississippi.

If there was no fabled Straits of Anian or Northwest Passage connecting east and west, Jefferson hoped for the ultimate development of such a route either by water or by land. Access to both oceans, Jefferson envisioned, necessitated a canal through Central America. Such ambitions lay in the future, however. At present, the United States had other problems, and the areas bordering its western frontiers fortunately belonged to a weak Spain. With patience, Jefferson declared, the United States could take the area "piece by piece."

The Spanish had long been apprehensive that America's westward movement would push them from North America. In 1794 the Spanish governor of Louisiana pinpointed the mainspring of U.S. expansionism:

> [The Americans'] method of spreading themselves and their policy are so much to be feared by Spain as are their arms. Every new settlement, when it reaches thirty thousand souls, forms a state, which is united to the United States, so far as regards mutual protection, but which governs itself and imposes its own laws.

Spain's worst fears became a self-fulfilling prophecy when Pinckney's Treaty of 1795 unleashed a drive toward northern Louisiana and the eastern bank of the Mississippi River. Americans in Tennessee, Georgia, and the Mississippi Territory, realizing that the Floridas controlled the main river entrances into North America, regarded West Florida as the key to the Gulf of Mexico. Although some day the United States would need New Orleans and the Floridas, its leaders were not worried as long as the areas were in Spain's hands. As Jefferson wrote in July 1801, "We consider [Spain's] possession of the adjacent country as most favorable to our interests, and should see with an extreme pain any other nation substituted for them."

France upset this comfortable relationship with Spanish Louisiana. For years rumors had circulated that the French intended to regain the territory lost to Spain during the French and Indian War. As shown earlier, the French minister to the United States during the late 1780s openly speculated about a restored empire in North America. Genet's efforts to wrest New Orleans from Spain were fresh in Americans' minds, and when France acquired the eastern half of Santo Domingo from Spain in the Treaty of Basel in 1795, stories spread in the United States that the French had tried to procure Louisiana as part of the agreement. Although France failed in this venture, it had gained complete control of Santo Domingo by securing the Spanish part of the island— an acquisition that stimulated interest in Louisiana as a granary for feeding the slaves on the sugar-rich Caribbean island. During the presidential campaign of 1796, Federalists accused Republicans of conspiring with the French to fuse areas west of the Appalachians with Louisiana. More than 100,000 Americans who had crossed the mountains by 1790 had reason to worry, for Talleyrand, now foreign minister under Napoleon, had again revived dreams of reestablishing the French empire in the New World.

On the same day that the Convention of 1800 settled the Quasi-War between the United States and France, Napoleon negotiated the secret treaty of San Ildefonso with Spain, which provided for the retrocession of Louisiana. Although many believed that the French had *forced* Spain to give up the territory, the truth was that the Madrid government had been anxious to sell because Louisiana had become a financial burden. The colony's revenue totaled only a fifth of the costs of holding it. Britons and Americans along the river were engaged in a thriving smuggling trade, and the Spanish had lost control over the right of deposit in New Orleans. As early as 1797 Spain's foreign secretary, Don Manuel de Godoy, remarked that "you can't lock up an open field." In a letter to the French on June 22, 1800, four months before the retrocession, he admitted that the area was a "parasite." According to the treaty of 1800, France promised an Italian kingdom

Charles Maurice de Talleyrand-Périgord
French foreign minister who negotiated the Louisiana Purchase with the U.S. diplomats and cagily urged them "to make the most of it" in answer to their question regarding the vast area's hazily defined boundaries. *Source unknown.*

for King Charles IV's brother-in-law, the Duke of Parma, in exchange for six warships and Louisiana. Napoleon's efforts to attach the Floridas failed. Talleyrand assured the Spanish king that French Louisiana would be a permanent barrier to both British and American encroachments. Spain had seemingly secured a buffer between its possessions on the continent and the United States, because Napoleon pledged never to sell Louisiana.

Rumors of a deal between France and Spain regarding Louisiana began drifting into Washington early in Jefferson's first administration. Signs of French activity in the New World had appeared in 1801 when French soldiers arrived in the Caribbean to put down a slave insurrection that had begun in Santo Domingo six years earlier. These fears seemed confirmed when America's minister to London, Federalist Rufus King of New York, informed Secretary of State

Madison in late March 1802 that France had promised an Italian kingdom to Spain, probably in exchange for Louisiana and the Floridas. The following November the British government, hoping to block French expansion in the New World, handed the U.S. minister a copy of a Franco-Spanish treaty of March 1801 (the Convention of Aranjuez), by which the Spanish king's nephew was to become king of Tuscany, later called Etruria. The treaty did not mention Louisiana, but the pieces of information so far received in Washington pointed to that area as the grand prize.

Jefferson reacted in several ways to the rumored sale of Louisiana to the French. He secured congressional authorization to construct fifteen gunboats and to federalize 80,000 state militiamen for duty along the Mississippi River; he warned French and Spanish diplomats in Washington of the anger of western Americans; and he publicly associated with the British chargé in Washington. The charade had effect. The French diplomat warned his home government that the Americans might seize Louisiana. Through a long-time friend then in Washington, Pierre Samuel duPont de Nemours, the president sent two letters to Paris, one addressed to the U.S. minister, Robert Livingston of New York. Dating it April 18, 1802, Jefferson declared his policy toward French ownership of Louisiana:

> [It] reverses all the political relations of the United States and will form a new epoch in our political course.... There is on the globe one single spot, the possessor of which is our natural and habitual enemy. It is New Orleans, through which the produce of three-eighths of our territory must pass to market.... France, placing herself in that door, assumes to us the attitude of defiance.... The day that France takes possession of New Orleans ... we must marry ourselves to the British fleet and nation.

Jefferson left the note unsealed, intending that DuPont read it and share its contents with the French court. France could avoid conflict, the president told Livingston, only by giving New Orleans and the Floridas to the United States. "Every eye in the U.S. is now fixed on this affair of Louisiana." In a covering letter Jefferson warned that the reestablishment of France in North America would be "the embryo of a tornado."

A few days later, on May 1, the president instructed Livingston to buy New Orleans and the Floridas. Although the minister was aged, nearly deaf, and unable to speak French, he was so tenacious in his entreaties that his French counterpart in the negotiations remarked afterward that the American ought to receive a certificate honoring his performance. The New Yorker had been the first secretary for foreign affairs under the Articles of Confederation and knew well the value of patience and persistence in diplomacy. Although Talleyrand denied that France had acquired Louisiana, Livingston ignored the disclaimer and continually reminded the French that control of Louisiana was meaningless without the Floridas. He

Robert Livingston
U.S. minister to France who worked with James Monroe in securing the Louisiana Purchase.
Portrait by John Vanderlyn; Collection of the New York Historical Society.

labeled New Orleans and the surrounding area "a desert and an insignificant town" and a "distant wilderness," and questioned whether the entire province would bring either wealth or power. In a suggestion that constituted the first official U.S. interest in lands beyond the Mississippi, he declared that if the United States owned the territory above the Arkansas River, it would serve as a buffer between French possessions below the river and British interests in Canada. Livingston also tried to tie in the reparations claims left unpaid by the Convention of 1800. A settlement regarding Louisiana, he insisted, should clear the air by including French reparations for damages incurred by American shippers during the Quasi-War of the late 1790s.

As Livingston hammered away at the French, the United States learned that in October 1802 Spain's acting intendant (fiscal officer) in New Orleans, Juan Ventura Morales, had suspended America's right of deposit. The move alarmed Americans, because it violated Pinckney's Treaty and appeared to confirm fears that France had regained Louisiana. A British observer declared that this decree had angered Americans more than any event since the Revolutionary era. Americans had reason for concern. Their wartime markets in Europe and the West Indies had grown tremendously by the late 1790s. Sugar, flour, and cotton from the Mississippi Valley entered the world market in steadily increasing volume not only because of the right of deposit but also because an ongoing slave rebellion in Santo Domingo wrecked the island's sugar industry and left a vacuum that Americans filled. In 1796 the value of exports down the Mississippi River was low, but by 1802 it had ballooned to $2 million. Cotton shipments through New Orleans had increased forty times over in three years, and by 1803 American shipping on the river more than doubled that of the Spanish and French combined. Particularly irritating to the Spanish was the flagrant American smuggling of gold and silver.

The order suspending the right of deposit did little economic damage, but the psycho-logical impact was instant and far reaching. It did not affect the Americans' right of free navigation of the Mississippi, nor did it prevent them from unloading their flatboats directly onto outgoing vessels. War, however, seemed imminent—if not with Spain, then surely with France. "The act justified war, to which ever government it might be imputed," Monroe declared, "and many were prepared to risk it by removing the obstruction by force." Although many inhabitants of the Mississippi Valley thought Spain and the United States on the verge of war, others regarded the suspension as Napoleon's first step toward closing the river to American commerce. If rumors were correct that he had secured the Floridas, the French could seal off the Gulf of Mexico and threaten the United States.

Fiction was more dangerous than truth in this instance, because the French had had nothing to do with suspending the right of deposit. Morales had followed a secret directive of July 1802 from Madrid, which instructed him to declare that under Pinckney's Treaty he could not extend the privilege of using New Orleans without direct approval of the Spanish king. The motive was clear: Spain intended to preoccupy France and the United States with one another and forestall American encroachments on Spanish territories in North America.

While irate westerners waited impatiently for Jefferson to take corrective action, the Federalists saw the opportunity for political gain and blasted the administration for failing to protect U.S. interests along the Mississippi River. In the Senate, Federalist James Ross of Pennsylvania demanded $5 million to finance a military expedition to take New Orleans. Alexander Hamilton urged the Republicans to occupy the city and the Floridas before even attempting to discuss the matter with France. The Federalists' strategy was transparent: Jefferson would have to either ask Congress for war with his beloved France (which he would never do) or betray his western constituents and drive them into the Federalists' camp.

Jefferson instead followed the advice of his friend DuPont, who had arrived in Paris and warned in December 1802 that a hard-line policy would worsen matters. Unaware of Livingston's exertions, DuPont recommended that the United States offer to buy New Orleans and the Floridas. Even if the effort failed, it would quiet the Federalists and convince westerners of the president's loyalty to their interests. The United States could not go to war with France. Jefferson, perhaps thinking that Ross's belligerence had unsettled the French and made them more amenable to recognizing U.S. interests in Louisiana, again turned to diplomacy.

In January 1803 the president nominated Monroe as minister extraordinary to France and Spain to assist Livingston in buying New Orleans and the Floridas. It was a wise political move. Monroe was popular among agrarians of the south and west, partly because he owned land in the west and had been a long-time advocate of free navigation of the Mississippi River. He would also have a favorable reception in Paris because of his pro-French stance during his ministerial stay there during the 1790s. Most important, he would have leverage. Should France refuse to negotiate, or should it close the Mississippi River, Monroe was to leave for England to negotiate an alliance.

The Senate only narrowly approved Monroe's appointment, but immediately afterward a House committee recommended an appropriation of $2 million for use in the negotiations and stipulated a demand for free navigation of the Mississippi River and access to all waterways in the Floridas that emptied into the Gulf. "If we look forward to the free use of the Mississippi, the Mobile, the Apalachicola, and the other rivers of the West," Jefferson insisted, "New Orleans and the Floridas must become a part of the United States, either by purchase or by conquest." In a striking move he privately authorized Monroe to go as high as $10 million for New Orleans and the Floridas. Shortly after the Ross resolution for taking the port city met narrow

defeat in the Senate, the special envoy left for France in early March 1803.

During the political controversy in Washington over Monroe's appointment, important changes on the diplomatic front worked to benefit the United States. In March Napoleon decided to break the Peace of Amiens of 1801 and resume the war against England. This monumental step required great amounts of money for the European campaign and for expected problems in the New World. Without French control of the Floridas, the British navy could seize New Orleans and close Louisiana. In the winter of 1802–1803 Napoleon had planned to seize Louisiana, but the army he assembled in the Netherlands for this purpose was iced in at port and later kept from the sea by storms. Even then, a British fleet waited in the English Channel to prevent any armada from sailing to Louisiana. Napoleon had failed to soothe U.S. fears of his intentions in the New World, and he now worried that uneasy Franco-American relations could lead to an Anglo-American alliance.

Failure to acquire the Floridas had weakened France's position by exposing Louisiana to the British, but a more immediate threat to Napoleon's New World plans was his inability to put down the slave insurrection in Santo Domingo. The island, rich in sugar, coffee, indigo, and cotton, was supposed to become the commercial center of a restored French empire in the New World. After the French had secured control over the entire island in 1795, a former slave and spokesman for the blacks, Toussaint L'Ouverture, had at first claimed loyalty to France, but that same year led an insurrection against white control. In November 1801, a month after a preliminary peace with England, Napoleon sent a first detachment of 20,000 men under command of his brother-in-law, General Victor Leclerc, to crush the rebellion. But everything went wrong for the French. In 1802, 24,000 soldiers died in the fighting and from yellow fever. Leclerc tricked L'Ouverture into captivity that year and shipped him to France, where in a dungeon he died of maltreatment and pneumonia.

Napoleon I
As emperor of France, he approved the sale of
Louisiana to the United States in an effort to
promote his war aims with England. *Source
unknown.*

The insurrection, however, raged on. In one
instance that horrified the world, 173 of 176
black captives hanged themselves overnight.
Leclerc estimated that another 70,000 soldiers
were necessary and proposed the following
macabre approach:

> We must destroy all the mountain Negroes, men
> and women, sparing only children under twelve
> years of age. We must destroy half the Negroes
> of the plains, and not allow in the colony a sin-
> gle man who has worn an epaulette. Without
> these measures the colony will never be at peace,
> and every year, especially deadly ones like this,
> you will have a civil war on your hands which
> will jeopardize the future.

A month later Leclerc died of yellow fever.
Notified of his brother-in-law's death, Napoleon disgustedly moved toward abandoning
his American plans: "Damn sugar, damn coffee, damn colonies," he angrily muttered at an

after-dinner gathering. Leclerc's successor ordered countless executions and imported 1500
bloodhounds from Jamaica in an attempt to
break the insurrection. But even these harsh
measures could not arrest the island's movement toward a chaotic form of independence.
With Santo Domingo gone (along with 50,000
French soldiers), the mainstay of the projected
French empire in the New World had slipped
from Napoleon's hands, and with it passed the
need for Louisiana.

With these events fresh in his mind, Talleyrand shocked Livingston in Paris on April 11,
1803, by asking whether the United States
would like to have all of Louisiana. Taken
aback, Livingston managed to reply: "No, our
wishes extended only to New Orleans and the
Floridas." But he agreed to discuss the matter
with Monroe, who was en route from Washington. Unknown to Livingston, Napoleon
had just the previous day notified two of his
ministers that he intended to part with Louisiana, and shortly before the offer to the U.S.
minister he had informed his own minister of
finance, François Barbé-Marbois. Whatever
the emperor's real reasons, his dream of a New
World empire lay shattered in the bloody aftermath of the slave revolt on Santo Domingo.

Several considerations influenced Napoleon's decision to sell, but the basic one was
his acceptance of reality. He had changed his
focus to building French power in Europe and
elsewhere. Money for the war with England
was vital, and he wished to avert a simultane-
ous conflict with the United States and thus
avoid the Anglo-American alliance that Jefferson seemed all too willing to negotiate. Most
important, however, Napoleon had recognized that the relentless nature of America's
westward expansion would turn its economic
dominance of Louisiana into political leadership as well. It seemed prudent to turn over
Louisiana, win American good will, and erect
an obstacle to continued British growth. Furthermore, he hoped that the competing interests of east and west in the United States
would lead to a battle over Louisiana and a climactic division of the nation into two weaker

powers. Perhaps at that undetermined time, the French could revive their imperial interests in the Western Hemisphere.

Two days after Talleyrand's offer to sell Louisiana, Monroe arrived in Paris, where Livingston swallowed his ill-concealed resentment of the Virginian's appointment and informed him of the radically changed situation. Neither man had authority to deal for territory beyond the Mississippi, but they quickly and wisely decided to approve the sale. After considerable dickering over the price, the two emissaries agreed that the United States would pay $11,250,000 for Louisiana and assume responsibility for $3,750,000 in reparations due to U.S. citizens for claims arising from the Quasi-War. In the treaty signed on May 2 but antedated to April 30, 1803, France ceded "the colony or province of Louisiana, with the same extent that it now has in the hands of Spain, and it had when France possessed it; and such as it should be after the treaties subsequently entered into between Spain and other states." Inhabitants of the province were to become U.S. citizens, and the United States guaranteed France and Spain access to Louisiana's ports for twelve years with the same regulations that applied to Americans.

Hardly able to contain their excitement, Livingston and Monroe waited until they signed the treaty to ask the dimensions of the territory. Did it, Livingston asked Talleyrand, contain West Florida? The wily French foreign minister replied in a statement certain to cause problems: "I can give you no direction. You have made a noble bargain for yourselves, and I suppose you will make the most of it." When the Americans persisted in their inquiries, Foreign Minister Marbois asked Napoleon, who remarked: "If an obscurity did not already exist, it would perhaps be good policy to put one there." It is probable that Livingston and Monroe wanted a vague boundary description in the treaty to enable the United States to claim West Florida. It is just as likely that Napoleon preferred the same ambiguity as the best means for ensuring continued trouble between the United States and its Spanish

and British neighbors. Whatever the truth, the United States had bought a huge territory containing thousands of American Indians and countless inhabitants of French, Spanish, and perhaps even British lineage.

Jefferson's celebration of the Louisiana Treaty was short-lived, for several constitutional and legal questions troubled him. The U.S. Constitution did not authorize the president to purchase land, nor did it permit him to convert a territory's residents into American citizens. He also had qualms about Napoleon's right to hand over Louisiana, because the Spanish minister in Washington emphasized that France had not yet transferred territories in Europe to Spain in accordance with the retrocession of 1800. No change of title to Louisiana had taken place, and it still belonged to Spain, he told Jefferson. Furthermore, the Spanish minister noted that Napoleon had promised the king of Spain that no third power would ever own Louisiana. But Jefferson's major worry was whether the United States had the constitutional right to make the purchase.

Jefferson considered a constitutional amendment to justify the acquisition. After Congress approved the treaty and paid for the area, he thought, it "must then appeal to *the nation* for an additional article to the Constitution." Albert Gallatin, secretary of the treasury, had sent a memorandum to Jefferson noting a constitutional justification for acquiring land as a means for expanding the republic. "The existence of the United States as a nation," Gallatin wrote, "presupposes the power enjoyed by every nation of extending their territory by treaties, and the general power given to the president and Senate of making treaties designates the organs through which the acquisition may be made." By the doctrine of implied or inherent powers, long rejected by Jefferson, Gallatin argued that in times of national need the president or Congress might go beyond the strict letter of the Constitution for the good of the nation.

Jefferson hesitated, but finally decided to forgo his rigid interpretation of the Constitu-

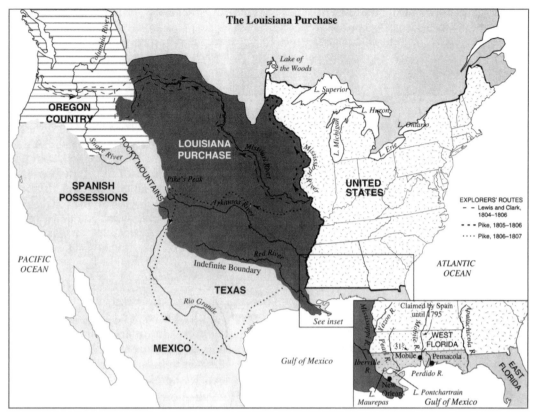

The Louisiana Purchase

Map 7
Clearly Jefferson's outstanding achievement as president, the purchase of Louisiana doubled the size of the United States and pointed the way to a continental empire.

tion in the interest of the nation. This was a wise move. In Paris, Livingston had warned that Napoleon seemed prepared to back out of the deal. The president received a letter from the minister in August declaring that France was "sick of the bargain," that Spain was "much dissatisfied," and that the "slightest pretense" could cause Napoleon to cancel the treaty. To Madison, Jefferson advocated overcoming the constitutional problems "*sub silentio.*" The president forwarded the treaty to the Senate, explaining that his purpose was to take advantage of a situation that might never present itself again. A "strict observance to the written laws is doubtless one of the *high* duties of a good citizen, but it is not the *highest*. The laws of necessity, of self-preservation, of saving our country when in danger, are of a higher obligation." Years afterward Jefferson agreed with Madison that the United States's acquisition of Louisiana had fully transformed the republic into an "empire of liberty" because it had joined freedom with expansion as a natural outgrowth of a Constitution that promoted "extensive empire and self-government."

The laws of politics dictated a battle over the treaty's approval. In a remarkable sleight of hand, Federalists reversed their stance exemplified in the Ross resolutions and now denounced the purchase for authorizing too much money for land the country did not need. They attacked its constitutionality and objected to admitting Louisiana into the Union as one or more states equal to the others. Yet these arguments were again transparent masks for their real concern that new western states would ally with the south to further undermine New England's political position in the nation. One Federalist senator sincerely concerned about the constitutionality of the purchase was John Quincy Adams, son of the former president, who asked whether the Constitution's treaty-making power permitted the involuntary addition of non-Americans to the Union. An amendment was necessary, he insisted. But his motion to establish a committee for this purpose failed, and Adams became the only Federalist to vote with the Republicans when the treaty won approval in October 1803 by a tally of 24 to 7.

On December 20, 1803, in a small ceremony at the Place d'Armes in New Orleans, the United States doubled in size when the French formally made the transfer of Louisiana, less than three weeks after receiving the province from Spain. In the presence of a few Americans and no French soldiers, the Stars and Stripes replaced French colors over American Louisiana.

Livingston had been correct in urging the president to approve the purchase without delay. Napoleon had acted illegally. He had not upheld his deal with Spain in 1800, for no nations recognized Etruria, and his soldiers remained in the kingdom. By transferring Louisiana to a third power, he broke his promise to Spain and violated the French constitution of 1799 by selling territory without the legislature's approval. Similarly, as Napoleon violated his word, his treaties, and his country's constitution, President Jefferson departed from his understanding of the U.S. Constitution in accepting the territory in the national interest.

Later, in 1828, the U.S. Supreme Court implicitly approved the constitutionality of the Louisiana Purchase in the case of *American Insurance Company* v. *Canter*. The nationalistic Chief Justice John Marshall, Jefferson's cousin but no friend or political ally, ruled (in regard to the purchase of Florida) that the government's treaty and war-making authority gave it the power to acquire territory and incorporate its inhabitants into the United States. Louisiana had already become the first state cut out of the vast territory; it was admitted to the Union in 1812.

The Louisiana Purchase laid the basis for a U.S. empire, even though some American citizens wanted more and wrongly claimed that past treaties gave the United States West Florida as part of the sale. "From this day," Livingston proudly declared, "the United States take their place among the powers of the first rank." The treaty affirmed the imprecision of the boundaries, for it defined Louisiana as "the same extent it now had in the hands of Spain and that it had when France possessed it [before the Treaty of Paris of 1763]." Livingston's efforts to determine the borders revealed that French and Spanish markings were different. Louisiana as defined under French control before the 1760s was larger than the area defined under Spanish ownership. French Louisiana enveloped all areas east of the Gulf shores to the Perdido River, including Mobile. Spanish Louisiana stretched east from the Mississippi River but only along the Iberville River and Lakes Maurepas and Pontchartrain. Lands between the Iberville and Perdido rivers, or much of West Florida, went to England in 1763 but were returned to Spain by the Treaty of Paris two decades later. The Louisiana dealt by Spain to France in 1800, and which Napoleon sold to the United States three years later, did not include West Florida.

The U.S. claim to West Florida was unfounded for other reasons as well. It is doubtful that at the outset of the negotiations, Livingston considered either of the Floridas part of Louisiana. At one point, he had written Madison that he favored exchanging Louisiana for the Floridas, because the latter area was more important. Yet after the negotiations, Livingston seems to have convinced himself that Napoleon had unwittingly included the Floridas in the sale of Louisiana to the United

States. Monroe recognized the weakness of this argument: Following the negotiations in Paris, he left for Madrid, where he attempted to deal for the Floridas. Even though the Louisiana Treaty did not include the Floridas, the ambiguity of the boundary provisions permitted the United States to make what it claimed was a legitimate argument for West Florida. Livingston and Monroe recommended that President Jefferson assume control over all lands between the Mississippi and Perdido rivers. Despite claims by both France and Spain that Louisiana's eastern border was the Mississippi and the Iberville, the United States insisted that the purchase included all of West Florida west of the Perdido and that the port of Mobile belonged to America.

The Jefferson administration lacked either legal or historical claim to the Gulf Coast east of the Mississippi River, and therefore it engaged in several dubious schemes intended to establish U.S. control over West Florida. In February 1804 Congress took the first step toward this objective by passing the Mobile Act. It authorized the president to extend jurisdiction over Mobile and set up customs controls on the bay, although the bay was Spanish territory. Protests from Madrid caused Jefferson to move the customs district inland to Fort Stoddard on the Mobile River, in U.S. territory north of the thirty-first parallel. The following April President Jefferson sent Monroe to join Charles Cotesworth Pinckney, now U.S. minister in Madrid, to persuade Spain to sell the Floridas. The timing seemed propitious, for Spain had allied with France in war against England. The two Americans sought East Florida and the Perdido River as the boundary of West Florida, but Spain had French support and refused to sell. In May 1805 Monroe and Pinckney proposed to Secretary of State Madison that the United States simply take the Floridas as indemnity for damage claims against Spain, which stemmed from the Quasi-War of the 1790s and from its decision to close the port at New Orleans in 1802. Jefferson found no problems with this high-handed approach.

In his message to Congress in 1805 he tried to force Spain into an agreement by warning of the possible use of 300,000 soldiers.

The war in Europe suddenly seemed to afford the United States an opportunity to purchase the Floridas from Spain. Napoleon needed money once again and no longer upheld Spain's position. In 1805 he intimated to the United States that he might persuade Spain to sell the Floridas for $7 million. The president seized the opportunity and convinced Congress in February 1806 to authorize a secret sum of $2 million to begin the acquisition process. But when the war suddenly shifted in France's favor, Napoleon withdrew the offer, and the negotiations never got under way. The Jefferson administration had one more chance in January 1808, when Napoleon tried to draw the United States into the war against England in exchange for the Floridas. But French armies seized Spain, and Napoleon again changed his mind when his brother Joseph, occupying the Spanish throne, opposed giving them up. Jefferson's hopes for acquiring the Floridas came to an end after an insurrection in Spain was followed by similar uprisings in its New World colonies.

The Louisiana Purchase, even without West Florida, proved to have monumental importance. The United States had acquired 828,000 square miles of territory for a mere three cents an acre. The negotiations had possibly prevented war with France and an entangling alliance with England. The new territory had widened the agrarian base of the Republican party, promoted national unity by deepening western loyalties to the Union, and offered Jefferson the opportunity to fulfill his dream of an empire of liberty. Indeed, the purchase had established a pattern for acquiring territories and gaining their inhabitants as citizens. The questionable chapters in the Louisiana story did not dampen the United States's territorial drive, as witnessed by its continuing interest in West Florida. Some expansionists even interpreted the Louisiana Treaty to include Texas, which they saw as a stepping-stone toward

California, Oregon, and the Pacific Ocean. The deal of 1803 helped advance the Anglo-American tradition of absorbing territories by linking freedom with expansion.

Jefferson fostered U.S. expansion in another important way. Less than a week after Monroe agreed to join Livingston in France, the president asked Congress to authorize an exploratory expedition into upper Louisiana territory that would set up trade with the Indians, compile information on the region and its inhabitants, determine whether whites could live in Missouri, examine the feasibility of an overland route from the Mississippi to the Pacific, and, most important, investigate the military strengths of the British and Spanish inhabitants of the huge area. The British must not be in the position to take upper Louisiana during a war with France, Jefferson declared.

The result of Jefferson's initial request to Congress was a series of expeditions led by army officers that greatly facilitated his efforts to control the North American continent. The first group—led by the president's private secretary Captain Meriwether Lewis, and assisted by William Clark, the younger brother of Revolutionary War hero George Rogers Clark—departed in the spring of 1804 and returned more than two years later with a claim to the continental interior stretching from the Mississippi to the Pacific coast. Meanwhile Jefferson sent army Lieutenant Zebulon Pike on two explorations. In 1805–1806 Pike failed in his stated purpose of locating the source of the Mississippi River, but he returned with valuable information on British influence in the surrounding area. He led another group southwest in 1806–1807, ostensibly to find the headwaters of the Arkansas and Red rivers, but probably under secret orders to determine Spanish strength in northern Mexico. These three explorers established America's overland ties with the Pacific coast and the Spanish southwest, and they helped to fulfill Jefferson's expansionist objectives in America. Meanwhile, by 1805, steadily worsening relations with England turned the president's attention to Atlantic affairs.

Deteriorating Anglo-American Relations

Resumption of the Anglo-French war in 1803 necessarily involved the United States because of its commercial interests in Europe and the West Indies and because of its efforts to protect the rights of neutrals at sea. British naval supremacy barred French and Spanish shipping to and from the Caribbean, so these two countries tried to recoup their losses by permitting U.S. vessels to take over the carrying trade. At first, in the early 1790s, Britain had sought to prevent this traffic by invoking the "Rule of 1756," which arbitrarily declared that ports closed in peacetime could not be opened in wartime. Since 1794, however, Britain had in effect waived the rule for American shippers by respecting the doctrine known as the "broken voyage." According to this doctrine, if carrier commanders "broke" a voyage from French or Spanish islands in the Caribbean by paying duties or posting bond in a U.S. port, they changed the status of their cargo to "neutral" or "American" and could legally reexport that cargo to Europe. The British Admiralty Court confirmed the principles of the broken voyage in the *Polly* decision in 1800. As a consequence, between the early 1790s and 1807, American exports increased fourfold, and imports doubled. Even so, President Jefferson and Secretary of State Madison, not content with the flimsy protection of the broken voyage, wanted more: They insisted on the principle that "free ships make free goods."

Instead, they were about to get less. With the renewed outbreak of war, Royal Navy officers complained that U.S. trade with Britain's enemies hurt the British war effort and deprived their merchants of profits. Moreover, they charged that U.S. ships were using the doctrine of the broken voyage fraudulently by docking but not actually off-loading cargo while in an American port, and then receiving a refund or drawback on the duties, which made them revert to their original status and further substantiated the phony conversion of the goods.

The beginning of the end of the United States's "first rapprochement" with England came with the *Essex* decision of 1805, which reversed the *Polly* case in an attempt to rectify the problems of the broken voyage concept. British naval commanders had seized the *Essex*, an American merchant vessel out of Barcelona, Spain, as it moved toward Havana after allegedly breaking the voyage in Salem, Massachusetts. The British Admiralty Court ruled that the mere claim of duty payment no longer sufficed in establishing that the ship's captain had broken the voyage; he must now *prove* his innocence. The *Essex* decision thus shifted the burden of proof from the capturing party (as under the *Polly* decision) to the captured party.

Evidence later showed that British suspicions were correct: The captain of the *Essex* had paid $5278 in duties and received a refund of $5080 before leaving for Havana. The stopover in Salem, the judge declared, had not neutralized the goods because the captain had not made a bona fide payment of duty. The voyage was "continuous" and a violation of the Rule of 1756 because its final destination was an enemy port.

The problems caused by the *Essex* case were attributable more to implementation of the decision than to the decision itself. Most nations recognized a belligerent's right to confirm a neutral's status and search for contraband, but the special irritant here was that the London government provided no advance notice that the *Essex* decision had changed policy. The Royal Navy had authorization to take suspicious ships to Halifax, Nova Scotia, for trial by an admiralty court already infamous for delaying shipments and ordering confiscations of cargo. British commanders thereupon stopped American vessels carrying French or Spanish goods headed toward either the Caribbean or Europe. Their decision to station warships near U.S. ports constituted a virtual blockade that enraged Americans.

Other events in 1805 also signified a hardening of British policy toward neutrals. In October the navy, under Lord Admiral Horatio Nelson, defeated the combined French and Spanish fleets near Trafalgar off southwest Spain and established British control of the seas; two months later the French armies rolled over Austrian and Russian forces at the Moravian village of Austerlitz, leaving Napoleon in control of Europe. The war stalemated, and the battle scene shifted to the commercial lanes. On the same day of Nelson's victory, October 21, a pamphlet in London gained instant popularity by urging a British clampdown on maritime restrictions. Sir James Stephen, an admiralty lawyer who was close to several British political leaders, wrote *War in Disguise; Or, the Frauds of the Neutral Flags*, which argued in behalf of the *Essex* decision and Britain's right to regulate the seas. Taxation, licensing, blockades, searches for contraband, impressments—*any* measures were justified to restrict a neutral's activities. The United States would not fight, Stephen insisted. Within a year the London government used the *Essex* decision, Nelson's victory, and Stephen's ideas in a concerted effort to shut off neutral trade to France.

As is so often the plight of neutrals, the United States found itself caught between the belligerent powers. In May 1806 the British announced the first of a series of Orders-in-Council that proclaimed a blockade of Europe from Germany's Elbe River to the French town of Brest. Napoleon retaliated with the Berlin Decree, which declared all British ports closed. The United States angrily denounced both measures as paper blockades in violation of international law. Early the following year the British announced two more Orders-in-Council, which ruled that trade carriers had to stop in England and pay duties on cargo before entering French ports. Napoleon countered with the Continental System, which, simply put, aimed at destroying British commerce. His Milan Decree of December warned that anyone submitting to Britain's rules would become a British possession subject to capture. His Continental System did not close all European ports to British shipping, for Spain, Sweden, and Russia kept trade lanes open; but from 1807 to 1812 the French captured more

American vessels than did the British. Thus, the British confiscated those ships not abiding by the rules, whereas the French seized those that did. Europe was a "great madhouse," moaned President Jefferson.

Although France likewise committed infractions that hurt American commerce, it was England's maritime supremacy, combined with its imperious treatment of neutrals, that made it the main object of U.S. complaints. The Royal Navy patrolled U.S. waters and met U.S. protests with ill-concealed arrogance, whereas the French could only stop ships in their ports or in the Caribbean. Besides, although they never paid reparations, the French implied that they were going to do so by apologizing for their seizures as mistakes. Britain's licensing system was an affront to the rights of neutrals, which the United States only grudgingly accepted because it profited from the sale of goods to the British Isles.

After the war resumed in 1803, Britain returned to the practice of impressment and quickly ignited the most emotional issue between the Atlantic nations. Desertions from the Royal Navy had dramatically increased during the first phase of the Anglo-French war; by the time the fighting ended in 1801, Nelson reported, 42,000 sailors had jumped ship. Many publicly denounced their officers, which encouraged British impressment gangs to be nondiscriminatory in rounding up alleged runaways. Abominable working conditions, heartless lashings at sea, wretched food, and miserable wages drove nearly 2500 a year from British ranks. Many signed on board American merchant ships, where treatment was more humane and wages far higher. Between 1793 and 1812 British commanders impressed nearly 10,000 seamen from private American vessels—more than 6000 of these after 1808 alone and many of them native U.S. citizens. The London government claimed that by 1812, 20,000 of its people were on American ships, about half the total on their rolls. The United States offered to bar British deserters from American vessels in wartime in exchange for the renunciation of impressments, but the

British government refused. The Royal Navy needed 10,000 additional men a year to maintain its ships at sea. A British commander had obstinately declared in 1797, "It is my duty to keep my Ship manned, and I will do so wherever I find men that speak the same language with me."

The impressment issue was so complex that the United States and Britain were both correct in their diametrically opposed positions. Few Americans questioned Britain's right to stop desertions, but they staunchly proclaimed that their country's naturalization process for granting citizenship protected former Britons from capture. The British held, instead, to their long-time argument for perpetual allegiance— "Once an Englishman always an Englishman"— which meant that a person born in England could not change citizenship and remained forever subject to fulfilling patriotic duties. Impressment, they declared, was a prerogative of the crown, grounded in common law and supported by acts of Parliament. Jefferson ardently disagreed. "I hold the right of expatriation [renunciation of allegiance] to be inherent in every man by the laws of nature." Thus did both sides in the controversy present convincing arguments based on national honor.

Enterprising Americans exacerbated the already raw situation by falsifying naturalization or "protection" papers and selling them for a small price. Britain's First Lord of the Admiralty, Lord St. Vincent, snidely remarked that "every Englishman . . . may be made an American for a dollar." Deserters bribed U.S. consuls and others in responsible positions and received bogus citizenship papers in return. The British never claimed the right to remove U.S.-born Americans, but they refused to recognize naturalized U.S. citizens and made a seemingly inordinate number of mistakes in distinguishing between Britons and U.S.-born Americans. These "mistakes," the United States noted, were often in direct proportion to the number of men needed to fit the British ship in question. The British offered to free those captives who could prove they were bona fide Americans, but such a laborious process required time and included no provision for reparation.

The question of sovereignty was central to both protagonists in the impressment controversy. The British argued that to command the perpetual allegiance of all their citizens was integral to national honor and security. Another country's flag provided no protective shield for deserters. The U.S. government insisted that any person could become a naturalized citizen of the United States and, as such, deserved the security afforded by the newly adopted government. Furthermore, *all* American ships at sea—whether private or public—were an extension of their country, protected by the flag overhead. Madison considered "a neutral flag on the high seas as a safeguard to those sailing under it." To this assertion, British Foreign Secretary Lord Harrowby replied in 1804 that the "pretension advanced by Mr. Madison that the American flag should protect every individual sailing under it on board of a merchant ship is too extravagant to require any serious refutation." The British claimed the right to visit and search *private* vessels at sea. Sovereignty rested in *naval* vessels and prevented such a search, they admitted, but a merchant ship was not a piece of U.S. territory simply because it flew the U.S. flag.

The two opposing arguments were nonnegotiable because of the high stakes involved on each side. The British regarded it as a matter of vital national interests: Renunciation of impressment would invite desertions, threaten supremacy at sea, and jeopardize the war effort with France. The Americans saw it as a matter of national integrity: Impressment of either naturalized or U.S.-born Americans was an infringement of the flag and sovereignty and a diminution of national honor. Had the United States been willing to accept something less than renunciation of the practice— perhaps Britain's adoption of precautionary measures to prevent abuses or mistakes and indemnification for those made—they might have resolved the issue. Had the British been amenable to U.S. assurances that deserters would not be welcome on merchant vessels, the two parties might have found grounds for settlement. But each side distrusted the other. British commanders eventually gave up trying to distinguish between native-born U.S. citizens and sailors born in England. They simply regarded all naturalization papers as forged or illegal under British law and arbitrarily selected those seamen deemed traitors and fit for duty. Mistakes occurred, and even when evidence convinced the British Foreign Office that U.S. citizens had been victimized, it refused to make reparation upon their release.

Peaceable Coercion as Possible Remedy

In 1801 President Jefferson wrote confidently that U.S. economic pressure would force Britain and France to respect the rights of neutrals. "Our commerce is so valuable to them that they will be glad to purchase it when the only price we ask is to do us justice. I believe we have in our hands the means of peaceable coercion." In truth, Jefferson's only choice was economic. His desire to cut taxes had restricted the navy to a bare flotilla of single-gun vessels, which were expected to safeguard the entire Atlantic coast. Gunboats, he wrote, were the "only *water* defense which can be useful to us, and protect us from the ruinous folly of a navy." He considered dry-docking ships-of-war near Washington and in times of crisis replacing them with gunboats manned by voluntary militia. The results of Jefferson's austere economic measures were evident in the country's lack of diplomatic leverage due to deficient military and naval power. Commercial pressures held little value without military support; gunboats were no match against warships.

The nation's military inadequacies highlighted two other shortcomings in Jefferson's policy: U.S. trade was *not* vital to Britain, as Jefferson had thought, and Americans were in no mood to make sacrifices for the administration's economic policies. Successful negotiations depended on military and economic strength. Power without willingness to negotiate leads to tyranny, but negotiations with no supportive power lead to protracted discussions that can bring frustration, defeat, and ultimately war. Jefferson's policies pointed toward the latter course.

In late 1806 Jefferson followed the example of his two predecessors in the Executive Office by sending a special mission to resolve all these maritime difficulties: Maryland attorney William Pinkney would join Minister James Monroe already in London. Congress had passed a nonimportation act the previous April, calling for restrictions on specified British goods after November 1, 1806, but the president withheld its implementation pending negotiations with England. In a situation sharply reminiscent of Jay's predicament in the 1790s, Monroe and Pinkney received instructions impossible to fulfill. Jefferson wanted England to renounce impressment and renew the maritime provisions in Jay's Treaty, due to expire in October 1807. Neither objective was feasible in wartime.

In the negotiations, Pinkney and Monroe proved more flexible than their superiors in Washington. They gave up the principle of free ships, free goods, in exchange for relaxed enforcement of the Rule of 1756. Britain ensured a return to the broken voyage concept of the *Polly* decision and agreed to permit U.S. ships into French ports if they first entered a home port of the United States. Foodstuffs were exempted from contraband, Britain allowed American ships to pass into European ports not under blockade, and the United States agreed to end nonimportation for a ten-year period. Negotiations over impressment were less promising. Britain agreed only to attach a note to the treaty that pledged greater care in removing seamen and ensured reparation for injuries. In practice these expedients would have alleviated the problem; in theory they did not. Monroe and Pinkney nonetheless signed the treaty on December 31, 1806, and forwarded it to the president.

Jefferson, however, refused to send the Monroe-Pinkney Treaty to the Senate because the terms included no disavowal of impress-ment. Furthermore, the treaty renounced for ten years what Jefferson considered to be his country's most effective leverage: commercial warfare. It is uncertain whether the British would have made a sincere effort to reduce the actual instances of impressments, but certainly the outcome of such a treaty could not have been worse than that which followed its unilateral rejection by Jefferson. Soon came tightened maritime restrictions by Britain and the fevered rush of events leading to war. The impressment question ended the possibility of a treaty settlement and soon became the central issue in Anglo-American relations.

On June 22, 1807, the United States and England seemed headed for war when a crisis over impressment occurred that Jefferson considered the most serious since the guns fired in Lexington. A U.S. naval vessel, the frigate *Chesapeake,* was en route from Norfolk to the Mediterranean. Its commodore, James Barron, had been in a hurry to leave the United States and had not prepared his guns or crew for action. Indeed, his men were not at their battle stations and the gun deck was strewn with naval stores to be put away while at sea. Ten miles off the Virginia shore, near Cape Henry, Captain Salusbury P. Humphreys of the British frigate *Leopard* signaled the *Chesapeake* that he had a message. Barron came to and granted permission to board but, in a nearly fatal blunder, he did not follow the prescribed naval procedure of readying his men for battle when moving alongside a foreign ship-of-war.

A British naval lieutenant boarded the *Chesapeake* and presented a note asking permission to search for and remove deserters, in pursuance of orders from a man well-known among Americans as the epitome of admiralty conceit: the commander of the British fleet in U.S. waters, Vice Admiral George C. Berkeley in Halifax. The 375-man crew of the *Chesapeake* included a number of Britons, or so rumor claimed. In fact, the previous February, some crew members from a British ship had escaped into Virginia and signed on board the U.S. ship. One of them, Jenkin Ratford,

H.M.S. Leopard *and U.S.S.* Chesapeake
This encounter at sea between the British and U.S. vessels brought attention to the impressment issue and ultimately helped cause the War of 1812. *Mariners Museum, Newport News, Virginia.*

had been a London tailor who enlisted on the *Chesapeake* and openly mocked British officers in the streets and wharfs of Norfolk. Barron refused to permit the search, and the British officer returned to his ship.

A battle seemed certain, but before Barron could prepare his men for action, Captain Humphreys ordered three broadsides fired into the *Chesapeake*. The Americans managed a single return shot, but in just ten minutes their ship lay helpless, with three men dead and eighteen wounded, including Captain Barron himself. Surrender followed, after which British sailors came aboard and seized four deserters, three of them U.S. born. The fourth was Ratford, who they pulled out of hiding and soon hanged at Halifax.

The most explosive aspect of this brief battle was that the British ship had violated U.S. sovereignty by impressing Americans from a *naval* vessel. Britons had searched naval vessels before. In 1798 the British had stopped the *Baltimore* near Havana, and in 1805 they had searched a gunboat and removed three

deserters. But this time Americans had died. When the *Chesapeake* limped back into Norfolk, the reaction was electric. A mob demanded revenge and in frustration angrily destroyed a huge supply of water headed for British sailors in Lynnhaven Bay.

President Jefferson could have had a declaration of war from Congress, but it was not in session, and the military weakness of the United States precluded such a request. Instead, he convened his cabinet and proclaimed that despite Jay's Treaty, U.S. ports were no longer open for provisioning by Britain's naval vessels. He then asked the states' governors for 100,000 militia and prepared the army and navy to defend the coast. These actions were smoke and not fire, however, because he did not call Congress into session until October, nearly four months after the *Chesapeake* affair. Jefferson meanwhile demanded an apology from Britain and warned the French minister in Washington that if the British made no reparations, the United States would seize Canada. Independence and national honor were at stake, declared Secretary of the Treasury Gallatin.

The British government attempted to calm the U.S. outrage over the *Chesapeake,* but that effort proved too little and too late. Britain's soft-spoken minister in Washington, David Erskine, warned his London office of the widespread anger in the United States, and the British government appeared ready to apologize but not to renounce impressment. It recognized that Captain Humphreys of the *Leopard* had overstepped bounds and seemed amenable to removing him from command, returning the impressed Americans, making reparations, and agreeing to leave U.S. warships alone. Indeed, Humphreys was put on half pay, although Berkeley received no punishment. But most of these concessions came years afterward—too late to atone for this flagrant violation of American honor.

Jefferson's only recourse was what he called "peaceable coercion": On December 22, 1807, after he had implemented nonimportation, Congress replaced it with a stronger measure called the Embargo Act. It closed U.S. ports to foreign vessels and restricted American ships to the coastal trade. Madison explained the rationale: "We send necessities to her [England]. She sends superfluities to us. Our products they must have. Theirs, however promotive of our comfort, we can to a considerable degree do without." The Jefferson administration authorized the confiscation of cargo and ships involved in illicit trade, required government approval before loading goods, and stipulated that captains involved in the coastal trade had to post bond twice the value of their cargoes to guarantee compliance with the law. By the following year the country's outgoing goods were a fifth of what they had been before the act; goods from England dropped more than half.

These police measures failed. Shippers accused of breaking the law were usually released, especially by New England courts overrun with jurors who disliked the administration's policies. Jefferson had called for a national sacrifice without instilling a sense of patriotic duty. He had not explained the objectives of the embargo to his constituents, nor had he tied its passage to a new British Order-in-Council, not yet publicly known, that increased restrictions on neutral rights. Unaware of this enhanced threat to their rights at sea, Americans could not understand why they must forfeit the rich profits of foreign commerce, dock hundreds of ships, and discharge tens of thousands of working seamen. Bitter denunciations of the Embargo Act came primarily from New Englanders, whose commercial prosperity had already suffered at the hands of the Republican administration. Many denounced the expansion of federal power. Some, in fact, warned of secession. Such behavior was treason, responded Jefferson, author of the Declaration of Independence and the Kentucky Resolutions, both of which had advocated the same remedy for oppression. Most Americans had another remedy: They simply ignored the Embargo Act. Smugglers sold goods in Spanish Florida, took them across Lake Champlain or overland into Canada (subsequently declared illegal), and blandly claimed that their ships had been blown off course into Canada or the West Indies, and even to Europe.

The Embargo Act threatened to revive the fallen Federalist party. To dramatize the situation, Federalists in Boston brought attention to the economic hardships by building soup kitchens for starving sailors. They claimed that the Embargo Act was unconstitutional because the government could only regulate trade, not stop it. The president, they bitterly charged, had taken sides with the French. They claimed that the measure actually augmented Napoleon's Continental System by preventing American merchants from carrying goods to Europe. The south and west, traditional Republican strongholds, did not protest as hotly because the British blockade had hurt their trade, and economic retaliation seemed appropriate.

The Federalists were correct in their central accusation: The Embargo Act damaged America more than England. In the United States, foreign commerce virtually came to a halt as businesses shut down, seamen lost their jobs, prices for manufactured goods soared, and farmers who had relied on the export trade were ruined. Admittedly, the act hurt British manufacturers who imported American cotton and tobacco, but British merchants compensated for these losses by taking over the U.S. carrying trade with the Continent. In a highly profitable venture, they sold products to Spain, whose people had rebelled against Napoleon, and to its colonies in Latin America. The embargo did damage the British West Indies and Newfoundland, both dependent upon American foodstuffs, and the shrinking supply of American cotton forced some British textile mills to close. But the attempt to extort changes in British maritime policy did not work. Those in Britain who suffered most lacked the franchise and could not influence the government. The British harvest of 1808 was plentiful and helped to offset food problems caused by the embargo.

Jefferson presented the weak argument that the Embargo Act stimulated U.S. manufacturing by reducing dependence on English goods. Albert Gallatin's *Report on American Manufacturers* in 1810 admitted that more money went into industry, but he warned that the public outcry against the administration and the costs in unemployment and trade outweighed any impetus to manufacturing. Evidence suggests that in the long run, U.S. manufacturing did grow faster with the Embargo Act. But in the short run, which mattered most to those most affected by the measure, Americans suffered from the embargo and attributed their suffering to Jefferson.

Napoleon welcomed the act because it caused Anglo-American difficulties by complementing his Continental System and because it had little impact on his transatlantic trade, which the Royal Navy had already nearly closed. In April 1808 he ordered the capture of vessels under U.S. colors found in French ports, on the specious ground that they had to be British because of the embargo. By mid-1809 the French had seized $10 million of American ships and goods. A Massachusetts Federalist disgustedly declared, "Mr. Jefferson

has imposed an embargo to please France and to beggar us!"

Had the embargo remained in effect a while longer, rising food prices and declining industrial sales might have forced the British to reconsider their maritime policy. In early 1809 the British government demonstrated an interest in restoring the Atlantic trade. But the embargo had already taken its place in history as a failure. Americans were not in a forbearing or long-suffering mood and demanded its repeal.

The Embargo Act was idealistic in conception but unrealistic in application. To be sure, it was idealistic because Jefferson and Madison had sought to protect the same rights of neutrals that Paine, Adams, and Washington had emphasized. But it was unrealistic for the United States to demand respect for neutral rights in a war having worldwide repercussions—especially when that neutral nation's only leverage was economic and when even that form of pressure was highly dubious. It was also unrealistic for Jefferson to expect Americans to support their government's wishes if such support meant compliance with a self-destructive law—particularly when a large number of the people expected to make such a sacrifice happened to be New Englanders and members of the opposition Federalist party. The Embargo Act caused deep national disunity.

The Jefferson administration had miscalculated in hoping that Britain would feel the effects of the embargo before the United States did. Although the ports of other nations remained open to British merchants, the president urged Americans to shut out *all* foreign trade. And yet, strange to say, Jefferson was realistic in recognizing that he had no alternative to economic pressure. His long-time opposition to a military buildup dictated peaceful measures, for his only other choice was submission. His economic program might have achieved some success if he had aroused a patriotic outcry by relating his objectives to British maritime measures that severely restricted U.S. neutral rights and insulted national honor. But almost matchless eloquence and reasoning would have been necessary to convince Americans to accept a policy more harmful to them than to those the act was intended to coerce. A potential saving factor was that the embargo bought preparation time for the United States by keeping it out of the European war; but time is valuable only if those in power use it to advantage.

Jefferson's Legacy

Jefferson's diplomacy was filled with paradoxes that make sense only when one realizes that he sought to reconcile the building of a U.S. empire with the protection of individual liberty. Thus did he advocate territorial and commercial expansion while opposing war and calling for a policy of peaceable economic coercion. Largely because of forces beyond his control, Jefferson warded off the French threat in Louisiana, but then, in a situation made more perilous because of the young nation's lack of military preparedness, he failed to safeguard American honor in the midst of the resurging Anglo-French war. On March 1, 1809, three days before Madison became president, Congress replaced the embargo with the Nonintercourse Act. It opened the export trade with all countries except Britain and France but provided that if either nation offered to respect U.S. rights at sea, trade would resume with that country immediately. That measure scarcely improved the situation, because most U.S. commerce was with the two countries at war, and the United States was still caught between them. Jefferson's legacy for Madison was a nearly certain war with England.

Selected Readings

Adams, Henry. *History of the United States during the Administrations of Jefferson and Madison.* 9 vols. 1889–1891.

Allison, Robert J. *The Crescent Obscured: The United States and the Muslim World, 1776–1815.* 1995.

Ambrose, Stephen E. *Undaunted Courage: Meriwether Lewis, Thomas Jefferson, and the Opening of the American West.* 1996.

Banning, Lance. *The Jeffersonian Persuasion: Evolution of a Party Ideology.* 1978.

Brant, Irving. *James Madison: Secretary of State, 1800–1809.* 1953.

Burt, Alfred L. *The United States, Great Britain and British North America.* 1940.

DeConde, Alexander. *This Affair of Louisiana.* 1976.

Dowd, Gregory E. *A Spirited Resistance: The North American Indian Struggle for Unity, 1745–1815.* 1992.

Egan, Clifford L. *Neither Peace nor War: Franco-American Relations, 1803–1812.* 1983.

Ellis, Joseph J. *American Sphinx: The Character of Thomas Jefferson.* 1996.

Hagan, Kenneth J. *This People's Navy: The Making of American Sea Power.* 1991.

Horsman, Reginald. *The Diplomacy of the New Republic, 1776–1815.* 1985.

Kaplan, Lawrence S. *Entangling Alliances with None: American Foreign Policy in the Age of Jefferson.* 1987.

———. *Jefferson and France: An Essay on Politics and Political Ideas.* 1967.

———. *Thomas Jefferson: Westward the Course of Empire.* 1999.

Ketcham, Ralph L. *Presidents Above Party: The First American Presidency, 1789–1829.* 1984.

Lang, Daniel G. *Foreign Policy in the Early Republic: The Law of Nations and the Balance of Power.* 1985.

Lewis, James E., Jr. *The American Union and the Problem of Neighborhood: The United States and the Collapse of the Spanish Empire, 1783–1829.* 1998.

Liss, Peggy K. *Atlantic Empires: The Network of Trade and Revolution, 1713–1826.* 1983.

Lyon, E. Wilson. *Louisiana in French Diplomacy, 1759–1804.* 1934.

McCoy, Drew R. *The Elusive Republic: Political Economy in Jeffersonian America.* 1980.

McDonald, Forrest. *The Presidency of Thomas Jefferson.* 1976.

———. *States' Rights and the Union: Imperium in Imperio, 1776–1876.* 2000.

Malone, Dumas. *Jefferson the President: First Term, 1801–1805.* 1970.

———. *Jefferson the President: Second Term, 1805–1809.* 1974.

Mannix, Richard. "Gallatin, Jefferson, and the Embargo of 1808," *Diplomatic History* 3 (1979): 151–72.

Owsley, Frank L., Jr., and Smith, Gene A. *Filibusters and Expansionists: Jeffersonian Manifest Destiny, 1800–1821.* 1997.

Perkins, Bradford. *The Creation of a Republican Empire, 1776–1865.* 1993. *The Cambridge History of American Foreign Relations,* vol. 1. Cohen, Warren I., ed.

———. *The First Rapprochement: England and the United States, 1795–1805.* 1955.

———. *Prologue to War: England and the United States, 1805–1812.* 1961.

Peterson, Merrill D. *Thomas Jefferson and the New Nation: A Biography.* 1970.

Risjord, Norman K. *Thomas Jefferson.* 1994.

Schom, Alan. *Napoleon Bonaparte.* 1997.

Sears, Louis M. *Jefferson and the Embargo.* 1927.

Sharp, James R. *American Politics in the Early Republic: The New Nation in Crisis.* 1993.

Smelser, Marshall. *The Democratic Republic: 1801–1815.* 1968.

Spivak, Burton. *Jefferson's English Crisis: Commerce, Embargo, and the Republican Revolution.* 1979.

Stuart, Reginald C. *United States Expansionism and British North America, 1775–1871.* 1988.

Tucker, Robert W., and Hendrickson, David C. *Empire of Liberty: The Statecraft of Thomas Jefferson.* 1990.

Tucker, Spencer C., and Reuter, Frank T. *Injured Honor: The* Chesapeake-Leopard *Affair, June 22, 1807.* 1996.

Varg, Paul A. *Foreign Policies of the Founding Fathers.* 1963.

———. *New England and Foreign Relations, 1789–1850.* 1983.

Walters, Raymond, Jr. *Albert Gallatin: Jeffersonian Financier and Diplomat.* 1957.

Watts, Steven. *The Republic Reborn: War and the Making of a Liberal America, 1790–1820.* 1987.

Weber, David J. *The Spanish Frontier in North America.* 1992.

Whitaker, Arthur P. *The Mississippi Question, 1795–1803.* 1934.

White, Leonard D. *The Jeffersonians: A Study in Administrative History, 1801–1829.* 1951.

Wright, J. Leitch. *Britain and the American Frontier, 1783–1815.* 1975.

CHAPTER 4

The War of 1812 and the Completion of American Independence, 1809–1817

Nation in Crisis

Historians have long disagreed over the causes of the War of 1812 with England, but many have found a unifying theme in the defense of national honor. In a real sense it was America's "Second War for Independence," because the new republic was still trying to convince other countries (especially Britain) that it deserved a respected place in the family of nations. Disputes developed over expansion into Canada and the Floridas, Indian troubles along the frontier, and maritime matters—impressment, search, paper blockades, freedom of the seas, and commerce. Bitter rivalries characterized the relationship between the internal political direction of the United States and international affairs. But the basic issue was Americans' desire to protect the republic against external *and* internal peril. In 1812 Republicans under President James Madison feared that the United States could collapse. As Madison saw things, the country had only two options: Submit to Britain's violations of U.S. rights and lose the people's support to Federalists, who seemed determined to curtail republican liberties in favor of a stronger form of government; or wage a war for the protection of liberty at home and abroad, but at the risk of almost

certain defeat. The Madison administration chose the latter course.

Madison's Policies

Madison's inauguration as president in March 1809 left the impression that U.S. foreign policy would continue to be as weak and irresolute as it had been under Jefferson. Despite his keen intellect and stubborn will, Madison cut an unimpressive figure of a man—five feet four inches tall, a scant hundred pounds in weight, self-effacing, and seemingly indecisive. His vivacious and much younger wife, Dolley, stood a head taller and affectionately called him "my darling little husband"; the writer-diplomat Washington Irving not so affectionately referred to him as "poor Jemmy" and "a withered little apple-john." Moreover, Madison owed his election to the Republican party caucus and the state party organizations, and he was bound to the party's "resistance-far-short-of-war" position. His Federalist opponents, for their part, appeared willing to capitulate to British pressure. Thus it seemed unlikely that Madison would change America's lackluster policy toward Britain unless the frustrations bequeathed by Jefferson continued to mount, leaving the only choice as either abject submission or an honorable war.

Appearances, however, were deceiving: But for the initiative of British Minister David Erskine, Madison might have been ready to accept war in 1809. Months before taking office he declared that as president he would call Congress into special session to consider war if the British did not change their policies toward America. At this point, however, the president was greatly encouraged about prospects for peace. A conciliatory offer had come from the mild-mannered and seemingly reasonable Erskine, who was married to an American and had friends in the country as well. Erskine opposed war and suggested that his government drop the Orders-in-Council in exchange for U.S. implementation of the Nonintercourse Act only against France. Under certain conditions British Foreign Secretary George Canning was amenable to such an arrangement. The United States must reopen trade with Britain, adhere to the Rule of 1756, and permit the Royal Navy to help the United States enforce the Nonintercourse Act against France. Canning even spoke of settling the *Chesapeake* affair with an "honorable reparation for the aggression."

Canning's stipulations were insulting, and Erskine knew it. Britain's participation in enforcing the Nonintercourse Act would imply U.S. subservience to the mother country because British warships would actually be capturing American vessels trading with France. Erskine therefore disregarded his instructions and in April worked out a pact with Secretary of State Robert Smith—*without* incorporating Canning's restrictions. Madison triumphantly announced the lifting of the Nonintercourse Act against Britain on June 10, the day Parliament was to repeal the Orders-in-Council, and nearly 600 American ships left for England as the Erskine Agreement went into effect.

The celebration was short. When Canning read the agreement, he hotly denounced Erskine as a "Scotch flunkey," called him home in disgrace, and repudiated the agreement, though allowing American ships already at sea to enter English ports. Madison felt tricked and embarrassed, and he reinstated the Non-

James Madison
President of the United States for two terms, he was commander-in-chief of American forces during the War of 1812. *T. Sully del/D. Edwin, ca. 1810; Library of Congress.*

intercourse Act against Britain on August 9. An angry national mood prevailed. Americans did not realize that Erskine had violated his instructions and thought that Canning's actions confirmed his well-known animosity for the United States. Negotiations over the *Chesapeake* came to an abrupt end, leaving disillusionment and bitterness as the chief features of Anglo-American relations afterward.

Relations with England further declined when Canning unwisely replaced Erskine with Francis James Jackson, who quickly distinguished himself by his haughty and offensive behavior toward Americans. Nicknamed "Copenhagen" because of his earlier participation in Britain's destruction of Denmark's navy and bombardment of its capital city, Jackson lacked Erskine's calm and trusting manner and soon alienated nearly everyone in Washington.

He arrived in Boston in September 1809 with eighteen servants and a wife who was an arrogant Prussian baroness, and he indiscreetly visited leading Federalists on his way to Washington. His contempt for Americans was undisguised. The president was a "rather mean-looking man," Dolley was "fat and forty, but not fair," and Americans were "all alike, except that some few are less knaves than others." Jackson called Erskine a "fool" for negotiating the treaty with Madison and implied that the president was a liar for denying having known of Canning's conditions for an agreement. Jackson received a number of threatening letters, and in April 1810 Madison demanded that he be recalled, which he was, but not until the end of the period for which he had already been paid. In a portent of the dark days lying ahead, Jackson returned home with honor, and the British waited almost a year to send a successor.

Relations with France were likewise on the verge of collapse. Napoleon complained that the Nonintercourse Act discriminated against the French and countered with two additional decrees—both announcing the resumption of seizures of American ships in French harbors. The second and more far-reaching of these measures, the Rambouillet Decree of March 1810, ultimately led to the confiscation of $10 million of American possessions and the imprisonment of hundreds of American seamen.

When the Nonintercourse Act expired in early 1810, Congress followed with a highly unorthodox measure called Macon's Bill Number Two. The first effort at a new approach to international affairs had failed to pass Congress. A virtual renewal of the Nonintercourse Act, Macon's original proposal would have allowed American trading vessels to enter any port, while keeping U.S. harbors closed to Britain and France until one of them terminated its maritime restrictions. But by 1810 few British vessels entered U.S. waters, and none did from France. The alternative, Number Two, went into effect on May 1, 1810. It opened U.S. trade with all nations but stipulated that if either Britain or France agreed to

recognize the United States's neutral rights at sea, the president could then reinstate the Nonintercourse Act against the other, after a three-month period of grace. Nathaniel Macon had bitterly opposed the attachment of his name to this measure, which he said reeked with capitulation and bribery and "held up the honor and character of this nation to the highest bidder."

The Madison administration's attempt at a European style of diplomacy resulted in an unconventional approach to foreign policy that is almost as difficult to explain as it was to implement. The measure was ill-advised because in an effort to preserve U.S. honor, it clumsily smacked of extortion. Worse, it opened the door for Napoleon's machinations. He considered Macon's Bill Number Two a surrender to England because its navy controlled the seas and because any concessions under the law could come only from London. He had nothing to offer—unless he could convince Madison that he had ended French restrictions on American shipping.

In August 1810 Napoleon directed his foreign minister, the Duc of Cadore, to inform the U.S. minister in Paris of France's willingness to repeal the Berlin and Milan decrees against the United States *if* Americans could convince the British to respect French rights as well. That goal in mind, Napoleon stipulated that either the British must repeal their Orders-in-Council or the United States must *force* them to respect U.S. rights at sea. Either way he won. Repeal of the Orders would open the sea lanes for American commerce—even those leading to France. Nonrepeal would mean war with England and by implication an alliance with France. Napoleon concluded with a transparent attempt at flattery that in less trying times would have received the inattention it deserved: "His Majesty loves the Americans. Their prosperity and their commerce are within the scope of his policy. The independence of America is one of the principal titles of glory to France." On November 2 Napoleon announced that his government would lift its restrictions on American shipping.

The president was not fooled by Napoleon's assurance and more than likely used it to justify a decision already made. He waited the promised three months before reimposing the Nonintercourse Act against Britain on February 2, 1811. The British complained that Napoleon had lied, and they probably were correct. If anything, however, the French were shrewd. Seizures by the Royal Navy totaled more than 900 vessels from 1803 to 1812; French violations numbered 560. But after the episode involving the Cadore letter, the number of incidents dropped dramatically to 34. The new secretary of state, James Monroe, denounced Britain for trying to control American trade and defame its honor. Retaliatory action was in order.

Perhaps Madison acted hastily, because Napoleon had not halted all confiscations of American ships. But one must note that the president did not like Macon's Bill because it surrendered control over American trade to England. The Cadore letter permitted a way out of a terrible dilemma. Madison used Napoleon's duplicity as leverage to unite Americans and to persuade Britain to retract the Orders-in-Council. He informed his attorney general that the Cadore letter provided an opportunity to escape either a humiliating peace or war with Britain *and* France. Britain could rescind the Orders or accept the possibility of war with the United States. But Britain maintained the Orders, and Madison's actions appeared to confirm the Federalists' charge that he was a mere pawn of French policy. In February 1811, when the Nonintercourse Act went back into effect against Britain, the U.S. minister in London, William Pinkney, returned home after five years of frustration.

As the diplomatic front continued to crumble, still another Anglo-American crisis developed at sea. In the darkened evening hours of May 16, 1811, the U.S. frigate *President* came upon a smaller British ship, the *Little Belt,* near the Virginia capes. Someone fired a shot, the origin of which remains uncertain, and when the fiery exchanges stopped almost an hour later, the *Little Belt* lay barely afloat with nine dead and twenty-three wounded. Americans suddenly found an outlet for their pent-up emotions over the *Chesapeake* and other violations of honor. Only one American was injured in the fray, leaving the widespread feeling that the United States had finally atoned for the *Chesapeake*.

Although many Britons spoke of war, the London government's major concerns were its own domestic crises and Napoleon, and hopes for peace turned to the efforts of a new minister en route to the United States, Augustus Foster. Arriving in Washington during the summer of 1811, Foster prepared to make a belated indemnification for the *Chesapeake,* but he quickly found Americans concerned about avenging the *Little Belt* affair and seizing Canada. Foster failed to understand that the president's warnings about British behavior were sincere and that war was a possibility. He befriended the Federalists, repeated that Napoleon had not revoked his decrees, and demanded that the United States reopen trade with his country. Monroe defended Napoleon and demanded that the British repeal the Orders-in-Council. Neither gave in. Foster secured the return of two of the three Americans impressed from the *Chesapeake* (the other had died in jail) and arranged for reparations. Americans considered these gestures to be too little and too late, and they grew increasingly incensed that the British government stubbornly refused to take their grievances seriously.

At this crucial juncture in Anglo-American relations, several events forced the British to turn their attention to internal affairs. Near the end of 1810 King George III went insane after his favorite child died, and a drawn-out political controversy developed over the rise to power of the prince regent. During the summer of 1812 shock again swept the nation when an assassin killed Prime Minister Spencer Perceval in the lobby of the House of Commons. A cabinet crisis ensued, forcing a postponement of the long-planned parliamentary discussion over repeal of the Orders-in-Council. Signs in Britain indicated that the ministry was moving, however unsteadily, toward ending maritime restrictions on the United States, but Pinkney's departure and a poor understanding of Britain's mood by the U.S. chargé in London led the Madison administration to believe that it should prepare to defend the nation's honor.

Meanwhile, the congressional elections of 1810 in the United States had brought into office a young and outspoken group of ardent nationalists who picked up the name "War Hawks." Among them were Henry Clay of Kentucky (by 1812 speaker of the House of Representatives), John C. Calhoun of South Carolina, and Felix Grundy of Tennessee. They were not warmongers as such, but like many Americans they were angered by British insults and considered war the only alternative to national humiliation. Clay valued the nation's honor and integrity above all else. "What nation," he asked, "what individual was ever taught in the schools of ignominious submission, the patriotic lessons of freedom and independence?"

Another onerous problem was the widespread belief in the United States that the British were inciting the American Indians of the Northwest to resist U.S. migration to the area. Crown officials in Canada kept the Indians supplied in case of a U.S. attack on the province. But the British could not provide Indians with military materiel for defense against an outright attack and then expect them not to use that same materiel in halting the equally dangerous threat of U.S. expansion. Americans interpreted British involvement as a calculated effort to stir up the Indians against them. To stop white expansion into the Ohio Valley, Tecumseh, the chief of the Shawnees, and his brother Tenskwautawa (known as the Prophet) organized an Indian confederacy throughout the vast region between the Appalachians and the Mississippi River. Americans attributed this growing frontier crisis to the British, who, according to popular belief, were paying bounties to the Indians for the scalps of white people.

Americans' fears about a British and Indian conspiracy were largely unfounded. The British actually wanted to avert war between Indians and whites and tried to buy the Indians' allegiance with nonmilitary gifts. But the frontier was resonant with rumor. In 1809 Governor William Henry Harrison of the Indiana Territory, through the expeditious use of whiskey and vague land markings, secured treaties with the Indians that opened 3 million acres of land to the United States and pushed the Indians all the way back to the Wabash River. When Tecumseh demanded that Harrison return the land, the governor refused.

The long-expected battle began when Harrison led a thousand men to the capital of the Indian confederacy at Prophetstown, a village where Tippecanoe Creek empties into the Wabash River near present-day Lafayette, Indiana. At dawn on November 7, 1811, the Indians, without Tecumseh (who was then in the south), attacked the encamped U.S. force. Harrison barely won the Battle of Tippecanoe, but his men inflicted numerous Indian casualties and held the field. Swiftly retreating Indians left weapons on the battlefield that bore the British monogram.

News of the Battle of Tippecanoe ignited a U.S. call to cleanse the entire frontier of British influence. A Kentucky newspaper attributed the Indian uprising to the British, and the young firebrand and Anglophile from frontier Tennessee, Andrew Jackson, challenged fellow Americans to avenge the bloodletting caused by Britain's secret agents. Canada was the North American headquarters for Britain and the objective of the Americans' anger, because their navy did not dare confront England at sea. Matthew Clay of Virginia boasted: "We have the Canadas as much under our command as she [England] has the ocean; and the way to conquer her on the ocean is to drive her from the land." Americans also talked about taking Florida, because it belonged to Britain's ally Spain and provided refuge for Indians who had attacked Americans in the south. Besides, Britain might use Florida as a base of operations against the United States.

Henry Clay agreed with Jefferson that taking Canada was "a mere matter of marching." Its acquisition would facilitate U.S. control of the Indian fur trade, provide access to the St. Lawrence River, furnish farmland, end troubles with the Indians, and rid the continent of Britain. Western Americans joined the cry for Canada but for a different reason: It could serve as a "hostage" and force the British to leave the Indians alone and relax maritime restrictions. Shortly after the Battle of Tippecanoe, Monroe told Congress: "Gentlemen, *we must fight*. We are forever disgraced if we do not."

In his annual message of November 1811, President Madison emphasized the overriding necessity of preserving national honor. The British government's maritime restrictions had "the effect of war on our lawful commerce" and violated "rights which no independent nation can relinquish." Moreover, Americans considered the Orders-in-Council only the *symbol* of Britain's willingness to trample their flag and defame their honor. The British had to change their supercilious attitude toward the United States. Furthermore, the president had paid a British secret agent $50,000 for a packet of letters that allegedly proved British collusion with the Federalists of New England. Although the charges were unfounded, Madison inflamed emotions by releasing the letters to the public in March. The following month he proposed a sixty-day embargo on all ships in port, an action generally regarded as preparatory to war. Congress went farther and extended the embargo to ninety days.

Ironically, although the Washington administration did not know because it had no minister in London, U.S. economic policies had combined with other developments to have their desired effect in England. Succeeding events did not prove Jefferson and Madison correct in arguing that economic coercion would force repeal of the Orders-in-Council. More important than U.S. policy was the two-year-old depression in England, which had become so severe by the spring of 1812 that

along with poor grain yields, threatened mob action, and reinstatement of the Nonintercourse Act in 1811 (which resulted from Napoleon's perfidy and not Madison's reasoning), it generated a demand among British manufacturers to reopen trade with the United States. In Birmingham a petition fifty feet long and bearing 20,000 signatures insisted on a reversal of maritime policies. The groups that had previously backed the stringent maritime laws—shippers and planters with interests in the West Indies—were now among those urging repeal.

In April 1812 the London government declared that it would repeal the Orders-in-Council if the Americans resumed normal trade and the French rescinded the Berlin and Milan decrees. Within a month the U.S. minister to Paris, renowned poet Joel Barlow, received a copy of a decree from the French foreign minister asserting that Napoleon had indeed dropped the decrees more than a year and a half earlier. The date on the new decree from St. Cloud was April 28, 1811. The paper was a fake, and Barlow knew it. But he intended to use it to provide the British with a means by which to save face and escape the ruinous Orders-in-Council. Less than two months later, the British minister in Washington informed his host government that "if you can at any time produce a full and unconditional repeal of the French decrees . . . we shall be ready to meet you with a revocation of the Orders-in-Council." The new foreign secretary in London, Lord Castlereagh, favored better relations with the United States and chose to regard Napoleon's clearly fraudulent decree as justification for taking a step he could not avoid. Therefore, on June 16, 1812, Castlereagh informed Parliament that his government supported a suspension of the Orders on condition that the Madison administration resume normal trade relations.

But the British action came too late. By the time the United States learned of the announcement, Congress had already declared war on Great Britain on June 18. Lack of speedy communications permitted this seemingly bizarre situation, but the causes of the U.S. decision actually went beyond the Orders-in-Council. The British expected Madison to suspend the move for war when news arrived of the repeal, but he refused to do so because, first, he interpreted the announced repeal as a trick to undermine the U.S. decision for war, and second, impressment and other trespasses on the nation's honor remained. The broader causes of the War of 1812 were evident in the president's message to Congress on June 1. Violations of U.S. rights at sea dominated the grievances, and impressment headed the list. Madison declared that Americans had been "dragged on board ships of war of a foreign nation" and forced to fight for their "oppressors." Confiscation of American goods and the proclamation of paper blockades infringed on U.S. maritime freedoms. The Orders-in-Council were attempts to monopolize the ocean lanes for British merchants. Madison closed with a denunciation of the British for inciting the Indians along the frontier. In a private communication he emphasized that the United States went to war to protect its sovereignty. War became imperative not because the American people wanted it but because, as one contemporary newspaper put it, they had no choice but to *surrender their independence, or maintain it by War.*

Disputes still continue over the causes of the War of 1812, but it seems clear that the drive to sanctify national honor provided the unifying theme for Americans. Some writers note that Madison's emphasis on maritime factors did not coincide with the voting pattern in Congress: Those for war were almost exclusively Republicans from the agrarian west and south, whereas all Federalists in the mercantile New England and Middle Atlantic states were opposed. This apparent paradox is explainable: British naval actions hurt western and southern grain and cotton sales and brought a depression in agriculture, but northern commercial interests profited from the wartime trade despite British restrictions. The British blockade undermined the American farmers' export trade and, as Calhoun

hotly proclaimed, threatened to destroy the republic by returning it to colonial status.

The voting distribution roughly corresponded with that of the presidential election of 1812. Madison's 128 electoral votes came primarily from the west and south (and Pennsylvania, whose residents were concerned about national honor and the welfare of the Republican party), whereas anti-administration Republican DeWitt Clinton's 89 votes came primarily from Federalists in the commercial New England and Middle Atlantic states. No evidence supports the Federalists' allegation that westerners and southerners entered an arrangement whereby they would maintain political control in Congress by securing Canada for the west and Florida for the south. It seems more likely that those concerned about these areas wanted to use them as defensive leverage in an effort to stop British insults to American honor. British infractions at sea hurt the United States economically, but the thread holding Americans together was widespread concern for their nation's sovereignty.

Americans came close to declaring war on France also and thereby bringing about what some imprudent enthusiasts were already calling a "triangular war." For a time Madison considered this possibility as a way to disprove the Federalists' charges of Republican partiality to France and to promote an earlier peace with either antagonist by threatening an alliance with the other. But the danger that neither England nor France would grant concessions led to the stark realization that the republic might have to fight the two most powerful countries in the world rather than one. In the Senate the Federalists failed by just two votes in bringing about a resolution for war on both England and France. And the sentiment for war with France was perhaps stronger than the narrow margin suggested. Some members of the opposition defiantly insisted that they wanted to fight the belligerents one at a time and that France would be next after Britain's defeat.

The Federalists were not justified in their accusations that Madison had worked with

Napoleon in pushing for war with England. As Jefferson explained, the British were a more immediate danger to U.S. integrity than the French. Only the Royal Navy had taken American lives. Only the British had stirred the Indians into killing Americans. Only Britain's attitude was condescending. Another factor was important: President Madison realized that with the United States at war with Britain, it could count on help from France without having to reciprocate. Napoleon would open ports to Americans and furnish free protection against the British.

For Americans, this second war with the former mother country would not only complete the work of the Revolution but also comprise another important chapter in the long power struggle between England and France. For the British, a war with the former colonies would provide a needless and frustrating obstacle to the central aim of destroying Napoleon. Britons were incensed that Americans did not recognize the evil that had descended on Paris. Why could they not see that British policies were geared only to creating a world without Napoleon in it? At the moment of U.S. entry into the European war, the French were sending more than half a million men into Russia, and England was preparing for the climactic phase of two decades of almost uninterrupted war. The American theater was thus peripheral to the grand scheme of the European war. The United States nonetheless felt it obligatory to establish its rightful place among nations and safeguard its share of the hemisphere from further European encroachments.

On the domestic level, the war with Britain threatened the American nation by endangering its republican form of government as well as its political party system. The Jeffersonians' political experiences in the past decade had convinced them that the Federalists intended to undercut the Republican party, disrupt republicanism, and establish a monarchical government. Perhaps Jefferson and Madison used the threat for political gain, but they believed that the republican experiment would collapse if the nation did not preserve the Republican party by guaranteeing national honor. As Jefferson and Madison saw it, national honor and the Republican party were inseparable, meaning that the very existence of the United States as an independent republic was at stake. To the Republicans, the choice was submission to Britain and the Federalists' return to power or war with England and the salvation of the United States from mother country and Federalists. War was the only alternative to a restored colonial status.

It was an unusual time in U.S. history, for politics had become synonymous with national destiny. The ideal meshed with reality, leading the Madison administration to choose war over submission.

War

The War of 1812 was widely unpopular among Federalists and their supporters in the United States. Opposition was so strong in New England that Americans loaned money to the enemy, aided British soldiers moving through the country, and traded with Canada and England during the war. Commanders of the Royal Navy reciprocated by looking the other way as America's merchant vessels broke the blockade and headed toward London or Liverpool, and the London government discreetly avoided actions that could alienate the northern states. Federalists bitterly spoke of "Mr. Madison's War," accused Virginia of conspiring to destroy New England, and warned of secession. Strife was so severe that during the controversy over the war declaration in the summer of 1812, a mob of Madison's supporters stormed a gathering of Federalists in Baltimore and killed and mutilated a number of them.

The Madison administration encountered a notable lack of national sentiment for war and therefore faced immense problems in raising money and an army. The charter for the Bank of the United States had expired in 1811, and state banks were unable to handle wartime needs. Congress raised the tariff and levied taxes on states and individuals, but it still had to borrow by issuing treasury notes and bonds.

The effects of Jefferson's military cutbacks became painfully clear in the early stages of the war. The army's rolls included 35,000 names, yet those in the field numbered no more than 10,000, many of whom were untrained and scattered along the frontier. The United States was not able to field its full force of 35,000 men until 1814. In the meantime American officers distinguished themselves by ineptness and cowardice. Few capable leaders appeared until Generals Jacob Brown, Winfield Scott, and Andrew Jackson came along late in the war. Furthermore, the famed fighting capacity of the revered U.S. citizen-soldier seemed to have burned out somewhere between the halcyon days of Lexington and Concord and the harsh reality of a war that to numerous Americans lacked a unified national purpose. Of 700,000 state militiamen supposedly ready for action, only 10,000 responded to the president's call for 100,000 in 1812. Many of these men refused to fight outside their home states, and hardly any considered leaving the country. Taking Canada and Florida became less important than preventing the British from taking the United States.

Yet the popular cry for Canada prodded the president to order the U.S. army into a series of attacks along America's northern frontier during the summer of 1812. Madison favored a drive to Montreal, which could have broken Britain's water connection between the St. Lawrence River and the Great Lakes and endangered its holdings in North America. But Americans were never able to amass such an ambitious assault. Invasion attempts through Lake Champlain, Niagara, and Detroit ended in the surrender of two U.S. armies because of incompetent military leadership and the militias' refusal to fight. The governor of Michigan Territory, General William Hull, briefly took part of Canada when he headed beyond Detroit, but he lost his belongings, private papers, and self-respect to the British during the campaign, all of which cost him his rank and almost his life afterward. In August the governor of Upper Canada, General Isaac Brock, warned Hull of an Indian

massacre of everyone with him in Fort Detroit, including women and children, and forced his humiliating surrender without resistance to an army half the size of his. Court-martialed and sentenced to hang for failure to fight, Hull received a presidential pardon because of his distinguished service during the Revolutionary War. Brock had meanwhile repulsed U.S. forces at Niagara under General Stephen Van Rensselaer. Although Brock died in an engagement at Queenston, Canada, New York militiamen refused to enter Canada to help the U.S. Army, and British forces rallied to drive the invaders back into the United States.

The following two years of the war were little better for the northern assault. In 1813 General William Henry Harrison's forces regained Detroit and at one time held Canadian territory after defeating the British and killing Tecumseh at the Battle of the Thames in October. The Indian confederacy collapsed, leaving the British with no ally and opening the Old Northwest to American settlers. In July 1814 Harrison and General Lewis Cass signed the Treaty of Greenville in Ohio with the Northwest Indians, establishing peace with the United States but requiring them to declare war on Britain. In a fourth and final campaign in Canada later that same year, American forces seized a small spot of Canada near Detroit, but were unable to launch an offensive.

Enthusiasm for expansion southward had meanwhile diminished, for shortly after the declaration of war and again in early 1813, northern members of Congress—Federalists and Republicans—defeated a bill that authorized the president to seize Florida. The United States took Mobile in 1813, which it wrongfully claimed was part of Louisiana, and in March of the following year Andrew Jackson defeated the Creek Indians, allies of Britain and Spain, at Horseshoe Bend in present-day Alabama. The following August, in 1814, the United States signed the Treaty of Fort Jackson with a small representation of the Creeks, gaining two-thirds of their lands by removing them from Mississippi Territory or later southern and western Alabama along with a large

Map 8

Although the war ended in a stalemate, the United States could claim victory in that it had overcome both internal and external perils to stay intact.

Andrew Jackson
He defeated Creek Indians at the Battle of Horseshoe Bend in present-day Alabama and, with the U.S. incorporation of Mobile, provided the only other expansionist acquisition during the War of 1812. *National Portrait Gallery, Smithsonian Institution, Washington, D.C.*

1812, including seven frigates. And U.S. naval officers had gained valuable experience during the Quasi-War with France and the war in the Mediterranean against the Barbary pirates of North Africa.

The United States shocked the British with its success at sea in the early part of the war. The U.S. frigate *Constitution* won several battles, including one that led to the seizure of the British frigate *Guerriere*. Commodore Oliver Hazard Perry defeated the British navy on Lake Erie and took Detroit in 1813. In one-on-one encounters, U.S. ships outmaneuvered the much larger British vessels, winning most of the initial engagements. Meanwhile, nearly 500 American privateers ran the blockade, seized about 1400 British commercial vessels (some even in the English Channel), and inflicted great damage on British shipping.

section of southern Georgia. But that was the extent of Americans' expansionist achievements. Northerners blamed southerners for failure to take Canada; southerners accused northerners of blocking the acquisition of Florida.

Surprisingly the Americans fared far better on the naval front. The British navy—receiving assistance from bases at Halifax, the Bermudas, Barbados, and Jamaica—proclaimed a blockade stretching from New England to the outlet of the Mississippi River and even into Chesapeake Bay and up the Delaware and Susquehanna rivers. The 170 U.S. gunboats along the Atlantic coast were virtually worthless; on one occasion, a storm tossed a gunboat out of the water and into a field. The navy, however, had sixteen seaworthy ships in

U.S. Constitution *and British* Guerriere
In one of the most surprising aspects of the War of 1812, the United States won several naval battles, including the *Constitution*'s seizure of the *Guerriere*. *Library of Congress.*

The President's House and Capitol Building
British forces set fire to the President's House, the Capitol, and other public buildings during their invasion of the United States in August and September 1814. *Library of Congress.*

Yet as the war dragged on, Britain's naval superiority began to assert itself. The Royal Navy minimized losses by convoying merchant ships through ocean lanes, avoiding engagements unless outnumbering the Americans by comfortable margins, and tightening the blockade to confine American merchants, privateers, and naval vessels to shore. At war's end the United States had only three warships left of the original sixteen.

The British carried out a holding operation in North America until the war in Europe climaxed with Napoleon's defeat in Russia and exile to Elba in April 1814. This strategy changed during the summer of that year, when they reassigned thousands of battle-seasoned troops from the Duke of Wellington's command in preparation for a three-pronged attack

on the United States. One force was to hit the Atlantic coast at Chesapeake Bay and move inland to Washington and Baltimore; the second was to pierce the continent by way of the St. Lawrence River and march toward Niagara and Lake Champlain and the Hudson Valley; the third was to launch an invasion through the Mississippi River at New Orleans.

The initial invasion, that into Washington itself, did not succeed. In the face of oncoming British troops, the U.S. forces panicked and, along with equally frantic government officials, fled Washington and encamped less than a mile away. The British took the nation's nearly deserted capital city by dark in August and burned the White House, the Capitol with the Library of Congress inside, other public buildings that included the war and treasury

Fort McHenry
The British launched an all-night bombardment of Fort McHenry outside Baltimore
in September 1814 that failed to bring its surrender and inspired Francis Scott Key
to write "The Star Spangled Banner." *John Bower, n.d. Color aquatint (restrike);*
I. N. Phelps Stokes Collection, Miriam and Ira D. Wallach Division of Art, Prints and
Photographs, The New York Public Library, Astor, Lenox, and Tilden Foundations.

departments, and a few homes before a storm forced their departure the next night for Baltimore. The president escaped by boat to the hills of Virginia after his wife had run from the White House clutching the huge portrait of George Washington. But Americans held the line at Fort McHenry outside Baltimore, despite an all-night bombardment. During the battle Washington lawyer Francis Scott Key, a witness at the scene, immortalized the U.S. flag by assigning new words to an English drinking song that eventually became "The Star-Spangled Banner."

The second and third British forces also met defeat. The Americans stopped the redcoats in Niagara, and on Lake Champlain in September 1814, Lieutenant Thomas McDonough drove them back at Plattsburgh, New York. In the third and last part of the British offensive, 8000 veterans led by General Sir Edward Pakenham (Wellington's brother-in-law) marched into New Orleans, where they encountered General Andrew Jackson and a ragtag force of 3500 men consisting of army regulars, militia, frontiersmen, Indians, black slaves, Louisiana French, and river pirates. After a two-week assault the British retreated on January 8, 1815, with numerous dead, including Pakenham.

The Battle of New Orleans has justifiably won a prominent place in U.S. history. Some observers have dismissed its importance because poor communications allowed the fighting to take place two weeks after the United States and Britain had signed a peace treaty in Europe. These critics argue that the British wanted to end the war in 1814 because of growing internal problems combined with the improved European situation and say that the British would not have fought for New Orleans unless the United States went after Canada or refused to ratify the treaty. Yet Americans could not have known this. As far as they were concerned, no peace pact had been ratified, and a British victory at New Orleans might have hardened their position and led to territorial demands as a prerequisite to peace. Americans have sanctified the battle with reason.

Peace

The Anglo-American peace negotiations were unusual in several respects. They began simultaneously with the onset of war, which meant that the tone of the discussions rose and fell in harmony with news from the battlefield. Until the British won the war in Europe, they sought no peace in North America and labored only to frustrate the negotiations. Thus, the failure of either antagonist to win a decisive battle necessarily prolonged discussions over matters that had no direct bearing on the causes of the war. The talks did not center on neutral rights, impressment, Canada, Florida, or national honor; instead, they swirled around secondary issues such as boundaries and fishing and navigation rights in North America. The end of the war in Europe in 1814 had actually made the causes of the War of 1812 academic, because Americans would not have gone to war with England had that country not been at

Battle of New Orleans and Death of Major General Edward Pakenham
In one of the great ironies of history, British Maj. Gen. Pakenham suffered a fatal injury during the Battle of New Orleans in January 1815—*after* his country's diplomats had signed the Peace of Christmas Eve with the United States in 1814.
Joseph Yeager, after William Edward West, 1817. Colored engraving; I. N. Phelps Stokes Collection, Miriam and Ira D. Wallach Division of Art, Prints and Photographs, The New York Public Library, Astor, Lenox, and Tilden Foundations.

war with France. The irritants that encouraged Anglo-American conflict were pique, anger, frustration, accusations of treachery, and mutual distrust and misunderstanding. Once these emotions had spent themselves and exhaustion from the Napoleonic Wars had set in, the Britons and Americans realized the senselessness of their war and worked toward ending it short of victory for either side. The treaty was ultimately an armistice by two countries that finally realized their best interests lay in peace.

The first call for negotiations in the Anglo-American war had come in the winter of 1812–1813, through a mediation offer from Czar Alexander I of Russia. Napoleon had just taken Moscow, and the czar wanted the United States out of the war to enable his English ally to save Russia from the French invaders. He also wanted American commercial goods. The Russian foreign minister made the mediation proposal in September 1812 to the U.S. minister in St. Petersburg, John Quincy Adams, but it did not arrive in Washington until the following March. By then the attempted U.S. invasion of Canada had gone sour, and Madison immediately showed interest in the czar's proposal. The president asked Secretary of the Treasury Gallatin and James Bayard, Federalist senator from Delaware, to meet Adams in Russia to negotiate an end to the war. But Madison had made a tactical mistake. With the war going poorly for the United States, he had accepted mediation without first notifying Britain. Castlereagh refused to participate, claiming that he wanted to negotiate only with the United States. In actuality, the London government was not on good terms with the Russians because they shared the Americans' views on neutral rights. The prime minister, Lord Liverpool, did not trust the czar and called him "half an American."

After some anxious months, Castlereagh notified the United States in November 1813 that he was ready to negotiate, but without the Russians. The president added Henry Clay, speaker of the House, and Jonathan Russell, former chargé to London and now minister to Sweden, to the Adams, Gallatin, and Bayard mission. They prepared to meet a three-member British delegation in Ghent, a Flemish town in the Lowlands across the channel from England, which was garrisoned by British soldiers.

The British team arrived in Ghent on August 6, 1814, and the talks began two days afterward. The three men Castlereagh sent to Ghent were Lord Gambier, an admiral who had participated in the burning of Copenhagen in 1807; Henry Goulburn, a member of Parliament who was strongly anti-American and held a minor government position as undersecretary for war and the colonies; and William Adams, who held a doctorate in civil law and specialized in admiralty matters. The men were capable but particularly notable for their lack of distinction. Having little authority, they had to send all matters to London, where Castlereagh kept tight reins over the talks. Castlereagh's main concern was the ongoing peace conference in Vienna, a fact the Americans realized. The foreign secretary also wanted to delay proceedings in Ghent until expected British military victories in the United States solidified his bargaining position.

Conflict had meanwhile developed among the U.S. negotiators themselves. Cramped quarters and the presence of five strong personalities almost inevitably caused trouble. Clay upheld his reputation for gambling, card playing, and drinking and in so doing caused hard feelings with Adams, who like his father preferred work to idle amusements. Adams found it annoying that at 5 A.M., when he began his workday with a quiet reading from the Bible, he heard Clay's card-playing partners rattling around the room next door after a long night. The straitlaced New Englander also became exasperated when Clay dozed during the day's lengthy peace discussions. Only Clay's charm, Gallatin's tact, Adams's hard work, and Bayard's congenial humor managed to keep the delegation together.

When the negotiations got under way in early August, both sides' demands ensured that the talks would be long and arduous. Secretary of State Monroe had originally instructed his delegates to demand British renunciation of impressment, cession of Canada, acceptance of the U.S. definition of neutral rights, indemnification for properties confiscated or damaged under authority of the Orders-in-Council, and the return of black slaves taken by the British. But the United States was not negotiating from a position of strength. It had no money, no allies, and virtually no military force. By the summer of 1814 President Madison and his cabinet had dropped their demand that Britain give up impressment and soon shelved their interest in Canada and Florida as well. The end of the war in Europe, Madison surmised, would bring a close to the impressment issue. And U.S. forces had proved unable to establish a valid claim to either of the areas bordering the republic. In the evening of August 8, 1814, after the first day of talks, revised directives arrived in Ghent. The Americans were to seek peace on the principle of *status quo ante bellum,* which meant a return to conditions before the war.

Britain's terms almost wrecked the negotiations because they suggested the arrogant attitude of a nation victorious in war. London's newspapers demanded abject submission from the United States. British negotiators were flushed with victories in Chesapeake Bay and expected the United States to withhold military installations on the Great Lakes, permit Britain's free use of the Mississippi River and Great Lakes, and give up land in eastern Maine, upper New York, and the northern sector of the Mississippi River near Lake Superior. Between Quebec and the St. John River, the British planned to build a military road, which would wind through New Brunswick before reaching the Atlantic. The British negotiators also wanted renewed fishing privileges off the Grand Banks and Newfoundland, which they claimed had terminated during the war. Goulburn even exceeded his instructions when, at the outset of the negotiations, he conditioned a settlement on the establishment of an Indian buffer state derived from U.S. territory in the northwest. Adams hotly rejected these terms and seemed amenable only to allowing British use

of the Mississippi River as a *quid pro quo* (an equivalent) for American fishing rights off the Atlantic coast. Clay indignantly opposed any concessions and Gallatin convinced the British to postpone both matters for future consideration. At that, the British delegates blandly remarked that if the negotiations broke down, Britain would feel free to alter its demands in accordance with the expected progress of the war.

The talks had deadlocked, leaving the Britons as the only ones who could salvage a settlement. The Americans had given up the issue of neutral rights and would accept the boundaries as they stood when war broke out in 1812. But instead of making a conciliatory offer, the British had countered with excessive demands that necessitated a surrender of U.S. sovereignty and honor. Castlereagh eventually relented on the Indian neutral zone and all questions involving the Great Lakes, but he offered peace on the principle of *uti possidetis,* that each belligerent would keep lands won during the war. Britain's invasion of Washington and occupation of territories in the northern parts of the United States made this proposal unacceptable to the Americans.

Fortunately for the heralds of peace, events in the United States combined with those in Europe to break the impasse in the Ghent negotiations. The monumental U.S. victory at Plattsburgh broke the British hold on Lake Champlain and required the Royal Navy to build a new fleet before another invasion attempt could take place. News of Plattsburg and the defense of Baltimore encouraged the delegates to renew their demands for the *status quo ante bellum,* even though Britain still retained upper Maine and parts of the northern Mississippi Valley. President Madison had also made the Britons wonder if their government were merely engaged in a war for territory when, in violation of customary diplomatic procedure, he made public the original demands of the British delegation. On the European side Castlereagh's dream of constructing a lasting peace in Vienna seemed to be shattering as Russia and Prussia insisted upon territorial concessions. Britain found itself engaged in a war that offered little value, even in victory.

Growing financial and economic problems in England and increasing talk in France about returning Napoleon from Elba necessitated a reassessment of the situation. The ministry sought the opinion of Wellington, who told a stunned Parliament that the war in America was unwinnable. Britain's failure to win decisively did not warrant a demand for territorial concessions, he emphasized. Exhausted by the war with Napoleon and fearing that the American war could wear on endlessly, the British government in November 1814 accepted Wellington's recommendation to accept the terms of *status quo ante bellum*. On Christmas Eve the two delegations signed the Treaty of Ghent, which ended the War of 1812 in a military stalemate.

The peace settlement, however, proved favorable to the United States even though it did not touch on any of the issues raised by President Madison's war message. The irrevocable fact was that the country was intact and independence reaffirmed. Factors beyond the new nation's control had again worked to its advantage, because the greatest stimulus to bringing the Anglo-American conflict to a close was Napoleon's defeat and the end of the European war. Continued hostilities between the Atlantic nations made no sense when both sides wanted peace and a resumption of trade. Impressment and neutral rights automatically disappeared from the debate, because they could not be issues in peacetime. Except for Mobile, the British and American forces returned all territories occupied during the war, granted amnesty to the Indians no matter which side they had supported, and called for the establishment of joint commissions to resolve boundary problems in the northeast around Maine and in the northwest between Lake Superior and the Rocky Mountains. The Treaty of Ghent did not resolve the questions of armaments on the Great Lakes and fishing rights in the North Atlantic, but it confirmed the

independence of the United States. On February 17, 1815, the Senate unanimously approved the treaty. The following day the war with Britain was officially over. John Quincy Adams expressed the feelings of Americans: "I hope it will be the last treaty of peace between Great Britain and the United States."

An unusual event occurred near the end of the war that encouraged Americans to believe that they had emerged victorious: The peace treaty arrived in Washington just ten days after the news came of Jackson's victory at New Orleans. The repulsion of the British seemed to have direct connection with the Ghent proceedings, because Americans considered the Battle of New Orleans to be retribution for the burning of Washington and the major factor in bringing the enemy to terms. The narrow line between stalemate and defeat escaped Americans. They remained under the erroneous impression that even an ill-trained militia was sufficient to defend the country and hailed Jackson as a living legend.

The confirmation of U.S. independence and honor enabled most Americans to dismiss the wartime discontent in New England as unimportant. But disgruntled representatives from Connecticut, Rhode Island, and Massachusetts had gathered in Hartford, Connecticut, in December 1814 to draw up constitutional amendments requiring a two-thirds vote of each house of Congress to declare war (except in case of invasion) or to pass an embargo. Extremists urging secession failed to win control of the convention, but the delegates approved several other amendments designed to protect the states from the federal government. To their chagrin, they arrived in Washington with their protests just as news of New Orleans and Ghent reached the capital. Shocked and dismayed by the turn of events, the Hartford representatives put up with ridicule for nearly a week before returning home. The end of the war and the appearance of victory put to rest this mild threat to the Union, permitting President Madison to ignore their proposals.

Reflections on the Treaty of Ghent

The Treaty of Ghent ended another era in U.S. foreign policy. Twice in the short history of the republic, outside forces had threatened its independence. In both instances, Americans had profited from events abroad that often had little to do with those at home. But whereas the first phase of the Anglo-French struggle helped to spawn a revolution in France that led to a resurgence of the European war, the second ended in a clear-cut British victory over Napoleon at Waterloo in 1815 and the establishment of a century of relative peace under the auspices of the *Pax Britannica*. Peace in Europe calmed the controversies over freedom of the seas, and by the time Madison left office in 1817, Americans could concentrate on domestic development and expansion westward. The war with England had taken 2260 American lives and had cost the nation $105 million. But the gains offered some solace: British troops had withdrawn from U.S. soil; Indian problems had sharply diminished both in the northwest and in the southeast; Americans had used their victories at sea as justification for a larger navy; impressment and violations of neutral rights had come to an end; and a long life of good Anglo-American commercial relations seemed guaranteed. Some Britons were unhappy that the war had failed to secure concessions from the United States, but most welcomed the easing of taxes at home, the reestablishment of the Atlantic trade, and the worldwide prestige that stemmed from Waterloo.

Skeptics have argued that the war and treaty were meaningless because they failed to resolve the causes of the war, yet those issues had ceased to exist once the fighting ended in Europe. The war made Americans aware of the need for a transcontinental network of defense that entailed expanding the nation's borders from ocean to ocean. It was also symbolically important in helping to establish respect for the United States both inside and outside the country, thus solidifying the nation. The War

of 1812 preserved the republic as the Jeffersonian Republicans saw it, affirmed U.S. character and independence, caused a surge of nationalism that stilled sectional division for a time, and left the National Anthem as a veritable monument to these successes.

Selected Readings

Adams, Henry. *History of the United States during the Administrations of Jefferson and Madison.* 9 vols. 1889–1891.

Berton, Pierre. *The Invasion of Canada, 1812–1813.* 1980.

Bird, Harrison. *War for the West, 1790–1813.* 1971.

Brant, Irving. *James Madison: Commander in Chief.* 1961.

———. *James Madison: The President, 1809–1812.* 1956.

Brown, Roger H. *The Republic in Peril: 1812.* 1964.

Burt, Alfred L. *The United States, Great Britain and British North America.* 1940.

Campbell, Charles S. *From Revolution to Rapprochement: The United States and Great Britain, 1783–1900.* 1974.

Carr, James A. "The Battle of New Orleans and the Treaty of Ghent," *Diplomatic History* 3 (1979): 273–82.

Coles, Harry L. *The War of 1812.* 1965.

Dowd, Gregory E. *A Spirited Resistance: The North American Indian Struggle for Unity, 1745–1815.* 1992.

Egan, Clifford L. *Neither Peace nor War: Franco-American Relations, 1803–1812.* 1983.

Engelman, Fred L. *The Peace of Christmas Eve.* 1962.

Goodman, Warren H. "The Origins of the War of 1812: A Survey of Changing Interpretations," *Mississippi Valley Historical Review* 28 (1941–42): 171–86.

Hagan, Kenneth J. *This People's Navy: The Making of American Sea Power.* 1991.

Hickey, Donald R. *The War of 1812: A Forgotten Conflict.* 1989.

Horsman, Reginald. *The Causes of the War of 1812.* 1962.

———. *The Diplomacy of the New Republic, 1776–1815.* 1985.

———. *Expansion and American Indian Policy, 1783–1812.* 1967.

———. *The War of 1812*. 1964.

Irwin, Ray W. *The Diplomatic Relations of the United States with the Barbary Powers, 1776–1882*. 1931.

Ketcham, Ralph L. *Presidents Above Party: The First American Presidency, 1789–1829*. 1984.

Lang, Daniel G. *Foreign Policy in the Early Republic: The Law of Nations and the Balance of Power*. 1985.

Lewis, James E., Jr. *The American Union and the Problem of Neighborhood: The United States and the Collapse of the Spanish Empire, 1783–1829*. 1998.

Liss, Peggy K. *Atlantic Empires: The Network of Trade and Revolution, 1713–1826*. 1983.

McCoy, Drew R. *The Elusive Republic: Political Economy in Jeffersonian America*. 1980.

McDonald, Forrest. *States' Rights and the Union: Imperium in Imperio, 1776–1876*. 2000.

Owsley, Frank L., Jr., and Smith, Gene A. *Filibusters and Expansionists: Jeffersonian Manifest Destiny, 1800–1821*. 1997.

Perkins, Bradford. *The Creation of a Republican Empire, 1776–1865*. 1993. *The Cambridge History of American Foreign Relations*, vol. 1. Cohen, Warren I., ed.

———. *Prologue to War: England and the United States, 1805–1812*. 1961.

Pratt, Julius W. *The Expansionists of 1812*. 1925.

Remini, Robert V. *The Battle of New Orleans*. 1999.

Rutland, Robert A. *The Presidency of James Madison*. 1990.

Schom, Alan. *Napoleon Bonaparte*. 1997.

Smelser, Marshall. *The Democratic Republic: 1801–1815*. 1968.

Stagg, J. C. A. *Mr. Madison's War: Politics, Diplomacy, and Warfare in the Early American Republic, 1783–1830*. 1983.

Steel, Anthony. "Impressment in the Monroe-Pinkney Negotiations, 1806–1807," *American Historical Review* 57 (1952): 352–69.

Stuart, Reginald C. *United States Expansionism and British North America, 1775–1871*. 1988.

Sugden, John. *Tecumseh: A Life*. 1998.

———. *Tecumseh's Last Stand*. 1985.

Taylor, George R. "Prices in the Mississippi Valley Preceding the War of 1812," *Journal of Economic and Business History* 3 (1930): 148–63.

Varg, Paul A. *Foreign Policies of the Founding Fathers*. 1963.

———. *New England and Foreign Relations, 1789–1850*. 1983.

Wallace, Anthony F. V. *The Long, Bitter Trail: Andrew Jackson and the Indians*. 1993.

Watts, Steven. *The Republic Reborn: War and the Making of a Liberal America, 1790–1820*. 1987.

Weber, David J. *The Spanish Frontier in North America*. 1992.

White, Patrick C. T. *A Nation on Trial: America and the War of 1812*. 1965.

Wright, J. Leitch. *Britain and the American Frontier, 1783–1815*. 1975.

CHAPTER 5

The Diplomacy of Hemispheric Order, 1817–1825

New Nationalism

The presidential administrations of Republican James Monroe of Virginia from 1817 to 1825 embodied the spirit of an awakened American nationalism. Independence had become a reality. The Federalists had become known as traitors because of their opposition to the War of 1812 and their support for the Hartford Resolutions, and the party's disarray afterward encouraged the nation's people to believe that to be an American was to be a Republican. Although most citizens rallied around President Monroe in the so-called Era of Good Feelings, Andrew Jackson became the symbol of this new nationalism, for his heroics at Horseshoe Bend and New Orleans had already become legendary expressions of a frontier individualism that glorified the killing of Britons and American Indians by raw recruits and state militias.

In truth, the young nation had barely escaped calamity by 1815, but this reality remained hidden amid the exultation over the first genuine feeling of freedom from the mother country. The country's new status would be short-lived, however, unless it resolved problems with Britain, Spain, Russia, and France; strengthened northern and southern border defenses; and expanded commerce

into Latin America. These objectives necessitated bringing order to the Western Hemisphere and establishing the United States as the New World's guardian against Old World political interference. Among the achievements in this period were smoothened Anglo-American relations, the Adams-Onís Treaty with Spain, and the Monroe Doctrine. Their common bond was a greatly enhanced feeling of national security that rested on the United States making itself the most influential power in the hemisphere.

Improved Anglo-American Relations

Anglo-American relations improved dramatically after 1815, largely through the efforts of British Foreign Secretary Lord Castlereagh and U.S. Secretary of State John Quincy Adams. In a real sense, Castlereagh took the lead in accepting the reality of U.S. independence and conducting diplomacy on the basis of equality. He knew that the United States was Britain's largest foreign market and that in return the Americans provided cotton and other agricultural goods essential to the British economy. He also recognized that in a war against the United States, Canada could be of little value in any offensive operations and was itself

James Monroe
He was a two-term president during the postwar Era of Good Feelings, when patriotism ran high and Americans made several foreign policy triumphs. *An 1817 engraving attributed to Stipple; National Portrait Gallery.*

Continent was vital to British security; Adams was convinced that his own nation's security depended on containing British expansion in the New World while expanding U.S. commercial and territorial interests.

Both men understood that their most weighty task was to resolve the great difficulties obstructing the development of trust between the Atlantic nations. Trade agreements were of the utmost importance. In July 1815 the two governments signed a commercial convention relating to trade in the Atlantic and India, which established reciprocity arrangements for four years, along the lines of Jay's treaty. But even though the agreement ruled out discriminatory duties and opened the East Indies to American vessels, it did not do the same with the West Indies because of continuing opposition from British merchants. Other problems appeared, some of which the Ghent negotiations had only postponed. Boundaries remained uncertain in

vulnerable to invasion. Finally, Castlereagh intended to focus on Europe, which required better relations with the United States.

On the other side of the Atlantic, Adams had recently served as minister to England, where he cultivated his long-time suspicions of that powerful nation into a sophisticated form of Anglophobia; nonetheless, he joined Castlereagh in recognizing the practical value of harmonious relations. A stern Calvinist and an ardent nationalist, Adams believed that the laws of nature would ultimately lead to U.S. control over Spanish possessions in the south and over British Canada in the north. To his colleagues in the cabinet, he insisted that the Europeans must understand "that the United States and North America are identical." Castlereagh argued that peace on the European

Lord Castlereagh
British foreign secretary who worked with John Quincy Adams in establishing an Anglo-American rapprochement. *National Portrait Gallery, London.*

John Quincy Adams
As secretary of state under Monroe, Adams was integral to several foreign policy achievements, including the Adams-Onís Treaty and the Monroe Doctrine. *Daguerreotype portrait; Metropolitan Museum of Art.*

the northeast around Maine and in the northwest above present-day Minnesota; the status of the huge Oregon Country was undetermined; questions lingered about the restoration of fishing liberties off British North America; a naval arms race threatened to erupt on Lake Champlain and the Great Lakes; complexities arose over the interrelatedness of recognition of new nations and the establishment of commercial relationships in Latin America. The Era of Good Feelings was a misnomer, but Adams and Castlereagh tried to fit international events to the label.

The most immediate problem in foreign affairs was a threatened arms race on the Great Lakes, which neither England nor the United States wanted or could afford. Canadians were upset that the Treaty of Ghent had not granted them direct control over coastal fishing areas and that it had failed to guarantee against an American invasion. Consequently, they put pressure on the London government to construct additional border fortifications. The United States retaliated against perceived aggression from the north by warning Canada against maritime encroachments, even though these threats seemed hollow in view of the demands by various groups in the United States that Congress cut taxes and the public debt. To most observers, peace was preferable to war.

Mounting tension on both sides of the North American border finally pushed the diplomats into action. Suspicions had risen when both Canadians and Americans stationed naval vessels on the Great Lakes. Britain prepared new programs to stop American smuggling operations along the frontier and to prevent British military deserters from joining the U.S. Army. The development of an Anglo-American naval race on Lake Ontario led the Department of State in Washington to make a suggestion that had come up before—mutual disarmament. In January 1816 Adams proposed negotiations and Castlereagh accepted. The British foreign secretary knew that the United States held the advantage because of its location near the troubled area and that Canada's safety was tied more to good Anglo-American relations than to an arms buildup. Besides, peace meant trade, and that was eminently more profitable than war.

An Anglo-American settlement took shape soon after talks began in Washington in April 1817 between Acting Secretary of State Richard Rush and British Minister Charles Bagot. The men exchanged notes establishing mutual disarmament, which the U.S. Senate approved a year afterward, and the Rush-Bagot agreement became a treaty. Both nations scaled down their naval commitments but maintained border defenses. The treaty, however, had no effect on land fortifications, for navy yards and land defenses stayed on the lakes for years. The Canadian-American border remained a guarded frontier until the resolution of the *Alabama* claims controversy between the United States and England, by the Treaty of Washington in 1871.

The Rush-Bagot Treaty reduced tension along the North American border and facilitated the resolution of other controversies between the nations. It set a precedent for mutual disarmament that resulted primarily from a reciprocal interest in establishing commercial relations and from each government's preoccupation with more pressing problems elsewhere.

The following year the United States and Britain settled a host of other problems by negotiating the Convention of 1818. Rush, now U.S. minister in London, and Albert Gallatin, who was in Britain as special emissary, renewed the Anglo-American commercial convention of 1815 (still excluding the West Indies) for ten years, resolved the controversy over slaves taken out of the country by British soldiers after the War of 1812, and granted Americans the "liberty" (not the right) to fish off British North American coasts forever. Trade was to be on a reciprocal basis, and the United States won most-favored-nation status in India, along with limited commercial rights in Canada. The British had argued that the War of 1812 terminated the fishing privileges granted under the Paris Treaty of 1783, and in the period afterward they had ordered the seizure of New England fishing boats engaged in the practice. They now proposed a compromise whereby Americans could fish along certain areas of Newfoundland and Labrador and in the waters around Magdalen Island if they gave up claim to inshore fishing along other parts of the British North American coast. Americans also agreed to restrict drying and curing (important in an era before refrigeration) to unsettled areas along the coast of Labrador and to regions in southern Newfoundland where fishing was allowed.

The remainder of the Convention of 1818 related to the northern boundary of the Louisiana Purchase and to the land beyond the Rocky Mountains. The source of controversy over the boundary east of the Rockies lay in the Paris Treaty of 1783, which had set the line from the northwesternmost reach of the Lake of the Woods due west to the Mississippi River. The border proved geographically impossible because the source of the river lay below the lake. The Louisiana Treaty of 1803 had not resolved the problem, and three years later, in the treaty that President Jefferson rejected because of the impressment controversy, James Monroe and William Pinkney had drawn the boundary at the forty-ninth parallel from the Lake of the Woods to the Rockies. The Americans at Ghent had called for the same boundary arrangement, but they dropped it when the British countered with a proposed *quid pro quo* of access to the source of the Mississippi and free use of its waters. In October 1815 Rush and Gallatin took advantage of England's preoccupation with other problems to draw the boundary of Louisiana south from the northwestern tip of the Lake of the Woods to the forty-ninth parallel and to the Rockies—thus terminating British navigation of the Mississippi River and acquiring (albeit unknowingly) the rich iron deposits of the Mesabi. But when the two American diplomats suggested extending the line to the Pacific, the British turned down the proposal and intimated that they preferred the Columbia River from its mouth rather than the forty-ninth parallel, as long as both nations could have commercial use of the river and harbor. England refused to give up claims to the Columbia River Basin.

Oregon was not an important issue in 1818, but both the United States and Britain recognized that this vast territory stretching from Alaska to California would not remain quiet for long. Four nations laid claims to the area, although those presented by Spain and Russia were weak. Arguments made by both Britain and the United States, however, were defensible. British fur trading interests had spread into the Pacific Northwest after the explorations of Captain James Cook and others, preceding U.S. entry. Americans based their claims on three events: the voyage of

Captain Robert Gray, who in 1792 discovered the mouth of the river named after his ship, the *Columbia;* the Lewis and Clark expedition of 1804 through 1806; and the construction of the fort and trading post at Astoria on the mouth of the Columbia River in 1811. During the War of 1812 the British occupied the fort, but in 1818 they returned it to the United States in line with the Ghent agreements. Castlereagh declared that the restoration of Astoria did not constitute recognition of U.S. control over the mouth of the Columbia, but he did not contest U.S. claims south of the river. Shortly after British withdrawal from the fort, Rush and Gallatin signed the Convention of 1818. Ignoring Spanish and Russian claims to Oregon, they approved an arrangement known as joint occupation whereby the territory would remain "free and open" to Americans for ten years, subject to renewal for the same period.

Adams-Onís Treaty

Improved relations with Britain enabled the United States to concentrate on resolving disputes with Spain over the Floridas, Louisiana, and Texas. The Floridas constituted the first major issue, because the status of their control affected the security of the southern coastal regions of the United States as well as its trade through the Caribbean. Pinckney's treaty of 1795 had set the thirty-first parallel as the northern border of the Floridas, and in 1803 Livingston and Monroe had made the specious claim that West Florida to the Perdido River should belong to the United States on the basis of Louisiana's uncertain boundary. "We shall certainly obtain the Floridas," Jefferson had predicted, "all in good time."

In the interests of U.S. security, Madison tried to make that good time come soon after assuming the presidency in March 1809. He wanted the Floridas so badly, according to a French diplomat in Washington, that they were "the object of all of Mr. Madison's prayers." The president, in fact, feared a British attempt to establish control over Spain's New World colonies and now supported a peaceable move to separate West Florida from Spain and bring it into the Union. Most residents of the province were Americans, and the new secretary of state, Robert Smith, all but invited them to sever Spanish ties when he offered the enticing assurance "that in the event of a political separation from the parent country, their incorporation into our Union would coincide with the sentiments and policy of the United States." In the autumn of 1810 presidential agents went farther than Madison's written directives and convinced Americans (some of them land speculators who had their own reasons for taking action) in West Florida to revolt. They seized the fort at Baton Rouge, raised a blue woolen flag with a single star that proclaimed the "Republic of West Florida," and requested annexation by the United States.

Rumors of the impending arrival of both Spanish and British troops forced Madison to act quickly. Within two days of receiving news of the West Florida uprising, he issued a proclamation instructing U.S. officials to extend jurisdiction over the area. In a highly questionable argument, Madison declared that the Louisiana Purchase of 1803 had included the Gulf Coast area to the Perdido River. To substantiate his position, he falsified dates on documents and ordered the governor of the Louisiana Territory to occupy as much of the new republic as possible short of causing a confrontation with Spanish soldiers. In December Americans entered the area west of the Pearl River, carefully averting a challenge to Spanish forces at Mobile by moving around the town to the Perdido River. The governments in both Madrid and London protested but could do nothing because of their involvement in the Napoleonic Wars. The Russian czar wryly commented to the U.S. minister in St. Petersburg, John Quincy Adams, that it was marvelous how the United States "keeps growing bit by bit in this world."

Madison was still apprehensive of British military intervention and now sought to use his newly won leverage in West Florida to acquire the eastern portion as well. American expansionists had wanted the Floridas for some time, and the imminence of war with England made their acquisition vital before they fell into enemy hands. Furthermore, the Spanish governor at Pensacola had informed Washington of his desire to give them up. Madison asked Congress for a declaration affirming the country's peculiar interests in the area, and that body responded with a secret resolution on January 15, 1811, which became known as the No-Transfer Resolution. It proclaimed that the United States "cannot, without serious inquietude, see any part of the said territory [East Florida] pass into the hands of any foreign power." That same day the legislature secretly authorized the president to order the "temporary occupation" of East Florida from the Perdido to the Atlantic if requested by local Spanish officials. Should a problem develop he had the army, navy, and $100,000 at his disposal.

The president, however, had larger goals in mind: He commissioned General George Mathews, a seventy-two-year-old veteran of the Revolutionary War and former governor of Georgia, as special agent to take *permanent* possession of East Florida. Madison attempted to justify the move on the grounds of the "national interest," which he defined as "self preservation" and the satisfaction of unpaid Spanish indemnities. But these arguments offered only weak justification for what the president intended to do, regardless of its propriety: annex East Florida. Spain *was* a decaying empire that had proved itself unable to prevent American Indians from crossing the province's northern border to raid U.S. settlements, and the province *was* vital to U.S. strategic and commercial interests. But the national interest did not hang in the immediate balance, however, and Madison would have been well advised to pursue the paths of diplomacy rather than those of poorly disguised aggression. But he did not. Mathews was to accept East Florida as U.S. territory if either the Spanish governor or "the existing local authority" (a term conveniently open to interpretation about whether it applied to

Spanish officials or to any *de facto* revolutionary group in control) showed interest in such an arrangement. If any foreign power threatened to seize the area, Mathews was to use his own judgment on whether to call in the army and navy to help him take control and drive out the intruder.

These instructions virtually invited Mathews to instigate a revolution while leaving the president room to repudiate his agent if events went awry. Mathews knew that Madison had assured Americans in West Florida that if they threw off Spanish control, he would welcome them into the United States. Mathews must also have realized the latitude of action afforded by the words "local authority." Had not the president followed the same strategy regarding East Florida? Madison, after all, had warned Mathews, "Hide your hand and mine."

In March 1812, with the assistance of U.S. soldiers and volunteers from his home state of Georgia (each promised 500 acres of land), Mathews fomented an insurrection. The first objective was Amelia Island, a British-American smugglers' haven lying just below Georgia's border off the Atlantic coast. Mathews persuaded U.S. naval officers in the area to put aside their fears of a war with Britain, Spain's ally, and they indiscreetly helped his "patriots" take the island. Although the revolutionary force failed to seize the Spanish fort at St. Augustine, Mathews established a government, installed a governor, and announced the cession of East Florida to the United States.

If the U.S. government's role in West Florida's revolution was ill-disguised, its saving grace was that no proof of complicity appeared. In East Florida, however, no veil of secrecy could conceal the bald fact that Mathews had engineered an outright invasion of Spanish territory that constituted an act of war. Madison realized that Mathews had gone too far and recalled him—but not before persuading Congress in the spring of 1812 to annex West Florida, that area lying between the Mississippi and Perdido rivers, and incorporate it into the Territory of Mississippi. The president then washed his hands of the East Florida affair, just as Mathews prepared to storm St. Augustine.

Events outside the United States finally rescued Madison from his discomfiting position. He confessed in early April 1813 of knowing no way to defend Mathews's actions in Florida. To Jefferson, the president moaned that Mathews had put the country in "a most distressing dilemma." But this dilemma quickly disappeared. War had broken out with Britain almost a year before, making it too risky to return East Florida to Spain. Defying congressional opposition, Madison sent U.S. soldiers to support the patriots still in control. The secretary of state, now Monroe, admitted afterward that the revolution in East Florida had embarrassed the United States, and yet the administration could not return the territory to Spain because of the growing crisis with England.

After war had begun with Britain in 1812, Congress empowered the president to seize all of East Florida, and in West Florida General James Wilkinson took Mobile in April 1813. The following year Andrew Jackson secured the town against the British and attacked the Spanish fort at Pensacola because it had served as Britain's base of operations. Spain demanded reparations for these acts and for the fact that Americans were opening ports owned by its rebellious New World colonies to privateers. By the time the war ended in December 1814, the United States controlled all of West Florida east to the Perdido River, although it agreed to return East Florida to Spain. The prognosis had changed, however: The Madrid government recognized that the war and ongoing insurrections in its Latin American colonies made it impossible to hold on to East Florida. The time had come to sell—if Spain could secure a satisfactory boundary between Louisiana and New Spain (Mexico).

The Floridas were in such turmoil after the War of 1812 that they were virtually uncontrollable by the Spanish governors in Pensacola and St. Augustine. Amelia Island remained a port of call for slave smugglers, adventurers, and pirates, who fitted the Indians with arms.

When Indians from East Florida swarmed over American surveyors near the Georgia border and renegades on Amelia Island defiantly asserted that East Florida belonged to Mexico, President Monroe ordered the island seized in 1817 on the basis of the no-transfer idea contained in the secret congressional resolution of January 1811. Other problems were developing. Creek Indians who survived Jackson's military expedition in 1814 had joined the Seminoles in the Floridas. Supplied by British merchants in East Florida, they and about 800 escaped slaves and a few white outlaws in the northern part of the province habitually raided American settlements, disrupting expansion into Georgia and Mississippi. The United States had to have order in East Florida, and it wanted Louisiana's borders set at the Perdido River to the east (incorporating West Florida) and the Rio Grande to the west. These were extreme claims, but Americans defended them on the basis of the vague boundary provisions of the Louisiana Treaty of 1803 and on Spain's inability to control the Floridas in accordance with Pinckney's treaty of 1795.

U.S. negotiations with Spain began in 1817, when Secretary of State Adams met with the Spanish minister in Washington, Don Luis de Onís. Adams was realistic and brilliant, a hardheaded diplomat whose objectives were to rid the hemisphere of Old World colonialism, spread U.S. republicanism over North America, and safeguard the nation's security. He must have recognized some of his own qualities in his talented adversary, for he observed the following of Onís:

> [He is] cold, calculating, wily, always commanding his own temper, proud because he is a Spaniard, but supple and cunning, accommodating the tone of his pretensions precisely to the degree of endurance of his opponent, bold and overbearing to the utmost extent to which it is tolerated, careless of what he asserts and how grossly it is proved to be unfounded. . . . He is laborious, vigilant, and ever attentive to his duties; a man of business and of the world.

The negotiations took place against a background of strong U.S. hostility toward Spanish colonialism and calls for accepting the newly independent states of Latin America into the world community. Adams resisted pressure from Henry Clay to grant *de facto* recognition to Spain's rebellious New World colonies, because he feared that such a move would insult Spain and abort the Florida talks. Adams noted two essential prerequisites to extending recognition to new states. First and foremost, the likelihood of Spain's regaining its possessions had to be absolutely remote. Second, these governments must conform to standards of international behavior. Adams knew that a delayed recognition could hurt U.S. commercial interests in Latin America and open the door to Britain; yet he realized that a hasty decision could cause war with Spain and arouse help for the Old World empire from antidemocratic European states also having commercial designs on Latin America. Recognition issues had caused war in other instances—as the French experience had shown in the 1770s. Adams probably agreed with his father, who remarked to him in 1818 that the South American peoples "will be independent, no doubt, but will they be free? General Ignorance can never be free, and the Roman Religion is incompatible with a free government."

Growing American sympathy for the struggling Latin Americans finally forced the Monroe administration to deal with the matter. Merchants from the United States carried copies of the Declaration of Independence and Constitution to the rebellious states and extolled the virtues of freedom. Clay's theatrical oratory on behalf of South America was difficult to counteract. "We behold there," he proclaimed on the House floor, "a spectacle still more interesting and sublime—the glorious spectacle of eighteen millions of people, struggling to burst their chains and to be free." Congressional passage of the Neutrality Acts of 1817 and 1818 failed to dissuade filibustering (private adventuring) and privateering out of New Orleans and Baltimore. But in late March of 1818, the Monroe administration won an important battle when

Congress overwhelmingly turned down a resolution for recognition of Spain's colonies, supported by westerners hostile to Spain.

Discussions with Onís nonetheless dragged on. Adams called for the cession of East Florida on the ground that Spanish officials had not stopped the Indian raids into U.S. territory as Pinckney's treaty had required. He also criticized Spain for failing to return runaway slaves and for aiding Britain in the War of 1812. In the spirit of a good bargainer, Onís countered by demanding that in exchange for East Florida, the United States must agree to a boundary at the Mississippi River (thereby negating the Louisiana Purchase), cancel all damage claims against Spain, and guarantee no interference in the revolts in Latin America. Adams responded with an equally unrealistic territorial proposal that called for the Rio Grande as the western boundary of Louisiana. After lodging their extreme demands, the two men took a slight turn toward compromise when Adams agreed to move the line northward to the Colorado River midway into Texas. Onís had no choice but to retreat from his earlier insistence on the Mississippi River as the western boundary: The state of Louisiana was already part of the Union. Even then, however, he called for a boundary that cut through Louisiana. Miles of contested territory still lay between, and neither man seemed willing to surrender anything more.

In the meantime the Spanish minister vainly tried to secure a favorable settlement by seeking mediation from his British ally. Onís warned Britain that if the European powers did not band together, the United States might take all of the Western Hemisphere. But in London Castlereagh rigidly held to his stance expressed two months before: Spain should give up East Florida in exchange for the best boundary possible between Louisiana and Mexico. He would consider mediation only if the United States also made the request, but he doubted (and correctly so) that such a request would transpire. Adams told Onís that the United States rigidly opposed any involvement in Europe's political swirls.

The Adams-Onís talks might have remained deadlocked had it not been for the dramatic entrance of General Andrew Jackson. The day after Christmas in 1817, President Monroe sent the Tennessean to resolve the Seminole Indian problem in East Florida. Jackson had authorization to cross the international border if necessary, but he was to stay clear of Spanish forts. He later claimed to have anticipated the president's request. On January 6, 1818, before Jackson's orders arrived in Nashville, he wrote Monroe: "The whole of East Florida [should be] seized . . . and this can be done without implicating the Government. Let it be signified to me through any channel . . . that the possession of the Floridas would be desirable . . . and in sixty days it will be accomplished." All he needed was some sign of approval from the White House.

In mid-February 1818, Jackson asserted, that sign came while he and more than a thousand men under his command were encamped along the Big Creek River in Georgia. His long-time friend, Representative John Rhea of Tennessee, wrote him a letter that the general later claimed had contained tacit approval from President Monroe to invade East Florida and settle the Indian problem—even if that meant seizing Spanish towns. Jackson declared that Monroe and Secretary of War John C. Calhoun approved the idea, despite their later denials. No evidence exists, because Jackson asserted that he burned the letter—if there was one—at Monroe's request. Rhea was confused. The elderly man later wondered if he *had* written the letter. By 1818 he admitted to writing a letter that could have left the impression that the government wanted Jackson to take East Florida.

The truth probably lies somewhere between. The president had condoned this type of activity twice before: while secretary of state during the abortive East Florida affair of 1811, and as secretary of war when Jackson conducted military operations in Pensacola and West Florida during the War of 1812. Monroe surely recognized the possibilities of trouble in sending the fiery general near a trouble spot inhabited by Indians and Spaniards he loved to hate. Jackson's hot-blooded and frontiersman character did not encourage him to observe diplomatic niceties in matters injurious to national honor. Nor did his past dealings with Indians or Spaniards (or anyone else who got in his way) suggest that he would use anything but brute force in achieving his aims. Monroe must have realized that Jackson would take care of the Indian and Spanish menace in his own fashion. And, like his predecessor Madison in dealing with the Floridas, Monroe left the way open to disavow any action by his general that went askew. The timing of Jackson's expedition was opportune, for numerous Spanish forces had moved to South America to put down the insurrections. Jackson assumed his mission was to take East Florida, and President Monroe never told him to stay out of the Spanish province. Each man knew what the other wanted without having to say it. Indeed, Monroe's very silence signified approval. The implications were enormous: The president and the general were preparing for war without consulting Congress.

In March 1818 Jackson's forces, now numbering 3000 troops and 2000 Indian allies, marched into East Florida and within two months brought the United States to the edge of war with both Spain and England. His men became enraged at finding fifty recently cut scalps of American settlers, all mounted on a pole in a small town's public square, and they occupied the greatly outmanned Spanish garrison at St. Marks in early April. They then replaced the Spanish flag with the Stars and Stripes, burned a nearby Indian village, executed two Indian prophets, and captured a seventy-year-old Scottish merchant named Alexander Arbuthnot, who had warned the Seminoles of Jackson's coming and was accused of selling them arms. In an Indian camp later on, Jackson's forces seized an English lieutenant suspended from the marines, Robert Ambrister, and charged him also with conspiring with the Indians. A quick court martial in St. Marks found both British subjects guilty and sentenced them to death. Thus had

Jackson laid the basis for an international storm by dispensing U.S. justice to two Britons in Spanish Florida. Uncertainty remains about whether Arbuthnot was involved in a dishonest trade, but Jackson ordered both men executed on the spot.

Jackson then headed toward Spanish headquarters at Pensacola, where he believed the governor was guilty of helping the Indians. On May 28, 1818, he took the town and fort, and the next day he confiscated the archives, appointed a U.S. officer as military and civil governor, and activated U.S. revenue laws in East Florida. On May 30 Jackson began the return to Tennessee, perhaps only partly satisfied because he had not taken St. Augustine and openly regretful that he had not hanged the Spanish governor. But he confidently assured the White House that after recovering from poor health resulting from the expedition, he would, with additional troops and a single ship, deliver St. Augustine to the United States and then rid Cuba of the Spanish.

Jackson's spectacular actions in East Florida caused an international crisis. The Spanish minister in Washington was livid. When news of Jackson's deeds arrived in April and May, Onís was at his summer retreat in Pennsylvania, but he returned to the capital early in the morning to interrupt Adams's Bible study and demand reparations and punishment for Jackson's conduct. The secretary coldly responded that he could make no reply until the president returned from his farm and could study the matter. But Onís was well aware of Britain's angry reaction to the executions of two of its subjects and now felt confident of British support against the United States in the Florida negotiations. Several times during the following week the two diplomats met in this heated atmosphere, Adams interspersing these bitter encounters with equally tense and almost daily meetings with the president and his cabinet. Secretary of War Calhoun led a scathing attack on Jackson. Furious that the general had circumvented his authority in seeking Monroe's approval to take East Florida, Calhoun demanded a court-martial. He even suggested

that Jackson had acted on behalf of friends interested in Florida land schemes.

Only Adams defended Jackson in the cabinet. The general's report to Calhoun contained statements that Adams found easy to accept. "I hope," Jackson wrote in florid frontier language, "the execution of these two unprincipled villains will prove an awful example to the world, and convince the Government of Great Britain, as well as her subjects, that certain, though slow retribution awaits those unchristian wretches who, by false promises, delude and excite an Indian tribe to all the horrid deeds of savage war." Adams insisted that the Florida assault was an act of self-defense against the chaos that had spilled over the border and into the United States; Jackson was correct in urging the United States to occupy all areas down to the thirty-first parallel. Indeed, the Spanish governor of East Florida and the Spanish commander at St. Marks deserved punishment for permitting the disorder to spread into U.S. territory. Adams reluctantly agreed that the United States should return Pensacola, but he believed that St. Marks should remain in U.S. hands as leverage for forcing the Spanish to establish control over the Indians. Self-defense, he told his cabinet colleagues, was part of the "common sense of mankind."

Adams made clear the administration's position to Spain. In one of his many discussions with Onís, the secretary indignantly declared that "we could not suffer our women and children on the frontiers to be butchered by savages, out of complaisance to the jurisdiction which the King of Spain's officers avowed themselves unable to maintain against those same savages." In his argument, later sent to Madrid, Adams charged that East Florida was "a derelict, open to the occupancy of every enemy, civilized or savage, of the United States, and serving no other earthly purpose than as a post of annoyance to them." The Spanish had a choice: either meet their international obligations, or cede the province to the United States.

President Monroe only appeared indecisive, because he recognized the opportunity to secure his nation's southern flank and was not above falsifying the record to justify Jackson's behavior. The Indian raids were a symptom of the real disease: the Spanish presence in the Floridas. The episode must not lead to war, he knew, but the fact was that Jackson had brought attention to a long festering problem that needed immediate resolution—and in the United States's favor. The president's sole reservation pertained to the *manner* in which Jackson carried out the assignment. Monroe said nothing about its results. He thought the posts should revert to Spain, and yet he was attracted by the prospect of taking both Floridas if his administration could escape the stain of aggression by persuasively pleading Adams's case for self-defense. He wrote Jackson that the U.S. stand would be defensible if he as president could show that the invasion directly stemmed from Spanish violations of U.S. rights. If Jackson approved, Monroe offered to alter documentation of the matter:

> You must aid in procuring the documents necessary for this purpose. Those you sent . . . do not, I am satisfied, do justice to the cause. . . . Your letters to the [War] Department were written in haste, under the pressure of fatigue. . . . If you think proper to authorize the secretary or myself to correct those passages it will be done with care.

Jackson refused the president's proposal.

In the meantime, while Americans hailed Jackson as a hero, Henry Clay, who was concerned about the Tennessean's burgeoning chances for the presidency, secured a congressional resolution of censure. Horseshoe Bend, New Orleans, and now East Florida—the possibilities seemed limitless as to what this crude and yet colorful American frontier Indian fighter would do. Tammany Hall in New York passed a resolution of praise, and Philadelphia and other cities wildly cheered him. Clay led a congressional inquiry into Jackson's conduct that hammered on for three weeks. He also delivered an impassioned three-day speech before a packed House of Representatives in support of several resolutions chastising Jackson for the invasion and for the executions of British subjects and Indian religious leaders. "Spare them their prophets!" he dramatically and half mockingly declared on behalf of the Indians. Even Rome respected the "altars and the gods of those whom she subjugated." Those great nations of the past—Greece and Rome—fell because "some daring military chieftain" extinguished their liberties. Such a calamity could happen to the United States, for "Greece had fallen, Caesar passed the Rubicon."

Jackson swore to "defeat these hellish machinations." To friends in the west, he wrote of Clay, "You will see him skinned here, and I hope you will roast him in the West." Stories circulated, perhaps started by Jackson's rabid followers, that he would cut off the ears of anyone who supported a Senate move for censure. Although some senators scoffed, others noticeably kept their weapons upon entering the chambers to debate the measure.

In February 1819 Congress decided against censuring Jackson for his conduct. But in vindicating his actions, it virtually admitted to having no control over him. Monroe had earlier assured that body that if Jackson entered Spanish territory he would *not* seize Spanish forts. When the general did so, both the president and Congress looked the other way.

Monroe's decision about the Florida episode hinged more on the British reaction than on American popular opinion. Initially, the British response angrily demanded an apology and reparations for the executions of their subjects. The U.S. minister in London, Richard Rush, warned that the atmosphere was explosive and Foreign Secretary Castlereagh feared that Parliament and the British people were in such an ugly mood that "war might have been produced by holding up a finger." But ameliorative factors were also evident. Castlereagh studied the evidence and agreed with the United States that Arbuthnot and Ambrister *had* engaged in illegal gunrunning and deserved no government protection. The foreign secretary was also preoccupied with preserving the peace in Europe and establishing closer economic ties with the United States. Indeed, he considered good Anglo-American relations as so imperative that he did not allow the Florida controversy to disturb the ongoing negotiations and ratification of the Convention of 1818 with the United States. Castlereagh refused to interfere on behalf of the two men, and Britain would not support Spain.

Castlereagh's assurances and Jackson's popularity in the United States eased the president's position. Monroe instructed his secretary of state to reject Spain's protests. Adams prepared a long paper and attached several documents justifying Jackson's actions as self-defense. The secretary intended to argue that Spain's failure to keep its house in order had forced the United States to take corrective action.

Adams reopened negotiations with Onís in October 1818. He first assured the Spanish minister that the United States would return both Pensacola and St. Marks to Spain. Then Adams announced an ultimatum: Maintain order in the Floridas, or cede them to the United States. The atrocities committed by the Indians justified Jackson's decision to execute both Englishmen—even without a trial, had he chosen to do so. Adams shocked Onís by demanding punishment of the Spanish officer responsible for the chaos in East Florida and compensation for the expenses of Jackson's expedition. If the United States did not receive satisfaction, Adams seemed to imply, Jackson (whom the Spanish bitingly referred to as "caudillo" and "the Napoleon of the woods") could ride again. Onís had no rejoinder: His government stood alone and had already instructed him to give up both Floridas. After four months of haggling over the Louisiana boundary, Monroe instructed Adams to settle on the Sabine River, thereby dropping claims to Texas and leading angry westerners to tag the secretary with blame. Spain could not go to war without British support, and it had to concentrate on putting down the ongoing insurrections in Latin America. The Spanish found it wiser to pull out with grace—and perhaps with money—than to lose everything in dishonor.

In Washington on February 22, 1819, the secretary of state signed the Adams-Onís Treaty, or what many would call the Transcontinental Treaty. The negotiators worded the transfer of the Floridas in a manner designed to satisfy each party's argument over whether the area west of the Perdido River had been part of the Louisiana Purchase of 1803. The United States received "all the territories which belong to him [king of Spain], situated to the eastward of the Mississippi, known by the name of East and West Florida." Furthermore, the United States gave up its shadowy claims to Texas based on the Louisiana Treaty, and Spain did the same with equally questionable claims to Oregon. Although the area beyond the Rocky Mountains was not an issue in 1819, Adams recognized the opportunity to solidify his country's argument for the Far West by removing Spain as a competitor. He had mentioned the forty-second parallel as a boundary in the course of a conversation with Onís the previous July. Now the two men drew the border in steplike fashion northwest from the mouth of the Sabine River in Louisiana until it reached the forty-second parallel near the Rockies and followed that line due west to the Pacific. No exchanges of money took place. Each side dropped damage claims against the other, and the United States agreed to assume its citizens' claims against the Spanish to a maximum of $5 million.

The treaty was a major stride toward Adams's goal of acquiring the Columbia River Basin and building a continental United States with secure borders. Such a window on the Pacific, he also knew, would expand American trade with Asia. Adams's diary entry for the day of the treaty signing recorded his intense satisfaction: "The acknowledgement of a definite line of boundary to the South Sea [Pacific Ocean] forms a great epocha in our history. The first proposal of it in this negotiation was my own, and I trust it is now secured beyond the reach of revocation." He joyously continued that "it was, perhaps, the most important day of my life." Adams attributed the triumph to "the work of an intelligent and all-embracing cause."

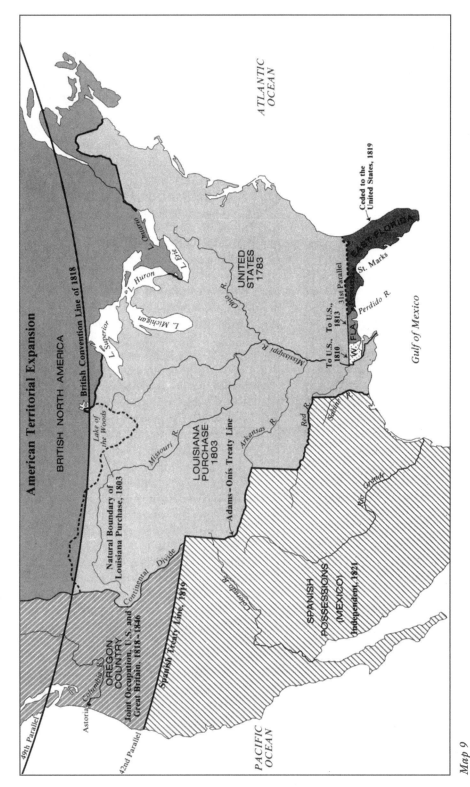

Map 9

The Adams-Onís Treaty, which John Quincy Adams considered his most outstanding accomplishment as secretary of state, was transcontinental in scope and vital to the nation's security.

Adams came under great criticism for not acquiring Texas in the negotiations, but the fact is that the slavery question precluded any demand for that huge area at this time. Unknown to Adams, Onís had received directives from Madrid to drop claims to Texas by retreating from the Sabine River as the boundary of Louisiana, but Monroe and his cabinet considered the Floridas vital and did not push for the additional southern territory. Not only did they and many southerners fear that a call for Texas might hurt the Florida negotiations, but they worried that it could lead to serious political repercussions over slavery. Coincidental with these talks, a bitter debate was under way in Congress over the admission of Missouri into the Union as a slave state; its entry would upset the delicate balance between free and slave states in the Senate. A national debate over slavery could also unravel the tenuous north-south alliance within Monroe's Republican party. Texas was potentially too dangerous an issue. It remained in Spanish hands, although Onís tied it to Mexico. When Mexico won independence in 1821, it claimed Texas as part of the new republic.

Problems in Spain caused a two-year delay in the treaty's ratification. The U.S. Senate unanimously approved the treaty in its original instance on February 24, 1819, despite criticism from Clay and other western members of Congress for the administration's failure to acquire Texas, and President Monroe ratified it the next day. In the meantime, however, some officials in Madrid objected that Onís had not received fair compensation for the great amount of land conceded. Others expressed concern about the absence of guarantees by the United States to enforce its neutrality laws and its refusal to withhold recognition of the Latin American insurgents. Jackson spoke for more than a few Americans upset over Spain's delays when he recommended that the United States use "the mouth of the cannon" to close the deal. In 1820 an uprising in Spain forced King Ferdinand VII to accept a liberal constitution, which further slowed ratification by requiring legislative approval of treaties.

The United States was also having second thoughts—and for good reason. A dispute had broken out over land grants in East Florida awarded by the king on the very day before the date set in the treaty (January 24, 1818) for the termination of such acts. Onís had cleverly outmaneuvered Adams in the negotiations. If validated, the grants would have denied U.S. ownership to all of East Florida except the east coast.

Spain, however, had to capitulate: The United States might simply seize the entire area in question, including Texas, and grant recognition to all the colonies claiming independence. These fears were justified. Monroe had already assured Adams that Congress would approve taking the Floridas *and* Texas if Spain did not revoke the royal charters and accept the treaty. These drastic measures proved unnecessary. The Madrid government canceled the grants, and the king ratified the treaty on October 24, 1820. Since the six-month time limit for ratification had expired, the Senate had to vote again on the treaty, and this time the senators approved it with four westerners dissenting on the basis of Clay's cry that "Texas was worth ten Floridas." On February 22, 1821, two years after the original signatures in Washington, the two countries exchanged ratifications and the Adams-Onís Treaty went into effect.

A little over a year later, in 1822, President Monroe drew widespread public approval when he recommended that the United States extend recognition to the new Latin American republics of Colombia, La Plata, Mexico, and Peru. The temptation to do so had come in June 1821, when Simón Bolívar's forces broke Spain's hold on Colombia and Venezuela, but Monroe had remained cautious. After more delay he made his move. He assured Congress in March 1822 that the probability of Spain's reestablishing control over its colonies was "most remote." In two months Congress approved Monroe's proposal and authorized $100,000 to send missions to the newly independent nations in Latin America.

Was the move justified? U.S. acquisition of the Floridas in 1821 had released that issue as a hostage in regard to recognition and permitted the Washington government to act primarily out of self-interest. The ideals of liberty propounded by the Latin American rebels drew a considerable following inside the United States, but the markets of these liberated colonies were of even greater importance to U.S. investors worried about England's expanding economic interests. In defense of the United States, international law contained no specific guidelines regarding how long a nation must wait to grant recognition to new states. The decision to do so was (and is) a judgment call based on that nation's determinations about whether the rebellious colonies had successfully thrown off the mother country and were, in fact, independent. The United States waited more than a year after the Adams-Onís Treaty to extend recognition. Spain's failure to restore control afterward proved U.S. actions correct.

The Adams-Onís Treaty has taken its rightful place as an outstanding achievement in U.S. diplomacy and a tremendous boost to the quest for continental security and economic growth. At virtually no cost, the secretary of state had rounded out the southeastern borders of the United States, drawn the western boundary of the Louisiana Purchase, improved his nation's chances for acquiring the Pacific Northwest by reducing its number of rival claimants to one—Britain—and pointed the way to a vast commercial market in the Orient. U.S. forces established a stable border between Georgia and East Florida; the people of Mississippi and Alabama had guaranteed access to the Gulf; and the cotton industry continued its epochal spread into the rich bottomlands. Furthermore, Adams had raised an issue that had the potential to justify additional land acquisitions: whether a nation had the right under self-defense to launch a preemptive strike when a desperate situation existed and no other recourse seemed available. The pattern of U.S. expansionism exemplified by Pinckney's treaty, the Louisiana Purchase, and now the Adams-Onís Treaty, suggested that national interest in Texas and

Oregon would not diminish. The only question was which issue would surface first.

Monroe Doctrine

The Monroe Doctrine of 1823 rivals the Adams-Onís Treaty in promoting expansionism by encouraging the acquisition of Texas, Oregon, and other areas in the transcontinental United States. More than any document of the time, it expressed the nationalist mood of an American people bold and perhaps foolhardy enough to warn Europe that the Western Hemisphere was no longer open for colonization. It marked the first official declaration of the country's unique character and a manifesto of political isolationism built on the natural protection of the Atlantic and Pacific oceans. The genius of the document lay in its balance between idealistic pronouncements regarding universal principles of right and realistic maneuvers intended to protect the national interest. The Monroe Doctrine left the impression that the United States opposed imperialism and sympathized with the new Latin American republics, and for those disinterested reasons it warned Europe to stay out of the New World. The reality was that the United States did not include itself in the restrictions, for its objectives were territorial and commercial expansion in the Americas that would further its own interests. Indeed, the United States had pronounced itself the guardian of the Americas. The Monroe Doctrine constituted a formal statement of U.S. independence and a declaration that the American republic intended to become the dominant power in the hemisphere.

The history of the Monroe Doctrine primarily began with the Congress of Vienna in 1815, which signaled the end of the Napoleonic Wars. Czar Alexander I of Russia had advocated the formation of a "Holy Alliance" in September, and within two months Russia, Prussia, Austria, and Britain renewed the "concert of Europe," or Quadruple Alliance, established the previous year. The purpose of the alignment, French Foreign Minister

Talleyrand declared, was to stamp out liberalism and restore monarchical governments overturned by constitutional revolutions. By 1818 the organization became known as the Quintuple Alliance when Bourbon King Louis XVIII returned to Paris and France joined the others as a keeper of order.

The Quintuple Alliance, led by Austrian foreign minister Prince Klemens von Metternich, prepared to fulfill its central mission when popular uprisings led to the establishment of constitutional governments in Naples, Piedmont, Spain, and Portugal. Britain was reluctant to participate. The London ministry did not favor liberal revolutions, but sentiments of this type were appearing among its own people, and Lord Castlereagh staunchly opposed intervention in European affairs because such a move might cause war. At the 1823 Congress of Verona in Italy, Britain broke with the European powers when they decided to send French soldiers to restore King Ferdinand VII to his pre-constitutional authority. Just before the meeting Castlereagh, in despair over the crumbling peace, committed suicide. His successor in the Foreign Office was George Canning, who also opposed the Spanish monarch's return to full power.

These events in Europe did not go unnoticed by the United States. The recognition question in Latin America was fraught with the danger of Old World interventionism in Spanish America—or so Americans feared. Simón Bolívar, Francisco de Miranda, José de San Martín, and Bernardo O'Higgins had launched a series of drives for independence that reached a climax when Mexico broke the Spanish bond in 1821. In the spring of 1822, as indicated earlier, President Monroe extended recognition to the new Latin American republics, shortly after the last of the Spanish armies pulled out of the New World. Adams and others in Washington sought to establish commercial ties with these new states before they fell under British control. But when France invaded Spain, the Monroe administration became alarmed that the French might try to restore Spanish rule in Latin America—and perhaps march on northward to the United States. Indeed, American fears were not off the mark in that Ferdinand had urged his European friends to help him regain control over the Spanish colonies in the New World. Rumors were widespread in the United States by the spring of 1823 that an arrangement existed whereby France would receive Cuba in exchange for restoring Spain's empire in Latin America.

These stories had a fortuitous effect on Britain. When the Latin American rebels threw off the mother country, they opened their ports to British merchants. The Washington administration could not have known that in late March Canning informed his ambassador in Paris that Britain would resist any French attempts to return Spain's New World possessions. The British foreign secretary sought to maneuver his country into a position of economic dominance in Latin America.

That objective in mind, Canning turned to the United States to secure either a convention or exchange of notes signifying Anglo-American opposition to Europe's intervention in Spanish America. In August 1823 he talked with Richard Rush in London about the French troops in Spain, and the U.S. minister remarked that he was certain the British would not allow the French to do the same in Latin America. Four days later, on August 20, Canning sent an "unofficial and confidential" note calling for a "joint disapprobation" of French intervention. Mutual interests in Latin America's independence, he insisted, pointed toward a cooperative policy. To relieve other nations' suspicions, Britain and the United States should take a public stand against territorial acquisitions. Less than a week later he again broached the idea, emphasizing that the two nations had an opportunity to "produce so unequivocal a good and prevent such extensive calamities." England could have enforced this idea without U.S. help, but Canning had other objectives.

The foreign secretary's motive was self-interest, and Rush knew it. Canning sought to rebuild his country's world influence, hurt

George Canning
British foreign secretary who, to many
Americans, epitomized the very worst in
arrogance. *National Portrait Gallery, London.*

Washington; but if Canning agreed to extend recognition to the new Latin American states, a move the United States had sought since 1815, Rush would initial a joint declaration that would "not remain inactive under an attack upon the independence of those States by the Holy Alliance." Conservatives in England opposed recognition, as Rush knew, but he hoped to use Canning's interest in a joint policy to secure a concession long wanted by the United States. The foreign secretary, however, only tentatively offered assurances of recognition. His evasive reply caused Rush to forward the issue to President Monroe.

The Monroe administration was divided in reaction to Canning's proposal. The offer was appealing, but the bearer was not. Canning was infamous for his anti-American behavior. Had he not pushed for harsher maritime restrictions in the tumultuous period before 1812? The president asked Jefferson and Madison for advice and, surprisingly, *both* favored acceptance. Jefferson argued that with British assistance the United States could maintain inviolability from the Old World. Madison agreed and recommended that the joint policy statement encompass a declaration in favor of the ongoing Greek revolution against the Turks. The Greeks' drive for freedom had attracted widespread support in the United States, and President Monroe knew that a pronouncement in their behalf would bolster a decision to accept Canning's invitation. In early November he told the cabinet that he had decided to accept Canning's offer. Adams, however, vigorously protested.

Adams was a realist and expansionist who distrusted the English and warned of strings attached to any so-called gift offered by the nefarious Canning. The secretary of state had no difficulty convincing his colleagues of Canning's cold and adversarial character. They remembered him as the wily diplomat who had angrily recalled his minister to the United States, the conciliatory David Erskine, in the stormy time before the outbreak of war in 1812. Britain sought commercial control of Latin America, Adams reminded fellow cabinet

badly by the French invasion of Spain, and even a weak ally like the United States would help restore a balance of power vital to peace. Canning also wanted to keep the newly opened markets of Latin America from reverting to Spain, and he recognized the economic advantages of drawing closer to the United States: Its consumers bought a sixth of Britain's exports and might exert pressure on Congress to reduce tariffs. The establishment of British influence in the Americas constituted the first step in this grand scheme.

Rush maintained a careful and detached composure. He would await instructions from

members, and the danger in Canning's proposal rested in the self-denying joint statement, "We aim not at the possession of any portion of them [Spanish states] ourselves." A U.S. signature would constitute a renunciation of claims to Cuba, Texas, and California.

But fear of European intervention in the New World threatened to override Adams's counsel. Restoration of the Spanish monarchy in Mexico and all South America horrified Calhoun, who, according to Adams's diary, was "perfectly moonstruck" at the prospect. Stories were circulating in the United States that French ships would soon leave for the New World to restore the Spanish colonies to the crown. To compound matters, Russia's minister in Washington, Baron Hendrik Tuyll, had informed Adams in mid-October that his country would not recognize the rebellious colonies in Spanish America and was satisfied with U.S. neutrality. This statement apparently constituted a warning that Russia would support Spanish and French intervention in Latin America if the United States joined England in a joint declaration of policy.

After several long discussions Adams finally persuaded the president to reject Canning's offer. Adams argued against the danger of European intervention; even if it materialized, the United States could rely on the British navy for assistance against intruders because Britain had too many economic interests in Latin America to allow anyone to intervene. A joint policy with England would do the United States no good. Latin Americans would thank the British for protection, not the Americans. It was better for the United States to act alone, Adams insisted, than "to come in as a cockboat in the wake of the British man-of-war."

Adams found it extremely difficult to put down the fear of Russian intervention in Latin American affairs. Russian traders had moved steadily down the northwest coast of North America after the voyages of Vitus Bering in the first half of the eighteenth century. In 1799 the Russian-American Company received a charter granting it sole commercial rights and governing control over the Alaskan area south

to 55° north latitude. The company then began a string of settlements, and by 1816 it had built a trading post above San Francisco Bay in Spanish California. These developments at first did not concern the Washington government because of its preoccupation with Britain and because of the remoteness of the Pacific coast. But in 1821 the czar issued a ukase (imperial decree) that broadened his country's claims south to the fifty-first parallel (thereby including much of Oregon) and restricted the waters within about a hundred miles of the coast to Russian vessels. The ukase seemed to mark a major step in Russian expansion southward into Oregon. To Calhoun and others, the threat lay in the czar's membership in the Quadruple Alliance. Britain protested, but the United States acted.

Adams raised the matter in a discussion with the Russian minister in Washington. The United States had received a note from the Russian Foreign Office praising the European alliance and declaring that the czar planned to maintain peace—even if such a move meant preserving Spain's control over its colonies, Tuyll pointedly told Adams. The secretary of state, however, did not believe the Russians would intervene. He had seen the scope and depth of their domestic problems when he served as minister in St. Petersburg and now seemed to use his colleagues' apprehensions over Russia to advance an idea he had been considering for some time. In July 1823 Adams wrote Tuyll that "we should contest the right of Russia to *any* territorial establishment on this continent, and . . . we should assume distinctly the principle that the American continents are no longer subjects for *any* new European colonial establishments." Adams then sent instructions containing this principle of "noncolonization" to the U.S. ministers in both Russia and England.

The idea of noncolonization was not new to England, because more than two years before, in January 1821, Adams had stated it in reply to the British minister's question about how far U.S. claims went in the Columbia River area. "To all the shores of the South Sea [the Pacific]," he declared. When pressed as to whether this affected Britain's holdings in North America, Adams answered: "No, there the boundary is marked, and we have no disposition to encroach upon it. Keep what is yours, but leave the rest of this continent to us." The secretary's dispatch to London in 1823 was stronger in tone, signifying that he was concerned more about England than Russia.

Adams's stand on noncolonization was hardly defensible, either in practical or theoretical terms. The United States was not strong enough to resist the European nations if they chose to establish colonies in the hemisphere. His associates in the cabinet also had doubts about the legal basis for such a pronouncement. European governments had long followed the practice that no country had exclusive claim to unsettled and unexplored areas. Adams knew this. In the Convention of 1818 he admitted to England's joint occupation of Oregon, although it is arguable that this arrangement did not necessarily involve *colonization*. But in 1824 he would agree to Russia's claim to the area above the 54°40′ line, and afterward in the same year he accepted the idea of resolving the Oregon boundary controversy by dividing the area along the forty-ninth parallel.

Perhaps, as some writers have suggested, Adams used the Russian matter to win support for his presidential bid in 1824. The opposition had accused him of giving away the west's interests by the treaties of 1818 with Britain and 1819 with Spain. A strong statement against future European colonization in the Americas might quiet his critics and rally voters around him. This may have been so, but the important point is that a strong declaration aimed at Russia would also implicitly warn *Britain* that outside interference endangered the U.S. interest.

Canning had not counted on the possibility of the Monroe administration declining his offer. To solidify his position he applied pressure on the French ambassador in London, Prince Jules de Polignac, to give him a memorandum in early October renouncing his

government's intentions to intervene in the Spanish colonies. Canning did not reveal the Polignac memorandum to Rush because he wanted to use the fear of European intervention to secure a U.S. commitment against seeking additional territories in the New World.

The question before the Washington government was how to inform other nations of its stance toward the Latin American republics. Adams wanted to send sternly worded notes to each foreign office but found no support in the administration. The president suggested including the ideas in his annual message to Congress in December. This approach drew approval, and Monroe prepared a draft that he brought before the cabinet on November 21, 1823. Adams, however, disliked its defiant tone and opposed the president's intention to warn the leading European powers to stay out of Greece and Spain. Adams wanted to make clear that the United States would be responsible for the western half of the world, and this necessitated mention of Russia's activities along the northwest coast. The message should warn against Old World interference in Latin America while offering assurances that the United States would reciprocate by staying out of European political affairs. Indeed, the popular frenzy generated in the United States by the pan-Hellenic movement contributed to Adams's determination to maintain that separation. Monroe gave in, although he remained convinced that the United States had a mission to spread republican principles. He insisted on expressing concern for the Greeks, but agreed to tone down criticism of French actions in Spain. Adams succeeded in making this an "American cause" that aimed at achieving national security through the establishment of political isolation on a hemispheric scale.

Those parts of the president's December 2 message to Congress that later became known as the "Monroe Doctrine" comprised only two pages of a total of thirteen and were separated into two brief passages by a long section on domestic matters. The message emphasized the uniqueness of America and the wisdom in political separation of the two hemispheres. The ideas meshed to form the central principle of political isolation: "We owe it, therefore, to candor and to the amicable relations existing between the United States and those powers to declare that we should consider any attempt on their part to extend their system to any portion of this hemisphere as dangerous to our peace and safety."

The principle of "noncolonization" associated with the Monroe Doctrine was an inseparable element of the United States's warning to Europe to stay out of the New World's political affairs. As pointed out earlier, Adams formulated the noncolonization principle in reaction to the Russian ukase of 1821. The secretary's influence was evident in the similarity between his note to the Russian minister in Washington during the summer of 1823 and the president's declaration to Congress that "the American continents, by the free and independent condition which they have assumed and maintain, are henceforth not to be considered as subjects for future colonization by any European powers." By not specifying Russia, this section left the implication that it applied to any foreign power—including Britain—that might consider intervening in the Americas. A corollary of noncolonization was the principle of "no transfer" that had risen in the congressional resolution over Florida in 1811: No changes could occur in the political control of colonies, and once a state became free, it remained so.

Monroe's message contained a related assurance by the United States that some have called the "hands-off" principle:

> With the existing colonies or dependencies of any European power we have not interfered and shall not interfere. But with the Governments who have declared their independence . . . we could not view any interposition for the purpose of oppressing them, or controlling in any other manner their destiny, by any European power in any other light than as the manifestation of an unfriendly disposition toward the United States.

A few months before the congressional message, Adams received word of Britain's interest in securing Cuba from Spain, and he immediately informed the governments in Madrid and Havana that the United States opposed a transfer of ownership. His central argument was that a Cuba independent from Spain would attach itself naturally to North America; his chief fear was England.

The other side of the Monroe Doctrine— the attempted *quid pro quo*—was the principle of abstention, or the guarantee of noninterference in Old World political affairs. The president drew upon Washington's Farewell Address in stating that "in the wars of the European powers in matters relating to themselves we have never taken any part, nor does it comport with our policy to do so." This was weak leverage, of course, because European powers were not concerned about U.S. interference in their affairs. The Monroe administration realized this: It left the way open for accepting Canning's proposed joint declaration against the Quadruple Alliance as soon as the state department could work out a suitable arrangement.

The Monroe Doctrine was a well-calculated bluff. The European governments had problems of their own and were unlikely to intervene in the Americas. The only teeth in the pronouncement was an implied U.S. alliance with England that rested on mutual interest in Latin American trade. A weak United States had to risk the entrapments of seeking British help, but it was correct in doing so without entering any type of formal arrangement. The new Latin American republics tried to band together against outside interference, while the European states decided to build commercial and banking ties without attempting to establish political control over the territories. Fortunately for the Western Hemisphere, the European governments were more interested in Asia and other matters than in challenging the claims made by the Monroe administration. These developments furnished time for the United States to mature to the point that it could actually defend its far-reaching assertions of 1823.

Latin Americans at first welcomed Monroe's declaration as a guarantee of U.S. protection against the Old World, but they quickly realized that deeds did not necessarily follow words. Various liberal thinkers in Latin America approved the message, and five of the new states—Argentina, Brazil, Chile, Colombia, and Mexico—asked the Washington government for treaties of alliance or assurances of aid should the European countries intervene. Adams turned them down with the admission that the United States would use force only with England's help. He explained to the representative of Colombia: "The United States could not undertake resistance to them by force of arms, without a previous understanding with those European powers whose interests and whose principles would secure from them an active and efficient cooperation in the cause."

Bolívar was skeptical about the president's declaration and recognized that the United States had acted out of self-interest. At the Congress of Panama, which he called in 1826 to arrange a common regional defense against Spain, the United States received only a belated invitation. Because of isolationist sentiment and political difficulties at home, the U.S. Congress so delayed its response that one delegate died before he could leave for the conference and the other arrived after it had adjourned. The Monroe Doctrine proved disillusioning to Latin Americans looking to the United States for assistance.

The Old World was hostile to the president's message because the United States had taken credit for preventing something that never would have materialized. Members of the Quadruple Alliance criticized the pronouncement as "arrogant" and "blustering." Metternich called it an "indecent declaration" that cast "blame and scorn on the institutions of Europe most worthy of respect," and Czar Alexander claimed it "enunciates views and pretensions so exaggerated, establishes principles so contrary to the rights of the European powers, that it merits only the most profound contempt."

Yet the United States could not have known that no member of the alliance seriously considered forcible intervention in Spanish America. The Monroe administration did not learn of France's noninterference guarantees in the Polignac memorandum until Canning revealed them to Rush almost two weeks after the president's message to Congress. The two powers most likely to intervene in Latin America—France and Russia—were not willing to do so. Canning had warned France against such action weeks before the president's message, and Russia was restrained by domestic and foreign problems. The Monroe Doctrine probably had little effect on the czar's decisions in 1824 to approve a treaty with the United States that withdrew Russia's claims in the northwest to the 54°40′ line, the present southern boundary of Alaska. The president's action did not deter the other European powers; they had already decided *not* to intervene.

The Monroe Doctrine constituted an implicit warning to Britain to stay out of New World political affairs. This was not clear at first, for both Canning and the British public thought the Monroe administration supported Latin American independence and hence open markets. The *Times* of London noted the similar interests of the United States and England and spoke of grand cooperative ventures in Latin America. Then the truth sank in. Canning recognized that the message could push the newly liberated Latin Americans into the U.S. camp and hurt British commercial interests. What is more, the United States received praise for what *he* had accomplished with the Polignac memorandum. Furthermore, he realized that the noncolonization principle applied to his country as well as Russia and feared that the Monroe administration had designs on Cuba.

To counteract pro-American feeling in Latin America, Canning circulated copies of the Polignac memorandum in the capitals of Latin American nations, which informed them that *Britain* had held off the Quadruple Alliance. This effort in the spring of 1824 came too late. It apparently convinced those already suspicious of the United States's objectives, but it was not enough to salvage Canning's political standing at home. In December he boasted to Parliament: "I resolved that if France had Spain, it should not be Spain 'with the Indies.'

I called the New World into existence to redress the balance of the Old." But Canning's attempt to undermine U.S. prestige in Latin America could not change the fact that the Monroe administration had outmaneuvered him. He must have seethed with anger at the caustic remark made by his enemy Lord Charles Grey: "Canning will have the glory of following in the wake of the President of the United States."

The Monroe Doctrine reflected the belief of the president and his secretary of state in national unity, even though the document had no legal sanction in the United States and no standing in the international community. Once Monroe rejected Canning's offer, he and Adams put together a monumental paper that satisfied the various sectional and economic divisions in the United States by facilitating its territorial and commercial expansion southward and westward. They realized that domestic politics were inseparable from foreign policy and formulated a broadly based policy statement that any successor to the Oval Office could support. The Republican party, an alliance of planters and merchants, could not quarrel with a policy that called for territorial expansion into the northwest and south at the same time it advocated the New England merchants' goal of open markets in Latin America. Monroe and Adams knew that their nation was vulnerable militarily and tried to turn the European powers against one another. This tactic would give the United States time to build an economic and military power base that the Old World would respect. They could not accomplish this objective with empty threats, but they did take advantage of the European powers' distrust of each other to promote an idea intended to safeguard U.S. security and promote the nation's hegemony throughout the hemisphere.

Consequences of Monroe's Diplomacy

The diplomatic achievements of the Monroe-Adams era included dramatically improved relations with Britain, the construction of a transcontinental boundary that yielded the Floridas and pointed to further expansion west, the chance for increased trade with Asia, and the declaration of the country's peculiar interests in the New World—all important contributions to the young nation's quest for security. The climactic event was the Monroe Doctrine, even though it lay dormant for over two decades, when Americans resurrected it to justify the wave of expansion west known as "manifest destiny." In the years between, the United States did not protest several French ventures in Latin America, nor did it dispute Britain's annexation of the Falkland Islands or its decision to broaden the borders of British Honduras. During the problems over Oregon and California in the 1840s, President James K. Polk stated what became known as the Polk Corollary of the Monroe Doctrine when in his first annual address to Congress he announced opposition to new European colonization in North America. The following decade, the Monroe Doctrine received its name. Then, during the Civil War, the Washington administration referred to the principles of the Monroe Doctrine in opposing French intervention in Mexico. Not until 1895 did a president, Grover Cleveland, again identify U.S. security with the independence of Latin America, and nine years later President Theodore Roosevelt declared that in cases of "chronic wrongdoing," the United States would assume the role of "international police power" in the Western Hemisphere. Nothing was new about the Roosevelt Corollary; President Monroe had set out its ideas more than eight decades before. The common feature of the two presidential declarations was the attempt to guarantee U.S. security by bringing order to the Western Hemisphere through the establishment of U.S. control.

Selected Readings

Ammon, Harry. *James Monroe: The Quest for National Identity.* 1971.

Bemis, Samuel F. *John Quincy Adams and the Foundations of American Foreign Policy.* 1949.

———. *The Latin American Policy of the United States*. 1943.

Bourne, Kenneth. *Britain and the Balance of Power in North America, 1815–1908*. 1967.

Brant, Irving. *James Madison*. 6 vols. 1941–1961.

Brooks, Philip C. *Diplomacy and the Borderlands: The Adams-Onís Treaty of 1819*. 1939.

Burt, Alfred L. *The United States, Great Britain and British North America*. 1940.

Campbell, Charles S. *From Revolution to Rapprochement: The United States and Great Britain, 1783–1900*. 1974.

Cunningham, Noble E. *The Presidency of James Monroe*. 1996.

Dangerfield, George. *The Awakening of American Nationalism, 1815–1828*. 1965.

———. *The Era of Good Feelings*. 1952.

James, Marquis. *Andrew Jackson: The Border Captain*. 1933.

Johnson, John J. *A Hemisphere Apart: The Foundations of United States Policy toward Latin America*. 1990.

Ketcham, Ralph L. *Presidents Above Party: The First American Presidency, 1789–1829*. 1984.

Kushner, Howard I. *Conflict on the Northwest Coast: American-Russian Rivalry in the Pacific Northwest, 1790–1867*. 1975.

Langley, Lester D. *The Americas in the Age of Revolution, 1750–1850*. 1996.

Lewis, James E., Jr. *The American Union and the Problem of Neighborhood: The United States and the Collapse of the Spanish Empire, 1783–1829*. 1998.

Liss, Peggy K. *Atlantic Empires: The Network of Trade and Revolution, 1713–1826*. 1983.

Logan, John A., Jr. *No Transfer: An American Security Principle*. 1961.

McDonald, Forrest. *States' Rights and the Union: Imperium in Imperio, 1776–1876*. 2000.

McInnis, Edgar W. *The Unguarded Frontier: A History of American-Canadian Relations*. 1942.

Masterson, William H. *Tories and Democrats: British Diplomats in Pre-Jacksonian America*. 1985.

May, Ernest R. *The Making of the Monroe Doctrine*. 1975.

Nagel Paul C. *John Quincy Adams: A Public Life, a Private Life*. 1997.

Nobles, Gregory H. *American Frontiers: Cultural Encounters and Continental Conquest*. 1997.

Owsley, Frank L., Jr., and Smith, Gene A. *Filibusters and Expansionists: Jeffersonian Manifest Destiny, 1800–1821*. 1997.

Pappas, Paul C. *The United States and the Greek War for Independence, 1821–1828*. 1985.

Parsons, Lynn H. *John Quincy Adams*. 1998.

Patrick, Rembert W. *Florida Fiasco: Rampant Rebels on the Georgia-Florida Border, 1810–1815*. 1954.

Perkins, Bradford. *Castlereagh and Adams: England and the United States, 1812–1823*. 1964.

———. *The Creation of a Republican Empire, 1776–1865*. 1993. The Cambridge History of American Foreign Relations, vol. 1. Cohen, Warren I., ed.

Perkins, Dexter. *The Monroe Doctrine, 1823–1826*. 1927.

Remini, Robert V. *Andrew Jackson and His Indian Wars*. 2001.

———. *Andrew Jackson and the Course of American Empire, 1767–1821*. 1977.

———. *Andrew Jackson and the Course of American Freedom, 1822–1832*. 1981.

———. *The Life of Andrew Jackson*. 1988.

Russell, Greg. *John Quincy Adams and the Public Virtues of Diplomacy*. 1995.

Sellers, Charles G. *The Market Revolution: Jacksonian America, 1815–1846*. 1991.

Stuart, Reginald C. *United States Expansionism and British North America, 1775–1871*. 1988.

Tatum, Edward H., Jr. *The United States and Europe, 1815–1823*. 1936.

Varg, Paul A. *New England and Foreign Relations, 1789–1850*. 1983.

Weber, David J. *The Spanish Frontier in North America*. 1992.

Weeks, William E. *Building the Continental Empire: American Expansion from the Revolution to the Civil War*. 1996.

———. *John Quincy Adams and American Global Empire*. 1992.

———. "John Quincy Adams's 'Great Gun' and the Rhetoric of American Empire," *Diplomatic History* 14 (1990): 25–42.

Whitaker, Arthur P. *The United States and the Independence of Latin America, 1800–1830*. 1941.

Williams, William A. "The Age of Mercantilism: An Interpretation of the American Political Economy, 1763–1828," *William and Mary Quarterly* 15 (1958): 419–37.

CHAPTER 6

To the Webster-Ashburton Treaty, 1825–1842

Ambivalent Anglo-American Relations

For a few years after the Era of Good Feelings, a state of general calm characterized U.S. foreign relations because of the country's preoccupation with internal matters and because of the relative peace in Europe. Perhaps this was fortunate, for the United States had entered a new phase in its history that featured presidents who were often inexperienced in foreign affairs. The irony was that John Quincy Adams, the most gifted diplomat of his time, had a disastrous four years as president, even in foreign affairs, and that the hot-blooded Andrew Jackson, his successor in 1828, achieved more in diplomacy than anyone could have predicted. It was also a time in which Americans exalted the principles of republicanism while denying these very principles to blacks and American Indians within the United States. During this era of paradoxes, the American nation reached its greatest heights by 1848 and then proceeded toward the fiery self-destruction of civil war.

The country's continued push for security through expansion still focused primarily on resolving problems with Britain, because relations between the Atlantic nations dominated the young republic's foreign affairs through-out the period following the Monroe Doctrine. Anglo-American commercial competition developed in Latin America, and arguments intensified over the trade of the British West Indies, the location of the Canadian-American boundary, and the suppression of the African slave trade. If familiarity breeds contempt, the classic example of this principle was Anglo-American relations. The British still seemed reluctant to accept the United States into the family of nations. Bitter resentment remained over the U.S. experiment in democracy because leaders in London believed the example unwholesome for the English masses; on the other side of the Atlantic, Americans viewed with disgust the arrogance of a nation that claimed a monopoly on culture and absolute control over the seas.

The Atlantic nations managed to maintain a relationship because the economic ties holding them together tended to counter the stresses and strains pulling them apart. The problem was that the bonds were tighter on the American side. By 1840 the United States was sending more than half of its exports to the British and receiving more than a third of its imports from them. England was not as dependent on the United States, even though it imported most of its cotton from the southern states. In 1825 British merchants exported a fifth of their products to the United States, but this figure fell to a tenth by 1840.

Several factors explain Britain's declining dependence on America. The British had moved toward free trade, which led to the end of imperial preference; Parliament had repealed the Corn Laws, opening the door to other markets; and manufacturers had emphasized goods for export. These changes encouraged an ambivalent relationship between the Atlantic nations. Although economic interests held them together, the resulting commercial rivalries threatened to drive them apart. In this fiercely competitive atmosphere, a number of seemingly unrelated political disagreements grew into potential sources of conflict by combining with one another and arousing emotional arguments over national honor and security.

Diplomacy of Adams and Jackson: Contrasting Styles

The presidential troubles of John Quincy Adams began with his close victory over Andrew Jackson in 1824 and extended through four turbulent years. No one received a majority of the electoral votes, and the election went to the House of Representatives, where in a state-by-state ballot Jackson's old nemesis, Speaker Henry Clay, cast his support for Adams. Shortly after his victory the new president appointed the Kentuckian as secretary of state. The outcome resulted from a "corrupt bargain," charged the disappointed and infuriated Jacksonians, a political payoff that stole the election from their hero and guaranteed Clay the presidency as heir apparent. From Adams's first day in office, Jackson's avid supporters opposed almost everything the president favored. The accusations and the failures in office were particularly difficult for Adams to accept. Like his father, he was often humorless, vain, and puritanical in behavior and outlook; but also like his father, the younger Adams was a devoted public servant and an ardent nationalist of unquestionable integrity.

In foreign affairs Adams ran into a bitter rivalry with British Foreign Secretary George Canning, who still resented the United States's independent stance in Latin America, as proclaimed in the Monroe Doctrine. Anglo-American competition over Latin America deepened as the London government extended recognition to the new republics in 1824 and sought control over the markets. "The deed is done," Canning boasted; "the nail is driven, Spanish America is free; and if we do not mismanage our affairs badly, *she is English*." Adams called the foreign secretary "an implacable, rancorous enemy of the United States."

President Adams's first venture in foreign affairs involved the Pan-American Congress, called by South American hero Simón Bolívar in 1826 to bring the Latin American nations together for protection against Spain and for the advancement of their own interests. The United States at first did not receive an invitation but eventually managed to procure one. Secretary of State Clay was a long-time advocate of Pan-Americanism and persuaded the president to send delegates. But instead of acting on his own, Adams tried to work through the Senate in securing the appointments and then turned to Congress for funds. The ensuing debate deteriorated into heated and long-winded political arguments bearing little relation to the business at hand. In addition, isolationists warned against foreign entanglements, and southerners feared that slavery might appear on the agenda. Northern newspapers supported the conference as conducive to U.S. economic interests in Latin America, but their realistic arguments could not override more pressing political considerations.

The affair turned into a fiasco that thoroughly embarrassed the Adams administration while enhancing Britain's stature in Latin America. Congress debated for four months before agreeing to fund the expedition to Panama. One envoy died of yellow fever as he made his way through Central America; the other waited for a safer season in which to travel, and the conference ended before he departed. Even if they had made it to the gathering, Canning had an agent present,

Edward Dawkins, to discredit the United States and prevent it from taking a leading position among the American states. Dawkins had several instructions: convince his Latin American hosts that Britain did not wish to prolong the war with Spain in the interests of British commerce; obstruct any effort to align the nations of the Western Hemisphere against the Old World; and oppose any move toward freedom of the seas. In particular he aroused resentment from Mexico and Colombia toward the United States by informing them that the U.S. minister in Madrid opposed their efforts to free Cuba from Spain. Despite the extreme optimism of the Panama meeting, the Latin American countries never adopted any proposals. No follow-up meetings took place, even though the call for Pan-Americanism surfaced again later in the century. Canning secured some measure of revenge for having been outmaneuvered earlier by Adams with the Monroe Doctrine.

Adams's second effort in foreign affairs was no more successful than the first. Interest in the trade of the British West Indies reappeared as an issue, because after the Napoleonic Wars, the United States's limited access to the West Indian markets came to an end. For the next decade the Washington government tried to gain commercial concessions. The Anglo-American commercial convention of 1815 permitted reciprocal most-favored-nation status in the British East Indies, but not in the West Indies. Castlereagh had proposed two years later to allow trade on a restricted basis, but this offer met resistance from the U.S. Congress, which had attempted to extract more concessions by repeatedly passing retaliatory trade laws that included cutting off direct commerce with the British West Indies and obstructing passage of the islands' goods into the United States through New Brunswick, Nova Scotia, Canada, and England. The legislation hurt American producers along with the British West Indies planters. In July 1822 Parliament yielded to pressure from the West Indies lobby and opened the islands to limited American trade, conditional on the allowance of British ships into U.S. ports. Adams, then secretary of state, pushed for more concessions, and in March 1823 Congress opened the nation's ports to British vessels carrying cargo from the West Indies but authorized retaliatory tariffs until American ships had equal access to the West Indies. The London government refused to drop its system of colonial preferences, and there the matter rested when Adams became president in March 1825.

Adams decided against compromise and ill-advisedly demanded U.S. access to the West Indies as a *right* instead of requesting it as a *privilege*. The tactic cost him any opportunity he might have had to open the islands to American merchants. Four months after Adams's inauguration, Parliament agreed to open more trade outlets to the United States, but with the stipulation that his government remove its restrictions on British trade. The president refused, hoping the West Indies planters would put pressure on the London government to give in. But the following July of 1826, Britain shut off the islands to American vessels until Washington agreed to end its retaliatory duties. Adams was unaware of this decision when he sent Albert Gallatin to England to work out a settlement of the issue, based on mutual suspension of restrictive laws. When Gallatin arrived in London, Parliament had closed the islands, and Canning refused to discuss the matter. Furthermore, he chided Gallatin for interfering in Britain's colonial affairs.

Adams's richly ingrained Anglophobia and personal animosity for Canning had gotten in the way of diplomatic sense. Americans justifiably criticized Adams for losing the trade, and even if he was now willing to accept the privilege short of full reciprocity, Congress would not go along. In March 1827 the president adhered to the law and announced the closing of U.S. ports to vessels arriving from any British possession in the hemisphere. Later that same year he recorded Canning's death in his diary with ill-concealed satisfaction. A bitter irony it was that a man so famed as a diplomat should lose his bid for reelection in 1828 at least partly because of his failures in foreign affairs.

Andrew Jackson
Before serving as president for two terms, Jackson was an Indian fighter and hero of the Battle of New Orleans. He symbolized the frontier individualism of the age. *William S. Pendleton, after painting by R. E. W. Earl; Library of Congress.*

Many feared that the new president, the short-tempered Andrew Jackson, would stir up war with Britain over the West Indies. Yet he was a firm proponent of commercial expansion as a vital ingredient of the nation's continued growth and surprised Americans by setting aside his long-standing distaste for the British. He instead sought U.S. access to the islands as a privilege, not a right. Jackson worked through Congress and his secretary of state, Martin Van Buren, to open the West Indies. The president agreed to repeal discriminatory tariffs even though the British had not ended their colonial preference system. His presidential proclamation of October

1830 opened U.S. ports to British vessels on an equal trade basis with American ships, and two days after the London government received news of this change, it granted access to the West Indies on condition that American merchants pay duties levied by London.

This was a major diplomatic victory for the new administration, although the success was attributable more to world events than to Jackson. Canning had died, and the new foreign secretary, Lord Aberdeen, was more conciliatory toward the United States. In addition, Britain had become disenchanted with the navigation system and was moving toward free trade. Moreover, people of the West Indies needed American foodstuffs and lumber. Americans overlooked these factors in praising the new president's ability to achieve so quickly what his predecessor had failed to secure for four years.

The president's reputation for diplomatic expertise did not last long, because the long-standing French spoliation claims issue brought out the real Jackson—an ultranationalist who viewed any insults to the United States as intensely personal and subject to retribution in an appropriate frontier manner. This festering claims problem had stemmed from damages inflicted on the American merchant marine by French vessels during the Napoleonic Wars. As part of the wartime settlement, France paid indemnities to European nations—but not to the United States. In July 1831, however, the Paris government relented to U.S. pressure and agreed to pay 25 million francs in six annual installments. But when the matter came before the French Chamber of Deputies, that legislative body thought the amount excessive and refused approval. In February 1833 the U.S. secretary of the treasury drew a draft for the first payment soon due, but the French minister of finance would not honor the request because the Chamber had not set aside the money. The king informed the U.S. minister in Paris that "unavoidable circumstances" had delayed the payment but assured him it would come. Over a year passed, however, and in April 1834 the Chamber again refused to approve a funding bill. By this time the president was irate because of what appeared to be a calculated slur on American honor. "I know them French," Jackson allegedly bellowed. "They won't pay unless they're made to."

The claims issue soon became a *cause célèbre*. The president took the issue before Congress in his annual message of December 1834 and requested support for sending an ultimatum to France. Jackson directed the navy to prepare for action and called for a law authorizing him to seize French vessels and property in the United States if the Paris government did not approve payment at the next legislative session. Jackson's Democratic followers supported this appeal to arms, but they encountered fierce opposition in the Senate from the newly formed Whig party, which was a mixed breed of National Republicans, states' rightists, and other dissidents who despised Jackson's growing executive power, and who now feared commercial losses from his French policy. The warning was clear to France, however. War talk resulted, securities dropped, insurance companies withdrew coverage of merchant houses, and the French government recalled its minister in Washington and suggested that his U.S. counterpart leave Paris. Relations remained tenuous at best, with only a chargé remaining in the French legation in Washington.

The French could not consider war because of ongoing European concerns, but neither could they retreat before the president's demands without risking national humiliation and the fall of their ministry. It was difficult to believe that such a matter could lead to war, but with the mercurial Jackson at the helm, no one could predict which course the ship of state might take. The president had just waged a long and bitter war against the Bank of the United States that had climaxed with his censure by the Senate for usurping legislative authority. Surely his fury knew no bounds. The Paris government sought an honorable way out of the entanglement. The Chamber appropriated the money but made payment contingent upon a satisfactory explanation from the president.

Jackson, however, refused any statement hinting at an apology, making a diplomatic break seem imminent. In November 1835 the United States closed its legation in France, and within two months the French chargé in Washington requested his passports and went home. The following month Jackson gave this statement to Congress:

> The honor of my country shall never be stained by an apology from me for this statement of truth and the performance of duty; nor can I give any explanation of my official acts except as is due to integrity and justice and consistent with the principles on which our institutions have been framed.

Both nations readied their navies for hostilities.

Fortunately, in January 1836, the London government offered to mediate the dispute. The British did not want their French ally to go to war and recommended that it simply regard the president's reference to the affair in his annual message to Congress of 1835 as an "explanation." By no stretch of the imagination was this an apology, but the Paris government prudently chose to interpret the address as a recognition of its honor and authorized the claims payments.

The French claims dispute had raised questions of national honor and for that reason caused talk of war. Jackson had unnecessarily made an issue of a subject better left to the sedate surroundings of the diplomats' table than to the counsel of warriors. His poorly advised stance was highly dangerous, for the French government was not in the political position to give in as quickly as he wanted. Admittedly, Jackson got the money and stoked the fires of nationalism by rallying Americans behind him and the flag. He probably won some measure of respect in Europe for the United States. But his brash policies had provoked a near confrontation over a matter that, with patience and time, the nation's diplomacy would doubtless have resolved without leaving a residue of hard feelings.

A third major issue confronting the Jackson administration concerned U.S. policies toward the American Indians, or Native Americans. The Constitution had left their status ambiguous, permitting the federal government to treat them as nations under its commercial, treaty, and war powers. Shortly after the War of 1812, the Washington government encouraged them to emigrate into the trans-Mississippi West. This arrangement was not satisfactory to southerners interested in acquiring Indian lands held under federal treaties. But Presidents Monroe and Adams refused to forcefully move them west. They instead argued for a gradualist approach of voluntary relocation, insisting that the nation abide by its treaties. Southerners complained that Indians had allied with the British during the war and that as barbarians, they could never be civilized and must be transplanted to areas not wanted by whites. In southerners' eyes the Indians were dangerous in two important ways: As irresponsible custodians of vast reaches of land, they had failed to promote the progress assured by superior white Americans; and as crude savages, the Indians posed a physical threat to Americans east of the Mississippi River.

During Jackson's presidency, Congress passed the Indian Removal Act of 1830, which provided for the forceful removal of the Indians of both North and South into the West. Jackson had favored a policy of separation by voluntary emigration; although agreeing with Monroe and Adams that the Indians were capable of assimilation, he believed that the hatred that land-hungry Americans felt for them made this process impossible. But voluntary relocation was no longer possible under the act of 1830. Already in Alabama, Georgia, Mississippi, and other states, Americans had violated federal treaties by simply moving into areas reserved for the Indians. Now the federal government had the authority to take these lands under the guise of new treaties that then evicted the tribes to areas beyond the Mississippi. By the time Jackson completed his two terms in office, the United States had concluded nearly a hundred of these confiscatory treaties with the Indians.

Many Indians refused to surrender their lands. In the north the outcome was the brief Black Hawk War of 1831–1832, which ended in the defeat of the Sac and Fox Indians and their deportation across the Mississippi. In the south, the U.S. government likewise drove out the five huge Indian tribes—the Cherokees, Chickasaws, Choctaws, Creeks, and Seminoles. Not all went peacefully. The Chickasaws, Choctaws, and Creeks agreed to treaties stripping them of their land and sending them west. The Seminoles rejected the treaty and pulled back into the Florida marsh to wage a long but futile war against the U.S. Army. In the end the government removed most of the Seminoles to Indian Territory in present-day Oklahoma; close to a thousand remained scattered in Florida.

The Cherokees of Georgia put up the most spirited opposition to removal. They had made every effort to establish themselves as an independent nation within Georgia by writing a constitution in 1827 and declaring themselves a sovereign state. But after the discovery of gold in the Cherokee lands two years later, the Georgia legislature ordered their confiscation. The Cherokees took their case to the U.S. Supreme Court. Did not the Constitution declare treaties part of the supreme law of the land? In *Cherokee Nation* v. *Georgia,* Chief Justice John Marshall declared in 1831 that the Cherokees were not a foreign nation but a "domestic dependent nation" subject to the exclusive jurisdiction of the federal government. Their treaty, however, still protected them from the state law appropriating their land. The following year Marshall ruled in *Worcester* v. *Georgia* that the Cherokees enjoyed territorial sanctions that the state of Georgia could not violate (making its law unconstitutional) and left the strong implication that the president bore the responsibility of upholding their rights guaranteed by federal law. But Jackson refused to follow these dictates. "John Marshall has made his decision," the president defiantly proclaimed; "now let him enforce it."

The Cherokees had no choice but to capitulate to the U.S. government. After a bitter split within the tribe, one faction came to terms in December 1835. The treaty turned over all lands east of the Mississippi to the U.S. government and stipulated that the Indians move west. But the vast majority of Cherokees refused to leave. Three years later, Jackson's successor and close cohort, Martin Van Buren, ordered the U.S. Army to work with the state of Georgia in forcing nearly 18,000 Cherokees westward. Inadequate provisions combined with a horrible drought to cause incredible suffering during the migration west. Nearly 4000 Cherokees died during what has become known as the "trail of tears."

Jackson's Indian policy provided a harbinger of what would come during the nation's continued westward movement. Indeed, the federal government suggested the rising prominence of Indian relations by establishing a Bureau of Indian Affairs in 1836. Jackson's paternalistic attitude toward the Indians was indicative of a strong racism practiced by local officials and legitimized by a national government that, through its acquiescence, effectively condoned the hardships and cruelties inherent in the removal program. The final report of the Cherokees' removal belied the truth by ignoring it: "Good feeling has been preserved, and we have quietly and gently transported 18,000 friends to the west bank of the Mississippi." Jackson praised the removal plan for safeguarding Americans and averting a decimation of the Indians. "This unhappy race—the original dwellers in our land—are now placed in a situation where we may well hope that they will share in the blessings of civilization and be saved from degradation and destruction." Jackson thus joined those Americans who regarded nonwhites as inferior and therefore susceptible to any kind of treatment that resulted in the advance of "civilization." It was not long before these same Americans would look upon the Mexicans too as aborigines and dismiss their opposition to westward expansion as unwarranted resistance to the spread of civilization. Jackson's administration did not inaugurate such policies, but it certainly promoted them.

Canadian Rebellions and the *Caroline* Episode

Besides the Indian controversy, President Van Buren encountered several diplomatic issues that threatened to embroil the United States in conflict. The first was Texas, a problem he inherited from Jackson, which is the topic of the following chapter. But the most pressing matter was the outbreak of the Canadian rebellions of 1837–1838.

Dissidents in Upper and Lower Canada, attempting to throw off British rule, attracted a considerable following in the United States by invoking the revolutionary ideals of 1776. William Lyon Mackenzie and other Canadian rebels aroused strong support from the U.S. side of the border. For one thing, the Panic of 1837 had thrown thousands of Americans into unemployment, leading them to accept the promises of cash and land in exchange for fighting the British. A broader consideration was that Canada's separation offered the prospect of U.S. expansion northward and the ultimate expulsion of the British from North America. President Van Buren responded to the growing border crisis with a neutrality proclamation in November 1837, but it lacked any means of enforcement and thus had little impact. The following month British loyalists drove Mackenzie out of Upper Canada and into Buffalo, New York, where he raised money and recruits for a "patriot" army to invade his homeland. Headquartered in the Eagle Tavern, he recruited nearly 500 Americans, who gathered under the command of Rensselaer Van Rensselaer of New York. The troops made their preparations at a dilapidated fortress in a densely wooded area on Navy Island, a small plot of land on the Canadian side of the Niagara River and about a mile above the falls.

Tensions mounted along the border as the rebels chartered a forty-five-ton, privately

Martin Van Buren
As president, he helped to defuse a dangerous border situation between the United States and British North America. *Library of Congress.*

owned American steamer, the *Caroline,* to transport American volunteers and war materiel from Buffalo to Navy Island. Exasperated by this open flaunting of U.S. neutrality, a Canadian officer and fifty militiamen determined to destroy the vessel. In the evening hours of December 29, 1837, they quietly rowed to the mooring spot of the *Caroline.* But it was not there. This setback did not stop the men; they crossed the river and found it tied to the dock at Schlosser—in U.S. waters. Using the blackness of the night as their shield, the Canadians stormed the vessel, wounding several crew members, killing an American named Amos Durfee, and seizing control in less than ten minutes. As a crowd of onlookers, awakened by the noise, collected along the shore, the captors forced everyone off the *Caroline,* pulled it to the middle of the Niagara, and set it afire. Moments later, the wooden-

hulled *Caroline* broke apart in the swift current and sank in flames, just above the falls.

Reaction to the *Caroline* affair along the border was electric. Newspaper reports dramatically—and erroneously—described the vessel hanging over the lip of the falls, its terrified passengers screaming for help just before plummeting to their deaths below. A poem made a monument of the incident:

> As over the shelving rocks she broke,
> And plunged in her turbulent grave,
> The slumbering genius of freedom woke,
> Baptized in Niagara's wave,
> And sounded her warning Tocsin far,
> From Atlantic's shore to the polar star.

Coffin-shaped circulars announced the public funeral of Amos Durfee, a grisly spectacle scheduled to take place three days later in the city square of Buffalo. In the meantime, amid speechmaking and shouts from a mob of 3000 armed men and numerous other spectators, the victim's remains lay on the courthouse steps, "its pale forehead, mangled by the pistol ball, and his locks matted with his blood!" according to the Anglophobic *New York Herald*'s lurid account. The *Rochester Democrat* trumpeted a call for war in the name of national honor.

The matter posed a severe challenge to the diplomats. Secretary of State John Forsyth denounced the *Caroline*'s destruction as an "extraordinary outrage" and demanded an immediate apology and reparations. The British minister in Washington, Henry Fox, called the act self-defense and declared that the rebellions in Canada were a crime and the *Caroline* a pirate subject to destruction in any waters. The London government refused to accept responsibility for the act. Forsyth countered by asserting that the Canadian rebellions constituted war and that those involved were belligerents. The United States had declared neutrality, and the *Caroline* could not have been a pirate.

The British minister detected a flaw in the U.S. argument that for some unexplained reason he failed to exploit. A note to his London

"The Caroline *Descending the Great Falls" by W. R. Callington*
The American steamer *Caroline* set afire by Canadian forces and, according to erroneous accounts, going over Niagara Falls on December 29, 1837. *Public Archives of Canada, Ottawa.*

office carried striking allusions to Jackson's invasion of Florida in 1817: "If the Americans either cannot or will not guard the integrity of their own soil or prevent it from becoming an arsenal of outlaws and assassins, they have no right to expect that the soil of the United States will be respected by the victims of such unheard of violence."

Even if the British government did not press the Jackson analogy, the Van Buren administration was caught in a dilemma. According to international law, the U.S. neutrality proclamation of 1837 defined the situation in the Canadas as a war between belligerents, which meant that contraband on board a neutral vessel was subject to confiscation. If the owners of the *Caroline* knew that it carried war materiel and volunteers for the rebel force (which, in fact, they did know), the boat was no longer neutral and should have gone to a prize court. In retrospect the British should have warned the U.S. government that if the *Caroline* continued its activities along the border, they would seize the

vessel; if this did not work, they could have disposed of the steamer quietly, not in a burst of flames before numerous witnesses on the Niagara River.

But hindsight was of no value in early 1838. Americans knew only that the British had invaded U.S. territorial waters, killed an American, and destroyed American property. President Van Buren asked the governors of New York and Vermont to call up their militias, and he dispatched to the troubled border a leading military figure of the War of 1812, the tall and august General Winfield Scott, to ascertain what terms each side would accept short of war. The following day, January 5, the president issued another neutrality proclamation, warning Americans that jail awaited those who violated his order. The president's efforts had little effect.

Despite the excitement, the outlook for peace was good. Emotional reaction to the *Caroline* affair diminished as one moved farther from the border, and it aroused little concern even in Britain. In Parliament the *Caro-*

line drew only a single reference; more than a few members expressed interest in allowing Canada to secede because it had become a liability. Americans capable of rational reflection realized that the problems concerning the vessel were frustrating to Britons trying to keep the empire intact, and they also believed that Canadian officials had overreacted. The *Caroline* had posed no threat to the British; although making three voyages to Navy Island on the day of the attack, the vessel carried only a small amount of contraband. In March 1838 Congress provided retribution for those involved in border raids, but the president still lacked the power of enforcement. General Scott faced the nearly impossible task of calming the hatred extending along 800 miles of border, but he was impressive in full dress uniform as he defiantly challenged dissidents: "Except if it be over my body, you shall not pass this line—you shall not embark."

Border tensions quickly dissipated after the British crushed the Canadian rebellions early in 1838, although incidents continued as a rash of secret societies appeared on both sides of the international boundary from Michigan to Vermont. The Canadian Refugee Relief Association of New York called for an invasion of Canada, and another secret organization, the Hunters' Lodges, first appeared in Vermont and boasted a membership of thousands who sought to free North America from British rule. Armed with secret handshakes, signs, and passwords, the Hunters infiltrated Canada and the southern part of the United States, elected leaders of a new Canadian republic, and dubbed the captain of the *Caroline* the "Admiral of Lake Erie."

Even though these patriot organizations had little chance for success, their existence suggested the growing need for the United States to establish stability along its northern frontier and thereby enhance the nation's security. Two times these groups attempted to invade Canada, only to encounter superior British forces who hauled off captives to a penal colony below Australia and encouraged remaining members of the societies to scatter to their homes. Both Mackenzie and Rensselaer had been arrested, and by the end of 1839 the border had calmed. President Van Buren had acted as forcefully as the law and national mood allowed. He had found it nearly impossible to maintain neutrality because of the vast area involved, the enormous American sympathy with the rebels' goals, the strong interest in expansion northward, the lax neutrality laws and inadequate federal enforcement, and the large number of Americans hurt by the depression and attracted to the patriot cause by economic inducements. Under these adverse conditions, Van Buren did all anyone could have expected.

Northeastern Boundary Controversy and Aroostook War

The most perplexing problem in Anglo-American relations since the Paris peace negotiations of 1782–1783 was the northeastern boundary that wound along the hump of present-day Maine. Arguments over the boundary's location eventually comprised thirty volumes of detailed and exhaustive information. The roots of the controversy lay in the theoretically sound, but practically unsound, wording of the Treaty of Paris ending the American Revolutionary War and supposedly defining the Canadian-American border. The map used by the negotiators (a Mitchell's Map of North America, 1775 edition) was flawed, because it proved impossible to match the treaty's words with the physical characteristics of the geographical terrain. But even more important, the Paris diplomats never intended their maps to show final boundaries. The heavy red lines found on all copies of the maps used in the negotiations were mere *proposals,* intended for use by joint commissions as bases for locating the final boundaries after the war had ended. Because the boundaries discussed in Paris were of a provisional nature only, the diplomats did not attach a copy of the map they used to the treaty. The result was a long history of ambiguity over the northeastern boundary.

The aftermath of the Paris negotiations is a story of continued frustration over the boundary that harried diplomats and threatened to swell into international conflict because of the infusion of national honor and Anglophobia. The initial problem was that no river fitted the description of one called the St. Croix in the treaty. Jay's treaty of 1795 provided for a joint commission to resolve the question. Three years later the commission agreed with the British claim and identified the Schoodic River as the one described in the treaty, not the Magaguadavic River lying a bit northward and advocated by the United States. But the rest of the line remained uncertain west to the St. Lawrence River. Anglo-American negotiators at Ghent also provided for mixed commissions; in case of disagreement, the issue would go before a third nation as arbiter, whose decision would be binding. Several attempts failed to resolve the matter, and in the meantime Maine became a state in 1820 (separated from Massachusetts) and further complicated the situation by insisting on *all* the territory in dispute.

In 1827 the boundary issue went to the king of the Netherlands, who was to act as arbiter in examining the opposing maps and arguments and making a binding decision between the competing claims. Four years later he declared that neither stand was definitive and proposed a compromise that divided the land in dispute. The British approved the Netherlands award of 1831, although they pointed out that the king's responsibility was to accept one of the two arguments, not split the territory between them. Maine, however, strenuously objected to any loss of territory, a stance that greatly reduced the likelihood of securing Senate approval of the treaty. The president seemed amenable to the king's proposal but was hesitant to get involved in an issue politically unpopular in New England, where his Democratic party was trying to build support. Jackson turned over the matter to the Senate without a recommendation, and in June 1832 that body voted against the award 21 to 20, leaving the question un-

resolved throughout the remainder of the decade.

At first glance the northeast boundary controversy seemed filled with petty disagreements over pine trees, countless streams, and harsh land basically unsuitable for large-scale farming and habitation; but this was an erroneous conception. Not only were the pine trees and much of the land valuable commodities, but both the British and the Americans had important security interests at stake. The British objected to extending the line to the watershed between the St. Lawrence River and the Atlantic Ocean (in accordance with the treaty) because that would cost them direct commercial and military access to the Atlantic. Such a line would also thrust the tip of Maine between the British provinces of Quebec and New Brunswick and deprive Britain of land for a military road leading directly into the Canadian interior. The War of 1812 (reinforced by the Canadian rebellions) made clear that such a road was vital—especially after the St. Lawrence froze over and British soldiers had to march through the area on snowshoes. The British wanted the line below the St. John River, because this would provide a strip of land suitable for a military road to run parallel between the St. Lawrence River and U.S. territory. The line sought by the Americans, however, would have divided the St. John River and isolated the British provinces from one another. The British insisted that their negotiators at Paris in 1782–1783 would never have agreed to a boundary that damaged their country's interests. The Americans countered that acceptance of the British claims would forfeit the rich soil and pine tree industry of the Aroostook Valley, alienate Maine and Massachusetts, which both had property interests in a boundary settlement, and enlarge the British domain in North America.

In early 1839 mounting exasperation over conflicting boundary claims and mutual distrust between Maine and New Brunswick led to the short-lived and nearly comical "Aroostook War." The New Brunswick government had extended jurisdiction over the area in dispute and granted land titles to its subjects. When Canadian lumberjacks moved into modern upper Maine, that state's legislature authorized the governor to dispatch militiamen to throw out the brawny "invaders." A mild skirmish led to the capture and imprisonment of fifty Americans. Reactions became hot and heavy on both sides of the border. The legislature of Nova Scotia appropriated money for war, New Brunswick sent troops to the troubled area, and the U.S. Congress allotted $10 million and empowered the president to call out 50,000 volunteers to defeat the "Warriors of Waterloo." Senator James Buchanan of Pennsylvania (later president) blustered that the choice was "war or national dishonor," and Anglophobia permeated the highly popular "Maine Battle Song":

> Britannia shall not rule the Maine,
> Nor shall she rule the water;
> They've sung that song full long enough,
> Much longer than they oughter.

After a few barroom brawls and numerous long hours of drilling and marching, emotions calmed, permitting General Winfield Scott, again sent by President Van Buren to the Canadian border, to arrange an uneasy truce. Maine and New Brunswick retained the areas then occupied, pending final resolution of the boundary. But the brief excitement along the border sent a message to Washington and London that if they did not negotiate a settlement of the boundary problem, the local governments might resolve it by force.

The Case of Alexander McLeod

In November 1840 a strange case involving a Canadian deputy sheriff named Alexander McLeod caused Anglo-American relations to take a sharp turn for the worse. Troubles left by the Canadian rebellions of 1837–1838 threatened to flare up again along the New York border when the story spread that McLeod, a loyalist during the uprisings, drunkenly boasted in a tavern in Buffalo, New York, that *he* had shot Amos Durfee during the *Caroline* raid. Furthermore, he opened his sheath at his side and drew out the still bloodstained sword used in gaining control over the vessel.

It was a fantastic tale, later shown to have no foundation in fact, but given the emberlike atmosphere along the Canadian border, the long-hated McLeod became the symbol of British ruthlessness and the object of bitter attack. New York authorities arrested him for murder and arson during the *Caroline* affair and prepared to bring him to trial. The Canadian government offered bail, but a mob aimed a cannon at the jail and blocked his release. A grand jury from New York indicted him, even though British Prime Minister Lord Palmerston demanded the prisoner's freedom on the basis that he had acted under government orders and could not be held personally responsible.

In a statement that actually reversed Britain's stand on the *Caroline* affair, the British minister in Washington, Henry Fox, declared that the vessel's destruction was "the public act of persons obeying the constituted authorities of Her Majesty's Province." The British had earlier refused to accept responsibility for the act, but the situation had changed, and they now found it advantageous to do so in an effort to win McLeod's release. President Van Buren and Secretary of State Forsyth were not "aware of any principle of international law, or indeed of reason or justice," granting sanctity to people who "acted in obedience to their superior authorities." They also recognized the limitations on their actions imposed by the states' rights doctrine. But they could not ignore Palmerston's ominous warning that McLeod's execution "would produce war, war immediate and frightful in its character, because it would be a war of retaliation and vengeance." Americans would stand guilty of a "judicial murder," Palmerston angrily declared to his minister in Washington.

As tempers rose along both sides of the North American border, the administrations in Washington and London changed hands,

Alexander McLeod
Britain threatened war with the United States
over this Canadian Loyalist who had allegedly
killed an American during the attack on the
Caroline. Charles Lindsey, The Life and Times
of William Lyon Mackenzie, *Toronto:*
P. R. Randall, 1862.

brightening chances for a peaceful settlement.
The new president (William Henry Harrison
had died after a month in office) was John
Tyler, and his secretary of state was Daniel
Webster. In April 1841 Webster reversed the
stand of the Van Buren administration by
agreeing with the British that McLeod had
acted under military orders and could not be
held responsible; but, like his predecessor, the
secretary of state could not arrange the prisoner's release because the federal government
lacked jurisdiction in the case. His efforts to
persuade New York to free McLeod or turn the
case over to a federal court had failed, and he
later claimed that, in the event of conviction,
he had been unable to secure a definite promise of pardon from the governor of New York,
William H. Seward. The New York Supreme
Court refused to grant his release but agreed

to a change of venue from Lockport to Utica.
Webster worried about McLeod's safety. "If a
mob should kill him, War w'd be inevitable in
ten days. Of this there is no doubt." The sole
saving grace in the tense situation appeared to
be the demise of Palmerston's rule. The Tory
ministry of Prime Minister Sir Robert Peel and
Foreign Secretary Lord Aberdeen took over
the London government in September 1841
and began working toward a peaceful resolution of the problem.

Finally, in early October, the long-awaited
McLeod trial began, dramatically complete
with federal soldiers stationed just outside
Utica and a sheriff's posse standing by to protect the accused from the large crowd of sullen
looking strangers that had ascended on the
town. Thus, in an atmosphere rife with threats
of violence and lynchings, lawyers furnished by
the Canadian government defended McLeod
in what surprisingly turned out to be an orderly affair. Alleged witnesses to his participation in the *Caroline* affair did not appear, and
McLeod established an alibi that convinced
the jury of his innocence. In less than twenty
minutes it returned an acquittal that instantly
lifted the pall of war that had settled over the
border.

The full year of excitement over the McLeod
affair suggested that several matters in Anglo-
American relations needed immediate rectifi-
cation. The diplomats had to clear the air of
numerous irritants, including the still smol-
dering *Caroline* matter. It is arguable whether
the McLeod episode would have led to war,
because the evidence strongly suggests that
Governor Seward, contrary to Webster's con-
clusions, had virtually assured a pardon to prevent an execution. In addition, the federal government would surely have intervened by force
to halt such a travesty of justice that would
have carried the added calamity of war with
England. Besides, a series of appeals would
have moved the case to higher courts and ultimately to the U.S. Supreme Court. There
the federal government could have secured
McLeod's release on a writ of habeas corpus
based on Britain's assumption of responsibil-

ity for the *Caroline*'s destruction. The lesson nonetheless was clear: The United States had to get its international affairs in order and prevent the states' rights doctrine from interfering with foreign relations. McLeod's personal culpability was not the issue; New Yorkers had placed Britain itself on trial.

Slavery and the *Creole* Revolt

Until the 1830s the American South was not actively involved in these ongoing Anglo-American controversies, but as slavery became an issue both inside and outside the United States, that section of the country became increasingly concerned about British behavior. Questions about slavery had not risen to the crisis level because no incident had occurred that brought focus to the matter. Yet a basis for trouble lay in the long-standing Anglo-American disagreements over the suppression of the African slave trade. The direct stimulus to a major controversy was a slave mutiny on board the American *Creole* in November 1841 as it engaged in the interstate slave trade from Hampton Roads, Virginia, to New Orleans. The African slave-trade issue and the *Creole* revolt soon became entangled with each other, threatening to cause an international confrontation over slavery itself.

Since 1808 the British government had tried to win U.S. cooperation in outlawing the international trade in slaves. The Founding Fathers had declared in 1787 that after a twenty-year period, Congress could move toward abolishing the traffic; but southern opposition based on racial and economic considerations had blocked any action until 1820. In that year Congress passed a law declaring that those who took part in slave trading were guilty of piracy, punishable by death. But no provision existed in international law that bound other nations, and no understanding had developed between the Atlantic nations that each could enforce the law against the other's subjects. Article X of the Treaty of Ghent provided that both governments would "use their best endeavors" to end the traffic,

and by the Convention of 1824 they agreed to reciprocal rights of search of vessels believed to be participating in the slave trade. But memories of impressment led to Senate action forbidding application of the law to North American waters and the convention never went into effect because the London government would not accept such an amendment.

In 1833 Britain abolished slavery in the empire and became leader of the world antislavery movement. The South, supported by outspoken northerners such as Senator Lewis Cass of Michigan, vehemently opposed British search of American vessels because the practice smacked of impressment. But by the latter part of the decade, British warships were stopping vessels off the African coast that flew the U.S. flag, and Secretary of State John Forsyth of Georgia and the U.S. minister to London, Andrew Stevenson of Virginia, vigorously protested these actions as interference in the nation's rights at sea.

The British found it difficult to defend the right of search in peacetime and tried to draw a distinction between a search and the right to *visit* a ship suspected of involvement in the slave traffic. Palmerston explained that such visits were necessary to enable British captains to determine whether the colors accurately identified the allegiance of the slave ships in question. Britain had signed treaties with several nations of Europe and Latin America and had to investigate whether slavers were using the U.S. flag as subterfuge. If denied this right of visit, the British could not hope to suppress the African slave trade. Stevenson countered that a "visit" was no different from a "search," in that both procedures constituted an inspection of the ship's cargo and perhaps the first step toward the impressment of American seamen. The United States would not permit a search of its ships, except for contraband in wartime.

By 1840 the United States was the only important seafaring nation that had refused to sign any treaty authorizing Britain to suppress the slave traffic. The governor of Liberia indignantly declared that the U.S. flag, flying illegally over slave ships, was the main obstacle to Britain's efforts to suppress the African slave trade. "Never was the proud banner of freedom so extensively used by those pirates upon liberty and humanity as at this season." But when the British minister in Washington had asked John Quincy Adams some years before if he knew of anything more horrible than the slave trade, even he, a staunch opponent of slavery, stoutly replied: "Yes, admitting the right of search by foreign officers of our vessels upon the seas in time of peace; for that would be making slaves of ourselves." The southern states' complaints about search and impressment perhaps camouflaged a deeper concern over slavery; but they had acquired unusual allies in northerners such as Adams and Cass, who were worried about U.S. rights at sea. All criticized England, however, as the source of their anger.

Thus, any incident that focused attention on slavery could inflame the South—and that event came in November 1841, when a slave named Madison Washington led eighteen others aboard the *Creole* in revolt, killing one man in the uprising, seizing command, and then seeking safety at Nassau in the British Bahamas. After numerous diplomatic exchanges with the Washington government, the Peel ministry in London infuriated the South by ordering the release of all 135 slaves from the American vessel on the ground that when they entered free British territory, they likewise became free.

A seemingly similar revolt on board the Spanish slaver *Amistad* had occurred just a little over two years before, causing southerners to perceive a pattern of behavior toward slavery that threatened its sanctity. In July 1839, black Africans led by Joseph Cinqué on the *Amistad* had mutinied in Cuban waters and made their way to New York, where U.S. naval officers seized the schooner, blacks, and cargo and took them all to an admiralty court in New London, Connecticut, for prize adjudication. But authorities placed the blacks under arrest to stand trial for murder. American abolitionists had meanwhile seen an

opportunity to expose the evils of the slave trade and slavery, and they arranged a court defense based on the natural right of self-defense against illegal detention. In March 1841, after a lengthy appeal process and just months before the *Creole* revolt, the U.S. Supreme Court declared the *Amistad* blacks free on the ground that their transport from Africa to Cuba had been in violation of Anglo-Spanish treaties against the African slave trade. They were "kidnapped Africans," entitled to strike for freedom by any means possible.

Although the *Creole* was engaged in the domestic traffic and the blacks aboard were unquestionably slaves by U.S. law, the emotions aroused by the two mutinies did not allow calm analysis. Both caused an uproar in the South. But what made the *Creole* affair more inflammatory was outright British interference in what the South considered a purely internal affair. Southerners demanded the return of their property, but Secretary of State Webster was in no position to comply because the only provision for extradition between the United States and England had been in Jay's treaty, which had expired in 1807. His only chance for reparations was an appeal to comity (hospitality), which offered little hope for return of the slaves. Thus, the South joined the growing number of Americans who felt provoked by British behavior.

The Webster-Ashburton Negotiations

Anglo-American relations were so severely strained by the early 1840s that they could have exploded in conflict. It was difficult to determine whether one factor was more dangerous than another, but the basic problem was a lack of trust that manifested itself in highly emotional disputes over national honor and security. Americans remained convinced that the British refused to grant them respect as a nation. London's *Edinburgh Review* disagreed, insisting that the U.S. republic was not "undervalued in England." But it admitted that "there is a nation by whom America is anxious to be esteemed—or, to speak more correctly, to be admired and feared—and that is England." [America thinks that by adopting a] "bold, or even a threatening tone towards England, she will obtain our respect." England despised America's "swagger or . . . bully."

Most Anglo-American difficulties after 1815 were loose ends left from the period before. Each nation remained suspicious of the other's economic and territorial intentions in the Western Hemisphere, primarily because of commercial rivalries in Latin America, continuing animosities along the Canadian border, disagreements over Texas, and growing questions concerning Oregon. No single event after the War of 1812 seemed capable of mobilizing the Atlantic peoples into war, but the combination of issues had that potential because of the pervasive element of mutual distrust.

Other irritants made matters worse. Longtime exchanges of biting insults across the ocean had worn on both nations' patience. Popular writers James Fenimore Cooper and Washington Irving led Americans in defending their country and lamenting British arrogance, whereas British travelers' accounts denounced American democracy and claimed it generated disgustingly uncivilized offshoots of fighting, tobacco chewing, drinking, stealing, slaving, hangings, and a general chaos resulting from rabble rule. Journals in both countries traded vicious jabs in what became known as the "War of the Quarterlies." A London journal acidly remarked that before the United States "can deserve the name of a wise nation, it must rid itself of its republicanism, its nationalistic 'fourth of July harangues,' [and its] nonsense about 'flying eagles and never setting stars,' . . . and the infinite superiority of the Yankee over all mankind, past, present, and to come."

The meshing of these with other issues created a volatile situation. During the Panic of 1837, Americans defaulted on interest payments and about $150 million in loans from the British that helped finance new roads, canals, and railroads in the United States. In addition, the absence of copyright laws in the United States permitted Americans to "borrow" from British writers without reimbursing them. One writer, Charles Dickens, was bitter on both counts: He had lost money from royalties *and* investments in the United States. Dickens received a warm welcome during his visit to the United States in 1842, but he returned home to publish his *American Notes,* which sharply criticized his hosts. Social, cultural, and economic ties seemed capable of holding the nations together, but these tenuous relationships needed strengthening by skillful diplomats.

In early 1842 the Peel ministry in London suggested that the two nations negotiate their differences, and the Tyler administration quickly agreed. The prime minister and his foreign secretary, Lord Aberdeen, recognized the commercial value of keeping peace between the Atlantic nations. But they also recalled the awful destruction of the Napoleonic Wars and were concerned that their country's recent problems with France would again lead to conflict. Improved Anglo-American relations, they hoped, might force the French to seek an accommodation with England.

These considerations in mind, Aberdeen appointed Lord Ashburton (Alexander Baring) as special emissary to the United States and authorized him to resolve all matters in dispute. He was an excellent choice. Six feet tall and sixty-seven years old, he was the retired head of the powerful Baring Brothers banking house, which had helped finance the Louisiana Purchase. He also was married to a Philadelphia lady and was known as a critic of British policies toward the United States before the War of 1812. Although he had no diplomatic experience, he had sat in Parliament for thirty years and was trusted in international political and financial circles as a man of unquestioned integrity. Americans were flattered by the British decision to send a special mission to the United States, especially because the envoy had such stature.

Britons also were pleased with Ashburton's counterpart in the United States, Daniel Webster. The bushy-browed and robust secretary

Lord Ashburton
British special emissary who helped to negotiate
the treaty in 1842 that promoted the mid-
century Anglo-American rapprochement.
Library of Congress.

of state, fifty-nine years old and majestic in
appearance, was a renowned spokesman for
nationalism, a firm believer in the inseparability
of domestic and foreign affairs, and a staunch
advocate of a pragmatic and realistic foreign
policy that rested on international law. He had
visited England three years before, where he
made many friends, including Ashburton himself. Webster had served as the Baring Brothers' legal agent in the United States and spoke
for New England mercantile interests. He was
also well-known for his desire to become U.S.
minister to the Court of St. James's in London. An English critic of the United States
once said of Webster that he was "a living lie,
because no man on earth could be so great as
he looked." Webster was on shaky political
ground because he was the only cabinet member not to resign when President Tyler's domestic policies veered sharply from those of

the Whig party and left him without a following. Webster explained that he wanted to complete the northeast boundary negotiations then
under way with England; but he probably also
believed that staying in office would afford him
a better position to outmaneuver Henry Clay
for the presidency in 1844.

Before the negotiations began, Webster
secretly worked to resolve the greatest obstacle to a boundary settlement—the opposition
of Maine and Massachusetts to a compromise.
He secured permission from President Tyler to
use his "secret service fund," a special annual
appropriation from Congress of $17,000,
which the executive could draw on at his dis-
cretion in matters affecting foreign affairs. With
the money, Webster hired a nondescript political figure from Maine named Francis O. J.
("Fog") Smith, who circulated newspaper editorials in New England warning that the alternative to a boundary settlement was war.

Webster's greatest boost came from an unexpected source—one Jared Sparks, a Harvard
historian. Sparks wrote the secretary of state
in February 1842 that while conducting research in the French archives, he had come
across a map bearing a heavy red line that Benjamin Franklin had apparently used in drawing the northeast boundary during the Paris
peace negotiations of 1782–1783. Much to
Sparks's surprise the marking supported the
extreme *British* claim to the area in dispute.
After wrestling with the dilemma of whether
to be a good historian whose loyalty was to
the truth or a good American whose loyalty
was to his country, he opted for leaving that
hard decision to someone else. Sparks returned to his lodging that evening and recon-
structed the line from memory onto a map of
Maine and forwarded it to Webster.

The secretary of state had received an unan-
ticipated boost to his chances for resolving the
boundary. He was not taken aback by Sparks's
revelation: An acquaintance had discovered
another map that belonged to Baron Friedrich
von Steuben of Revolutionary War fame, and
it contained a red line corresponding to the
one on Sparks's map. Believing that a diplo-

mat, like a lawyer, had no obligation to reveal incriminating evidence to his opposition, Webster put both of them away; but when the negotiations with Britain approached, he put them to use. Again with secret service money, he dispatched Sparks, since returned to the United States, to Augusta, Maine, to inform the state's legislators of the two maps and convince them that refusal to compromise *now* might be costly. If copies of either red-line map turned up later, the British would have claims to *all* territory in dispute. The completion of Webster's "grand stroke," as he called it, was to persuade both Maine and Massachusetts to send commissioners to the negotiations in Washington.

Ashburton had meanwhile arrived in Washington in April 1842 and had soon become involved in secret talks of his own. Without notifying his home government, he contacted officials in New Brunswick to determine their minimum expectations on the boundary. A secret delegation arrived in Washington sometime later to discuss the matter with Ashburton, and to his regret its demands were more stringent than those of the Peel ministry. Ashburton's lack of diplomatic experience had put him in a precarious position: It enmeshed him in the local interests he sought to avoid. Ashburton found it more difficult to reach an amicable settlement now that he had talked with New Brunswick's representatives. He had unknowingly erected another barrier to compromise.

The Webster-Ashburton talks finally got under way in June 1842. The British emissary suggested that the two men dispense with formal diplomatic procedure and hold open, friendly meetings designed to reach a compromise. Webster agreed, and they dropped protocol and exchanged few diplomatic notes. This decision confounded historians who later investigated these proceedings in Washington, but several bits of evidence make clear that the negotiations had already fallen into the byzantine style of traditional diplomacy and that they did not progress as smoothly and amicably as both men had hoped. Ashburton found the

Daniel Webster
U.S. secretary of state who negotiated the Webster-Ashburton Treaty with England that resolved several issues, including the long-standing northeast boundary dispute. *Library of Congress.*

repeated delays, long-winded arguments, and hot and fetid Washington weather almost unbearable. He had come to the United States without his wife because of her poor health and had hoped to return home in a month. The presence of the Maine and Massachusetts commissioners proved especially exasperating. Ashburton never came to understand the practical politics involved in Webster's decision to include them in negotiations between nations, and he refused to talk with them.

After considerable discussion Ashburton retreated on his boundary claims and agreed to a settlement later that month. His instructions were to secure a line as close as possible to that of the Netherlands award of 1831, because even if it left the Aroostook Valley to the United States, such a settlement would discourage U.S. expansion northward by guaranteeing enough land for a British military road extending from the Atlantic to the Canadian interior. To secure this line, Ashburton conceded free navigation of the St. John River to the United States, along with land totaling 7000 of the 12,000 square miles in dispute. This was about 893 square miles less than the Netherlands award, although the United States received four-fifths of the assessed value of the entire territory in question, including an important military position at Rouses Point located near the top of Lake Champlain. To mollify Maine and Massachusetts for consenting to give up part of their land claims, the agreement specified that the United States pay those states $150,000 each. Finally, the two negotiators settled another section of the Canadian boundary farther west. Ashburton conceded U.S. claims to 6500 square miles of territory stretching from Lake Superior to the Lake of the Woods. This arrangement turned out to be an unexpected bonus for the United States: In the latter part of the century, Americans discovered that this area (upper Minnesota) contained the rich iron ore deposits of the Vermilion and eastern Mesabi ranges.

The northeast boundary was clearly the most nettlesome problem facing Webster and Ashburton, but other issues were also difficult to resolve. Southerners demanded a favorable settlement of the African slave-trade question and indemnity for the slaves liberated during the *Creole* affair. Ashburton had told Aberdeen that the United States's central concern in both matters was impressment and asked for authorization to renounce the practice. But the foreign secretary could not do this without encouraging desertions and endangering the crown's authority over its subjects. Ashburton nonetheless assured Webster by a carefully reasoned note attached to the treaty (but not part of the formal agreement) that impressment in peacetime had "wholly ceased" and would not be "under present circumstances renewed." Webster and Ashburton then tried to remove the necessity for a reciprocal right of search in halting the African slave trade. Article XIII of the treaty established joint-cruising squadrons along the African

coast "to enforce, separately and respectively, the laws, rights, and obligations, of each of the two countries, for the suppression of the slave trade." Each squadron must have a minimum of eighty guns and would operate independently but "in concert and cooperation, upon mutual consultation, as exigencies may arise."

Webster and Ashburton were unable to reach formal agreement on the *Creole* controversy, but they attached notes to the treaty containing Ashburton's guarantee that British officials in the islands were to avoid "officious interference" with American ships driven into their ports for reasons beyond their control. In a move to prevent future cases like that of the *Creole* but to placate antislavery groups in the United States and Britain, Webster and Ashburton included a provision in the treaty that established mutual extradition of fugitives accused of seven specified crimes. The list, however, did not include mutiny.

These decisions did not still the growing controversies over slavery and the African slave trade. The United States failed to enforce the joint squadron clause, largely because of southern influence in key government positions. Until 1857 the British shied away from ships flying the U.S. flag, but finally, out of exasperation, they resorted to search tactics in trying to halt the slave traffic. Lewis Cass, then secretary of state, bitterly criticized the "right to visit," and the following year the British agreed to drop the practice in peacetime unless specifically permitted by treaty. In 1862, during the American Civil War, the Anglo-American nations signed an agreement allowing mutual search in peacetime. The end of the Civil War brought an end to slavery in the United States and at long last resolved the controversy. In the meantime an Anglo-American claims commission in 1853 closed the *Creole* matter by awarding southerners $110,330 for slaves lost in the mutiny.

Webster and Ashburton also resolved the *Caroline* and McLeod affairs. In an exchange of notes attached to the treaty, Ashburton emphasized that on the *Caroline,* "there were grounds of justification as strong as were ever presented in such cases," but he insisted that

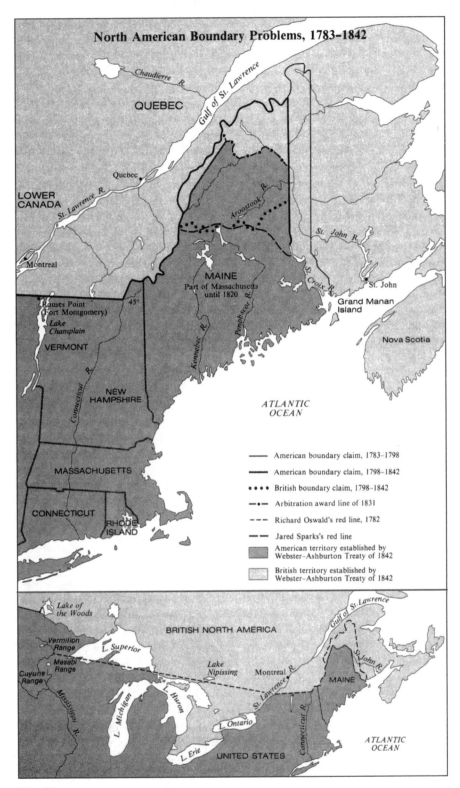

North American Boundary Problems, 1783–1842

Chaudierre R.

QUEBEC

Gulf of St. Lawrence

Quebec

LOWER
CANADA

St. Lawrence R.

Montreal

Aroostook R.

St. John R.

St. Croix R.

St. John

MAINE
Part of Massachusetts
until 1820

Grand Manan
Island

Nova Scotia

Rouses Point
(Fort Montgomery)

Lake
Champlain

45°

VERMONT

Kennebec R.

Penobscot R.

Connecticut R.

NEW
HAMPSHIRE

ATLANTIC
OCEAN

MASSACHUSETTS

CONNECTICUT

RHODE
ISLAND

——— American boundary claim, 1783–1798

━━━ American boundary claim, 1798–1842

•••• British boundary claim, 1798–1842

—•— Arbitration award line of 1831

––– Richard Oswald's red line, 1782

— — Jared Sparks's red line

▓ American territory established by
Webster-Ashburton Treaty of 1842

░ British territory established by
Webster-Ashburton Treaty of 1842

Lake of
the Woods

BRITISH NORTH AMERICA

Gulf of St. Lawrence

Vermilion
Range

L. Superior

Mesabi
Range

Cuyune
Range

Lake
Nipissing

Montreal

St. Lawrence R.

MAINE

St. John R.

Mississippi R.

L. Michigan

L. Huron

St. Lawrence R.

Connecticut R.

L. Ontario

L. Erie

UNITED STATES

ATLANTIC
OCEAN

Map 10
The Webster-Ashburton Treaty resolved two sets of Canadian boundary problems, but
the settlement was even more important in establishing a mid-century rapprochement
between the United States and England.

the British had intended "no slight of the authority of the United States" in destroying the vessel. He then added a statement that Webster later stretched into an apology: Ashburton expressed regret "that some explanation and apology for this occurrence was not immediately made" and hoped that "all feelings of resentment and ill will, resulting from these truly unfortunate events, may be buried in oblivion, and that they may be succeeded by those of harmony and friendship." Webster made no demands for reparation because he knew that the *Caroline* had been trafficking in contraband. On the McLeod matter Webster expressed regret for the incident, and it too was closed. In late August 1842 the secretary of state, with Tyler's support, drafted a bill that Congress quickly enacted. The so-called McLeod law (or Remedial Justice Act) established federal jurisdiction over cases involving aliens accused of criminal acts committed under government orders.

One subject discussed but not considered an issue at the time was Oregon, a huge expanse of land that sprawled from the southern tip of Alaska to Spanish California and from the Rockies to the Pacific. Ashburton had instructions to propose the Columbia River as a boundary between the nations, but Webster rejected this reminder of British imperial days. Yet the secretary of state was not overly concerned about acquiring the Pacific Northwest, and as a Whig he favored commercial over territorial expansion because the latter was injurious to American unity and contributory to war. In late June 1842 he explained to an acquaintance: "In seeking acquisitions, to be governed as territories, and lying at a great distance from the United States, we ought to be governed by our prudence and caution; and a still higher degree of these qualities should be exercised when large Territorial acquisitions are looked for, with a view to annexation." Ashburton did not believe that American settlements in Oregon would be substantial for some time and was willing to postpone the subject for fear that it might interfere with the delicate discussions over the northeast bound-

ary. "It must, therefore, I fear, sleep for the present," he wrote Aberdeen.

Ratification of the Webster-Ashburton Treaty, signed in Washington on August 9, 1842, faced serious obstacles because it got entangled in political battles on both sides of the Atlantic. In the United States, Anglophobe Senators James Buchanan of Pennsylvania and Thomas Hart Benton of Missouri, both Democrats, criticized the settlement as a "solemn bamboozlement" that sacrificed part of Maine to Britain. Yet within two weeks the Senate overwhelmingly approved the treaty. Most Americans welcomed the news, although people in Maine and Massachusetts remained disgruntled until Webster's continued newspaper editorials finally convinced them that the only option to the treaty was war.

The matter was even more complicated in Britain. Canadians bitterly denounced the treaty, and in England the political "outs," led by Palmerston and his Whig mouthpiece, the *London Chronicle,* caustically assailed it as a "pitiful exhibition of imbecility" and the "Ashburton capitulation." During the ensuing debates in Parliament in February 1843, news arrived of the Sparks map supporting Britain's extreme boundary claims, causing Britons to unleash another barrage of criticism of Webster's duplicity and Ashburton's stupidity. Meanwhile, Ashburton himself uncovered another red-line map in the British Museum (the Richard Oswald or King George III map), which substantiated the equally extreme U.S. claims. Although the existence of the two contradictory maps again underlined the wisdom of the Webster-Ashburton compromise, the discovery of the map in England nonetheless embarrassed the Peel ministry and threatened to unravel its diplomat's handiwork. Aberdeen took it upon himself to convince the U.S. minister in London, Edward Everett, that the ministry had not been aware of the Oswald map during the Washington negotiations. The irony is that each side in the dispute had held maps supporting the boundary claims of its adversary. The difference was that Webster knew what he had and used it to

PUNCH'S PENCILLINGS.—Nº. LIII.

FAIR ROSAMOND; OR, THE ASHBURTON TREATY.

London **Punch**
According to the London *Punch,* the barbarian Americans offered the British the choice of either accepting the Webster-Ashburton Treaty or facing war. *London* Punch.

advantage in the negotiations, whereas Ashburton came across his map too late to affect the treaty terms but in time to promote the ratification process in England.

Ashburton's discovery took the fire out of the political abuse aimed at the treaty—especially when succeeding events showed that *Palmerston* had come across the map some years before and had hidden it in the archives. With the opposition now in total disarray, Parliament easily approved the treaty and voted a formal expression of appreciation to Ashburton for his public service.

The Importance of the Webster-Ashburton Treaty

Lingering suspicions about the Webster-Ashburton Treaty have obscured its contribution toward easing Anglo-American tensions and bringing security to much of the United States's northern border. Some writers still insist that Webster retreated too easily on the northeast boundary: Had he held out a while longer, their argument goes, the red-line map discovered in England would have substantiated the U.S. claim, and *all* the disputed territory would have become part of the United States. Yet, as noted earlier in this chapter, a careful examination of the Paris negotiations of 1782–1783 shows that all maps referred to contained only *proposed* boundaries and that the diplomats' intention was for a joint commission to construct the final markings after the war. Hence the Webster-Ashburton boundary compromise (in which the United States received the better part) was the most feasible route to a settlement.

Another controversy has arisen, even more difficult to lay to rest. Some historians have accused Webster of taking money during the negotiations in exchange for a boundary settlement favorable to Britain. Indeed, some of Webster's contemporaries in 1846 went so far as to attempt to impeach him retroactively for illegal activities during the negotiations that included embezzlement from the state department and unauthorized use of the president's secret service fund. Webster's inexhaustible need for money was well known, but even though this reality had led to hot disputes over his integrity, the critics have never proved their charges. A House committee heard testimony on his behalf—including that of former President Tyler, who declared that he had approved the secretary's draws from the secret service fund—and exonerated the secretary on all counts. Webster had bitter political enemies who, in seeking to discredit his performance as secretary of state, have had long-lasting effects on those writers later analyzing his achievements in office.

A fair evaluation must take into account all aspects of the negotiations, for the treaty was a package agreement that set forth a compromise in which neither party surrendered vital interests and both achieved objectives considered important to national security. The

Webster-Ashburton Treaty promoted a mid-century rapprochement that promoted Anglo-American interdependency. It also helped remove the British obstacle to a better border relationship in the northeast, which in turn permitted Americans to focus on westward expansion. In a broader perspective, the treaty proved integral to the formation of an Atlantic friendship whose ramifications have reached to the present.

Selected Readings

Baxter, Maurice G. *One and Inseparable: Daniel Webster and the Union.* 1984.

Belohlavek, John M. *"Let the Eagle Soar!" The Foreign Policy of Andrew Jackson.* 1985.

Bemis, Samuel F. *John Quincy Adams and the Foundations of American Foreign Policy.* 1949.

———. *John Quincy Adams and the Union.* 1956.

Blumenthal, Henry. *A Reappraisal of Franco-American Relations, 1830–1871.* 1959.

Bourne, Kenneth. *Britain and the Balance of Power in North America, 1815–1908.* 1967.

Campbell, Charles S. *From Revolution to Rapprochement: The United States and Great Britain, 1783–1900.* 1974.

Chitwood, Oliver P. *John Tyler: Champion of the Old South.* 1939.

Corey, Albert B. *The Crisis of 1830–1842 in Canadian-American Relations.* 1941.

Curtis, James C. *The Fox at Bay: Martin Van Buren and the Presidency, 1837–1841.* 1970.

Debo, Angie. *A History of the Indians in the United States.* 1970.

Ehle, John. *Trail of Tears: The Rise and Fall of the Cherokee Nation.* 1988.

Eisenhower, John S. D. *Agent of Destiny: The Life and Times of General Winfield Scott.* 1997.

Elliott, Charles W. *Winfield Scott: The Soldier and the Man.* 1937.

Hargreaves, Mary W. M. *The Presidency of John Quincy Adams.* 1985.

Horsman, Reginald. *Expansion and American Indian Policy, 1783–1812.* 1967.

———. *The Origins of Indian Removal, 1815–1824.* 1970.

James, Marquis. *Andrew Jackson: Portrait of a President.* 1937.

Johnson, Timothy D. *Winfield Scott: The Quest for Military Glory.* 1998.

Jones, Howard. "Anglophobia and the Aroostook War," *New England Quarterly* 48 (1975): 519–39.

———. "The Attempt to Impeach Daniel Webster," *Capitol Studies* 3 (1975): 31–44.

———. "The *Caroline* Affair," *The Historian* 38 (1976): 485–502.

———. "Daniel Webster: The Diplomatist," in Shewmaker, Kenneth E., ed., *Daniel Webster: "The Completest Man,"* 203–29. 1990.

———. *Mutiny on the* Amistad: *The Saga of a Slave Revolt and Its Impact on American Abolition, Law, and Diplomacy.* 1987; 1997.

———. "The Peculiar Institution and National Honor: The Case of the *Creole* Slave Revolt," *Civil War History* 21 (1975): 28–50.

———. *To the Webster-Ashburton Treaty: A Study in Anglo-American Relations, 1783–1843.* 1977.

———, and Rakestraw, Donald A. *Prologue to Manifest Destiny: Anglo-American Relations in the 1840s.* 1997.

Jones, Wilbur D. *The American Problem in British Diplomacy, 1841–1861.* 1974.

———. *Lord Aberdeen and the Americas.* 1958.

Ketcham, Ralph L. *Presidents Above Party: The First American Presidency, 1789–1829.* 1984.

Klunder, Willard C. *Lewis Cass and the Politics of Moderation.* 1996.

McDonald, Forrest. *States' Rights and the Union: Imperium in Imperio, 1776–1876.* 2000.

McInnis, Edgar W. *The Unguarded Frontier: A History of American-Canadian Relations.* 1942.

Merk, Frederick. *Fruits of Propaganda in the Tyler Administration.* 1971.

Nagel, Paul C. *John Quincy Adams: A Public Life, a Private Life.* 1997.

Parsons, Lynn H. *John Quincy Adams.* 1998.

Perkins, Bradford. *The Creation of a Republican Empire, 1776–1865.* 1993. The Cambridge History of American Foreign Relations, vol. 1. Cohen, Warren I., ed.

Peterson, Norma L. *The Presidencies of William Henry Harrison and John Tyler.* 1989.

Reeves, Jesse S. *American Diplomacy under Tyler and Polk.* 1907.

Remini, Robert V. *Andrew Jackson and His Indian Wars.* 2001.

———. *Andrew Jackson and the Course of American Freedom, 1822–1832.* 1981.

———. *Daniel Webster: The Man and His Time.* 1997.

Richards, Leonard L. *The Life and Times of Congressman John Quincy Adams.* 1986.

Rogin, Michael P. *Fathers and Children: Andrew Jackson and the Subjugation of the American Indian.* 1975.

Russell, Greg. *John Quincy Adams and the Public Virtues of Diplomacy.* 1995.

Satz, Ronald M. *American Indian Policy in the Jacksonian Era.* 1975.

Sellers, Charles G. *The Market Revolution: Jacksonian America, 1815–1846.* 1991.

Stevens, Kenneth. *Border Diplomacy: The* Caroline *and McLeod Affairs in Anglo-American Canadian Relations, 1837–1842.* 1989.

Stuart, Reginald C. *United States Expansionism and British North America, 1775–1871.* 1988.

Varg, Paul A. *New England and Foreign Relations, 1789–1850.* 1983.

Weeks, Philip. *Farewell, My Nation: The American Indian and the United States, 1820–1890.* 1990.

Weeks, William E. *Building the Continental Empire: American Expansion from the Revolution to the Civil War.* 1996.

———. *John Quincy Adams and American Global Empire.* 1992.

Whitaker, Arthur P. *The United States and the Independence of Latin America, 1800–1830.* 1941.

Wilson, Major L. *The Presidency of Martin Van Buren.* 1984.

CHAPTER 7

Destiny and Annexation: Oregon, Texas, and the Mexican War, 1842–1848

Manifest Destiny

New York lawyer and journalist John L. O'Sullivan colorfully expressed the ebullient mood of Americans in 1845 when he proclaimed "the right of our manifest destiny to overspread and to possess the whole of the continent which Providence has given us for the development of the great experiment of liberty and federated self-government entrusted to us." O'Sullivan had earlier declared that America's "floor shall be a hemisphere—its roof the firmament of the star-studded heavens, and its congregation an Union of many Republics, comprising hundreds of happy millions . . . governed by God's natural and moral law of equality."

The term *manifest destiny* suggested a mystical, almost religious belief that a higher power had mandated U.S. expansion in the name of liberty. Although pronounced a crusade to civilize backward peoples, the doctrine aroused a mixed reaction. Opponents derided its arrogant attempt to rationalize aggression and territorial thievery, arguing that racism permeated the doctrine and left no room for nonwhites. Supporters used it to persuade Britain and others to stand aside for U.S. expansion into Oregon, Texas, California, and the Southwest—the issues over these latter

three areas leading to war with Mexico in 1846. The truth seems to be that manifest destiny provided a cloak of idealism that fitted comfortably over realistic territorial and commercial objectives. Following the American Revolution's call for individual freedom and patterned after Jefferson's justification for the Louisiana Purchase as an "empire of liberty," the gospel of manifest destiny offered the best of foreign policies in that idealists supported its republican objectives while realists applauded its expansionist results.

When O'Sullivan wrote his editorials, he at first referred only to Texas but then expanded his claims to include the United States's "true title" to Oregon. Manifest destiny thus became the symbol of an age of expansion, when Jacksonian Americans spoke optimistically about spreading their republican way of life while engaging in both territorial and commercial pursuits. Many Americans argued that ever since the Puritans came to the New World, God had ordained these special people to promote a millennial vision having no earthly boundaries. Washington Irving and other writers exalted western expansion as a means of furthering the American mission by the peaceful acquisition of territory and the incorporation of self-government. Meanwhile, on the religious front, American missionaries penetrated the west as well as Asia, eastern Europe, and the Ottoman Empire. As part of the blessings of this providential trust, the United States would promote its national security interests by enlarging its territorial and commercial claims. The Webster-Ashburton Treaty had eased relations with Britain on the Atlantic side of the continent and allowed Americans to concentrate on expansion toward the Pacific and beyond. Such expansion would spread the experiment in republicanism, afford opportunity for everyone by calling for little or no government restraints, encourage the growth of states' rights, facilitate the acquisition of rich farmland, lead to a plentiful trade in furs that could reach the Orient, and help to safeguard the country's security by driving out foreign intruders and closing the last gaps in its continental borders. Pinckney's treaty, the Louisiana Purchase, the Adams-Onís Treaty, the Monroe Doctrine— all fitted the developing pattern, and the decade of the 1840s marked its fulfillment.

Oregon

The Oregon dispute captured the romantic imagination of Americans more than any other expansionist issue. Americans had first laid claim to that vast area beyond the Rockies in the early 1790s, when Captain Robert Gray discovered the mouth of the Columbia River. The Lewis and Clark expedition of 1804–1806 had solidified this claim, and in 1811 New York businessman John Jacob Astor established the fort and fur post called Astoria on the banks of the Columbia River. Two years later he sold Astoria to the British North West Company when it appeared he would lose the post during the War of 1812. But the Treaty of Ghent restored Astoria to the United States in 1818, and the following year Spain relinquished claims to Oregon by signing the Adams-Onís Treaty. In 1824 Russia agreed to withdraw north to the 54°40′ line. By the 1840s, then, the United States and England had become the chief rivals over this one-and-a-half million square miles of territory bounded

by the Rockies on the east, the Pacific on the west, the 54°40′ line to the north, and the forty-second parallel to the south. Indeed, the huge area included parts or all of five present states and half of British Columbia.

America's continental expansion had two economic dimensions: agricultural and commercial. When Americans spoke of Oregon they primarily meant the Willamette River Valley, a hundred-mile stretch of fertile and timber-rich lowland running north to south below the Columbia River. British references to Oregon meant the territory lying above the Columbia. That site contained the headquarters of the Hudson's Bay Company, a parliamentary chartered monopolistic enterprise that dealt not only in furs but also in agriculture and cattle raising, and which had merged with the British North West Company in 1821. Under the leadership of Dr. John McLoughlin, the Hudson's Bay Company operated out of Fort Vancouver and discouraged U.S. settlements north of the Columbia River. Americans also saw maritime advantages in Oregon. Commercial interests would prosper from the Pacific's abundant supply of whales, salmon, and fur-bearing animals; Oregon would provide a stepping-stone to Asia.

By the practical reality of possession, British claims to Oregon were stronger than those of the United States. Their explorers had entered the waters of the region long before anyone else. Furthermore, they had enhanced their claims by promoting occupation. Sir Francis Drake had sailed along the coast during the sixteenth century, Captain James Cook had landed in the northwestern waters during the 1770s, and Captain George Vancouver had done the same nearly twenty years later. The British did not claim all of Oregon but preferred an equitable division of the area with the United States. They rejected the U.S. argument for the principle of "contiguity," that Oregon was a "natural extension" of the Louisiana Purchase and therefore belonged to the United States, and they dismissed the argument for Oregon implied by the boundary line to the Pacific contained in the Adams-Onís

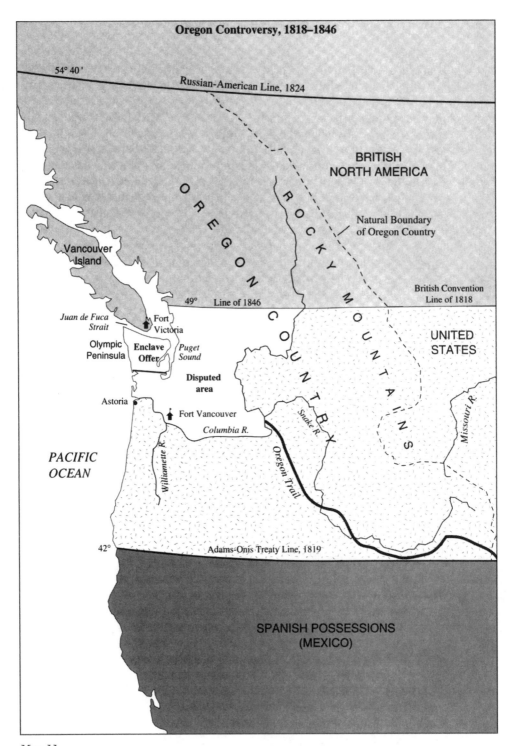

Map 11
The Oregon Treaty of 1846 was one of President Polk's central achievements, but it came only after threats of war between the United States and England.

Treaty of 1819. The Nootka Sound Convention of 1790 with Britain itself, they declared, had canceled Spain's right to Oregon and also invalidated U.S. claims because, by the convention, Spain gave up exclusive jurisdiction over the region. On the explorations issue, Britain countered that it had a stronger claim to the land above the Columbia. Both sets of claims seemed to offset each other, except that by 1821 the Hudson's Bay Company was the most powerful economic and political entity in the northwest.

Before the 1840s those few Americans who had any interest in Oregon were confident that, as had happened with Louisiana and the Floridas, time and American settlers would decide its ownership. Lewis and Clark had not described the area in a way conducive to settlement, and in the 1820s Senator Thomas Hart Benton of Missouri expressed satisfaction with the Rocky Mountains as the "everlasting boundary" of the United States. The Convention of 1818 with England had set up a "free and open" arrangement for ten years, which became known as joint occupation, and Britain had later turned down the U.S. suggestion to divide Oregon east and west at the Rockies, instead proposing the Columbia River as the boundary. In August 1827 an Anglo-American convention had extended joint occupation indefinitely, with the stipulation that abrogation required a year's notice. The British again declined a partition at the forty-ninth parallel and failed to entice Americans to accept the Columbia River by offering an enclave, or small piece of land, on the Olympic Peninsula, which would have permitted them to construct a fort and use the harbors of Puget Sound.

U.S. interest in Oregon remained alive during the late 1830s, largely through the efforts of Senator Lewis F. Linn of Missouri, who sponsored resolutions calling for the United States to provide military protection over the road west and offer 640 acres of land in Oregon to white males who farmed the tract for five consecutive years. As Congress again debated Linn's bill in 1841, Lord Palmerston warned the House of Commons that the bill's passage "would be a declaration of war." Senator John C. Calhoun of South Carolina temporarily defused the dangerous situation by urging a policy of "wise and masterly inactivity" that would follow the traditional pattern of allowing the natural course of settlements to resolve the matter.

During the Webster-Ashburton negotiations in Washington in 1842, President Tyler proposed a compromise of the Oregon question. Ashburton informally told Webster that Britain still adhered to the Columbia River, and Webster replied that the United States would accept that boundary if Britain persuaded Mexico to sell Upper California to the United States and recognize the independence of Texas. Ashburton had no instructions to accept this tripartite arrangement and refused. That same year the Tyler administration likewise found the Columbia River boundary unacceptable. Captain Charles Wilkes of the U.S. Navy had returned from an exploratory expedition and warned that a dangerous sandbar crossed the mouth of the river and that its waters were navigable only to the falls a hundred miles inland. The United States had to have the harbors of Puget Sound, and this arrangement required an international boundary northward at the forty-ninth parallel.

The Tyler administration's attempt to resolve the matter left a bitter taste with many Americans. Webster and Ashburton chose to drop it, but people in the West and Upper Mississippi Valley had heard rumors of the White House's tripartite proposal and held "Oregon conventions," angrily denouncing the government for its willingness to sacrifice the area above the Columbia River. In July 1843 more than a hundred representatives from six states gathered in Cincinnati to claim all of Oregon from the forty-second parallel to the 54°40′ line. The "imperative duty" of the federal government, they declared, was to extend jurisdiction over the territory. Their demands went to the president, Congress, and all state governors.

The issue became serious when a burst of expansion west known as "Oregon fever" sprang on the national scene in 1843. The Panic of 1837 drove many Americans westward in search of a new life; others went simply for adventure. Expansionists boasted of wresting the area from England, staking out the land for American farmers, and acquiring a stepping-stone to the East Asia. Oregon's population in 1841 numbered only about 500, which included fur traders, farmers, and missionaries. Nearly one hundred Americans migrated to the area in 1842, but a thousand more went the following year. In 1845 the census showed more than 2000 settlers in Oregon, but after the rapid influx of that year, approximately 5000 Americans lived below the Columbia. This number became more imposing since only a scant 700 British subjects lived above the river. In July 1843 the Americans in Oregon established a provisional government, and two years later they passed an amendment with a highly suggestive preamble declaring that the governing provisions would apply until the federal government proclaimed jurisdiction over the area. This was a virtual invitation to the Washington government to act. But despite the Senate's approval of Linn's fortification bill, the House refused support. Representative John Floyd of Virginia and Senator Benton of Missouri, the latter now a converted expansionist, touted Oregon's importance to the Pacific Ocean trade. The Columbia River, Benton declared, was the "North American road to India."

The presidential election of 1844 made western expansion the central issue of the campaign. Henry Clay of Kentucky captured the Whig nomination, and James K. Polk, a Jacksonian Democrat from Tennessee, became his party's compromise candidate. The Whigs quickly found the answer to their campaign jibe, "Who is James K. Polk?" when he attracted a groundswell of popular support by calling for expansion into both Oregon and Texas. The Democratic platform adopted in Baltimore issued a sharp challenge to Britain by declaring that U.S. title to all of Oregon was "clear and unquestionable" and calling for the immediate "reoccupation of Oregon"

James K. Polk
Although president for only a single term, he resolved the Oregon boundary dispute with England, solidified the U.S. claim to Texas, and acquired the great southwest as a result of the Mexican War. *Library of Congress.*

and "reannexation of Texas." The Democrats had ingeniously linked the two expansionist issues and thereby won the support of northerners and westerners seeking Oregon as a free-soil area and southerners interested in Texas for spreading slavery.

Few Americans laid serious claim to all of Oregon before the election, and no one had connected it with Texas. But the Democratic platform satisfied both the free-soil and slavery interests in the party, and the simple attachment of the prefix "re" to occupation and annexation furnished the United States a respectable defense against the charges of imperialism. By the time Clay recognized the popularity of his opponent's platform, it was too late. Polk's narrow victory in New York gave him the election. It is difficult to interpret the outcome as national approval for western expansion, but the election stirred a British call for arbitration of the Oregon issue and fed the expansionists' cry for territory. In January 1845 Secretary of State Calhoun turned down the British proposal for arbitration, and President-elect Polk triumphantly hailed the election returns as a mandate for U.S. expansion.

The new president was a realist and an expansionist. He sought to rid the west of England and other foreign influences by the skillful use of bluff and public statements calculated to arouse the fiercest expressions of Anglophobia. In his inaugural address of March 1845 Polk threw down the gauntlet to London's leaders by asserting that the U.S. right to all of Oregon was "clear and unquestionable." Political rhetoric perhaps, but the British considered presidential declarations to be official policy statements and were deeply offended by what one journal called the "*manner*, not the matter in dispute." The *Times* of London proclaimed that only war could tear Oregon from Britain. Polk's declaration was risky, but it achieved the desired effect: After fulfilling the Democratic platform's expansionist cry, he prepared to compromise on Oregon.

In July 1845 Polk authorized his secretary of state, James Buchanan, to inform the British that the United States would accept the forty-ninth parallel as the boundary in exchange for the southern half of Vancouver Island. When pressed to explain why the president had retreated from campaign declarations, Buchanan replied that Polk felt bound by the actions of his predecessors. At this point, the British minister in Washington, Richard Pakenham, should have forwarded the proposal to his London office for advice, but he could foresee no change in his superiors' policy and refused it on his own. Pakenham reasoned that Buchanan's offer had not included the long-time call for free British use of the Columbia River, and he was still upset over Polk's previous demand for all of Oregon. The president, however, considered Pakenham's reaction an affront and was irate. He

ignored Buchanan's warnings to defuse the issue because of the growing troubles with Mexico over Texas and in late August again demanded the 54°40′ line. In withdrawing his offer of the forty-ninth parallel, Polk defiantly declared that "if we do have war it will not be our fault." British Foreign Secretary Lord Aberdeen had meanwhile disavowed Pakenham's unilateral action, and his minister twice suggested arbitration, but Polk now insisted on a British concession.

The focus of U.S. attention in the autumn of 1845 alternated between Oregon and the ongoing crisis with Mexico, but in December the president again challenged the British presence in the Pacific Northwest. His annual message to Congress clarified U.S. objectives as Texas, California, and Oregon. Congress, he declared, should inform Britain that the United States was ready to give the required one-year notice for ending joint occupation in Oregon. In what has become known as the Polk Corollary of the Monroe Doctrine, he proclaimed that the United States opposed European involvement in North America and stood "ready to resist it at any and all hazards." Polk specifically invoked the noncolonization principle in asserting that "no future European colony or dominion shall with our consent be planted or established on any part of the North American continent." Although he included France and others in the warning, his main concern was Britain. The president wrote in his diary in early 1846 that "the only way to treat John Bull [England] was to look him straight in the eye."

The country's ongoing situation with Mexico was steadily worsening, however, causing Polk to leave the door open for a British counterproposal to a line at 54°40′ He had to be careful because of domestic political considerations. Northern and western expansionists were upset with Calhoun and other southerners, because after Congress admitted Texas into the Union as a state in December 1845, they seemed willing to compromise on Oregon at the forty-ninth parallel. Several Democrats demanded all of the disputed territory to the

54°40′ line, and when they thought that Polk was softening on Oregon, Senator Edward Hannegan of Indiana warned, "I shall hold him recreant to the principles which he professed, recreant to the trust which he accepted, recreant to the generous confidence which a majority of the people proposed in him."

Polk was playing a dangerous game, both at home and abroad. A mistake could alienate fellow Democrats who had only narrowly won office in 1844; worse, it could lead to war with Britain—and at the same time as a nearly certain war with Mexico. But political considerations also bore heavily on his mind. If the Democrats came to believe that the president was not upholding their aims in Oregon, the party would lie in shambles, and he would be its chief casualty. Pressure on Britain, if not handled well, could have dire consequences. The United States could not afford war, and certainly not in concurrence with a Mexican conflict. Polk must have been bluffing: He did not make any military preparations during these crisis-ridden months.

The Oregon dispute had actually narrowed in focus to a small triangular-shaped territory lying between the Columbia River and the forty-ninth parallel and including Juan de Fuca Strait. In four instances—1818, 1824, 1826, and 1844—the British had called for the Columbia River as the boundary, but each time the United States argued for the forty-ninth parallel. After the furor over Tyler's tripartite suggestion and the revelations of Wilkes's voyage, the United States could not consider anything less than the forty-ninth parallel. Even Whig commercialists, who opposed Polk's expansionist policies, recognized the necessity of controlling Juan de Fuca Strait and the harbors of Puget Sound.

Both Britain and the United States wanted to resolve the Oregon question short of war, but neither could compromise national honor. Aberdeen, like Polk, had to protect his political flanks, and to do so he mobilized the country's military forces. The U.S. minister in London, Louis McLane, was alarmed about the buildup and brought the matter before Aberdeen. The foreign secretary explained that the president had renounced compromise and demanded the entire area in dispute. His government could not take a chance on Polk's real intentions and had to defend Canada, even if that necessitated "offensive operations." McLane finally convinced Polk that he had gone too far. War with Mexico was imminent and conflict with Britain was unthinkable. Buchanan's dispatch arrived by return steamer in late February 1846, offering some hope for a peaceful settlement. The secretary of state first informed Aberdeen that Polk "would accept nothing less than the whole territory unless the Senate should otherwise determine," but he then added that the president was ready "with reluctance" to discuss any British recommendation for a boundary at the forty-ninth parallel and Juan de Fuca Strait. In the meantime the House passed the bill serving notice of the termination of joint occupation; the Senate then entered a lengthy, acrimonious debate highlighting manifest destiny and bitter sectional division between northerners and southerners over the Oregon boundary.

The way to compromise in the Senate came through the efforts of a strange combination of southern Democrats and northern Whigs. Commercial groups from both parties wanted peace; Calhoun joined Webster in calling for an amicable settlement; and the aged Albert Gallatin published a seventy-five-page essay opposing war. The Senate finally passed the House bill announcing the end of joint occupation, but in a tone noticeably milder than that found in Polk's message. The original House measure had brusquely instructed the president to announce the notice of abrogation, whereas the amended Senate version of late April made no reference to the country's "clear and unquestionable" right to the 54°40′ line. It instead called for "a speedy adjustment" of the opposing Anglo-American claims. The Senate's approval by a wide margin demonstrated that most members favored compromise. Within a week of the congressional action, Buchanan sent notice of the treaty's abrogation to Aberdeen but notified him also of the president's expressed desire for compromise.

Aberdeen likewise wanted a compromise over Oregon at the forty-ninth parallel. Besides problems with France and growing popular feeling at home against colonialism, his country was dangerously divided by the raging controversy over repeal of the Corn Laws—or the high protective tariff on grain. In addition, Britain needed U.S. cotton, and the potato shortage in Ireland was threatening to become acute. But despite these pressures for a settlement, Aberdeen could not leave the appearance of backing down before the United States. The only serious concern in the controversy was the Hudson's Bay Company, but it had lost popularity in England because of its high prices on furs. An unexpected coincidence worked to Aberdeen's advantage. By early 1845 the company had decided to move its headquarters from Fort Vancouver on the Columbia River to Fort Victoria on Vancouver Island. The company's spokesmen explained that trappers had cleaned the mainland of fur-bearing animals and that apprehension had grown about U.S. encroachments from below the river. As late as 1846 fewer than ten Americans lived above the Columbia, but many work-hardened pioneers in the Willamette Valley had a reputation for fighting and seemed ready to overrun the Northwest—especially if that action entailed destroying the hated Hudson's Bay Company and running out the British.

Aberdeen's treaty proposal on Oregon arrived in Washington in early June and drew Polk's restrained support. It accepted the forty-ninth parallel as the boundary from the Rockies to the waters touching Vancouver Island and the mainland, but it allowed Britain to retain the island by continuing the line around its southern side. Polk approved these provisions but did not favor Aberdeen's stipulation that use of the Columbia River from the boundary to its mouth would be "free and open to the Hudson's Bay Company, and to all British subjects trading with the same." The charter for the trading company would

soon expire, however, and, because Parliament showed no real interest in granting a renewal, British use of the river would also come to an end. Even more important, the United States had gone to war with Mexico the previous month, and the conciliatory British ministry, Polk realized, maintained only shaky political control over those clamoring for a stronger Oregon policy. The president followed his cabinet's advice to submit the matter to the Senate for its opinion *before* he accepted or rejected the British treaty. This approach constituted a break with the procedure established during the first years of the republic, but the move was good politics, and Polk was a good politician.

Polk's strategy worked. On June 12 the Senate voted 39 to 12 to advise him to accept Aberdeen's proposals. The formal signing ceremony for the Oregon treaty took place three days later, and on June 18 the Senate approved by the wide margin of 41 to 14. All the opposition came from Democrats, and mostly from the Middle West. The president ratified the treaty the following day.

Not all Americans were happy with the settlement, however. Democratic Senator William Allen of Ohio disgustedly resigned as chair of the Foreign Relations Committee, and Benton delivered a sarcastic assessment that probably contained more than a kernel of truth: "Why not march up to 'Fifty-four Forty' as courageously as we march upon the Rio Grande? Because Great Britain is powerful, and Mexico is weak." But, Benton seemed unwilling to admit, few Americans demanded *all* of Oregon, and most supported the forty-ninth parallel.

War over Oregon was preventable because both the United States and Britain were willing to compromise once they had satisfied the demands of national honor. Also, the British fortunately again had other more pressing domestic and foreign concerns. If Polk had counted on these developments, he had calculated correctly. Probably good fortune had looked kindly on him—and his nation. War with Britain at the same time that the country was at war with Mexico conjured up images too terrible to ponder. Admittedly, the stakes in the British struggle were high—perhaps superseded only by the risks. British removal from the Pacific Northwest, the opening of a North American highway to Asia, and the heightened opportunity to acquire Polk's prime objective of California—all these grand hopes seemed fulfilled by the Oregon Treaty of 1846. In retrospect, Polk's risky strategy seems sound because it worked. He got what he wanted all along—the forty-ninth parallel as the boundary and the harbor at Puget Sound—and without war.

The Texas Question

The Mexican War of 1846–1848 had its roots in the long-standing Texas question, for the U.S. annexation of Texas in 1845 had catalyzed several other issues and ultimately led to conflict. The boundary dispute magnified the central issue of annexation: Texans argued for the Rio Grande River from its mouth west to its source and then north to the forty-second parallel. The Mexican government countered for the Nueces River, lying more than 150 miles north of the Rio Grande and winding through largely uninhabited territory. The land was not so much the question as it was a series of grievances that grew into questions of honor between the Americans in Texas and the government in Mexico City. Texans believed that the Mexican government had become oppressive; Mexicans feared that in the name of manifest destiny the United States intended to swallow all their holdings in the hemisphere. The Texas issue, American damage claims against Mexico, President Polk's desire for California, and manifest destiny— all these combined to drive the United States into war with Mexico.

The events in Texas that culminated in the Mexican War actually began during the 1820s. By the Adams-Onís Treaty of 1819, the Washington government had given up claims to areas west of Louisiana's border at the Sabine River, but the situation dramatically changed

when two years later Mexico won independence from Spain. The Mexican government proved unstable and its empire so expansive that leaders found it nearly impossible to maintain authority in the provincial hinterland so far from their capital of Mexico City. The country of Mexico spread north and west to Oregon and included thinly populated areas stretching hundreds of miles east to Louisiana. About 60,000 nationals lived in a republic housing six million poor and illiterate Indians and people of mixed nationalities who felt no allegiance to any central governing body. Whereas Mexicans of Spanish descent preferred living close to their capital, great numbers of Americans did not. They had migrated into the upper provinces of Mexico—Texas, New Mexico, and California.

Like the Spanish before them, the Mexicans used the empresario (contractor) system to attract settlers into Texas. Officials opened the area to anyone, hoping to create a buffer against U.S. encroachments, but proximity dictated that the greatest influx would be from the United States. Missouri's Moses Austin (who soon died) and his son Stephen were the first empresarios to lead the stipulated 300 families into Texas in 1822. Migrants were to swear allegiance to the Mexican government, meet tax obligations, convert to Roman Catholicism, and pay ten cents an acre under easy credit terms—a small fraction of the going price in the United States of $1.25 cash per acre. The Panic of 1819 had restricted credit arrangements in the United States, and the cheap land in Mexico, along with its liberal constitution of 1824, encouraged more than 30,000 Americans to migrate into Texas by the mid-1830s.

Problems had already developed by this time, however. Americans maintained their former personal and national loyalties and showed little interest in becoming Catholic. They complained when Mexico prohibited the further introduction of slaves, levied tariffs on American imports into Texas, used convicts in its armies, and barred further migration of Americans into Texas. Moreover, the government had passed into the hands of General Antonio López de Santa Anna. Although elected on a liberal ticket, Santa Anna, ironically, suspended the constitution in 1834 and established a military dictatorship. Texans protested infringements of their rights under the constitution and presented a "Declaration of Causes" modeled after America's great document of 1776. By the autumn of 1835 the Texans had engaged in a series of confrontations with Mexican troops that led to the establishment of a provisional government and an army under Sam Houston, a robustly tall frontiersman who had embraced the image of the Noble Savage after living with the Cherokee Indians and becoming known as Kalanu, a war title meaning "The Raven."

Both the Washington government and its citizens closely followed the growing crisis in Texas. American ministers had tried to purchase Texas on two occasions. During the 1820s Joel Poinsett of South Carolina had worked with liberals in the Mexican congress but had failed, and President John Quincy Adams had authorized his secretary of state, Henry Clay, to buy the area. In one of Clay's meetings with the Mexican minister in Washington, he had presented the outlandish argument that the sale of Texas would work to Mexico's advantage by lopping off its far northern sector and thereby placing its capital city closer to the center of the country, where all capitals should be. One of President Jackson's appointees, Anthony Butler, was even more blunt. He suggested that the United States follow standard procedure in Mexico and offer a bribe of $500,000. The Washington government's clumsy efforts at acquiring Texas forewarned Mexico. Most Americans, however, were discreet: They argued that time and the steady course of U.S. settlement in Texas would determine its fate as these same factors had done so with the Floridas.

The heightening tensions led to the outbreak of the Texans' War for Independence in 1836, which aroused widespread interest throughout the United States. Despite President Jackson's invocation of neutrality, "Texas

General Antonio Lopez de Santa Anna
Led Mexican forces in field during the Texans' War for Independence and returned ten years later to lead his country again as president during the Mexican War. *Library of Congress.*

meetings" drummed up considerable support for volunteer soldiers and for economic and financial assistance in fighting the Mexican government. During the previous November of 1835, an uprising by a few Texans had forced out the few Mexican forces left in the province and had caused Santa Anna to lead troops into Texas to reestablish control. He and his large force first engaged the Texans at an old mission in San Antonio called the Alamo. On March 6, 1836, after almost a two-week siege, 5000 Mexican soldiers broke the resistance of Colonel William Travis and 200 companions and killed all survivors, including legendary figures James Bowie and Davy Crockett. Three weeks later James Fannin and 400 Texans, including many volunteers from the United States, surrendered to Mexican forces at Goliad, only to be summarily shot. More Americans joined Houston's

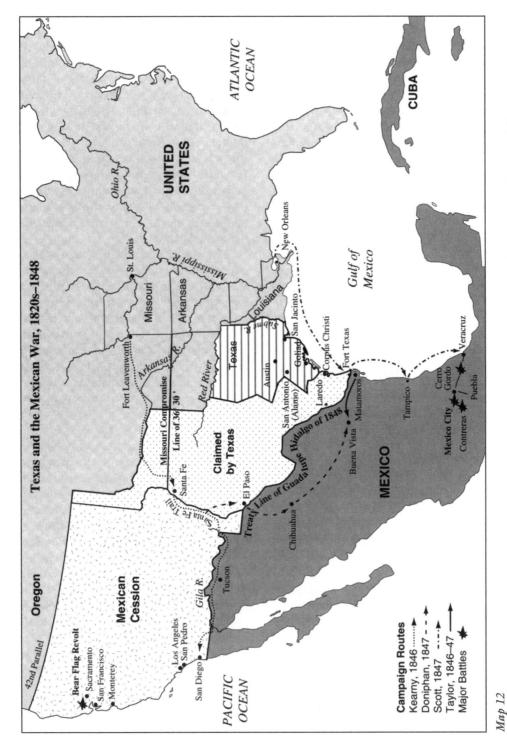

Map 12

The United States acquired the great Southwest by a war with Mexico that many critics attribute to aggressive imperialism.

army as terrified Texan refugees fled across the Sabine River and into Louisiana to escape Santa Anna's advancing army.

On April 21, 1836, at a spot near present-day Houston called San Jacinto, the Texan army of 800 men suddenly attacked the Mexicans, who were then in afternoon siesta. Shouting "Remember the Alamo," Houston's forces charged across an open field, scattering many of Santa Anna's men and killing more than 600. After a lengthy search, they found the general disguised in the dress of a common soldier and hiding in a tall clump of grass. On May 14 he signed two treaties with Houston that recognized Texan independence, required Mexican troops to evacuate Texas, and proclaimed the Rio Grande as the western and southern boundary of the new republic. The terms only appeared final on paper. When freed, Santa Anna later disavowed the agreements as made under duress, as did the new government in Mexico City, which had recently overthrown Santa Anna.

The new independent republic of Texas promptly sought annexation by the United States, and with Houston's close friend Jackson in the White House, prospects looked good. As early as April 1836 a proposal lay before Congress to extend recognition to Texas, but the abolitionists bitterly fought the move as the first step toward annexation and the eventual division of Texas into several slave states. Indeed, the terms in Texas's request for annexation had included the acceptance of slavery. The president understood the political realities of the situation and turned his back on annexation. His Democratic party rested on a loose alliance of northerners and southerners who could remain united only as long as slavery did not become an issue. Abolitionists already accused southerners of conspiring to extend the peculiar institution into Texas, and even though no evidence has appeared to substantiate such a plot, the impression was far more real than the truth. The greatest number of migrants into Texas were from the South, and this was proof enough of that region's overriding intention to spread

slavery. The president personally favored annexation, but the number of free and slave states in the Union stood balanced at thirteen, and it seemed safer to leave matters that way.

As in 1820, when the debate over Missouri's admission raised the slavery issue and forestalled claims to Texas, the question of territorial expansion again proved complex. In a paradoxical sense, the westward movement was two-headed: It carried the seed of liberty and empire while also bearing the seed of slavery and self-destruction. The potential for sectional trouble had jumped astronomically because the spread of republican institutions was now in unhappy wedlock with the extension of slavery. Although the two contradictory ideas might coexist in precarious balance, the admission of Texas into the Union would throw the advantage overwhelmingly to slave owners because the huge area could be carved into as many as five slave states. Jackson turned his back on a friend, although on the day before he left office—March 3, 1837—he extended recognition to Texas and appointed a chargé d'affaires—almost a year after the Texans won independence at San Jacinto. The following July the United States established diplomatic relations with the "Lone Star Republic," which claimed status as a country under the presidency of Sam Houston.

Continued tensions between Texas and Mexico forced the new republic to turn to Europe for help. The strife-torn government in Mexico City repeatedly warned that it would invade Texas, and twice in 1842 its forces raided areas north of the Rio Grande. Mexico's population outnumbered that of Texas about one hundred to one, and Texas's military and governmental needs threatened to sink the country in debt. In August 1837 the Texas minister in Washington had made a formal proposal of annexation, only to withdraw it when the new Democratic president, Martin Van Buren, refused support for the same political reasons given by his predecessor. The president of Texas, Mirabeau Bonaparte Lamar, meanwhile tried to expand Texas's interests to the Pacific by sending the Santa Fe Expedition in 1842. Its members, primarily traders, got lost and became prisoners of the Mexicans, who killed some of the Texans en route to Mexico City. That same year Houston returned to the presidency after a brief time out of office. Texas was in deep financial trouble and in danger of another assault by Mexico. The republic had two choices: annexation by the United States, which seemed out of the question, or independence under a British protectorate, which was not. Houston, in fact, decided on a clever ruse to force the Washington government to act: He left the impression that Britain's good offices had achieved the present truce between Texas and Mexico and that Texas and Britain were moving closer together.

Britain and France favored an independent Texas for several reasons. A Texan republic would block the United States's southward expansion, help protect British holdings in the Caribbean, build a balance of power in the hemisphere, encourage further division in the United States, and aid British expansion in the New World. Texas would also furnish cotton and a tariff-free market for British goods that might encourage the United States to repeal its duties. British abolitionists hoped for an end to slavery in Texas, some seeking to provide a wholesome example for the southern states in the Union, others thinking that the move might attract slaves to leave those states and become free citizens of the new republic. Still others had self-interest in mind: Pursue abolition as a means for undercutting foreign competition from cheap slave labor. To promote these objectives, Britain extended recognition to Texas in 1840 and negotiated treaties of commerce and friendship. France likewise granted recognition and signed treaties of amity and trade. On one occasion, in 1842, Britain intervened to preserve the uneasy peace between Mexico and Texas.

The Tyler administration tried to bring about the annexation of Texas, even though the slavery question continued to complicate the issue. After Webster resigned as secretary of state in May 1843, Tyler no longer faced such staunch opposition to expansion from within his administration. He justified Texas's annexation as a means for preventing it from falling under British control and becoming free from slavery. Tyler appointed Abel Upshur of Virginia to the state department, who agreed with the president's fears about British influence in Texas and worked to advance the negotiations.

In September 1843 Upshur informed Houston that the United States was ready for annexation, but the Texan was reluctant to ask again. Yet he relented in mid-February 1844 and wrote Jackson that for the third time Texas would request annexation; however, he pointedly warned that another rejection would force it to "seek some other friend." But before Tyler could act, Upshur was killed in the accidental explosion of a huge cannon on board the U.S. warship *Princeton*, forcing the president to appoint a new secretary. Tyler unwisely chose John C. Calhoun of South Carolina. Unlike Upshur, Calhoun was not moderate on slavery, and his very presence immediately revived suspicions of southern intentions. On April 12 Tyler signed the treaty of annexation with Texas and forwarded it to the Senate. But that body then made an unfortunate move. It postponed action until after the political party nominating conventions of May 1844, and Texas became a pawn in the political game.

Just before the conventions the front-running candidates, Democrat Martin Van Buren of New York and Whig Henry Clay of Kentucky, published statements opposing the quick annexation of Texas. It became evident, however, that neither man understood the national mood in the United States. As indicated earlier, a dark horse Democratic candidate, James K. Polk of Tennessee, advocated a program of expansion that included Texas and won him the nomination. But the Texas question had become a political issue and therefore less subject to a settlement based on the national interest.

In early June the Senate divided along party lines and voted 35 to 16 against Tyler's Texas treaty. Of twenty-nine Whig senators, all but one opposed annexation; the others came from Van Buren Democrats upset with Polk's nomination. The outcome was perhaps encouraged by an indiscreet note from Secretary of State Calhoun to the British minister, which an antislavery senator had procured and given to the press. In the note Calhoun advocated the treaty because of British efforts to end slavery in Texas. Annexation, he declared in an ill-advised remark, was "the most effectual, if not the only means of guarding against the threatened danger" of abolitionism. He also included a lengthy defense of slavery that cited statistics purporting to prove that liberty for blacks was injurious to their morale and health. Calhoun's pseudoscientific defense of slavery infuriated antislavery groups and threatened to undermine Texas's chances for annexation.

While the Texas question smoldered, Americans went to the polls in November 1844 and elected Polk on the Democrats' platform calling for the "reoccupation of Oregon" and the "reannexation of Texas." Thus did the Democrats bolster the fiction that Texas at one time belonged to the United States and that John Quincy Adams had shamelessly returned it to Spain during his negotiations with Onís in 1819. Polk's party interpreted the election results as approval of expansion and prepared to carry out the Democratic platform once he assumed office in March 1845.

The outgoing president had not given up on acquiring Texas. Tyler's states' rights principles had put him at odds with the nationalists in the Whig party, and Clay had joined others in effectively riding the Virginian out of the party. Tyler had nothing to lose by supporting the annexation of Texas. Without a party and now a lame duck, he decided to act on Texas before leaving office. In his annual message to Congress in December 1844, he reiterated his fears of British and French interests in the republic and argued that the previous month's election showed that a "controlling majority of the people, and a large majority of the states, have declared in favor of immediate annexation." Instead of follow-

ing the usual path through the Senate, however, Tyler unleashed a political furor by calling on Congress to annex Texas through the highly unorthodox procedure of a joint resolution. Method lay behind what his opponents bitterly denounced as madness. Legislative approval required only a simple majority in each House rather than a two-thirds vote in the Senate. Whigs in the Senate controlled the Foreign Relations Committee and opposed a joint resolution on the ground that the United States could acquire territory only through a treaty. Tyler countered by seeking the admission of Texas as a *state,* not as a territory, and he justified his action by the constitutional provision declaring that "new States may be admitted by the Congress into this Union."

The ensuing battle focused on slavery again, for abolitionists believed that Tyler the Virginian was determined to spread his section's favorite institution. The truth probably lies somewhere between Tyler's wish for political retaliation and his fear of British interference in Texas, with weight on the latter. Piqued with those who had made him a political outcast, he found it easy to favor a bill that denied Jacksonian Democrats the opportunity to acquire Texas and at the same time overcame the Whigs' opposition to it. The independent political status thrust on Tyler permitted him to rise above party and defend annexation as important to the national interest.

Tyler encountered numerous obstacles. John Quincy Adams warned Bostonians that the annexation of Texas would set off a "deadly conflict of arms" between the "spirit of freedom" and the "spirit of slavery." Former President Jackson wrote the newspapers that "you might as well attempt to turn the current of the Mississippi as to turn the democracy from the annexation of Texas. . . . [O]btain it the U. States must—peaceably if we can, but forcibly if we must."

Concern also developed over whether Texas would consent to annexation. The province remained under Houston's influence, although he left the presidency in December 1844 and with fellow Texans remained deeply disgruntled over past rejections. In fact, Houston had warned before the last rebuff that if it happened again, Texas would *"remain forever separate."* Tyler and Calhoun tried to soothe his frustrations by sending Jackson's nephew to Texas as chargé d'affaires in August 1844, while Jackson reminded Houston that a good Texan's loyalties lay with the United States and not with Britain. Proponents of annexation suggested various political plums—including the presidency of the United States—if Houston would support the treaty. He eventually took the politically prudent course of informing Jackson that he would "not interpose any individual obstacle to its consummation."

On January 25, 1845, the House approved the annexation measure 120 to 98 and sent it to the Senate, where Benton, a Democrat, recommended an alternate measure designed to reestablish that body's control over the Texas question. He called for the admission of Texas as a state, but under conditions reached through negotiations with Texas, rather than by those arbitrarily set by the United States. If the Senate accepted Benton's proposal, the president would have to work out an arrangement with Texas that contained the safeguard of requiring that same Senate's approval. The Missourian later claimed that Tyler had agreed to turn over the matter to President-elect Polk, who offered assurances of accepting Benton's approach.

The political wrangling was still not over. During the night of February 27, 1845, the Senate approved the amended version of the House bill by the slim margin of 27 to 25, all Democrats and three southern Whigs voting for it. After the House concurred with Benton's changes, President Tyler signed the bill on March 1. But two days later, the day before Polk took the presidency, Tyler decided to thrust presidential authority in the process. Secretary of State Calhoun directed the chargé in Texas to invite Texas into the Union under provision of the House resolution. Benton was infuriated, but the new president eventually went along with his predecessor's decision.

Thus, Texas became part of the Union through the unusual procedure of joint resolution. Under the annexation treaty, Texas was to become a state that included "the territory properly included within, and rightfully belonging to the republic of Texas." The United States and "other governments" would resolve any boundary problems. Texas was to send Congress a republican constitution by January 1, 1846, and with Texas's approval, four more states might be created from its territory. Above the Missouri Compromise line of 36°30′, no slavery could exist in new states; below it, the people of the states would decide whether to allow slavery. Britain made a last-ditch effort to dissuade Texas from accepting the annexation treaty when in May it placed pressure on Mexico to extend recognition. But that summer Texas opted to join the United States rather than rely on British assurances that seemed all the more weak as Mexico made preparations for an invasion intended to win back its lost territory. On July 4, 1845, Texans ratified the annexation treaty and took the first step toward eventual statehood.

The United States was justified in annexing Texas, if for no other reason than the fact that its occupants invited the move and several countries had extended recognition to the republic, including the United States, Britain, France, and the Netherlands. It was a mutually profitable arrangement. The incorporation of Texas bolstered U.S. security in the Southwest, and annexation afforded Texas protection against Mexico, even though fears on that score were imaginary because Mexico had proved itself incapable of reestablishing control over its former province. The United States had made little effort to remain neutral in the period after the Texas revolution of 1836: Its laws were too weak to stop Americans in the United States from assisting transplanted Americans in Texas. The Washington government realized that the longer Texas remained independent, the greater the chances were for trouble with Europe and along the Mexican border. Americans believed it too dangerous and too lucrative to turn down the acquisition of Texas.

However convincing such arguments were to those above the Rio Grande, they carried little weight below it. On March 6, 1845, Mexico's minister in Washington broke relations with the United States by securing his passports and returning home.

War with Mexico

President Polk's aggressively expansionist policies ultimately combined with Mexico's unrealistic stand on Texas to bring war in 1846. The Mexican government had warned of a break in relations if the United States annexed Texas, although this position was untenable given Texas's nine years of independence. But Polk had also adopted a provocative stand: He openly favored the province's highly debatable Rio Grande boundary claim on the basis of the treaties at San Jacinto in 1836. Opponents argued that the treaties were worthless because Santa Anna had signed under pressure and a successor government had repudiated them. Proponents countered that nearly all treaties were the result of some form of pressure and that Houston had negotiated with Mexicans representing the regime then in power. Another related point is that the longtime accepted border of Texas had been the Nueces River, located a considerable distance north of the Rio Grande; from 1836 to 1845 neither Mexico nor Texas had attempted to occupy the area between Corpus Christi on the mouth of the Nueces and the Rio Grande. If the area was disputed, neither nation showed much interest in seizing it during Texas's long period of independence. Perhaps the two nations would have been wiser to forgo occupation of the area until they had attempted a negotiated settlement. But Polk's assertive policies had hardened the differences and quickened the likelihood of a confrontation. He simply regarded all land above the Rio Grande as part of the United States and worked to solidify that claim. Both nations thus moved toward a war that neither could

Major General Zachary Taylor
His military victories during the Mexican War catapulted him into the presidency in 1848. *Library of Congress.*

have wanted had their leaders taken time for reflection.

After Texas agreed to annexation terms during the summer of 1845, Polk escalated pressure on Mexico to surrender areas desired by the United States, either at the tip of a pen or the barrel of a gun. In July he ordered General Zachary Taylor and 3900 regulars to defend the newly acquired U.S. territory against expected Mexican invasion. Trouble was likely, for Taylor had earned the label "Old Rough and Ready" and came from the same temperamental mold as Andrew Jackson.

Problems of a political nature soon developed: Taylor was a Whig, and Polk was a cold and aloof Democrat with a devout distrust for Whigs. Both men could be invincibly stubborn, and often were—especially in their animosity for one another. Polk had not been enthusiastic about sending Taylor, and later events seemed to confirm his suspicions that the general was incompetent, uncooperative, and, most of all, interested in the presidency in 1848. Taylor, however, did act with restraint. His instructions were to affirm the U.S. title to the disputed territory by moving below the Nueces River and as close to the Rio Grande "as prudence will dictate." He was to take no offensive action and avoid areas controlled by Mexican officials. By August his force was on the west bank of the Nueces at Corpus Christi, where it stayed until March of the following year.

In the meantime Polk took other secretive actions. That same summer he sent agents to Texas who apparently urged its president, Anson Jones, to occupy the disputed area below the Nueces. U.S. military and naval contingents in the region seemingly understood that their "defensive" orders included support for any attempts by Texas to secure all territory to the Rio Grande. Polk had already secretly dispatched the commander of the Pacific Squadron, Commodore John D. Sloat, to occupy California's major ports if Mexico attacked Texas.

Polk feared British intentions in California—perhaps even more so than in Texas, which by now was fairly safe. U.S. interest in California had originated before the new president came to office in March 1845. Ten years earlier President Jackson had failed in an attempt to buy San Francisco Bay and Upper California, and, as previously mentioned, President Tyler had offered a tripartite deal in 1842 whereby the Columbia River would become Oregon's southern boundary if Britain could persuade Mexico to sell Upper California to the United States. That same year, in October, Commodore Thomas ap Catesby Jones of the U.S. Navy received unconfirmed reports that the United States and Mexico were at war, and he seized the capital of California at Monterey and annexed the Mexican province. When he learned the next day that war had not been declared, he apologized, returned the harbor to Mexican officials, and ultimately received a

temporary suspension from command. Secretary of State Webster termed Jones's act "a freak of his own brain" and likewise apologized to Mexico, but that government terminated all talks about San Francisco.

The United States's direct involvement in California developed slowly. Settlers had begun to penetrate the vast region off the Oregon Trail during the early 1840s, but by that time seafarers, fur traders, and "mountain men" had been there for two decades. In 1845 interest grew in California because of the enthusiastic reports of exploratory expeditions. Captain Charles Wilkes of the U.S. Navy visited Oregon and California in 1841, and his published accounts lauded San Francisco as having "one of the finest, if not the very best harbour in the world." The Mexican government was weak, he declared, and the area would doubtless become independent and provide a pathway to the trade of the Pacific and Orient. A second report came from the famous explorer and son-in-law of Senator Benton, Lieutenant John C. Frémont of the U.S. Army's Topographical Corps, who entered California during the winter of 1843–1844 and wrote glowing accounts of rich farmland. A third series of reports came from Thomas O. Larkin of New England, who had lived in Monterey as a businessman since the early 1830s. By the opening of the next decade he wrote articles for the eastern press in praise of California and in 1843 became the first U.S. consul. Three years later he estimated that close to a thousand U.S. citizens lived in California, but he thought this figure would rise dramatically.

Mexico tried to stop U.S. migration into California and persuade those settlers already there to leave. But as was the case with Texas, local officials in California were too few to carry out their government's wishes. As late as 1846 no more than 7000 people of Spanish lineage lived in California; Mexico controlled no areas above San Francisco and nothing farther inland than the coast. Most Spanish settlers were engaged in sheep and cattle raising, and a few were missionaries.

Polk's California policy was to buy it from Mexico or, failing that, to encourage its residents to seek annexation by the United States. Consul Larkin confirmed the president's fears about British intentions in California by uncritically passing troublesome rumors to Washington. In mid-October 1845 Polk designated Larkin a private agent under orders to encourage separatism in California and bring about its annexation by the United States. Secretary of State Buchanan ordered Larkin to assure the people of California that if they won independence from Mexico, "we shall render her all the kind offices in our power as a sister republic." The United States would "make no effort and use no influence" to induce California to join the Union, but if its people chose to do so, "they would be received as brethren, whenever this can be done without affording Mexico just cause of complaint." Buchanan's letter provided an unmistakable incentive to revolution.

In the meantime Polk inquired whether Mexico would welcome a minister to discuss the nations' problems, and in mid-October 1845 he learned that Mexico's president, José Joaquín Herrera, would receive a commissioner from the United States to resolve the Texas issue. Polk, however, ignored Herrera's stipulations of sending a low-ranking *commissioner* to discuss only the Texas boundary. He appointed Democrat John Slidell of Louisiana, a known expansionist, as envoy extraordinary and minister plenipotentiary to open negotiations over Texas, California, and the long-standing claims issue. Slidell was to recommend a border from the mouth of the Rio Grande to El Paso, then north to the forty-second parallel and west to the Pacific, which would award eastern New Mexico and Upper California to the United States. He had authority to pay $25 million for New Mexico and California, although he could go as high as $40 million. The other issue concerned more than $2 million of damages awarded but not yet paid to U.S. citizens that stemmed from the insurrections in Mexico. In exchange for the Rio Grande as boundary, the United States would assume these claims, which the Mexican government had found financially impossible to honor. Slidell's instructions contained some flexibility, but the absolute minimum was the Rio Grande as border.

Slidell arrived in Mexico City in early December 1845, amid an atmosphere of threatening violence. Herrera's government could not appear conciliatory without risking its own overthrow. News of Slidell's secret mission had reached Mexico even before he received the appointment, drawing a wrathful reaction in Mexican newspapers and handbills charging the Herrera government with treason. Moreover, because Slidell's title exceeded commissioner status, any official dealings with him would have implied the restoration of relations with the United States and Mexico's willingness to accept the United States's annexation of Texas. In sum, political reality dictated that Mexico could not engage in talks involving Texas or California.

The irony is that despite its rebuff of Slidell, Herrera's government fell. By March the special envoy ignored the troubles that his own presence had caused and indignantly assured Buchanan that "nothing is to be done with these people, until they shall have been chastised." War was desirable, he wrote the president. "Depend upon it," he declared; "we can never get along well with them, until we have given them a good drubbing."

After news of Slidell's rejection reached Washington, Polk made an effort to establish physical claims to the area below the Nueces River. On January 13, 1846, he ordered General Taylor to move south out of Corpus Christi and occupy the east bank of the Rio Grande. The president probably intended to force negotiations, but Mexico understandably regarded the move as an act of provocation. After a near skirmish with a small contingent of Mexican cavalry, the U.S. forces reached the southern edge of the disputed territory on March 28 and encamped a few miles above the mouth of the Rio Grande at present-day Brownsville. There Taylor established quarters at what became known as Fort Texas. On the other side of the river was Matamoros, a Mexican settlement garrisoned by 3000 soldiers.

Meanwhile in mid-February a friend of Santa Anna's approached President Polk with an enticing proposal: The former Mexican chieftain, then in exile in Havana, would accept a boundary satisfactory to the United States if it facilitated his return to power. To persuade the Mexican people to comply, Santa Anna recommended that the U.S. forces move to the Rio Grande (which Polk had already arranged) and that Slidell board a U.S. warship at Veracruz and present an ultimatum to the Mexican government.

Polk liked the proposal, even though he could not act on it immediately. He presented the idea to his cabinet with the suggestion that if the Mexicans failed to meet its conditions, the Americans were "to take redress into our own hands by aggressive measures." The concurrent Oregon crisis slowed the president's hand, because Buchanan warned against taking any action that might provoke Mexico until relations with Britain improved. Polk temporarily withdrew the idea of an ultimatum and instructed Slidell to delay his return to Washington until the diplomats resolved the Oregon question. Slidell's experience in Mexico, the president feared, would alarm Americans and, by suggesting imminent hostilities with Mexico, conceivably harden Britain's stance on Oregon.

Growing tensions along the Rio Grande meanwhile exploded in conflict during late April. For almost three uneasy weeks American and Mexican soldiers had glared menacingly at each other across the muddy river, and then the Mexicans brought in 2000 more forces. On April 12 Mexico warned Taylor to pull back to the Nueces River, which in itself seemed to imply approval of Texas's annexation by the United States and a reduction of the dispute to the area between the rivers.

When Mexico cut off Taylor's access to the Rio Grande, he established a blockade at its mouth that closed the river to Matamoros and, under international law, constituted an act of war. It was a "defensive precaution,"

Taylor explained. Less than two weeks later, the Mexican president declared that Taylor's blockade had forced his country into a "defensive war" against the United States, and the following day 1600 Mexican troops crossed the Rio Grande above Taylor's quarters. That same day Taylor sent a small number of dragoons to investigate a suspected "invasion" of U.S. territory. Although they returned a few hours later with nothing to report, that evening Taylor dispatched another sixty-three men. The next day, April 25, the long-expected confrontation occurred. Mexican soldiers attacked the Americans north of the Rio Grande, killing eleven and taking the rest prisoner. Two days later, in the early morning, Taylor learned of the clash. "Hostilities may now be considered as commenced," he wrote the president.

Before news of the bloodshed had reached Washington, President Polk had called a cabinet meeting on May 9, a Saturday, to discuss his intention to ask Congress to declare war on Mexico. According to his diary, he assured his cabinet that "we had ample cause of war, and that it was impossible . . . that I could remain silent much longer; that I thought it was my duty to send a message to Congress very soon and recommend definitive measures." All members of the cabinet except Buchanan and Secretary of the Navy George Bancroft agreed that the president should ask Congress for a declaration of war. Both men feared congressional opposition and British hostilities on behalf of Mexico. Buchanan reluctantly gave in to the president, but Bancroft held fast. He noted that "if any act of hostility should be committed by the Mexican forces he was then in favor of immediate war." Polk nonetheless retired to his office after the adjournment to write a war message that he would present to Congress the following Tuesday.

Around 6:00 P.M. that same Saturday evening, however, Taylor's message arrived, stating that fighting had taken place on the Rio Grande. The president immediately reconvened his cabinet. Somehow the *Washington Union* had procured the news and carried the story in its evening edition under the blaring headline: "American blood has been shed on American soil!" Amid the uproar in the streets, Polk's cabinet members gathered and *unanimously* advised him to ask Congress for a declaration of war. All the following Sunday, except the time he took to attend church services, Polk worked on the address. By noon of Monday, May 11, 1846, he had incorporated the suggestions of military, congressional, and cabinet figures and submitted his call for war to Congress. The original message had focused on the alleged "breach of faith" concerning the Slidell mission and mentioned the boundary and claims grievances, but Taylor's dispatch dramatically changed the thrust of the argument. Mexico, Polk declared, "has invaded our territory and shed American blood upon the American soil."

The wide support in Congress for war with Mexico gives a misleading view of the popularity of the decision. The legislative scene in no way resembled a healthy and honest debate over the president's message. The ruling Democratic party in the House restricted the period of debate to two hours, despite the Whigs' demand for additional time to study the materials Polk submitted with his request for war. The House speaker refused to recognize members seeking more information, although two opponents managed to secure the floor long enough to berate Polk's explanation as an "utter falsehood." Others bitterly called the military action "Mr. Polk's War," and abolitionist Joshua Giddings of Ohio denounced it as an attempt to spread slavery. "I will not bathe my hands in the blood of the people of Mexico," he declared, "nor will I participate in the guilt of those murders which have been and will hereafter be committed by our army there." Outside Congress, the renowned writer and abolitionist Ralph Waldo Emerson of Massachusetts warned that war with Mexico would highlight the horrid issue of slavery and ultimately destroy the Union.

Despite the vocal opposition, Congress moved irrevocably toward war. The House voted in favor of the resolution 174 to 14.

The next day, May 13, the Senate discussed the measure a little longer than did the House, but the margin for war was also wide—40 to 2. The war bill empowered the president to call out 50,000 volunteers and approved a $10 million military appropriation.

Presidential disclaimers notwithstanding, much of the war's unpopularity was attributable to the issue of whether slavery would extend into territories that the United States might acquire from Mexico. Polk argued in vain that the war bore no relation to slavery. He wrote in his diary that "its introduction in connection with the Mexican War is not only mischievous but wicked." The war nonetheless opened a debate over slavery's expansion that centered on an attempt by antislavery groups in Congress to pass the Wilmot Proviso. House Democrat David Wilmot of Pennsylvania sought to bar slavery from any areas taken from Mexico during the war, and he affixed the measure as a rider to the war appropriations bill of August 1846. Northern support was not sufficient to override the opposition of southern Whigs and Polk Democrats; but Wilmot and others inflamed emotions by repeatedly introducing the proposal over the next few years. The Wilmot Proviso never passed Congress, but its very discussion caused numerous angry debates over slavery and the Union.

The Polk administration meanwhile remained convinced that Santa Anna's restoration to power would ensure a rapid victory. To guarantee a quick peace, the White House directed the U.S. naval commander off Veracruz to facilitate Santa Anna's return to Mexico at the proper time. Some weeks afterward, Santa Anna assured the president that he intended to "govern in the interest of the masses." In late July Buchanan wrote the Mexican foreign minister that the United States wanted an honorable peace; but before his message arrived in Mexico City, Santa Anna had received permission to pass through the U.S. blockade at Veracruz in August and during a revolution in Mexico took over the "Liberating Army." When Santa Anna's foreign

Polk as War President
This cartoon showed Polk using "manifest destiny" as a sword intended to spread democracy into the "backward" areas held by Mexico. *Library of Congress.*

minister replied to the missive from Washington that peace considerations would have to await a new Mexican legislature in December, Buchanan realized that the United States had been duped and irately proclaimed that it would "prosecute the war with vigor." As Santa Anna raised an army of 25,000 men and prepared to move north against General Taylor, it became unmistakably clear that Polk's ill-advised backdoor maneuverings had succeeded in restoring to power Mexico's most capable military leader.

The president's goal in the war became, he declared, to "conquer a peace." This fine-sounding objective would not be easy to achieve, for Mexico's standing army was five times larger than that of the United States, and Mexicans were supremely confident that the Americans lacked the ability and will to fight. Moreover, a war on Mexico's home soil instilled higher morale among its forces, and

many Mexicans believed that the United States's preoccupation with Britain and the Oregon question would work to their advantage.

Taylor received orders to move south from the Rio Grande into the Mexican heartland, and a second contingent was to leave Fort Leavenworth and pass through Santa Fe. At that point Colonel Alexander W. Doniphan broke off down the Rio Grande to El Paso and by March 1847 had occupied Chihuahua. Colonel Stephen W. Kearny led a force from Fort Leavenworth toward New Mexico and then onward to California.

Meanwhile, in May 1846 Californians overthrew Mexican rule in a strange series of events known as the "Bear Flag Revolt," which involved Army Captain John C. Frémont in some shadowy and still undetermined way. Frémont had appeared on the scene during the winter of 1845–1846 with an exploratory expedition of sixty-two armed men,

Captain John C. Frémont
His activities in revolutionary California remain shrouded in mystery, but his hame has become virtually synonymous with the founding of the "Bear Flag Republic" in 1846. *Library of Congress.*

ostensibly under orders to ascertain the best land passage to California. The Mexican commander at Monterey had ordered him and his armed force to leave the province. After some disagreement the Americans moved up the Sacramento Valley and into Oregon. That same May of 1846 a marine lieutenant arrived from Washington with messages for Larkin and Frémont. The contents of these messages remain unknown, but soon afterward Frémont made a timely return to the San Francisco area and assisted the small group of Californians who led the successful revolt.

In July, after receiving unofficial word that the United States and Mexico were at war, Frémont joined forces with Commodore Sloat and Captain Robert F. Stockton in occupying

California. By the end of the month the United States controlled all regions above Monterey, and soon Stockton, Frémont, and Larkin enlarged the occupation to include San Diego, San Pedro, and Los Angeles. When Washington sent official news of the war, Stockton announced his country's annexation of California, but he then encountered a rebellion that broke out in Los Angeles in September. Three months later Kearny and a hundred cavalry arrived, and with the help of Stockton and Frémont they regained control of the settlement in early January 1847. California belonged to the United States.

On the southern front, the Polk administration prepared to take the war to the Mexican people by sending an amphibious force, under the renowned Major General Winfield Scott, by water from New Orleans to Veracruz and then overland to the capital at Mexico City. The president had serious misgivings about sending a Whig to do a Democrat's bidding. The two men, in fact, had had troubles before—and not only because of their competing egos and clashing personalities. Polk had received support for the presidency from Andrew Jackson, who was Scott's longtime enemy; the general, as mentioned, was a Whig—with political ambitions. But after Polk searched in vain for a Democratic military leader, he finally gave in and ordered Scott and 10,000 men to prosecute the central campaign of the war. In March 1847 they left their ships along the shores of Veracruz and on March 29 won the city's surrender. Scott then faced the major arm of Mexican troops under Santa Anna, who had just suffered defeat at the hands of Taylor at Buena Vista and was eager for a victory. U.S. forces again won a hard-fought battle at Cerro Gordo. Next the town of Puebla fell, and Scott soon headed toward Mexico City.

In the tradition of the Spanish conquistadors who first invaded Mexico, President Polk sent both an olive branch and a sword to Mexico City in 1847. When Santa Anna demanded that the Americans pull out of Mexico as a prerequisite to negotiations, Polk attempted

to use the victories at Buena Vista and Veracruz to bring Mexico to the peace table
through the efforts of a special commissioner,
Nicholas Trist. Chief clerk in the state department, he was the former consul in Havana
and had a knowledge of Spanish, but his most
important qualification was his status as a loyal
Democrat who could report directly to the
president on Scott's political intentions. Trist
received instructions in mid-April to offer as
much as $30 million for New Mexico, Upper
and Lower California, the Rio Grande as
boundary of Texas, and transit rights across
the Isthmus of Tehuantepec. The money
would also count toward assuming U.S. damage claims against Mexico to a maximum of
$20 million. The least Trist could accept was
New Mexico, Upper California, and the Rio
Grande border. If this obscure peacemaker
succeeded in his mission, the Polk administration could take the credit; if he failed, it
could disavow him at no cost.

In early May Trist caught up with Scott's
forces, but difficulties immediately arose between the men. Scott believed that Polk had
intentionally insulted him by sending a civil-
ian to deal with military matters. Trist's orders
to make peace at the earliest possible moment,
Scott insisted, interfered with his authority
to wage war. The general felt humiliated by
Trist's semi-independent status and by a sealed
letter he carried to Mexican authorities that
Scott was not allowed to see. For almost two
months the Scott-Trist feud continued, with
each man refusing to talk to the other.
Though in the same camp they communicated
only through bitter letters (some thirty pages
long). But when Trist became ill in July, the
two men reconciled their differences.

Scott and over 10,000 U.S. troops marched
out of Puebla toward Mexico City in early
August 1847. They had first made a sincere
effort to end the war short of invading the
capital. Trist had established communications
with Santa Anna through the British minister
in Mexico City and had learned that the general would accept peace on the receipt of
$10,000 now and an assurance of $1 million

General Winfield Scott
Led U.S. forces in seizing Mexico City in
September 1847, forcing Mexico's defeat
in the war. *Library of Congress.*

after the treaty's ratification. Scott agreed and
made the initial payment from his secret service fund, but like Polk earlier, he too became
a victim of Santa Anna's duplicity when the
dictator announced that the Mexican legislature opposed peace talks. The only way to
end the war was to take Mexico City. Santa
Anna's army was much larger than Scott's,
but it was divided by political infighting and
demoralized by insufficient food and war
materiel. Near the city Scott encountered his
first military resistance, but after veering
south to avoid the enemy's strongholds, he
won battles at Contreras and Churubusco,
and on August 20, 1847, he prepared to enter
the capital city.

Three days later Santa Anna notified Scott
through the British legation that he wanted a
cease-fire. The two sides accepted an armistice
until the signing of a treaty and, if the peace

effort failed, agreed to give forty-eight-hour notice before resuming fire. But Scott's experiences with Santa Anna raised suspicions about whether he was stalling for time, and when the Mexican general refused Trist's conditions for peace, Scott abruptly terminated the talks and prepared to storm the city. On September 13 the Americans seized the fortress at Chapultepec and the next day took Mexico City. Two days afterward Santa Anna resigned as president, and a new provisional government took over.

President Polk had meanwhile become increasingly concerned over a growing "All-Mexico Movement" in the United States. Before news of Mexico City's fall reached Washington in early October, he called Trist home and ordered Scott to take the capital and end the war. Polk was extremely sensitive about charges of his waging a "war of conquest," and he realized that the all-Mexico demand would prolong the fighting and entail undetermined results, both on the battlefield and in the political wars. He was also apprehensive over the political meaning of better relations between Trist and Scott and upset that Trist had forwarded a peace recommendation from Mexico that demanded the Nueces River as the border of Texas.

Encouraged by Scott's victories in the field, the president prepared to broaden the war aims to include more but not all of Mexico. He thought that the United States should keep New Mexico and California and that Scott's forces should help install a republican government in Mexico that would favor a just end to the war. Two cabinet members, Buchanan and Secretary of the Treasury Robert Walker, favored U.S. conquest of all of Mexico. The secretary of state recommended that the president announce in his annual message to Congress that the United States "must fulfill that destiny which Providence may have in store for both countries." Polk's words were less prophetic in tone but seemed to be identical in meaning when he declared that the United States should "take the measure of our indemnity into our own hands."

Some contemporaries erroneously believed that southern slaveholders were the major proponents of acquiring all of Mexico. Writer and abolitionist James Russell Lowell recorded his antiwar, anti-South stance in the famed *Bigelow Papers* and warned that California would be divided into slave states. Yet most southerners did not want territories from Mexico: Slavery was illegal and the climate and soil ill suited for its introduction. But northerners failed to grasp this reality and proclaimed their opposition to the spread of slavery through the hotly debated Wilmot Proviso.

Those who led the all-Mexico movement were primarily from New York and the west, and nearly all were Democrats who defended their position on the basis of manifest destiny. John L. O'Sullivan's *Democratic Review,* in which the term first appeared, called on the United States to take all North America. The *New York Herald,* the *Sun,* and the *New Orleans Picayune* agreed that the Mexican people needed U.S. guidance because of their inability to govern themselves. The *New York Evening Post* did not mince words. "The aborigines of this country have not attempted and cannot attempt, to exist *independently* alongside of us. . . . The Mexicans are *aboriginal Indians,* and they must share the destiny of their race." *Niles' Register* of Washington referred to "'Manifest Destiny' Doctrines" in defending the country's harsh treatment of Mexico.

Trist received notice of his recall in mid-November, but he hesitated to leave because Santa Anna's successor government in Mexico seemed eager for peace. When Trist unofficially informed the Mexican leaders of his order home, they urged him to complete the negotiations first. Scott and a member of the British legation agreed, and Trist decided to remain, on the condition that Mexico approve the minimum demands of the United States. He realized that no Mexican government could survive if it sent a delegation to Washington, and he also knew that he had to negotiate a treaty with the Moderate party before it fell from power. Those less amenable to a settlement would take over, Trist feared, if suspicions developed that Polk favored the all-Mexico movement. Trist opposed a long guerrilla war that might end with the United States in control of the entire country, but burdened with costs and responsibilities impossible to meet. He wrote Polk a sixty-five-page letter defending his decision to remain in Mexico despite orders to return home.

The president became livid upon receiving Trist's note on December 6. "I have never in my life felt so indignant," he recorded in his diary. "Mr. Trist, from all I can learn, has lent himself to Gen'l Scott and is his mere tool, and seems to be employed in ministering to his malignant passions." Still fuming in mid-January, Polk bitterly denounced Trist's dispatch as "arrogant, impudent, and very insulting to his Government, and even personally offensive to the President. . . . If there was any legal provision for his punishment he ought to be severely handled. He has acted worse than any man in the public employ whom I have ever known."

Polk's obstinence was as strong as Trist's arguments were correct. The emissary on the spot clearly understood the realities far better than did the president thousands of miles away in Washington. Continuation of a war for greater parts of Mexico than authorized in the original peace offering would have ensured a long and potentially devastating desert war. In the six weeks that it took for Polk's orders to reach Trist, the Mexican people had elected an interim president who wanted to end the war. Indeed, just as the disheartened diplomat prepared for his return to Washington, word came from the foreign office in Mexico City that the government had named commissioners to begin peace talks. To reject this overture would surely undermine the peace group, prolong U.S. occupation of the Mexican capital, and encourage much more vicious fighting. Like many sound decisions, Trist's did not come easily—particularly when it violated directives from the president of the United States.

Treaty of Guadalupe Hidalgo

At Guadalupe Hidalgo outside Mexico City, Trist signed a treaty on February 2, 1848, that ended the war with Mexico. The terms comprised the minimum requirements set up in his original directives of April 1847, in that the United States received California, New Mexico (the Mexican Cession, which constituted the present states of New Mexico, Arizona, Utah, and Nevada), and recognition of the United States's annexation of Texas with the border at the Rio Grande. In return, the United States paid Mexico $15 million and assumed the damage claims made by its citizens of $3.25 million. The sum of money awarded Mexico seems large in that Polk considered the territorial gains an indemnity for the war caused by Mexico, but the payment enabled the Mexican government to tell its people that it had forced the United States to award an indemnity. The money might also allow the Polk administration to escape the charges of imperialism already leveled at the United States.

Polk disapproved of the treaty but had to send it to the Senate, both because of mounting opposition to the war and because the growing all-Mexico movement might prevail and cause renewed fighting. The Whigs had captured a majority in the House of Representatives after the election of 1846, and in January 1848 the Whig-led Senate narrowly passed a resolution denouncing the war as "unnecessarily and unconstitutionally begun by the President of the United States." Young Illinois Congressman Abraham Lincoln joined the swelling discontent by criticizing the "war of conquest" and introducing the "spot resolutions," which challenged the president to show the spot where Americans' blood had stained American soil. Henry David Thoreau wrote his essay "Civil Disobedience" in nonviolent protest against paying taxes to support what he denounced as an unjust war.

Polk's central problem became clear. "If I were now to reject a treaty," he told his cabinet, "made upon my own terms, as author-

ized in April last, with the unanimous appro-
bation of the Cabinet, the probability is that
Congress would not grant either men or
money to prosecute the war." Should Polk
turn down a treaty that fulfilled his own directives, he would have to pull U.S. troops from
Mexican territory and lose New Mexico and
Upper California, and the Whigs would doubtless win the White House in November. Polk
sent the treaty to the Senate on February 22
with a guarded recommendation for approval.

The Treaty of Guadalupe Hidalgo encountered serious obstacles in the Senate. Its passage was uncertain because of that body's divisions over the territorial question. At one time
a coalition of fifteen Whigs wanted to return
all lands west of the Rio Grande to Mexico,
while eleven Democrats (ten from the South
and West and one from New York) favored
enlarging the conquered territories to include
part or all of the northern provinces of Chihuahua, Coahuila, Nuevo León, and Tamauli-
pas. None favored the treaty without amendments. But the strange alignment fell apart
during the treaty vote, and on March 10,
1848, the Senate approved 38 to 14, with 26
Democrats and 12 Whigs comprising the
majority and the parties splitting evenly in
opposition. On May 30 the two governments
exchanged ratifications and President Polk
declared the treaty in effect on July 4, 1848.

Polk remained intensely bitter over Trist's
rebellious behavior. He refused to approve
payment for Trist's salary or expenses after the
date of his recall, and the emissary disappeared
into poverty after losing his job in the state
department. More than two decades afterward, Congress reimbursed him for the salary
and expenses incurred after his recall from
Mexico, and President Ulysses S. Grant (who
had fought in the Mexican War but opposed
it as "the most unjust war ever waged by a
stronger against a weaker nation") appointed
him postmaster in Alexandria, Virginia. This
was small recompense for Trist's services in
halting the war.

Assessments of the treaty have varied. Whig
Philip Hone denounced it as "negotiated by

Nicholas Trist
This picture, taken years after the Mexican War,
shows the U.S. chief clerk in the state department
who ignored President Polk's recall directive and
negotiated the Treaty of Guadalupe Hidalgo with
Mexico in 1848. *Library of Congress.*

an unauthorized agent, with an unacknowl-
edged government, submitted by an accidental President, to a dissatisfied Senate." This
wry comment overlooked the dire alternative
to Trist's treaty, which was protracted guerrilla
warfare brought by the growing popular push
for all of Mexico. The United States had
already lost 1721 men in battle and 11,550
to disease and other factors (out of nearly
105,000 in the army, which constituted the
highest death rate of any war in America's history). Mexico lost 50,000 men and the chance
for empire by giving up one-half of its territorial possessions and becoming landlocked
between its Yankee neighbor to the north and
the rest of Latin America to the south. The
events of 1846 through 1848 contributed to

continued political disorder in Mexico that encouraged a quarter-century of civil war and led to repeated instances of outside intervention in its affairs.

The Mexican War greatly enhanced the power and border security of the United States, and yet it paradoxically exposed serious weaknesses in the country's domestic structure. Immense danger came from mixing slavery with expansion, because with the repeated failures of the Wilmot Proviso to pass Congress, the highly charged question remained of whether the newly acquired territories would be slave or free. The war also raised the race issue in the acquisition of new lands, thereby providing a preview of the nation's later problems in the Pacific and Caribbean. The conquest of Mexico opened all areas above the Rio Grande and encouraged U.S. expansion across Indian territories. During the 1820s and 1830s the Americans had moved into areas east of the Mississippi, and those Indians forced to relocate in Missouri and Oklahoma would soon feel the pressure of Americans pushing beyond the mighty river. An American critic of the Mexican War caustically remarked, "If just men should ever again come into power, I believe they ought not to hesitate to retrocede to Mexico the country of which we have most unjustly despoiled her."

Consequences of Polk's Diplomacy

If one judges a president strictly on his accomplishments in office, Polk's administration was a resounding success. Most important, he solidified U.S. security by achieving every territorial objective: the annexation of Texas with the Rio Grande as border, and the acquisition of Oregon, New Mexico, and California. The United States owned the Pacific coast from Puget Sound to San Diego and had therefore opened the commercial road to Asia. It had acquired huge plots of rich farmland, vast timber resources, and great expanses of grazing land for cattle. In a scant three years the republic had acquired 1.2 million square miles

of territory and expanded its size by two-thirds. Polk had served as a most effective agent of manifest destiny.

Yet serious misgivings lingered over the issues raised by Polk's territorial acquisitions as well as his aggressive and dangerous style of diplomacy. The incorporation of so much territory had exposed the inherent contradiction in an expansionist policy that rested on an uneasy marriage of slavery and freedom. In retrospect, the bitter debates over the Wilmot Proviso provided a clear indication of the tragic path the nation was taking toward deepening sectionalism and ultimate civil war. In the meantime, contemporaries blasted "Mr. Polk's War" and, in an interesting political twist, elected a hero of that war to the presidency in 1848, General Zachary Taylor of the Whig party. Congressman John Quincy Adams of Massachusetts was a life-long continentalist and yet had been unable to support the president's war message. Adams darkly warned that "it is now established as an irreversible precedent that the President of the United States has but to declare that War exists, with any Nation upon Earth and the War is essentially declared. . . . It is not difficult to foresee what the ultimate issue will be to the people of Mexico," he proclaimed, "but what it will be to the People of the United States is beyond my foresight, and I turn my eyes away from it."

Selected Readings

Bauer, Karl Jack. *The Mexican War, 1846–48.* 1974.

Bergeron, Paul B. *The Presidency of James K. Polk.* 1987.

Billington, Ray A. *The Far Western Frontier, 1830–1860.* 1956.

Bourne, Kenneth. *Britain and the Balance of Power in North America, 1815–1908.* 1967.

Brack, Gene M. *Mexico Views Manifest Destiny, 1821–1846: An Essay on the Origins of the Mexican War.* 1976.

Brauer, Kinley J. *Cotton Versus Conscience: Massachusetts Whig Politics and Southwestern Expansion, 1843–1848.* 1967.

Campbell, Charles S. *From Revolution to Rapprochement: The United States and Great Britain, 1783–1900.* 1974.

Campbell, Randolph B. *An Empire for Slavery: The Peculiar Institution in Texas, 1821–1865.* 1989.

Connor, Seymour V., and Faulk, Odie B. *North America Divided: The Mexican War, 1846–1848.* 1971.

Davis, William C. *Three Roads to the Alamo: The Lives and Fortunes of David Crockett, James Bowie, and William Barret Travis.* 1998.

De Bruhl, Marshall. *Sword of San Jacinto: A Life of Sam Houston.* 1993.

Drinnon, Richard. *Facing West: The Metaphysics of Indian-Hating and Empire Building.* 1980.

Eisenhower, John S. D. *Agent of Destiny: The Life and Times of General Winfield Scott.* 1997.

———. *So Far from God: The U.S. War with Mexico, 1846–1848.* 1989.

Elliott, Charles W. *Winfield Scott: The Soldier and the Man.* 1937.

Fuller, John D. P. *The Movement for the Acquisition of All Mexico, 1846–1848.* 1936.

Goetzmann, William H. *When the Eagle Screamed: The Romantic Horizon in American Diplomacy, 1800–1860.* 1966.

Graebner, Norman A. *Empire on the Pacific: A Study in American Continental Expansion.* 1955.

Griswold del Castillo, Richard. *The Treaty of Guadalupe Hidalgo: A Legacy of Conflict.* 1990.

Hague, Harlan, and Langum, David J. *Thomas O. Larkin: A Life of Patriotism and Profit in Old California.* 1990.

Harlow, Neal. *California Conquered: War and Peace on the Pacific, 1846–1850.* 1982.

Hietala, Thomas R. *Manifest Design: Anxious Aggrandizement in Late Jacksonian America.* 1985.

Hopewell, Clifford. *Sam Houston: Man of Destiny.* 1987.

Horsman, Reginald. *Race and Manifest Destiny: The Origins of American Racial Anglo-Saxonism.* 1981.

James, Marquis. *The Raven: The Life Story of Sam Houston.* 1929.

Johannsen, Robert W. *To the Halls of the Montezumas: The Mexican War in the American Imagination.* 1985.

Johnson, Timothy D. *Winfield Scott: The Quest for Military Glory.* 1998.

Jones, Howard, and Rakestraw, Donald A. *Prologue to Manifest Destiny: Anglo-American Relations in the 1840s.* 1997.

Jones, Wilbur D. *The American Problem in British Diplomacy: 1841–1861.* 1974.

Lack, Paul D. *The Texas Revolutionary Experience: A Political and Social History, 1835–1836.* 1992.

Lander, Jr., Ernest M. *Reluctant Imperialists: Calhoun, the South Carolinians and the Mexican War.* 1980.

Mahin, Dean B. *Olive Branch and Sword: The United States and Mexico, 1845–1848.* 1997.

Matovina, Timothy M. *The Alamo Remembered: Tejano Accounts and Perspectives.* 1995.

McCaffrey, James M. *Army of Manifest Destiny: The American Soldier in the Mexican War, 1846–1848.* 1992.

McDonald, Forrest. *States' Rights and the Union: Imperium in Imperio, 1776–1876.* 2000.

Merk, Frederick. *Albert Gallatin and the Oregon Problem.* 1950.

———. *Fruits of Propaganda in the Tyler Administration.* 1971.

———. *Manifest Destiny and Mission in American History.* 1963.

———. *The Monroe Doctrine and American Expansionism, 1843–1849.* 1966.

———. *The Oregon Question: Essays in Anglo-American Diplomacy and Politics.* 1967.

———. *Slavery and the Annexation of Texas.* 1972.

Morrison, Michael A. *Slavery and the American West: The Eclipse of Manifest Destiny and the Coming of the Civil War.* 1997.

Nelson, Anna K. *Secret Agents: President Polk and the Search for Peace with Mexico.* 1988.

Nevins, Allan. *Frémont: The West's Greatest Adventurer.* 2 vols., 1928.

Nobles, Gregory H. *American Frontiers: Cultural Encounters and Continental Conquest.* 1997.

Ohrt, Wallace. *Defiant Peacemaker: Nicholas Trist in the Mexican War.* 1997.

Perkins, Bradford. *The Creation of a Republican Empire, 1776–1865.* 1993. *The Cambridge History of American Foreign Relations,* vol. 1. Cohen, Warren I., ed.

Perkins, Dexter. *The Monroe Doctrine, 1826–1867.* 1933.

Peterson, Norma L. *The Presidencies of William Henry Harrison and John Tyler.* 1989.

Pletcher, David M. *The Diplomacy of Annexation: Texas, Oregon, and the Mexican War.* 1973.

Pohl, James W. *The Battle of San Jacinto.* 1989.

Price, Glenn W. *Origins of the War with Mexico: The Polk-Stockton Intrigue.* 1967.

Proctor, Ben H. *The Battle of the Alamo.* 1986.

Raat, W. Dirk. *Mexico and the United States: Ambivalent Vistas.* 1992.

Rakestraw, Donald A. *For Honor or Destiny: The Anglo-American Crisis over the Oregon Territory.* 1995.

Reeves, Jesse S. *American Diplomacy under Tyler and Polk.* 1907.

Remini, Robert V. *Henry Clay: Statesman for the Union.* 1991.

Robinson, Cecil. *The View from Chapultepec: New Writers on the Mexican-American War.* 1989.

Rohrbough, Malcolm J. *Days of Gold: The California Gold Rush and the American Nation.* 1997.

Rolle, Andrew F. *John Charles Frémont: Character as Destiny.* 1991.

Ronda, James P. *Astoria and Empire.* 1990.

Santoni, Pedro. *Mexicans at Arms: Puro Federalists and the Politics of War, 1845–1848.* 1996.

Schroeder, John H. *Mr. Polk's War: American Opposition and Dissent, 1846–1848.* 1973.

———. *Shaping a Maritime Empire: The Commercial and Diplomatic Role of the American Navy, 1829–1861.* 1985.

Sellers, Charles G. *James K. Polk: Continentalist, 1843–1846.* 1966.

———. *The Market Revolution: Jacksonian America, 1815–1846.* 1991.

Singletary, Otis A. *The Mexican War.* 1960.

Slotkin, Richard. *Regeneration Through Violence: The Mythology of the American Frontier, 1600–1860.* 1973.

Smith, Justin H. *The Annexation of Texas.* 1911.

———. *The War with Mexico.* 2 vols., 1919.

Stanton, William R. *The Great United States Exploring Expedition of 1838–1842.* 1975.

Stenberg, Richard R. "The Failure of Polk's Mexican War Intrigue of 1845," *Pacific Historical Review* 4 (1935): 39–68.

Stephanson, Anders. *Manifest Destiny: American Expansionism and the Empire of Right.* 1995.

Stuart, Reginald C. *United States Expansionism and British North America, 1775–1871.* 1988.

Varg, Paul A. *New England and Foreign Relations, 1789–1850.* 1983.

Weber, David J. *The Mexican Frontier, 1821–1846: The American Southwest under Mexico.* 1982.

Weeks, William E. *Building the Continental Empire: American Expansion from the Revolution to the Civil War.* 1996.

Weinberg, Albert K. *Manifest Destiny: A Study of Nationalist Expansion in American History.* 1935.

Winders, Richard B. *Mr. Polk's Army: The American Military Experience in the Mexican War.* 1997.

CHAPTER 8

Between the Wars, 1848–1861
YOUNG AMERICA AND THE
PARADOX OF SLAVERY AND FREEDOM

Prelude To Civil War:
The Turbulent 1850s

In retrospect, the turbulent decade of the 1850s provided the necessary prelude to the Civil War. All the elements of sectional divisiveness characterized the period, driven by a deep and bitter distrust between North and South that focused on diametrically opposed definitions on what was morally right and morally wrong. U.S. foreign policy became an almost forgotten casualty of this hatred, for domestic disunity virtually ensures a weak and ineffective performance in foreign affairs. Both North and South supported a republican form of government, but they violently disagreed over whether a republic could house both slavery and freedom. The nation continued to unravel over this fundamental and timeless issue of individual liberty, and with this relentless unraveling came a foreign policy that lacked order and purpose. Just as North and South radically differed on domestic matters, so did they find that many of these same issues jeopardized foreign policy by making it impossible to agree on what constituted the national interest.

Young America

Manifest destiny in the United States did not run its course with the Mexican War, for expansionist efforts continued during the 1850s under the label of "Young America," though repeatedly running afoul of the paradox between slavery and freedom. As controversy over the peculiar institution began to dominate the American domestic scene, so did the democratic revolutions of 1848 in Europe fire Americans' imagination about spreading freedom abroad, particularly when tens of thousands of immigrants entering the United States pleaded for help against Old World oppression. Even while slave owners sought to spread their property into the new areas acquired from Mexico, they joined numerous other Americans in praising the antimonarchical revolutions in Europe as proof of the virtuous working power of republicanism.

By 1852 the predominant Democratic party advocated an expansionist-interventionist foreign policy that actually contributed to its own undoing. Before the nation's internal differences reached a thunderous climax in civil war, the United States had celebrated the nationalist efforts of Hungary, Italy, and Ireland; acquired still another piece of land from its already shrunken Mexican neighbor; brought about a mild but noteworthy improvement in British relations; unofficially supported filibusters (private adventurers) in Latin America who sought the annexation of Cuba, Nicaragua, and

THE CHAMPION OF THE LIGHT WEIGHTS ON HIS GUARD.

M——d P——(having shied his castor over the rope, and followed it up himself.)—BRING ON YOUR MAN, AND PUT HIM ON THIS SIDE OF THE LINE YOU LIKE. *Cartoon published in "Young America" in 1856, emphasizing Fillmore's national position.*

MASON & DIXON'S LINE

"Young America"
This cartoon emphasizing President Millard Fillmore's national position captured the spirit of expansionism during the 1850s. Young America *magazine, 1856.*

along with the interests of business. Still, the only expansionist effort that approached the aggressive pattern of the previous decade—the South's desire to build a Caribbean empire—collapsed because of the all-consuming sectional division over slavery. Altogether it was a swashbuckling, adventuresome time. Americans, like the buccaneers of old, felt free to grab everything within reach while attempting to ignore the very real and nearly fatal contradiction embedded within an expansionist thrust that aimed at reconciling the irreconcilable differences between slavery and freedom.

Thus, slavery, a major irritant to expansionism in the 1840s, ultimately crushed that regenerative spirit in the 1850s. The United States's acquisitions of Oregon and California had laid the path to Asia. The California gold rush of 1849 had sparked a great new wave of westward migration, which had raised interest in constructing a canal or railroad across the isthmus of Central America. Yet the slavery issue impeded territorial interests in both Canada and Latin America, because southerners realized that Canada would become free, and northerners recognized that Latin America would become slave territory. Many Americans lamented slavery's interference in the nation's manifest destiny. But just as the republican ideal created the illusion of a unified nation, so did the reality of slavery threaten to leave in its stormy wake two nations—one free and one slave. Illinois attorney and rising politician Abraham Lincoln perceptively complained in 1854 that the institution of slavery hurt the nation's image abroad by depriving "our republican example of its just influence in the world" and exposing Americans to the charge of hypocrisy.

Weak national leadership during the 1850s along with the growing internal strife over slavery thoroughly undermined the country's foreign policy. Presidents and secretaries of state followed whatever expansionist whim seemed popular at the time. Filibusters roamed Latin America, often with the Washington government's tacit blessing, and diplomats threatened Spain with the use of force in an effort to

Mexico; and, largely because the slavery issue bore no relation to U.S. expansion in the Pacific, made substantial commercial advances in both China and Japan. The most important aspect of the decade, however, was the bitter sectional division that developed over the question of slavery's extension into newly acquired U.S. territory. The slavery issue destroyed the southern dream of a Caribbean empire and helped bring on the Civil War.

The slavery controversy repeatedly blocked nearly every territorial expansionist attempt during this chaotic decade. U.S. expansion took another form, however: Americans came to regard Asia as a special domain for the spread of republican and missionary ideals,

acquire Cuba. Some leaders sought to involve the United States in the upheavals in Europe, and most welcomed the opportunities for increasing trade with China and opening Japan. Hardly anyone, however, spoke of the responsibilities that came with international involvement. Nearly all became caught up in the swelling national concern over slavery and its spread into the newly acquired lands from Mexico. Young America was younger in maturity than in years during the 1850s.

The surge of popular feeling for Hungary provided an illustration of the ultranationalist, free-wheeling spirit of the times. When the Hapsburg regime in Austria received Russia's help in putting down the Hungarian revolt in 1849, American sympathy for the rebels proved too strong for the new administration to ignore. In June President Zachary Taylor extended recognition to the rebels and drew a vehement protest from the Austrian chargé in Washington, Chevalier Hülsemann. The revolution collapsed before a U.S. emissary reached Hungary, but Secretary of State Daniel Webster, in that office for the second time, feared the rapidly developing internal division in the United States and tried to use the Hungarian cause to unite Americans around the principles of freedom. In late 1850 he denounced Austria in the "Hülsemann Note." Events in Hungary, the secretary declared, "appeared to have their origin in those great ideas of responsible and popular governments on which the American constitutions themselves are founded. . . . The power of this republic, at the present moment, is spread over a region, one of the richest and most fertile on the globe, and of an extent in comparison with which the possessions of the House of Hapsburg are but as a patch on the earth's surface." Webster's lecture drew the support of most Americans, but it infuriated the Austrian monarch and did nothing to ease the burgeoning sectional clash at home between slavery and freedom.

The excitement over Hungary continued, because in 1851–1852 its exiled rebel leader, Louis Kossuth, visited the United States, seeking aid. Support for Kossuth swelled throughout the country on his arrival in New York in early December 1851, and at a huge bipartisan banquet held in his honor by Congress, Webster rejoiced at the "American model upon the Lower Danube and on the mountains of Hungary." These florid public pronouncements perhaps enhanced Webster's prospects for the presidency, but they also kept relations strained with the Austrian government until his death in October 1852. In the meantime, the exhilaration of the parades, speeches, parties, and gifts finally gave way to the realization that the United States had to stay out of Europe's concerns.

In Mexican affairs, the 1850s took on the character of the previous decade, probably arousing a sense of *déjà vu* among Americans. The source of trouble was the United States's old nemesis, Santa Anna, who had again seized power in Mexico City and was again in desperate need of money. The gold recently discovered in California had increased U.S. interest in constructing a transcontinental railroad. Realizing that the United States wanted land in the southwest for a railroad to the Pacific, Santa Anna instructed the Mexican minister in Washington to inform President Franklin Pierce that a generous monetary offer, accompanied by well-publicized threats to the regime in Mexico City, would yield territorial concessions. Toward that end, Pierce followed the advice of his secretary of war, Jefferson Davis of Mississippi, in sending James Gadsden as minister to Mexico, authorized to secure the southern boundary. As former president of the South Carolina Railroad Company, Gadsden had long expressed interest in building a transcontinental railroad that took the southern route. He assured Santa Anna of the desired cash outlay for any of five boundaries stipulated by the United States, and the Washington government made a mock show of force by sending soldiers to the Rio Grande.

At this point similarities with the past suddenly ended. Santa Anna kept his word, even though he agreed to only the minimum boundary that Gadsden had authority to accept. In late December 1853 the U.S. minister secured an agreement that went through a major revision in the U.S. Senate before winning approval the following April as the Gadsden Treaty. Antislavery senators fought against the pact, arguing for a northern railroad passage west. They failed. The United States paid $10 million (cut from $15 million) to Mexico in exchange for about 50,000 square miles of land between the Colorado and Rio Grande rivers (the so-called Gadsden Purchase, a narrow strip of land south of the Gila River and comprising lower Arizona and New Mexico) and transit rights across the Isthmus of Tehuantepec. The latter provision had resulted from the work of C. L. Ward, a special agent hurriedly sent by the administration to the negotiations (without state department authorization), who had verbal instructions to secure private claims across the isthmus in which his New York business firm had expressed interest. In addition, the United States won a release from the obligations of the Treaty of Guadalupe Hidalgo which had held it responsible for damages in Mexico caused by Indians living on the U.S. side of the border. The two governments exchanged ratifications in Washington in June 1854, making it possible for the United States to build the Southern Pacific Railroad.

Improved Anglo-American Relations

For several reasons relations with Britain improved during the late 1850s, but only after the outbreak of serious differences in the first half of the decade. The U.S. acquisition of Oregon and California had underlined the potential of the East Asian trade, and the United States now sought to build a canal or railroad that would link the Atlantic to the Pacific. The obvious passageway was through either Panama, the narrowest point on the isthmus, or Nicaragua, which was a day closer to the United States and had a series of rivers and lakes that interconnected across most of the country. But U.S. hopes for transit rights across the isthmus of Central America ran into

difficulties because of competing British interests in the region.

The United States had taken a major step toward gaining access to Central America in 1846, when it had negotiated a treaty with New Granada (later Colombia) allowing U.S. use of Panama. New Granada feared that Britain would seize the isthmus and was willing to exchange transit rights for U.S. promises to safeguard the neutrality of the route, maintain freedom of passage, and protect New Granada. The U.S. minister to New Granada, Benjamin Bidlack, received this surprising offer from his host government and, without authorization from Washington, signed the treaty. President Polk endorsed his diplomat's action and forwarded the pact to the Senate where, despite a lengthy discussion caused by fear of foreign entanglement, it met approval in June 1848. The treaty of 1846 ultimately led to the completion of the Panama railroad in 1855, which was less than fifty miles in length.

The treaty of 1846, however, aroused British concern because of the apparently concerted U.S. push toward the Caribbean and Latin America. Commercial considerations worked to hold the Atlantic nations together. Britain's economic ties with the United States had grown at such a rapid pace that by the 1850s it received one-half of its imports and 80 percent of its cotton from the U.S. South. On the other side of the ledger, American merchants imported nearly one-half of their goods from Britain, and they welcomed British investments in railroads and other business enterprises. Yet these tenuous economic links could snap if U.S. expansion endangered British interests in Latin America. The treaty of 1846 therefore posed a threat to Britain's maritime control in the Caribbean and its holdings in the southern half of the hemisphere.

In January 1848 the British tried to rectify the rapidly deteriorating situation by seizing the little settlement at San Juan in Nicaragua, renamed Greytown, which sat at the mouth of the San Juan River that cut across the isthmus to the Gulf of Fonseca on the Pacific side. The British had already established a protectorate

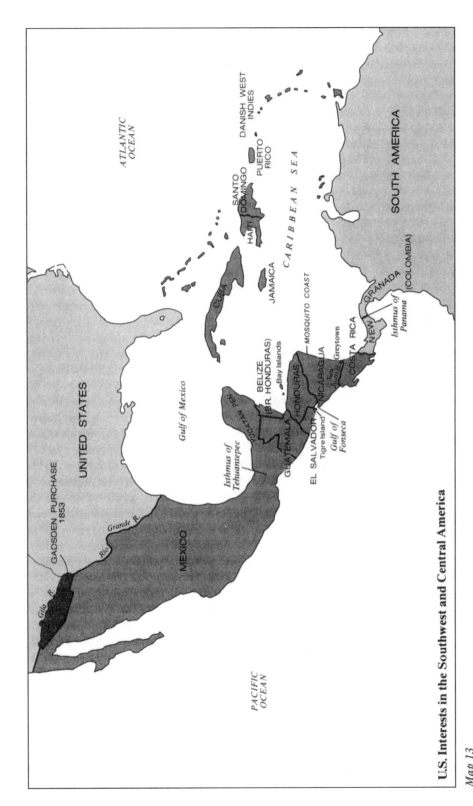

U.S. Interests in the Southwest and Central America

Map 13

U.S. interests in this part of the hemisphere came into direct conflict with the British.

over the Mosquito Indians along Nicaragua's east coast, and they owned Belize (later British Honduras), the Bay Islands, and a naval center at Jamaica. The occupation of Greytown thus solidified their claims in Central America. In October of the following year a British naval officer acted without orders in seizing Tigre Island near the Pacific terminal point of the projected canal route. The London government renounced that rash act, but Americans were incensed. At almost the same time the British took Greytown, gold was discovered in California, and the ensuing rush of "forty-niners" necessitated the immediate construction of a passageway west through the isthmus of Central America. Despite the blusterings of Anglophobes, war was out of the question. The United States had to negotiate with Britain.

The Clayton-Bulwer Treaty of April 19, 1850, marked the culmination of U.S. efforts to set up an Anglo-American arrangement for an isthmian canal. Secretary of State John Clayton won Lord Palmerston's support in opening transit rights to all nations and signed a pact in Washington to that effect with British Minister Sir Henry Bulwer. The treaty specified that the two nations must cooperate in building any isthmian canal and that neither would exercise "exclusive control" afterward. In the words of the treaty, "neither will ever erect or maintain any fortifications commanding the same, or in the vicinity thereof, or occupy, or fortify, or colonize, or assume, or exercise any dominion over Nicaragua, Costa Rica, the Mosquito Coast, or any part of Central America." The United States expected the British to withdraw from Greytown and the Mosquito Coast, but the London government refused. Neither side could back down for political reasons, but the two parties managed to conceal their disagreements in a document remarkable for its ambiguous language. Clayton had meanwhile kept members of the Senate informed throughout the negotiations, a shrewd move that allowed them to read their own meanings into the treaty and which thereby encouraged its quick approval.

Despite a wide margin of support in the Senate, the settlement became the object of sharp criticism in the United States at large. Several members of the opposition Democratic party accused the Taylor administration of caving in to the British; others complained that the United States had given up its own right to expand south by promising not to take any of Central America. In the dispute over the Clayton-Bulwer Treaty, Americans for the first time referred to President Monroe's address of 1823 as the Monroe Doctrine. Critics fumed that the United States should have required the British to relinquish areas taken by force; defenders more rationally pronounced the agreement a victory for the Monroe Doctrine because Britain had promised not to acquire additional territories in the hemisphere.

Before the president ratified the treaty, the two negotiators exchanged secret notes explaining their conflicting understandings of the agreement and, in doing so, virtually altered its meaning. Bulwer claimed that it meant no *new* colonization and would not approve his nation's withdrawal from present holdings; Clayton argued that the pact was retroactive in intention and required the British to pull out of the hemisphere. The secretary of state defiantly warned that the United States had secured exclusive transit rights in several other Central American countries and that he was prepared to take these treaties to the Senate. Indeed, some of the republics, he told Bulwer, sought U.S. protection against the British. "There is not one of these five Central American states that would not annex themselves to us tomorrow, if they could," Clayton declared, "and if it is any secret worth knowing you are welcome to it—*Some of them have offered and asked to be annexed to the United States already.*" These notes remained confidential because public exposure of their reservations would have undermined the treaty or at least made it almost meaningless. Thus, the treaty approved by the Senate differed considerably from the exceptions outlined by each diplomat. In a strict sense the U.S. secretary of state had violated the Constitution's treaty-making stipulations in arranging the pact with Britain.

Anglo-American relations in Latin America remained uneasy despite the Clayton-Bulwer Treaty. Within three months the London government claimed that in addition to the exemptions of the Bay Islands and Belize, the treaty's provisions had no effect on the British presence in either Greytown or the Mosquito Coast. The situation worsened in 1852 when the British established a colony in the Honduran Bay Islands, and in the summer of 1854 when a mob attacked a U.S. diplomat in Greytown. After a U.S. naval officer failed to win reparations for the assault, he bombarded the town. No one died in the assault, but the incident threatened to have international repercussions because British and French properties were among the losses. The Washington government upheld the act despite a heated protest from London, but the crisis blew over when Britain's leaders backed off from demanding indemnification and instructed their nationals to present damage claims to Nicaragua on the ground that that government was responsible for all events occurring within its territories.

The British had no choice but to bend to U.S. pressure. They had allied with France against Russia in the Crimean War that broke out that same year of 1854, and the Mosquito Coast was not worth war with the United States. In October 1856 the British foreign secretary, Lord Clarendon, signed a convention with the U.S. minister in London, George Dallas, which provided for British withdrawal from the Bay Islands and the Mosquito territory. In December 1857 the ever-pragmatic Palmerston explained his willingness to retreat in Latin America: "[The Americans] are on the spot, strongly, deeply interested in the matter, totally unscrupulous and dishonest and determined somehow or other to carry their point. We are far away," he continued, "weak from distance, controlled by the indifference of the nation ... and by its strong commercial interest in maintaining

peace." But the U.S. Senate attached amendments to the Dallas-Clarendon Convention that Britain rejected, and the attempted settlement failed.

The obscure language of the Clayton-Bulwer Treaty led to continued disagreements over Central America, but the pact relieved much of the tension by discouraging U.S. annexation efforts. The treaty constituted a victory for the Monroe Doctrine and the United States in that the Americans had won the right to build a canal (albeit a cooperative enterprise) through a British-controlled area. Shortly afterward, the American railroad magnate Cornelius Vanderbilt established a steamship and railroad line through Nicaragua that eventually competed with the railway across Panama. In 1857 President James Buchanan asked Congress to authorize troops to keep both routes open, but the slavery issue again intervened in foreign policymaking and blocked the measure.

Anglo-American relations improved further with the movement toward a reciprocity treaty between the United States and Canada. Near the opening of the decade, U.S. interest in Canada revived when British colonial policies threatened to drive the North American provinces from the empire. Repeal of the Corn Laws in 1846 had cost Canada its advantageous position in the grain market, encouraging political leaders to push for a peaceful break with the London government and annexation by the United States. Britain at first responded by lifting many commercial restrictions between Canada and other parts of the empire, but U.S. tariff laws contributed to Canada's difficulties and suggested the benefits of incorporation.

Opposing factors were at work, however. Canadians accused Americans of violating the fishing provisions contained in the Convention of 1818 and tried to stop them from coming closer than three miles from shore and from buying fishing materials in British ports. Americans insisted that the Canadians were unreasonably strict in interpreting the provisions of the Convention. In June 1852 the

British navy provided protection for the Canadians' fishing rights in North America. The Americans retaliated by arming their fishing vessels, and the president dispatched ships to the troubled area with instructions to safeguard his nation's rights at sea. In May 1854, after nearly a year of angry controversy, Britain accepted Washington's invitation to discuss these problems.

A number of considerations ensured the success of the ensuing negotiations between Secretary of State William Marcy and the governor general of British North America, Lord Elgin. Americans wanted fishing rights, and Canadians wanted lower tariffs. Ironically, northerners in the United States favored a pact because it pointed to the ultimate annexation of Canada, whereas southerners approved because they believed that an agreement would ease Canada's economic problems and thereby *reduce* the chances for annexation. Southerners had also just won a victory for slavery (the Kansas-Nebraska Act of late May 1854, which terminated the ban on slavery's spread into these territories), making some of them amenable to a treaty with Canada that northerners wanted. Finally, the state department hired a lobbyist, who later claimed to have distributed over $200,000 in U.S. and Canadian funds in Congress and Canada to promote the treaty. Elgin's secretary, Laurence Oliphant, arrogantly claimed that the treaty "floated through on champagne," which was, he sarcastically added, the only way "to deal with hogs."

The Marcy-Elgin Treaty of June 1854 rested on the principle of reciprocity and was to remain in effect for ten years, after which either nation could abrogate the pact with a one-year notification. It removed duties on numerous goods and allowed Americans to fish in areas closed by the Convention of 1818; in return, Canadians secured fishing rights along the Atlantic coast of the United States above the thirty-sixth parallel. The United States received free navigation of the St. Lawrence River and its canals in exchange for giving the British reciprocal rights to Lake Michigan. The United States withdrew from the pact in 1866, in part because of its belief that Canada had pursued pro-Confederate policies during the Civil War, but also because of its claim that Canadians had gained more from the treaty than had Americans, a belief encouraged by the support for protective tariffs by the controlling Republican party.

The Crimean War of 1854–1856, which found Britain and France on one side and Russia on the other, provided the backdrop for a sudden but temporary decline in U.S.-British relations. Americans sympathized with Russia because of a past history of stable relations, but also because of recurring Anglophobia. The situation became more confusing when the British minister in Washington, John Crampton, recruited U.S. volunteers for the war, who were soon en route to Halifax and then off to the Crimea. Marcy lodged a vigorous protest, and when that brought no results, he sought Crampton's recall. The British Foreign Office refused to comply, but in May 1856 the United States expelled Crampton and three consuls involved in recruiting. The Pierce administration's decision was partly political, because the Democratic convention met less than a week after the Crampton episode, and the president's anti-British action had enormous appeal to the substantial number of Irish-Americans and Anglophobes who belonged to his party.

Despite these problems, Anglo-American relations became fairly stable by the latter half of the 1850s. Many British observers pondered the economic benefits derived from U.S. control: It seemed to bring stability to the region and thereby further trade. The Atlantic cable laid in 1858 promised closer contact between the English-speaking nations, as did growing cultural ties. That same year British searches of American ships suspected of engaging in the African slave trade caused a brief flare-up over an age-old controversy; but when the Buchanan administration sent warships to the Gulf of Mexico to stop such practices, the British made a modest retreat in June 1858 by renouncing the right of search in peacetime (but not wartime, when the British would more likely exercise the practice). The London ministry then eased tension in Central America the following year by signing an agreement with Honduras recognizing its control over the Bay Islands. In 1860 it negotiated an arrangement with Nicaragua relinquishing the Mosquito protectorate. Buchanan praised the settlements as triumphs for the Monroe Doctrine.

Anglo-American relations had become progressively smoother throughout the 1850s because both governments recognized the overriding importance of maintaining commercial ties. Toward that end, the British government had realistically ended its attempt to halt the spread of U.S. interests into Central America. Not unrelated to this altered policy was Britain's confidence that the Webster-Ashburton and Oregon boundary treaties of the preceding decade had safeguarded its interests in upper North America. Survival of the mid-century rapprochement would prove important as the two Atlantic nations encountered even more serious challenges during the Civil War.

East Asia

U.S. policy in East Asia focused on commercial rather than territorial expansion and therefore proceeded virtually unnoticed by most Americans due to their preoccupation with domestic political events relating to slavery. Equally noteworthy, because the peculiar institution bore no relation to the United States's interests in Asia, it posed no obstacle to commercial advances in East Asia. American popular interest in this area of the world surpassed the government's active involvement. Romantics joined missionaries in describing the exotic charms of the Orient, both in paintings and sculptures and in numerous sermons and religious publications. The nation's low-key commercial penetration of this vast region proved valuable primarily in opening the door for the nation's more active economic involvement during the latter part of the century.

The United States's initial thrusts into East Asia were only partly successful, largely because Orientals regarded Westerners as foreign devils and hesitated to open commercial doors. In the eighteenth century China allowed foreign trading vessels to enter only at Canton and, in an effort to prevent foreign contamination, required them to conduct business only within "factories," or trading posts lying outside the city. For years the United States followed Britain's lead by seeking most-favored-nation status—the right to the same commercial privileges accorded other countries. As trade avenues gradually opened, European powers pushed for colonization and spheres of control. The United States, by contrast, sought to keep China and Japan open to everyone in general and to American merchants in particular. Thus, the United States's earliest policies in Asia were forerunners of the "open door" of the late nineteenth century. Most Americans rejected the use of force, as employed by Europeans, and preferred peaceful means for obtaining the same economic privileges enjoyed by other nations.

U.S. trade with the Orient had begun shortly after the American Revolution. By the turn of the nineteenth century numerous American ships had followed the lead of the *Empress of China*, which had left New York for Canton in 1784 with furs, cotton, lead, and ginseng (a root believed capable of restoring virility) and returned a year later with a rich cargo of silks, spices, and tea. By the 1820s China's interest in cotton seemed to guarantee a huge Asian market for the South's chief product.

During the 1830s the U.S. penetration into East Asia deepened. The first American missionaries arrived in China, and merchants from New England and the Middle Atlantic states, along with southern cotton exporters, broadened their commercial contacts in Asia. In 1832 the United States sent a special agent to East Asia, Edmund Roberts, who had instructions to negotiate trade agreements with Cochin China (Indochina), Siam (modern Thailand), Muscat (along the Arabian Sea), and

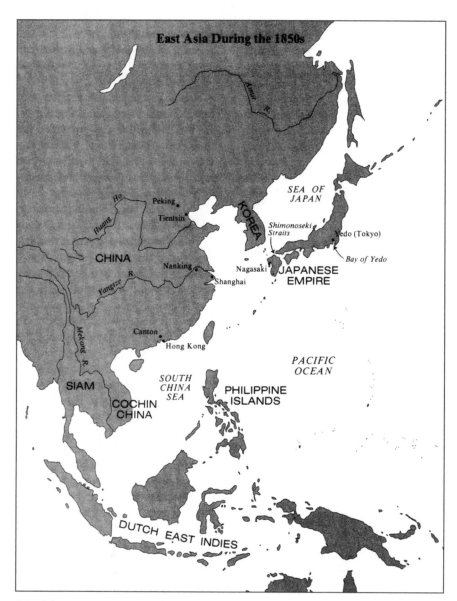

Map 14
America's involvement in East Asia was restricted primarily to a few contacts with China and Japan.

Japan. Few observers attached importance to the mission; in fact, Roberts had no directives to deal with China for fear of disturbing the existing trade. The following year Roberts signed commercial treaties with Siam and Muscat, but he decided not to talk with Japan until he had a larger delegation and more money for gifts. The Senate approved the two treaties, but Roberts died before he could negotiate a pact with Japan.

Britain's Opium War with China from 1839 to 1842 ultimately broke down restrictions on trade. For some time British merchants had sold India-grown opium in China after paying a nominal tax to governing authorities. But in 1839 new leaders in China, who despised the sale of the drug to their people, confiscated a huge supply from British traders and set off a conflict that ended with China's defeat three years later. In August 1842 Britain and China signed the Treaty of Nanking, which awarded Britain the island of Hong Kong, the opening of five new trading posts on the coast, the power to help set tariff rates, extraterritoriality in civil cases (right of foreigners to trial in their own courts), and war reparations. More important, the outcome of the Opium War opened China to the West.

The United States took advantage of Britain's commercial gains in China to seek most-favored-nation status. In the summer of 1843 Congress approved a special mission led by Massachusetts Whig Caleb Cushing, who negotiated the highly favorable Treaty of Wanghia (a village near Canton) in July 1844. According to terms, the United States could expand its trading activities to the five recently opened ports in China, establish consular posts, claim extraterritoriality in civil *and* criminal cases, and help determine tariff rates. Cushing had secured unconditional most-favored-nation treatment, giving the United States the same commercial privileges that China had awarded to Britain after the Opium War. His treaty provided a major impetus to American commercial expansion and to the growth of manufacturing in the northeast.

The treaties negotiated by Britain and the United States violated China's integrity as a nation and became a long-standing grievance against the West. Anglo-American claims to extraterritoriality and involvement in the establishment of tariff rates constituted infringements of China's sovereignty. Americans argued that extraterritoriality was necessary in criminal as well as civil cases in view of the great differences between their system of law and that of the Chinese: Laws in China, Americans claimed, were unjust and inconsistent. If so, the responsibility for criminal judgments given to U.S. consuls (seldom trained in such matters) resulted in numerous abuses as well. These unequal provisions remained in effect until the United States required China's assistance in World War II and agreed to bring them to an end.

The Taiping Rebellion of 1850–1864 threatened to undo U.S. relations with China as established by Cushing's treaty. Americans at home sympathized with the rebels because their leader was a Christian convert seeking to overthrow the conservative Manchu dynasty in Peking. Americans in China, however, agreed with the British that the government's collapse would invite European intervention and upset trade in China. British and Chinese forces clashed at Canton in November 1856, and a U.S. naval launch took fire from the Chinese forts. The U.S. Navy, without Washington's authorization, shelled and destroyed the forts. Within a year both Britain and France were fighting in the Chinese civil war, while the United States and Russia maintained official neutrality but cooperated with the British and French in sending diplomatic representatives to the negotiations.

In 1858 all four nations gathered with China at Tientsin to negotiate an end to the war. Americans won lower tariffs and the use of additional ports on the Chinese coast and the Yangtze River, while China agreed to tolerate Christianity and permit the United States, Britain, France, and Russia to establish diplomatic headquarters at Peking. Two years later Britain and France secured more commercial concessions by the Convention of Peking, which then benefited American merchants through the most-favored-nation principle established under Cushing's treaty. The emperor finally accepted the Tientsin treaties that same year of 1860, when British and French forces occupied Peking and left him no choice.

The Treaty of Tientsin of 1858 exemplified the United States's efforts to guarantee its commercial objectives by opposing any nation's establishment of permanent control in China. The most-favored-nation approach constituted the United States's only effective instrument for preventing a partition that would end Chinese sovereignty and obstruct trade. Throughout the Taiping Rebellion the U.S. commissioner in Canton worked to protect U.S. interests by safeguarding the empire against British and Russian exploitation. Three years later, in 1867, the U.S. minister to China, Massachusetts Congressman Anson Burlingame, accepted an invitation from the Chinese government to head a mission sent to persuade the major powers to limit their demands. He succeeded in winning assurances from Britain, France, and Russia not to seek special advantages during China's period of distress. The following year he again represented China in securing a treaty in Washington that dealt with travel, commerce, consuls, and other matters. The Burlingame Treaty of 1868 also permitted unrestricted Chinese migration into the United States, a provision that reflected its need for cheap labor to build the nation's first transcontinental railroad.

U.S. interest in Japan grew more slowly than it did in China, largely because of the island nation's self-imposed seclusion from the outside world. In the early seventeenth century Japan had come under control of the shoguns (military chieftains) of the Tokugawa family, who barred most outsiders as barbarians. The situation began to change after the Treaty of Wanghia of 1844 as U.S. trade in Shanghai made Japan a natural port of call to and from China. Stories circulated about Japan's brutal treatment of shipwrecked Amer-

Commodore Matthew C. Perry
Opened the U.S. commercial door to Japan in 1854. *Library of Congress.*

ican seamen driven into port, and although the allegations were largely untrue, the Washington government intended to guarantee the safety of the seamen. American steamships also required a coaling station in Asian waters, making Japanese coal a major attraction. The United States was unsuccessful in opening Japan during the 1840s, but its efforts received renewed impetus in the following decade because of the increased commercial interest in Asia brought on by the recently acquired Pacific coast.

In early 1852 Commodore Matthew C. Perry, veteran of the War of 1812 and younger brother of the hero of Lake Erie, became commander of the East India Squadron and received orders to establish commercial relations with Japan. Perry was to secure trade agreements, a coaling station, and assurances of hospitality for Americans forced into Japanese waters. In July 1853 four U.S. warships under his command entered the Bay of Yedo (later Tokyo). Only two were steamers, but they blew out heavy black smoke and caused one onlooker to remark that Japan was being overrun by "barbarians . . . in floating volcanoes." The "black fleet" waited in the bay for nearly a week with the commodore remaining out of sight to add mystery and importance to the visit. Finally Perry and his entourage came ashore, greeting the Japanese with a thirteen-gun salute and accompanied by 400 armed men and two black bodyguards. A band played "Hail, Columbia" as Perry handed Japanese officials a letter for the emperor calling for a treaty, but the bewildered Japanese simply ordered him to leave. Perry announced that he would return the following year with a larger squadron to pick up the emperor's reply.

Perry's second visit to Japan made a greater show of military force than did the first. In March 1854, after a two-week wait in the harbor with seven warships, he again landed, this time with a seventeen-gun salute followed by three bands playing "The Star-Spangled Banner" while Perry marched in with 500 men, their bayonets and guns noticeably on display. The Japanese were more amenable this time, even exchanging gifts with their visitors. Perry's offerings included a model train, a telegraph, and a history of the U.S. war with Mexico that suggestively contained drawings of the U.S. navy shelling Veracruz.

Japan's attitude had softened for several reasons. The country was undergoing great internal change as a new urban-merchant class saw commercial benefits in dealing with the United States. Western weapons were impressive, as a Japanese official would attest after looking into the mouth of an eight-inch gun and trying to lift a sixty-four-pound cannon ball. The Japanese were also wary of Russian intentions. In August 1853, shortly after Perry's first visit, the Russians inadvertently promoted U.S. interests by maneuvering close to Nagasaki with four ships. Their presence in Japanese waters had become too regular, the Japanese believed, encouraging an understanding with the United States.

Perry negotiated the Treaty of Kanagawa with Japan on March 31, 1854. This treaty was only a limited success, however, because it dealt primarily with the problem of shipwrecked seamen and did not establish broad commercial relations. Signed by the shogun, the treaty opened only two isolated ports for coal and supplies and granted consular privileges in each, and it contained no guarantees of coaling stations or extraterritorial rights. The Japanese promised to assist shipwrecked Americans and extend most-favored-nation privileges, but they stipulated that business transactions had to take place through Japanese officials, not private merchants.

Americans nonetheless regarded Perry's venture in East Asia as a major success. Weighed against Japan's past isolation, the pact of 1854 was instrumental in bringing the country into world affairs and raising U.S. chances for a general trade agreement. Perry's treaty won unanimous approval at home. Congress voted him a bonus, Boston businessmen awarded him a medal, and the New York Chamber of Commerce gave him nearly 400 pieces of silver dinner settings.

The United States attempted to open the door wider to Asia after Perry's treaty with Japan. The following year Dr. Peter Parker, a medical missionary, became U.S. commissioner to China and immediately sought additional concessions in East Asia. The United States sent its first diplomatic representative to Japan in August 1856. Townsend Harris, a New York businessman who had visited Asia on several occasions, became consul general with the responsibility of opening the commercial door to Japan. But he lacked military support, and the Japanese refused to welcome him. Harris and his secretary lived in seclusion for over a year until a U.S. vessel arrived, and he heard nothing from the state department for a year and a half. The Japanese meanwhile blamed him for several natural disasters that they interpreted as divine dissatisfaction with Perry's treaty and urged him to return home.

Yet Harris patiently reminded his hosts that the European nations were more dangerous than the United States and that it would be more advisable to give America what it wanted than to have the others wrench concessions at the cost of blood.

Harris eventually earned Japan's trust. In June 1857 he secured a convention that broadened U.S. commercial privileges, and in July of the following year he signed the first major treaty of amity and commerce permitted by Japan with the West. Of no small consequence was British and French intervention in the ongoing Chinese civil war, because the act highlighted concern about their designs in Asia and probably encouraged the Japanese to come to the negotiating table. The Harris Treaty of 1858 widened commercial privileges, authorized the appointment of consuls in all ports open for trade, permitted the exchange of diplomatic representatives, drew up fixed tariff schedules, and approved extraterritoriality. The following year Harris became minister to Japan and headed the new U.S. legation in Tokyo.

The United States's opening of Japan did not come without stirring up massive unrest on the island. Japanese isolationists were unhappy with the shogun for dealing with foreigners and rallied around the emperor in resisting outside intervention. By June 1863 the emperor wanted all foreigners out of Japan, and even though his wishes went largely unfulfilled, violence ensued and took the life of the secretary of the U.S. legation. In the Straits of Shimonoseki in 1864 a Japanese officer, without authorization, fired his cannon on foreign vessels and brought retaliatory action through a joint punitive expedition in which the United States took part. By the Convention of 1864 the Japanese made reparations. The U.S. portion of the indemnity was much higher than the costs of the venture, however, and in a gesture of good will Congress later reimbursed the full amount to Japan. In 1868 the emperor regained power from the shogunate in the Meiji Restoration and soon welcomed Western ways and technology. By the turn of the twentieth century the United States had agreed to grant Japan full control over tariffs and over foreigners within its borders.

By the outbreak of the Civil War, the United States had made economic inroads into Asia that focused primarily on China and Japan. Neither country had opened its commercial doors willingly or totally; but Americans of the early nineteenth century had laid the basis for their successors by pointing the way to the famed though mythical "China market."

The Southern Dream of a Caribbean Empire

In a curious twist, slavery became both the central stimulus and the chief obstruction to the South's efforts during the 1850s to build an empire in the Caribbean that might lead to the admission of slave states and the restoration of a political balance in the Congress. Much of the economically poor area seemed ready for the taking, and yet any attempt to accommodate slavery with the unfurling of the U.S. flag appeared destined to failure. Opposition to the spread of slavery into new territories, embodied in the Wilmot Proviso and growing stronger in intensity as the decade became increasingly unstable, ensured that any expansionist proposals would set off sharp and bitter debates growing out of mutual suspicions between North and South. Both sections had recognized the necessity of incorporating Texas, California, and the Mexican Cession, but they now had to confront the trouble that erupted over the status of the newly acquired areas: Would they be slave or free? By the 1850s northerners were so wary of southern motives that they preferred to restrict the size of the Union rather than see it grow to the benefit of the South.

It is doubtful that support for manifest destiny had ceased to exist among northerners, but the idea's internal contradictions ultimately encouraged the two sections to adopt radically different positions. Both agreed that the driving spirit of territorial expansion was republicanism and the spread of civilized institutions, but they sharply disagreed over whether slavery was reconcilable with freedom and thus an integral part of that civilization. Not all Americans looked at slavery from a moral point of view. Yet they soon realized that its political aspects were inseparable from its morality. When the two sections finally focused on this latter issue, the possibility of compromise eluded the antagonists, and the nation moved toward the Civil War.

The only way for the South to enhance its political power was to expand into the Caribbean; the only way for the North to retain its political power was to block such a move. Senator William H. Seward of New York argued that the prerequisite for the country's spread into the Caribbean was the abolition of slavery. But this price was too high for southerners. The Compromise of 1850 encouraged the southern drive toward the Caribbean by requiring California's admission as a free state and by opening the Mexican Cession to "popular sovereignty" in allowing its inhabitants to decide the slavery question. Expansion southward seemed to be the only remedy to the South's continued decline in political power. The Gulf of Mexico, according to expansionist James D. E. B. DeBow of the widely read *DeBow's Review,* was the "great *Southern* sea." Slavery would thrive in Cuba, Mexico, Central America, and perhaps in the rest of Latin America. If thwarted in this drive toward the Caribbean, the South's choice would become obvious: Free the slaves, which was out of the question, or leave the Union, which was not.

The first apparent opportunity for southward expansion arose in Yucatan. In 1848 the white government of the Yucatan peninsula, which considered itself independent of Mexico, faced certain revolt by its native Indians. A spokesman for that government notified the Polk administration in Washington that Yucatan would grant the United States "dominion and sovereignty" in exchange for military assistance against the Indians. The president

seemed interested, especially when it appeared that Britain and Spain might intervene in Yucatan's troubles. Polk told Congress in late April that the United States must oppose the transfer in ownership of any area in the hemisphere, even if its residents favored such a change. This pronouncement gave added meaning to the "Polk Corollary" of the Monroe Doctrine, because the original statement had opposed a transfer *without* the approval of people in the area. Further action proved unnecessary when the Yucatan government managed to settle its problems without a revolution.

Cuba, however, was the grand prize and the focal point of southern expansionist aims. The United States had a long-standing interest in the island. Romanticized as "The Ever Faithful Isle" because it (and Puerto Rico) did not break from Spain along with the rest of its Latin American possessions, Cuba was also known as "The Pearl of the Antilles" and "The World's Sugar Bowl" because of its enormous production of molasses and sugar. For several decades Cuba had attracted American investment and trade. By mid-century it had become strategically important as well, involving U.S. interests in the Caribbean, Gulf of Mexico, Mississippi River, and the isthmus of Central America. Finally, to many southerners, Cuba presented the distinct danger of becoming another Haiti—especially if Spain carried through on its threats (done only to undermine filibustering) to emancipate Cuba's slaves. A black nation so close to the Gulf states would set an example that might foment slave revolts in the South.

The U.S. failure to acquire Yucatan, along with the Pierce administration's later inability to secure a naval base in the Dominican Republic, dramatized Cuba's centrality. Indeed, the island became an important way station to Oregon and California. President Polk had the support of Lewis Cass, Stephen A. Douglas, John L. O'Sullivan, and other prominent "Young Americans" in his Democratic party in trying to buy Cuba for $100 million, but Spain had the support of Britain and France in staunchly refusing the offer. Cuba remained a natural object of manifest destiny in the 1850s, furnishing southerners a potential outlet for expanding slavery and gaining political control in Congress.

The North's political dominance in Washington obstructed the formal development of a southern empire in the Caribbean, but that did not rule out measures that operated either just outside the law or barely within it. Filibusters offered a means for taking Cuba. Such private ventures were well rooted in the American expansionist tradition: West Florida, Texas, and California had been at least partly "liberated" and acquired by that means. Another method was through the Pierce administration's expansionist policies, which relied on highly unorthodox diplomatic procedures or gave unofficial blessing to filibustering. Yet no approach could circumvent the slavery issue. Many followers of filibusters came from the South because of proximity, and more than a few members of the Pierce and Buchanan administrations were southerners or southern sympathizers. The widespread impression among northerners was that the South had allied with the expansionist Democratic party to spread slavery.

The first Cuban filibustering expedition of note was led by General Narciso López, a Venezuelan-born officer in the Spanish military. López had been a businessman in Cuba, and as a Spanish refugee he had tried several times to win the island's independence from Spain as a step toward annexation by the United States. Having married into a slaveholding family in Cuba, López made northerners apprehensive that he was part of a southern conspiracy to extend slavery. He aroused great support from Cuban exiles in New York City and attracted a number of volunteers in New Orleans, some of whom were veterans of the Mexican War and wanted to free Cuba and acquire property on the island. For their services López offered all they could drink and smoke and whatever they pillaged from captured areas—including women. In the event of success, each man would receive a bonus of $1000 and 160 acres of land on the island. López had several hundred volunteers in his filibustering force on Round Island off Louisiana in September 1849, but the U.S. Navy prevented their departure for Cuba. He did not give up. Turning primarily to southerners for assistance, he won the support of John Quitman, a successful cotton and sugar grower, former general in the Mexican War, and soon governor of Mississippi. López also received help from Laurence Sigur, editor of the *New Orleans Delta,* former Mississippi Senator John Henderson, and the man whose name had become synonymous with the term manifest destiny, John L. O'Sullivan of New York's *Democratic Review.*

All of López's filibustering attempts were fiascos. In May 1850 he led 700 forces out of New Orleans for Cuba—their mission unmistakably clear from the red shirts they wore in honor of the European revolutions of 1848. Spanish regulars in Cuba drove them away. When López's followers returned to the United States, government officials arrested them under the Neutrality Act of 1818. All participants went to trial in New Orleans, but after three mistrials for Henderson, the prosecution dropped the cases. In August 1851 López tried again. With a band of 500, he sought to fulfill the promise of a proclamation calling for the acquisition of Cuba according to "inevitable destiny." Once more López ran into trouble, but this time he could not escape the consequences. Spanish forces on the island swarmed over the invaders and put them in prison. Authorities kept more than 100 in jail and, in a move that shocked Americans, executed López and 50 of his cohort, including Colonel William Crittenden of Kentucky, nephew of the U.S. attorney general.

López's actions had finally drawn international attention. People of New Orleans were infuriated over the executions, because many of the victims came from southern families. Unrest spread to Key West and northward to Cincinnati, Philadelphia, and Pittsburgh. Mobs stormed the Spanish consulate in New Orleans and the U.S. legation in Madrid. Secretary of

State Webster extended apologies to Spain and admitted to his government's failure to act forcefully against filibustering. The next year the Spanish queen pardoned the imprisoned members of the López expedition, and Congress appropriated a small reparation for damages to the Spanish consulate in New Orleans.

U.S. interest in Cuba did not end with López's death. In April 1852 the governments in London and Paris followed the promptings of the Madrid regime and invited the United States to join them in a self-denying pact intended to ensure Spain's continued control over the island. Although Webster supported the tripartite proposal, he died in October and his successor in the state department, Edward Everett, rejected it with the argument that Cuba was primarily an *American* question. The elections of the following month convinced the new president, Franklin Pierce, that Americans were still fervent expansionists. "The policy of my administration," Pierce declared in his inaugural address, "will not be controlled by any timid forebodings of evil from expansion. Indeed . . . our attitude as a nation and our position on the globe render the acquisition of . . . [Cuba] eminently important for our protection, if not in the future essential for the preservation of the rights of commerce and the peace of the world." Both Secretary of State William Marcy and the minister to England, James Buchanan, were former members of Polk's cabinet and continued to work for Cuba's acquisition, as did the new minister to Spain, former Senator Pierre Soulé of Louisiana, and the minister to France, John Mason, also a cabinet member under Polk. At first Marcy attempted quietly and unofficially to buy Cuba from Spain, but these efforts soon gave way to Soulé's designs to take the island by force.

If the president's inaugural address did not provide ample warning of U.S. intentions regarding Cuba, his appointment of Soulé as minister to Spain left no doubt. Soulé's well-known calls for Cuba made his selection for the post at Madrid an outright affront to that government. To make matters worse, just before departing for Spain, Soulé delivered a fiery speech in New York calling for Cuba's annexation. France had already exiled the hot-tempered and outspoken southerner because of his extreme views on republicanism. And now, soon after his arrival in Madrid, he had alienated fellow diplomats. The French ambassador, the Marquis de Turgot, did not conceal his contempt for Soulé, and eventually the American challenged Turgot to a duel over an alleged insulting remark about Mrs. Soulé's low-necked dress. Soulé shot him in the leg and crippled him for life. The *New York Herald* moaned, "We wanted an ambassador there, we have sent a matador." Yet the administration in Washington did not recall Soulé—perhaps because many Americans exuberantly praised his conduct.

By late February 1854 a crisis developed with Spain that involved Soulé and U.S. interests in Cuba. Spanish authorities in Havana had clamped down on maritime laws and on February 28 seized the cargo of the American merchant steamship *Black Warrior* as it passed between New York and Mobile. The vessel, Havana officials declared, failed to carry adequate identification of cargo, an admitted infraction of customs law but one overlooked numerous times in the past. Many Americans were incensed, and Soulé seized the moment to justify a demand for Cuba. He handed a provocative note to Spanish officials in Madrid and followed it with an ultimatum demanding the removal of all Spanish officials involved in the seizure and giving the government forty-eight hours to make $300,000 in reparations to the ship's owners. President Pierce meanwhile sharply criticized Spain in a message to Congress. Marcy had instructed his minister to seek only an indemnity, but Soulé had gone beyond.

While Soulé fumed over the *Black Warrior* episode, the Spanish foreign minister in Madrid worked to resolve it peacefully. He thought Soulé had exceeded Washington's orders and wrote a justification of Spain's behavior that the Pierce administration could not refute. At the same time Spanish officials in Madrid contacted the owners of the American vessel and authorized $53,000 in reparations. The *Black Warrior* returned to its coastal trade, and port officials in Havana thereafter treated it with deference. Once again the two nations escaped a serious confrontation over Cuba. Soulé continued to believe that the episode had stained his country's honor.

In April 1854 the Pierce administration initiated another effort to buy Cuba that culminated in one of the most outlandish documents in the history of U.S. foreign policy—the Ostend Manifesto. Marcy had directed Soulé to offer a maximum of $130 million for the island. If Spain declined the offer, the secretary of state included a follow-up instruction that, in the hands of a man of Soulé's fiery temperament, contained dangerous implications. In the tradition of Presidents Madison in West Florida and Monroe in East Florida, Marcy told Soulé that upon Spain's refusal to sell, "you will then direct your efforts to the next desirable object[,] which is to detach that island from the Spanish dominion and from all dependence on any European power." Marcy later instructed Soulé to meet *privately* with Ministers Buchanan in England and Mason in France to "compare opinions as to what may be advisable, and . . . adopt measures for perfect concert of action in aid of [the] negotiations at Madrid."

Instead of keeping the proceedings private, as Marcy had directed, the three U.S. ministers came together with other U.S. diplomats in a series of well-publicized meetings in October at Ostend in Belgium and Aix-la-Chapelle in Rhenish Prussia. There they eventually produced a dispatch that they sent to Washington by secret messenger. Although it was a private report to the secretary of state, portions of its contents had already appeared in European and American newspapers before Marcy received the packet in November. For political reasons if nothing else, the Washington administration had dismissed the idea of using force to acquire Cuba and preferred some type of financial acquisition. But its ministers in Europe had misinterpreted Marcy's

aggressive notes following the *Black Warrior* episode to mean that war remained a viable instrument for securing the island. The manifesto warned that if Spain refused to sell Cuba, the United States would be justified in seizing it by force. One contemporary writer expressed feigned amazement that the Washington government had "planned a burglary of great proportions and published a prospectus in advance."

The so-called Ostend Manifesto set out the importance of Cuba to the United States, explained why Spain should sell, and then declared that "self-preservation is the first law of nature, with states as well as with individuals." If Cuba became "Africanized," it would emerge as a "second St. Domingo, with all its attendant horrors to the white race, and suffer the flames to extend to our own neighboring shores, seriously to endanger or actually to consume the fair fabric of our Union." Should the Madrid government refuse to part with the island, the United States would be justified "by every law, human and divine," in "wresting it from Spain . . . upon the very same principle that would justify an individual in tearing down the burning house of his neighbor if there were no other means of preventing the flames from destroying his own home." In a note accompanying the dispatch, Soulé stoically declared that if the effort to acquire Cuba were to "bring upon us the calamity of a war, let it be now."

Several stormy cabinet meetings led to Marcy's decision to reject the use of force in obtaining the island. In doing so, he referred to the "robber doctrine," and Soulé, now thoroughly discredited by the Pierce administration, angrily resigned as minister. The president's enemies in the House of Representatives were not satisfied. They arranged publication of the report in March 1855, causing a northern outcry against an alleged southern plot to expand slavery into Cuba. Even then, the situation could have been worse. The president and his secretary of state had turned most of the heat toward their ministers in Europe by managing to delete from the documents Marcy's reference to the United States possibly having to "detach" the island from Spain.

The excitement caused by the Ostend Manifesto was attributable to the heated political atmosphere engendered by the almost fanatical distrust between North and South. Otherwise, the document would have received the ridicule it deserved. But the Pierce administration's proslavery stance on the Kansas-Nebraska Act of that same year had made northerners extremely suspicious of any attempts to annex Cuba. Congress's decision to permit slavery's expansion into Kansas and Nebraska on the basis of popular sovereignty had further divided the nation by intensifying the South's efforts to acquire Cuba, Nicaragua, and Mexico. The sheer timing of the Ostend Manifesto also contributed to the national uproar. The paper was not actually a "manifesto" because the United States delivered no ultimatum to Spain, but as with other events of the decade, newspapers and politicians preferred exaggeration to truth.

Marcy's April instructions to Soulé were partly responsible for the trouble. His meaning, as made clear in the rest of the note, was to help Cuba achieve independence through negotiations, making the island available for U.S. annexation. But he ill-advisedly used a word in his instructions that was subject to varying interpretations—*detach*—and that virtually opened the door for the more direct and seemingly synonymous word that appeared in the manifesto—*wrest*. Perhaps Marcy preferred the diplomatic approach. If so, his instructions should have been more specific and carefully written. But given Soulé's past performance in Madrid, one has to wonder what Marcy really had in mind. It would not be the first time (nor the last) that unspoken or unwritten wishes became inferred policy in the hands of rash acting diplomats.

With the expansionist Democrats slowed by the slavery issue, attention again turned to the filibusters. John Quitman, who had supported López's attempts to take Cuba, had meanwhile resigned his position as Missis-

sippi's governor in 1851 because of the controversy over filibustering and had decided to seize the island himself. Should Spain abolish slavery in Cuba, he feared, the South's institution would be in danger. Besides providing a dangerous example of freedom, a new black nation could grow out of Cuba and block the South's spread into the Caribbean. In 1854 Quitman prepared to lead a force of 3000 to take the island, but he could not overcome the federal government's opposition, the lack of financial support, and the failure to arouse help among the Cubans themselves. A year later Quitman gave up on filibustering because of what he called the "humbug administration" in Washington.

The most persistent and colorful filibuster was William Walker of Tennessee, who tried four times—in 1855, 1857, 1858, and 1860—to invade Latin America and in the process greatly heightened the southern effort to spread slavery into that region. Indeed, at one time he installed himself as head of Nicaragua. Known as the "Grey-Eyed Man of Destiny," Walker appeared to be the fulfillment of an ancient folk tale of the Nicaraguan Indians—that a "grey-eyed man" would lead them to freedom. Walker hardly cut an impressive looking figure, and his record suggested only the remotest chance of lasting success. He stood five feet, six inches tall, weighed a mere hundred pounds, and was heavily freckled and shy. He had earned a degree in medicine before losing interest in that profession and switching to law in Louisiana. But his practice did not do well, and he changed his focus to journalism. In New Orleans he became co-editor and co-owner of the *Crescent*. After the death of his wife in 1849 he moved to California and soon became interested in filibustering. In 1853 he and a small crew of adventurers seized from Mexico the capital of Lower California at La Paz, but after declaring it a republic with himself as president, he had to withdraw because of infighting and poor discipline. Eventually caught by U.S. authorities and tried for violating the Neutrality Act of 1818, he won acquittal in San Francisco.

U.S. interest in building a canal through Nicaragua attracted Walker's attention to Latin America throughout the last half of the 1850s. Hired to keep order in the small country by an American business that transported passengers across Nicaragua to California, Walker was so successful that he finally took control of the republic in 1855 and declared himself president. His band of filibusters was bisectional in origin, with a slight majority coming from the North and including entrepreneurs and financial agents. Their chief motives, Walker believed, were a search for adventure and a chance to gain the spoils of war. At this point Walker was only mildly opposed to slavery, but he shifted his public position out of pure self-interest when he came to realize that his major hope for U.S. support lay among southern slave holders. Encouraged by a recent visit and promised investments in Nicaragua's land by none other than Pierre Soulé himself, Walker's government soon reestablished slavery and prepared to resume the slave trade. Furthermore, it swore to bind "the Southern states to Nicaragua as if she were one of themselves." With the assistance of the U.S. minister in Nicaragua, Walker's group turned the country's attention to cotton, sugar, rice, and other crops well suited to the warm climate and cheap labor. Walker now appeared to be the leading proponent of expanding slavery into the Caribbean.

Walker's activities in Nicaragua aroused widespread suspicions. Many British thought him the agent of American expansionists in violation of the Clayton-Bulwer Treaty, a belief the U.S. government encouraged by its half-hearted efforts to stop filibustering. But even more explosive were northerners' suspicions that Walker was a southern instrument for spreading slavery. Indeed, the Democratic party fostered those suspicions in 1856 by inserting a statement in its platform endorsing Walker's desire to "regenerate" Nicaragua. That same year the Pierce administration extended recognition to the Walker government in Nicaragua, partly because it

was the only group having authority but also because the move might prove politically beneficial at home.

But Walker's rapid rise to the top in Nicaragua was followed by an even faster fall from power. Shortly after becoming president of Nicaragua, he alienated its people by his oppressive rule, and his followers turned on one another or fell victim to liquor and disease. Anglo-French opposition to Walker's regime further undercut his government, and eventually he alienated railroad baron Cornelius Vanderbilt by taking the side of Charles Morgan (who had earlier assisted Walker) in their bitter fight over transit rights in Nicaragua. Vanderbilt's enmity proved costly, because he ultimately aided Costa Rica, Guatemala, Honduras, and San Salvador in forcing Walker to flee to the United States in the spring of 1857. Walker still did not give up. By November of that year he was headed back toward Nicaragua, but U.S. naval officers took him into custody near Greytown. He won his release and in 1858 was trying again to reach Nicaragua when his ship struck a reef off British Honduras. In the spring of 1860 he tried a fourth time to regain the presidency of Nicaragua, but in an attack on Honduras he was routed and turned for help to a British official, who handed him over to the Hondurans. In mid-September 1860 Walker died before a firing squad.

Walker's legacy lay in the impetus his filibustering exploits gave to the growing sectionalism in the United States. The South saw a potential avenue for spreading slavery into the Caribbean, but the North rigidly opposed any move in that direction. The irony is that whereas some newspapers accused Walker of trying to wreck the Union by establishing a "Southern Slave Empire," others insisted that he would have saved the Union by acquiring enough land in Latin America to allow the South to send its excess slaves and thereby remove the danger of secession. Whatever the truth, Walker used the southern cause to advance his own personal interests and in the process deepened North-South suspicions.

Cuba, however, remained the chief object of southern expansionists, and soon the Buchanan administration too fell victim to the slavery issue in making a last-ditch effort to acquire the island. Immediately after Buchanan's inauguration in 1857, the U.S. Supreme Court handed down the ill-fated Dred Scott decision, which sharpened hostilities over slavery by removing all restrictions on its extension and, as a matter of course, further reduced the United States's chances for taking the island. Republicans sought the Homestead Act to attract Americans westward, but southern Democrats held out for Cuba. Buchanan kept trying. He appointed a wealthy New York banker, August Belmont, to the ministerial post in Madrid, only to have the Senate refuse confirmation because Belmont had earlier suggested that the United States bribe Spain into giving up the island. In December 1858 Buchanan asked Congress to set aside money to buy Cuba lest European powers intervene. The Senate Foreign Relations Committee recommended $30 million for that purpose, but abolitionists in the Republican party blocked a decision until Congress adjourned. Buchanan tried and failed again in 1859 and 1860, and U.S. efforts to annex Cuba came to an end with Abraham Lincoln's election to the presidency: The Illinois Republican opposed the move.

If Buchanan's Caribbean policy was more national than sectional, it nonetheless appeared to lean toward the South and slavery. He sought to buy Cuba, to place U.S. soldiers in Nicaragua and Panama for safeguarding transportation facilities, and to send the army to Mexico to restore domestic order. Admittedly, these measures would have warded off European intervention in the New World and established respect for the Monroe Doctrine. Furthermore, Cuba's acquisition might have slowed the move toward civil war. According to later Confederate president Jefferson Davis, "The end, regret it as we may, the inevitable end of continuance in such hostility between the States must be their separation. This brings me to . . . the importance of the Island

of Cuba to the Southern States if formed into a separate confederacy." Commercial gains would be important, "but the political necessity would be paramount, and the possession would be indispensable." It is highly doubtful that the incorporation of the Caribbean states would have completely defused the move toward secession: The fact is that their acquisition would have benefited the South and therefore infuriated the North. This cold realization killed all expansionist proposals while suggesting that neither success nor failure in acquiring these areas would have affected the onrushing Civil War.

With neither section willing to compromise, the South announced secession, effectively turning attention away from Cuba and other expansionist enterprises in Latin America. Slavery ceased to exist in the United States by 1865, and for almost three decades so did active U.S. interest in Cuba and the Caribbean. Outside the United States, the principal legacy of the filibustering expeditions was a deep distrust in Latin America that marred relations between the Americas for years. Inside the country, the activities of Walker and others had bequeathed a greatly intensified sectional controversy that would culminate in the Civil War.

Reflections on the 1850s

The United States's confusing and disjointed foreign policy of the 1850s is understandable only within the context of slavery and the coming of the Civil War. The nation's involvement in foreign affairs lacked cohesion because North and South were bitterly divided over several issues, including what each section defined as the national interest. Many Americans from both sections were concerned with whether slavery was compatible with the republican ideals associated with manifest destiny. Americans agreed that territorial expansion was the means toward empire, but they differed on whether slavery was reconcilable with freedom and hence an integral part of the nation's destiny. Expansion northward was blocked by an alien majority and by a climate unsuited for cotton and slavery; expansion southward was both driven and repressed by the existence of slavery. Northerners feared a conspiracy to spread slavery and successfully shattered the southern dream of a Caribbean empire. Perhaps a number of Americans wanted Cuba in the national interest, but suspicion of the South's motives was so widespread in the North that any expansionist program benefiting the South was subject to attack. Such a chaotic decade provided a fitting prelude to the tragic domestic conflict that erupted in the spring of 1861.

Selected Readings

Bauer, K. Jack. *Zachary Taylor: Soldier, Planter, Statesman of the Old Southwest.* 1985.

Binder, Frederick M. *James Buchanan and the American Empire.* 1994.

Bourne, Kenneth. *Britain and the Balance of Power in North America, 1815–1908.* 1967.

Brown, Charles H. *Agents of Manifest Destiny: The Lives and Times of the Filibusters.* 1980.

Burns, E. Bradford. *Patriarch and Folk: The Emergence of Nicaragua, 1798–1858.* 1991.

Campbell, Charles S. *From Revolution to Rapprochement: The United States and Great Britain, 1783–1900.* 1974.

Chaffin, Tom. *Fatal Glory: Narciso López and the First Clandestine U.S. War against Cuba.* 1996.

Cohen, Warren I. *America's Response to China: An Interpretive History of Sino-American Relations.* 2000.

Donald, David H. *Charles Sumner and the Rights of Man.* 1970.

Downs, Jacques M. *The Golden Ghetto: The American Commercial Community at Canton and the Shaping of American China Policy, 1784–1844.* 1997.

Dowty, Alan. *The Limits of American Isolation: The United States and the Crimean War.* 1971.

Dulles, Foster R. *Yankees and Samurai: America's Role in the Emergence of Modern Japan, 1791–1900.* 1965.

Ettinger, Amos A. *The Mission to Spain of Pierre Soulé, 1853–1855: A Study in the Cuban Diplomacy of the United States.* 1932.

Fairbank, John K. *Trade and Diplomacy on the China Coast: The Opening of the Treaty Ports, 1842–1854.* 2 vols. 1953.

Fay, Peter W. *The Opium War, 1840–1842.* 1975.

Findling, John E. *Close Neighbors, Distant Friends: United States–Central American Relations.* 1987.

Freehling, William W. *The Road to Disunion.* 1990.

Fujita, Fumiko. *American Pioneers and the Japanese Frontier: American Experts in Nineteenth-Century Japan.* 1994.

Gara, Larry. *The Presidency of Franklin Pierce.* 1991.

Garber, Paul N. *The Gadsden Treaty.* 1923.

Gibson, Arrell M. *Yankees in Paradise: The Pacific Basin Frontier.* 1993.

Goldstein, Jonathan. *Philadelphia and the China Trade, 1682–1846: Commercial, Cultural, and Attitudinal Effects.* 1978.

Graham, Gerald S. *The China Station: War and Diplomacy, 1830–1860.* 1978.

Gulick, Edward V. *Peter Parker and the Opening of China.* 1973.

Hagan, Kenneth J. *This People's Navy: The Making of American Sea Power.* 1991.

Henson, Curtis, T. *Commissioners and Commodores: The East India Squadron and American Diplomacy in China.* 1982.

Horsman, Reginald. *Race and Manifest Destiny: The Origins of American Racial Anglo-Saxonism.* 1981.

Hunt, Michael H. *Ideology and U.S. Foreign Policy.* 1987.

———. *The Making of a Special Relationship: The United States and China to 1914.* 1997.

Johannsen, Robert W. *Stephen A. Douglas.* 1973.

Johnson, Robert E. *Far China Station: The U.S. Navy in Asian Waters, 1800–1898.* 1979.

Jones, Wilbur D. *The American Problem in British Diplomacy, 1841–1861.* 1974.

Klein, Philip S. *President James Buchanan: A Biography.* 1962.

LaFeber, Walter. *The Clash: A History of U.S.-Japan Relations.* 1997.

Langley, Lester D. *The Cuban Policy of the United States: A Brief History.* 1968.

———. *Struggle for the American Mediterranean: United States–European Rivalry in the Gulf-Caribbean, 1776–1904.* 1976.

Layton, Thomas N. *The Voyage of the "Frolic": New England Merchants and the Opium Trade.* 1997.

Long, David F. *Gold Braid and Foreign Relations: Diplomatic Activities of U.S. Naval Officers, 1798–1883.* 1988.

May, Robert E. *John A. Quitman: Old South Crusader.* 1985.

———. *The Southern Dream of a Caribbean Empire, 1854–1861.* 1973.

McDougall, Walter A. *Let the Sea Make a Noise: A History of the North Pacific from Magellan to MacArthur.* 1993.

Morison, Samuel E. *"Old Bruin": Commodore Matthew C. Perry, 1794–1858.* 1967.

Neu, Charles E. *The Troublesome Encounter: The United States and Japan.* 1975.

Neumann, William L. *America Encounters Japan: From Perry to MacArthur.* 1963.

Nichols, Roy F. *Franklin Pierce: Young Hickory of the Granite Hills.* 1958.

Pérez, Louis A. *Cuba and the United States: Ties of Singular Intimacy.* 1997.

Perkins, Bradford. *The Creation of a Republican Empire, 1776–1865.* 1993. The Cambridge History of American Foreign Relations, vol. 1. Cohen, Warren I., ed.

Perkins, Dexter. *The Monroe Doctrine, 1826–1867.* 1933.

Perry, John C. *Facing West: Americans and the Opening of the Pacific.* 1994.

Potter, David. *The Impending Crisis, 1848–1861.* 1976.

Rosenstone, Robert A. *Mirror in the Shrine: American Encounters with Meiji Japan.* 1988.

Saul, Norman E. *Distant Friends: The United States and Russia, 1763–1867.* 1991.

Schoonover, Thomas D. *The United States in Central America, 1860–1911: Episodes of Social Imperialism and Imperial Rivalry in the World System.* 1991.

Schroeder, John H. *Shaping a Maritime Empire: The Commercial and Diplomatic Role of the American Navy, 1829–1861.* 1985.

Shewmaker, Kenneth E. "Daniel Webster and the Politics of Foreign Policy, 1850–1852," *Journal of American History* 63 (1976): 303–15.

———. "Forging the 'Great Chain': Daniel Webster and the Origins of American Foreign Policy toward East Asia and the Pacific, 1841–1852," *American Philosophical Society* 129 (1985): 225–59.

Silbey, Joel H. *The Partisan Imperative: The Dynamics of American Politics Before the Civil War.* 1985.

Smith, Elbert B. *The Presidencies of Zachary Taylor and Millard Fillmore.* 1988.

———. *The Presidency of James Buchanan.* 1975.

Spencer, Donald S. *Louis Kossuth and Young America: A Study of Sectionalism and Foreign Policy, 1848–1852.* 1977.

Stuart, Reginald C. *United States Expansionism and British North America, 1775–1871.* 1988.

Treat, Payson, J. *Diplomatic Relations between the United States and Japan: 1853–1895.* 2 vols. 1932.

Van Alstyne, Richard W. *The United States and East Asia.* 1973.

Varg, Paul A. *New England and Foreign Relations, 1789–1850.* 1983.

Wall, James T. *Manifest Destiny Denied: America's First Intervention in Nicaragua.* 1981.

Walworth, Arthur. *Black Ships Off Japan: The Story of Commodore Perry's Expedition.* 1946.

Warner, Donald F. *The Idea of Continental Union: Agitation for the Annexation of Canada to the United States, 1849–1893.* 1960.

Wiley, Peter B. *Yankees in the Land of the Gods: Commodore Perry and the Opening of Japan.* 1990.

Williams, Mary W. *Anglo-American Isthmian Diplomacy, 1815–1915.* 1916.

CHAPTER 9

The Civil War,
1861–1865

The International Dimension

On April 12, 1861, Confederate forces in Charleston opened fire on the federal garrison in Fort Sumter, and the Civil War began. Tensions had risen dramatically after the election of Abraham Lincoln to the presidency. To the South the tall and lean man from Illinois posed a significant threat: whether an abolitionist who, according to misguided perceptions, fitted the mold of the radical John Brown, or, in reality, a Republican who would eventually bring an end to slavery by opposing its expansion. In rapid time South Carolina led six other southern states in announcing secession from the Union. After the shots at Fort Sumter, the seven states drew the support of four more states in joining the Confederate States of America, which had already drawn up a constitution and set up a provisional government in Montgomery, Alabama. President Lincoln called for 75,000 militiamen to put down what he termed an insurrection "too powerful to be suppressed by the ordinary course of judicial proceedings."

Although the domestic aspects of the Civil War have attracted their deserved attention, the international dimension of that same war has rarely received its due. Lincoln's central purpose was to preserve the Union by amassing sufficient military forces to defeat the South on the battlefield; but no less important, and integrally related to this objective, was the need to prevent a European intervention in the war that would confer legitimacy on the South and greatly facilitate its move toward independence by opening the door to foreign assistance. Whether intervention took the form of a mediation offer, a call for an armistice, or an outright recognition of nationhood, such foreign involvement would raise the South's status and help determine the war's outcome. Not only would the Confederacy attract greater financial investment at home, but it would gain access to European ports and pocketbooks, and perhaps even negotiate military and commercial alliances. Foreign intervention was particularly perilous to the Union during the first eighteen months of the war, when its verdict hung in the balance.

Several considerations would affect the war's direction. If the conflict became sustained, the North's superior manpower and industrial resources would ultimately prove decisive. Some 22 million people resided in the area above the Mason-Dixon line; only 9 million, including 4 million slaves, lived below. And the North's economic advantages were even more distinct. Besides a great number of shipping and manufacturing concerns,

Abraham Lincoln
Although urged by Republican party members
to declare that the Civil War was over slavery,
he insisted that his objective was to preserve
the Union. *Photo by Lewis E. Walker, ca. 1863;
Library of Congress.*

its agricultural Midwest yielded bountiful supplies of wheat and corn that often made their way into British and other foreign markets. But southerners had stronger and more capable leadership at the outset, and in a short war they would benefit from higher morale (a war for southern independence), a rich military tradition, and a frontier type of existence that better acclimated them to the rigors of army life. Many southerners were hunters who knew the terrain and could fire rifles with considerable skill, and more than a few were trained officers and soldiers. The image of the northerner, so often accurate, was that of a laborer or mechanic who knew little or nothing about guns, military strategy, and battlefield tactics. But these factors were important primarily in a short war. The major hope for the Confederacy lay in using its vast cotton

resources as leverage—"King Cotton Diplomacy"—to win European recognition of its independence and then to secure loans, war materiel, and perhaps even an ally. It was critical to the Union to prevent this catastrophe.

The question of diplomatic recognition by Britain became vital to the war. As that nation went, so would go France and perhaps the rest of the European Continent. The widespread belief among Americans was that the British favored the breakup of the Union as a major step toward their gaining an upper hand in North America. If the United States suffered a mortal blow, Britain could safeguard its holdings in the Western Hemisphere while thankfully witnessing the demise of manifest destiny. Lest there be doubt about the British attitude, Americans found the ultimate proof in the prime minister—the aggressive and saber-rattling Lord Palmerston, who had threatened

Lord Palmerston
British prime minister who thought southern independence a fait accompli. *Massachusetts Historical Society.*

war over the McLeod affair and remained a staunch and outspoken critic of the United States.

Thus, to the Union, British intervention loomed as the most serious danger in foreign affairs. Although the presence of slaves in the South complicated matters for the antislavery British, President Lincoln unintentionally relieved them of that dilemma by denying that slavery bore any relation to the war and arguing instead that his sole purpose was to preserve the Union. What is more, British intervention seemed imminent because of the widely expressed feeling in that country—including among its leaders—that southern separation was a fait accompli. How could the Washington government hope to subjugate a Confederacy so large in both numbers and territory? The Union considered the intervention question so explosive that it warned Britain of war if it extended recognition to the South.

1861: Union Diplomacy

Union diplomacy in the Civil War lay in the hands of the president and his secretary of state, William H. Seward of New York. After their fierce political rivalry at the Republican convention of 1860, Lincoln's invitation to Seward to become secretary of state was almost as surprising as Seward's acceptance. Seward remained a deeply disgruntled, embittered man who believed the presidency rightfully belonged to him and made little effort to hide his feelings. Henry Adams, son and secretary of the Union minister in London, Charles Francis Adams, described Seward as a "slouching, slender figure" with a "head like a wise macaw; a beaked nose, shaggy eyebrows, unorderly hair and clothes; hoarse voice; offhand manner; free talk, and perpetual cigar." Seward regarded Lincoln as a clumsy buffoon who had stolen the nomination and eked out the election in a campaign heralded by divisiveness. Seward had been a frontrunner for the presidency until a statement he had made sometime earlier—that the sections were heading for an "irrepressible conflict"—

William H. Seward
As secretary of state under Lincoln, Seward's major objective was to prevent England from extending recognition to the Confederacy. *National Archives.*

came back to haunt him; but if he could not lead the deeply troubled nation from the highest position in the land, he could occupy the second most important seat as heir apparent to the presidency and act as an English-style prime minister possessing both the power and the will to protect Americans from Lincoln's numerous shortcomings. The president had breathed new life into Seward's political aspirations by appointing him secretary of state; the New Yorker was not about to let the opportunity pass.

Seward's outspoken and brusque manner at first threatened to disqualify him from the position as the president's chief diplomat. Seward had earned his Anglophobe reputation before joining the cabinet. Britons remembered his outspoken anti-British role in the McLeod war scare of 1841, and as recently as 1860 he had thoroughly offended his Atlantic cousins by making derisive remarks to the visiting Duke of Newcastle. Even more disconcerting was Seward's first attempt to win control of the administration's foreign policy and keep Europe out of American affairs. In effect he suggested that the administration resolve the sectional crisis at home by involving the entire nation in a crisis abroad. A hard line by the Lincoln administration, he believed, would rally all Americans around the flag and convince British and other European leaders that intervention on behalf of the Confederacy meant certain war with the Union.

On April 1, 1861, appropriately enough "All Fool's Day," Seward sent the president a memorandum entitled "Some Thoughts for the President's Consideration," which claimed that Lincoln was "without a policy either domestic or foreign" and suggested a way to reunite the Union. As secretary of state, Seward offered to "demand explanations" from France and Spain for interfering in Mexico and Santo Domingo. If their replies were not satisfactory, he would expect Congress to declare war and thereby rouse North *and* South against their common enemy. Although Seward denied interest in leading this policy, he admitted that "I neither seek to evade nor assume responsibility."

Lincoln's response to this preposterous idea received the attention it deserved. He formulated a tactful and private reply to the note that made his opposition clear without embarrassing Seward or driving him from the administration. The president emphasized that whatever policy the administration adopted, "*I* must do it." The suggested ultimatum he ignored, and it quietly died.

The president's problems with his secretary of state did not end with this episode. Late in May Seward prepared a dispatch for London so threatening that Lincoln found it necessary to make revisions before allowing it to leave the country. Seward's missive of May 21 warned of war if Britain recognized

Confederate independence, but the president toned down its impact by directing Charles Francis Adams in England not to give the actual dispatch to his host government but to regard it as only a guide for his behavior.

Seward's initial diplomatic ventures rested on a highly questionable assumption. Although it would have been foolish for a *united* country to foment a war with any or all of the European powers, and although it appeared infinitely unwise for a divided nation to risk such a war, he hoped that the external danger would cause a surge of patriotism that would smooth over internal differences. But, given the intense animosity that had led to such a monumental step as secession, Seward had dangerously underestimated the depth of southern commitment. Lincoln had no assurance against the South's simply signing a peace treaty with any European antagonist and leaving the North to fend for itself.

With these dangerous flirtations behind him, Seward turned to a more reasoned policy that nonetheless carried its own unexpected complications: He advised the president to impose a blockade of the entire southern coast from the Chesapeake Bay to the Rio Grande. On April 19 Lincoln issued a proclamation announcing his intention to do so. Thus, the Union navy of fewer than 100 vessels, two-thirds of which were in need of repairs or were outmoded sailing ships, prepared to close about 185 bays or inlets stretching over 3500 miles of Atlantic and Gulf coastline. Many foreign observers joined the South in calling it a "paper blockade," which was contrary to international law, but as the blockade steadily tightened throughout the war, Union vessels captured or destroyed more than 1500 ships and ultimately seized control of all major Confederate ports. The South urged the British to ignore Union vessels by entering its ports; the British feared a confrontation at sea that could lead to war. They eventually accepted the legality of the blockade when, as British Foreign Secretary Lord John Russell allowed, it posed an "evident danger" to any ships attempting to challenge the Union navy.

Lincoln's blockade proclamation, combined with his increasing references to the South's actions as a rebellion, created a paradox that plagued the administration throughout the war. His declaration of a blockade implied the outbreak of war, which automatically defined both antagonists as belligerents and made it possible, under international law, for neutral nations to trade with North *and* South. Furthermore, even though Lincoln meant rebellion to refer to a purely domestic matter involving the punishment of treason, his use of the term, again under international law, constituted an admission to a southern effort that was more highly organized than a mere insurrection and thereby categorized the Confederacy as a belligerent. Lincoln sought to maintain the fiction that the American conflict was a purely internal proposition. If defined in that manner, the ongoing events in North America would necessarily be of no concern to other nations, and the president could exercise his constitutional powers of restoring domestic order by putting down the rebels. But to do so, he also believed, required the full use of his powers as commander in chief—including the establishment of a blockade. Thus did the president add further complexities to an already confusing situation out of his effort to exhaust all remedies in preserving the Union.

Lincoln had assigned a dual status to the war. On the one hand, as he well knew at the outset of the fighting, the existence of an insurrection permitted him, as president, to put it down under his constitutional duty of guaranteeing a republican form of government throughout the country. On the other hand, his reference to a rebellion implied that the South had resorted to war in an effort to break from the parent state; as commander in chief, he could exercise military powers that included the installation of a blockade. In either case, however, the danger was clear: The South's newly won belligerent status left it barely a step away from nationhood.

The British chose not to exploit this contradiction in Lincoln's dual policy—primarily because of their desire to stay out of the American war by adopting a course of neutrality, but also because the precedent of ignoring a blockade might work against *them* in a future war. Under international law, legally blockaded ports were closed to other nations. Consequently, the Palmerston ministry adhered to international law by interpreting the blockade as affirming the existence of war. On May 13, 1861, the queen announced a neutrality proclamation that set the standard for France and other European governments to follow.

At first glance the British declaration of neutrality took on the appearance of an undisguised act of favor for the South. In accordance with Lincoln's blockade and his use of the term *rebellion*, the British neutrality proclamation confirmed the South's status as a belligerent. Confederate vessels—including privateers that President Jefferson Davis of the Confederacy had offered to commission two days before Lincoln issued the blockade proclamation—could plunder Union merchant vessels and procure goods in neutral ports, and the Confederacy itself could float loans and purchase war materiel in Europe. In addition, British vessels (as neutrals) could challenge the effectiveness of such a sweeping blockade, thereby enhancing the possibility of a confrontation with Union ships that could bring an Anglo-American war and, as a matter of course, southern independence. The British, however, rejected southern calls to ignore the blockade.

Perceptions quickly took precedence over reality, leading the Union to mistakenly denounce the British policy of neutrality as prosouthern. Britain's overriding concern in declaring neutrality was to prohibit its subjects from participating in any activity that might pull their nation into the American conflict; but it also realized that unless the Confederacy were accorded belligerent status, British naval officers would have been bound to treat its privateers as pirates. Union supporters believed, however, that the London government had willfully and maliciously granted belligerent status to the Confederacy as the prelude to recognition of its independence.

Jefferson Davis
President of the Confederate States of America.
National Archives.

London's policy seemed to highlight pro-South sympathies in Britain, encouraging both northerners and southerners to believe that formal British recognition would soon follow. Yet the truth is that British neutrality actually worked to the Union's advantage by adding credence and authority to the blockade and providing an opportunity for superior northern resources to take their toll on the South. Moreover, the furor in the North over the British stance caused the London government to exercise even greater care in its relations with the Union. But these considerations did not enter the Union's calculations in 1861. Northerners condemned Britain's neutrality proclamation as a spiteful and hostile attempt to undermine the Union.

Seward tried to rectify the dangerous situation. He realized that after the Crimean War the Declaration of Paris of 1856 had, among other things, abolished privateering; he also knew that the United States had turned down an invitation to join Britain and more than forty other nations in signing the pact. Before the Civil War the Washington government approved privateering because the practice benefited small-navy nations like the United States. In addition, the other features of the declaration fitted U.S. ideas of maritime rights advocated since the Revolution: "free ships, free goods" (no confiscation of any cargo on neutral or belligerent vessels except contraband) and no paper blockades. But these attractive maritime guarantees had not been sufficient to compensate for the provision against privateering. Now, however, Seward saw an advantage in accepting the prohibition against privateering. He suggested to the British minister in Washington, Lord Lyons, that he would initial the Declaration of Paris if the United States could seize all belligerent goods at sea, including those of a *non*contraband nature.

Lyons was dubious about the offer—and with good reason. Not only would the unrestricted seizure of goods invite trouble, but Lincoln's rejection of secession left the Union intact and made the South's use of privateers an act of piracy. Accordingly, all signatories of the Paris pact—including England—would become silent partners of the North by bearing the responsibility of enforcing its provisions against the South. Furthermore, the police action afforded by the European powers would free the Union to enforce its blockade—against those very same European powers. Dismissing Seward's proposal as "rather amusing," Lyons advised Russell in London to turn it down. In the meantime Lyons asked Seward whether his government had the capacity to make the South comply with a new policy against privateering. Seward blandly responded that southerners would adhere to the Declaration of Paris because they were part of the United States. Lyons looked quizzically at Seward and made a comment that laid bare the inconsistencies in the Union's maritime policy: "Very well. If they are not independent then the President's proclamation of

Lord Lyons
As British minister to the United States, he felt certain that Seward would advocate a war with Britain if it recognized the Confederacy. *Lord Newton, Lord Lyons: A Record of British Diplomacy, 2 vols., London: Edward Arnold, 1913, 1: frontispiece.*

blockade is not binding. A blockade, according to the convention, applies only to two nations at war."

Lyons could not overlook the incongruities in the Union's policy because of the potential damaging impact of the blockade on his nation's trade and maritime rights in general. Lyons's behavior infuriated Seward. "Europe must interpret the law our way or we'll declare war," the secretary of state stormed at him. We will "commission enough privateers to prey on English commerce on every sea." This was a bluff, and Lyons knew it. The Confederacy had a coastline impossible to seal off. The Union navy was under the able leadership of Secretary of the Navy Gideon Welles, but even he was unable to perform miracles with

a mere forty-two seaworthy warships—only eight of which were in American waters when the war began. When Seward's request for conditional adherence to the Declaration of Paris arrived in London, Russell approved, but with the important stipulation that this would not "have any bearing . . . on the internal differences now prevailing in the United States." In other words, the prohibition against privateering would not apply to the present war. As events turned out, the Confederacy had little success in privateering because the European governments soon prohibited the entry of captured ships and their prizes.

The Union's major legal means for enforcing the blockade was to invoke the doctrine of "continuous voyage" in determining whether a ship's cargo was subject to seizure. Under this argument, which the British established in the *Essex* case of 1805 and used against the United States in the Napoleonic Wars, the Union could seize vessels entering any neutral port if it decided that the ultimate destination of their cargo was the Confederacy. Thus, British ships en route to Nassau, Bermuda, and Havana were open to capture, and, in fact, Union ships on numerous occasions seized British vessels or confiscated their cargoes.

The most celebrated case involved the privately owned British steamship *Peterhoff.* In 1863 a Union cruiser seized the *Peterhoff* near the Danish West Indies and charged the captain with engaging in a continuous voyage to the Confederacy, even though he had already unloaded his cargo of military supplies at Matamoros on the Mexican side of the Rio Grande and the goods were to go overland to the Confederacy. Indeed, the South had come to rely on Matamoros as a trading center for marketing cotton in exchange for contraband. The U.S. Supreme Court eventually supported the Lincoln administration's stand, although ruling in 1866 that only the contraband (and not the vessel itself) was subject to capture: The noncontraband goods were sanctified because they were to have gone from a port not located within the blockade limits (Matamoros) and by land to the Confederacy.

Yet the court added that if the ship's owners had been in collusion with the subterfuge, the *Peterhoff* itself would also have been a suitable prize. After the war, in the cases of the *Bermuda* in 1865 and the *Springbok* of the following year, the court approved Union confiscation of the vessels because their final destination was a Confederate port.

Perhaps surprisingly, the British Foreign Office never lodged a formal protest against the Union's use of continuous voyage doctrine. Although numerous British observers joined several prominent European jurists in complaining about the practice, the London government took the longer view. As a maritime nation, the role of precedent was critical to Britain's livelihood. Palmerston and his colleagues were satisfied that the United States supported a doctrine beneficial to belligerents seeking control of the seas.

Lincoln knew that the Union's success depended heavily on Britain's attitude; and he also realized that the question of slavery would determine a large measure of that British attitude. The British press had initially supported the Union in the war because its only purpose (or so it seemed from 3000 miles away) could be to stamp out slavery. But regardless of Lincoln's personal repugnance toward the peculiar institution, he repeatedly insisted that his prime goal was to preserve the Union. In his inaugural address he had expressed the will of his Republican party in declaring that "I have no purpose, directly, to interfere with the institution of slavery in the States where it exists." Lincoln realized that the law was on the side

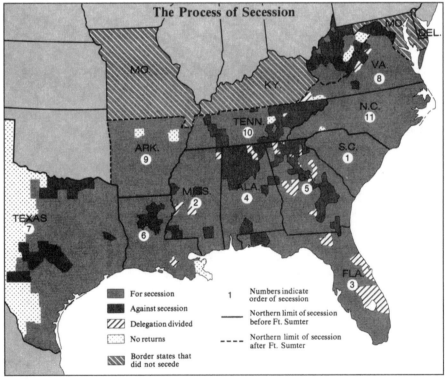

Map 15
One reason why Lincoln refused to declare slavery as the reason for the war was the certainty of driving the border states (slave states that had not seceded) into the Confederacy.

of slave owners and chose instead to undermine the institution by blocking its spread into new territories and bringing about its "ultimate extinction." His central concern, as emphasized in the address, was to establish that "no State, upon its own mere motion, can lawfully get out of the Union."

Political realities, of course, played a large role in Lincoln's public stance on slavery. He knew that a war to end slavery might give victory to the Confederacy by alienating Unionists in the South and causing the secession of the border slave states of Maryland, Kentucky, Missouri, and Delaware. He also realized that strong anti-black sentiment in the North would prevent most of his countrymen from taking up arms against slavery. Yet Lincoln also regarded the issues of slavery and Union as inseparable: Union victory depended on resolving *all* issues threatening its existence. But the resolution of the slavery issue, Lincoln believed, could not come through abolition without incurring enormous physical and material costs. Nor was the matter open to the suggestion of Russell and others in London— that the Union permit the South to establish its own slave nation and allow the existence of free territory on all sides to bring about slavery's eventual demise. The British failed to understand Lincoln's precarious political position. When he called only for the preservation of the Union, they insisted that the South's cry for independence was morally defensible.

In France, Napoleon III saw numerous advantages resulting from a permanently divided America but was reluctant to take any action without a British initiative. The emperor hoped to achieve his ancestors' dream of reestablishing a French empire in the New World, and in October 1861 he proposed joint mediation of the war, a move motivated by his designs toward tipping the outcome to the Confederacy and, as a result of winning its favor, implanting French colors in strife-torn Mexico. The French people supported Napoleon's mediation suggestion, although for different reasons. Textile workers needed southern cotton, although not at the cost of conflict. The upper classes detested American democracy and, like the English, identified more with southern aristocracy. Although working classes and liberals opposed slavery and favored the Union's republicanism, they had no influence on the French government. Napoleon later welcomed the Confederate minister, but kept the Union representative at a distance. He also permitted French shipbuilding firms to construct and arm vessels for the South, although these efforts did not work out. Mediation seemed the desirable course, but Napoleon realized that success in that endeavor depended on the London government taking the lead.

1861: Confederate Diplomacy

The South was greatly encouraged by Britain's view of the war as a struggle for independence against northern aggression, and not as a war for slavery. Confederate propagandists worked in England to dismiss slavery as an issue and to convince the upper classes that the South's only objective was freedom and that its cotton resources were vital to their country's textile industries. Ironically, Britons compared the North to the British empire under King George III and the South to the American colonies in 1776. The failure of English liberals to understand that a Union victory would necessarily mean the end of slavery perplexed and infuriated American antislavery proponents who wished Lincoln would make plain the inescapable outcome of the conflict. When both the *Times* and *Punch* of London reflected upper-class sentiment and blasted Lincoln and the North, the Anglophobic *New York Herald* led the counterattack in a bitter newspaper exchange that intensified Anglo-American animosities but did nothing to allay the prevailing British feeling that southern independence was inevitable.

Palmerston and Russell exemplified the upper-class belief that a lengthy war meant the senseless destruction of life and property. Many of society's leaders found nobility in the southern aristocracy and considered Davis a gentleman in the British tradition and Lincoln the uncivilized product of a degenerating democratic North. "Wonder to relate," a writer with the *Times* noted after an interview with Davis; "he does not chew and is neat and clean-looking, with hair trimmed, and boots brushed." But in the person of Lincoln, the predicted results of mob rule in the United States had reached fulfillment: The experiment in republicanism had sunk into chaos and spewed forth one of its own—a gangly, ax-swinging rube who had risen from the Illinois prairies to determine the destinies of millions of mediocre Americans like him.

Britons thought the sheer size of the United States proved its greatest enemy, because they believed that expanding republics faltered in proportion to the amount of freedom awarded their citizenry. Thus, the prospect of Lincoln's success in the war was unsettling. Many in England were concerned about rising popular demands for democratic changes at home and feared that Union victory could set a dangerous example that might heighten these demands and lead to anarchy.

Admittedly, in the first stages of the war, government leaders in London saw practical benefits stemming from a southern victory that divided the American empire. Russia's ambassador in London explained in 1861 that "the English Government, at the bottom of its heart, desires the separation of North America into two republics, which will watch each other jealously and counterbalance one the other. Then England . . . would have nothing to fear from either; for she would dominate them, restraining them by their rival ambitions." Palmerston realized that the existence of two American countries would reduce commercial competition, diminish the U.S. threat to Canada and other British holdings in the New World, and frustrate manifest destiny. In early 1861 the U.S. Congress had passed the Morrill Tariff, which raised duties and seemed indicative of further moves toward protectionism. British free traders thought that Congress had aimed the bill at them and looked to

the advantages of having a southern agricultural nation without tariff walls. They realized that nearly 80 percent of the cotton in their textile mills came from the South. The Civil War provided an opportunity for Britain to spread its influence in the Americas.

Britain's reaction to the Civil War was thus mixed, but as the hard reality of the war sank in, most groups opposed intervention on behalf of the South and favored neutrality. Conservatives believed that Lincoln stood on the side of stability and order and that it was not politic to support a government built on insurrection. Reformers John Bright and Richard Cobden were among a few who recognized that Union victory would, as a matter of course, end slavery. Bright declared in Birmingham, England, in December 1862, "I blame men who are eager to admit into the family of nations a State which offers itself to us, based on a principle . . . more odious and more blasphemous than was ever heretofore dreamed of." He continued: "The leaders of this revolt propose this monstrous thing— that, over a territory forty times as large as England, the blight and curse of slavery shall be forever perpetuated." Some British merchants wanted to stay out of the conflict because northern privateers would raid their ships; but, in a significant and far-reaching development, increasing numbers gradually began to realize that a protracted war between North and South would seriously damage Britain's main commercial rival and that Anglo-American trade would gain more from a Union intact than from one mortally divided. Another large group favoring neutrality was the working class. These people were aware of the morbid descriptions of slavery found in Harriet Beecher Stowe's best-selling novel *Uncle Tom's Cabin* and resolved that if the Union freed the slaves, the example would benefit all labor groups. The North took on the image of an egalitarian democracy; the South appeared to be a closed society built on white wealth and black labor.

Confederate diplomats in Europe found that despite their best efforts to sidestep the issue, slavery severely hampered their attempt to win recognition. Indeed, the British had abolished slavery in the empire almost three decades before the Civil War. The South tried to play down the subject of slavery, but it could not hide public statements made by its spokesmen. In March 1861 the vice president of the Confederacy, Alexander Stephens, proclaimed in Savannah that slavery had caused "the late rupture and present revolution." The Confederate government, he continued, rested "upon the great truth that the Negro is not equal to the white man; that slavery, subordination to the superior race, is his natural and moral condition." When Lincoln declared that the war was to preserve the Union, Britons who favored the South could remain in that camp; but if the president changed the war's purpose to destroy slavery, these same people would have to decide whether they could favor a society whose very cornerstone was the peculiar institution.

The South pinned its hopes for British recognition on King Cotton Diplomacy, or the threatened withdrawal of the product as economic pressure to achieve Confederate aims. As early as 1858 Senator James Hammond of South Carolina had declared that if Britain was denied the South's cotton, it "would topple headlong and carry the whole civilized world with her, save the South. No, you dare not make war on cotton. No power on earth dares to make war upon it. Cotton is king!" In June 1861 the Charleston *Mercury* exalted cotton as the key to Confederate victory: "The cards are in our hands! and we intend to play them out to the bankruptcy of every cotton factory in Great Britain and France or the acknowledgment of our independence." The logic seemed impeccable. Nearly one-fifth of the British people drew their livelihoods from textile production, and the great bulk of their cotton came from the South. By 1860 the British received almost 2 million bales a year. Any obstruction to this flow, the South thought, had the potential of affecting about 5 million British subjects in a business that held up an empire.

The South's reliance on cotton diplomacy set off a flurry of activity abroad. In March 1861 President Davis sent three unofficial agents to Europe to seek recognition, float loans, circulate propaganda, and purchase ships and goods. Their *quid pro quo* was tariff-free trade with the South and the assurance of broadened European economic influence in the New World. The Palmerston ministry's reaction was reserved, because it had already decided to stay out of American affairs and allow the war to render its own verdict. Lyons in Washington advised his home government to grant only an informal audience to the Confederate ministers. "I shall see the Southerners when they come," Russell replied, "but not officially, and keep them at a proper distance."

News of the Confederate commissioners' presence in Europe led Seward to send the prominent Massachusetts lawyer and congressman Charles Francis Adams as Union minister to London. This was a master stroke, for this descendant of two presidents was a learned and cultured gentleman who was calm in demeanor and gifted in the art of diplomacy. Adams had been educated in an English public school and was so British in manner that he was able to mingle socially with Russell and others. Adams's appointment served to balance Seward's hot temperament and thereby defuse many Anglo-American problems.

Adams's work was ready for him when he arrived in London on May 13, 1861. That same day the queen had announced neutrality, which caused him to fear that this admission to the South's belligerent status was the prelude to recognizing its independence. The British government had not authorized the sale of military goods or the fitting of privateers, but these developments now seemed likely. Russell was evasive when Adams tried to discern how much influence the Confederate emissaries had won in England, but he avoided the temptation to break diplomatic relations. The British, after all, had not extended recognition to the South. And, Adams knew, war with Britain could prove fatal to the Union.

Charles Francis Adams
As Union minister to England during the Civil War, Adams's most difficult task was to prevent British recognition of the Confederacy. *Massachusetts Historical Society.*

Trent Affair

The Confederates' hopes for victory jumped dramatically in July 1861 after they routed Union forces at the Battle of Bull Run (Manassas Junction) in Virginia. Indeed, news from the battlefield seemingly ensured British recognition of the South. Whereas Palmerston and others in England regarded what they snidely called the "Bull's Run Races" and "Yankee's Run" as further proof of the irrevocable nature of southern separation, those who had been studied skeptics suddenly became exuberant believers.

The ramifications of this first pitched battle of the Civil War were instantaneous and far-reaching. The head of President Davis's secret-service operations in Europe, James D. Bulloch, found a welcome hearing in England when he sought contracts with private firms for building a Confederate navy. Davis acted quickly to take advantage of the Confederacy's favor. To win European recognition and disavowal of the Union blockade, he dispatched James Mason of Virginia as minister to England and John Slidell of Louisiana as minister to France. Mason was colorful and controversial. He had served as senator a decade earlier and had infuriated northerners by writing the Fugitive Slave Law of 1850 and staunchly supporting the Kansas-Nebraska Act of four years afterward. While minister to England, however, he would not leave a good impression. Often chewing tobacco during heated debates in the House of Commons, he spit the juice across the carpet, only some of which reached the cuspidor. Slidell also was well-known: He had called for war with Mexico as Polk's envoy to that country during the tumultuous days of late 1845, and he had earned a reputation as one of the most rabid secessionists in Congress on the eve of South Carolina's announced departure from the Union.

Now, in mid-October 1861, Mason and Slidell slipped through the blockade at Charleston and headed for Havana, where they transferred to the British steamship *Trent*, expecting to board another steamer at St. Thomas and then enjoy safe passage to Europe under neutral colors.

Meanwhile, Captain Charles Wilkes of the U.S. Navy, already renowned for his reports on Oregon, waited aboard his U.S.S. *San Jacinto* outside Cuban waters. *Without orders from Washington,* he stopped the *Trent* in the Bahama channel on November 8, after firing two warning shots across its bow. He sent an officer aboard for Mason and Slidell, who Wilkes claimed were the "embodiment of dispatches" (contraband) and therefore traitors to the United States. Mason and Slidell refused to leave the ship, and Wilkes ordered a small detachment of marines to remove them. As they seized Mason in his cabin, Slidell tried to squeeze through a porthole in his quarters and likewise was captured. Wilkes allowed the *Trent* to resume its voyage to England but

British H.M.S. Trent *and U.S.S.* San Jacinto
According to numerous historians, this encounter
in the Bahamas came closer than any other
incident during the Civil War to causing war
between the Union and Britain. *National
Archives.*

not an enemy port. But Wilkes's rash and
unauthorized behavior would soon cause
great trouble. Had he searched the *Trent,* he
might have discovered that Mason had collaborated with the British commander in hiding the Confederate mail packet from the
boarding party; the British vessel would have
lost its neutral status and become subject to
capture and adjudication before a prize court.
The entire episode was fraught with legal difficulties, but these were of no consequence to
northerners who were frustrated with the war
and regarded Wilkes's behavior as a welcome
reassertion of U.S. honor at home and abroad.
The governor of Massachusetts triumphantly
declared that Wilkes had "fired his shot across
the bows of the ship that bore the British lion
at its head." Banquets were held in his honor,

took the two captives and their two secretaries
on board the *San Jacinto,* where he gave them
his cabin and welcomed them to his table for
meals. A week later the *San Jacinto* arrived
at Fortress Monroe in Virginia, and Union
forces transferred the captives to Fort Warren
in Boston.

Northerners at first wildly rejoiced at
the news, boasting that Wilkes had not only
avenged the disaster at Bull Run but in the
process had righted a long succession of British
wrongs at sea. To them, it mattered little that
Wilkes had violated international law by removing Mason and Slidell: Never had any admiralty court interpreted human beings as
contraband, and the vessel's destination was

Captain Charles Wilkes of the Union Navy
As commander of the *San Jacinto,* he fomented a
war scare between the Atlantic nations by acting
without Washington's orders in seizing two
Confederate emissaries from the British steamer
Trent in November 1861. *Library of Congress.*

the *New York Times* suggested setting aside another Fourth of July commemoration, the secretary of the navy rewarded him with a promotion and special praise, and the House of Representatives voted him a gold medal.

In Britain the response to the *Trent* affair unleashed a storm of criticism focusing on a flagrant violation of national honor. The stock market plunged as the English accused Seward of trying to instigate a war. "Good God," Henry Adams wrote his brother in Massachusetts. Wilkes had committed the same horrendous maritime sins that England had long practiced. "What's got into you all? What do you mean by deserting now the great principles of our fathers, by returning to the vomit of that dog Great Britain?" War seemed certain, Adams believed. Indeed, Palmerston

John Slidell
Also seized from the British *Trent,* he was a fervent supporter of southern independence while in Congress on the eve of secession. *National Archives.*

opened an emergency cabinet meeting with a near call to arms: "I don't know whether you are going to stand this, but I'll be damned if I do!" The following day the cabinet recommended that Lyons make three demands: reparations, the immediate release of Mason and Slidell, and a formal apology "for the insult offered to the British flag." In an ominous series of moves, the government put the navy on alert, readied military supply operations, and sent 11,000 troops to Canada, who left England to the sound of a band playing "Dixie." Russell prepared to direct Lyons to set a seven-day deadline on the demands; if not met, the minister was to break relations and return home.

These harsh words might have brought the nations to war had it not been for a timely

James Mason
Seized from the British *Trent,* he was despised by northerners for sponsoring the Fugitive Slave Law in 1850. *National Archives.*

problem in communications. The Atlantic cable that had been laid in the late 1850s was not working, and it took nearly two weeks for news to travel between England and the United States. British officials did not know whether the United States had retreated on the matter and did not want to see war develop if it had. The British note did not arrive in Washington until a month after Americans learned of the *Trent.* Delays on both sides of the Atlantic in receiving news of the *Trent* episode allowed emotions to peak and then cool. The chair of the Senate Foreign Relations Committee, Charles Sumner, recognized the potential disaster awaiting the Union and called on the Lincoln administration to free the two Confederate ministers.

The president was in an unenviable position. Compliance with British demands could undermine the already waning support for his government; refusal could bring war with England and a certain end to the Union. Lincoln searched for a middle ground. Seizure of the *Trent,* he knew, had been a welcome corrective for the widespread despair resulting from Bull Run and, used carefully, might serve to warn the British that recognition of the Confederacy could mean war with the Union. He was hesitant to throw away such a potent remedy without examining all factors involved.

In the meantime Prince Albert, who was the queen's consort, searched for an honorable way out of the crisis. Opposing war, he rose from his sickbed to tone down Russell's ultimatum: Lyons was to *ask* about the *Trent* matter and seek reparations. He also told Lyons to accept an explanation rather than demand an apology. Most important, Lyons was to give the United States a face-saving way out of the crisis by allowing its government to reply that Wilkes had acted without orders, "or, if he did, that he misapprehended them." When the revised instructions reached Lyons, he learned that he was "to abstain from anything like menace" when seeking the men's release and "to be rather easy about the apology." The seven-day deadline remained, however, and if the United States refused to comply, Lyons was to break diplomatic relations and return home—but *without* warning of war. As fate would have it, Prince Albert passed away in mid-December 1861, leading to nationwide mourning and allowing further time to defuse the dangerous situation.

On December 19 Seward received the note from Lyons on an informal basis (therefore gaining some time before the seven-day clock began to run) and delivered it to Lincoln for a decision. The first public outburst of satisfaction over Wilkes's actions had proved to be the last, and many influential northerners were now calling on the administration to release Mason and Slidell and grant reparations and an apology. In addition, spokesmen from France, Italy, Prussia, Denmark, and Russia recognized that the *Trent* precedent would endanger *all* vessels at sea and condemned the U.S. action as wrong. Charles Francis Adams in London assured his home government that Palmerston's ministry would not retreat from its demands, and the French minister in Washington reiterated his government's position that it would not oppose Britain's stand in the crisis. On Christmas Day Lincoln's cabinet met and was unable to resolve the matter, but the following day it reached a unanimous decision. Lincoln summed up the administration's position when he commented, "One war at a time." He instructed Seward to tell Lyons that Wilkes had the right to search the *Trent* "as a simple, legal and customary belligerent proceeding," but his failure to take the captured ship as a prize necessitated the prisoners' release.

That same day Seward presented the note to Lyons and then publicized his reply in the press, explaining to the American people that the United States had won a major diplomatic victory because Britain had finally recognized the maritime rights that Americans had fought for during the War of 1812. He declared that Wilkes had acted correctly in searching the *Trent,* but he then added an argument not substantiated in international law: The seizure of Mason and Slidell, Seward asserted, was justified because "persons, as well as property, may become contraband." Although Wilkes had failed to take the *Trent* before a prize court for adjudication, he brought attention to a welcome change in British maritime policy that constituted a major advance for free-trade nations like the United States that sought to protect the rights of neutrals. "If I decide this case in favor of my own government," Seward explained, "I must disavow its most cherished principles, and reverse and forever abandon its essential policy." Yet, he added, "If I maintain those principles, and adhere to that policy, I must surrender the case itself. . . . We are asked to do to the British nation just what we have always insisted all nations ought to do to us." Seward concluded that surrender of the men, who after all were of "comparative unimportance," would have no impact on the "waning proportions of the existing insurrection." The Lincoln administration had escaped a highly volatile situation and at the same time left the erroneous impression of having gained a U.S. victory at sea by insisting that the *Trent* outcome had safeguarded the nation from maritime actions (including impressment) that violated the grand principle of freedom of seas.

Seward's highly convoluted note on the *Trent* achieved its purpose of averting a conflict with Britain. It received a favorable reception in the North, but not from either London's leaders or southerners and their sympathizers. Russell called it a victory for Britain because Mason and Slidell won their freedom, but he cautioned that he did not approve Seward's argument. Spokesmen for the Confederacy complained that the British had failed to intervene and now considered Russell "an avowed enemy." Seward's earlier belligerent style of diplomacy had been risky because it convinced Lyons that the United States wanted to instigate a war; in the end it eased relations between the Union and Britain while allowing *both* governments to claim victory.

A third and critical message became clear: The outcome of the *Trent* affair signaled a warning that the Palmerston ministry intended to remain neutral, a stand that satisfied neither the Confederacy nor the Union. According

to the Confederate agent in England, Henry Hotze, the crisis had actually hurt the southern cause by permitting the British government to claim a major diplomatic victory and become less subject to popular pressure for intervention. Charles Francis Adams offered the same observation, though adding a word of caution. The ministry, he wrote Seward, had gained a much stronger position at home, making it critical that the Union avoid any issue that might provide the British a pretext to exploit America's domestic problems. Britain, Adams warned a friend, would continue to "sit as a cold spectator, ready to make the best of our calamity the moment there is a sufficient excuse to interfere." No other Anglo-American event had had such potential for war, and yet Britain maintained neutrality and let the trouble blow over.

The Crisis over Intervention: 1862

On the Union's military front 1862 started well. General Ulysses S. Grant took Forts Donelson and Henry in Tennessee, and New Orleans fell to Commodore David G. Farragut, thereby exposing the Mississippi River to northern control and threatening to separate the West from the rest of the Confederacy. In the East the Union blockade steadily tightened, and a well-publicized assault on Richmond began under the all-too-careful and plodding leadership of General George B. McClellan.

Internationally, developments were mixed. Despite high hopes, King Cotton Diplomacy was proving to be a dismal failure. Confederate leaders had not been aware of the huge reserves of cotton that Britain had when the war started, thanks to record southern crops during the three preceding years. Indeed, Britain's overproduction of textiles had resulted in the closing of many factories and the unemployment of thousands of mill workers. In a desperate effort to create a shortage in England, the South destroyed or embargoed 2.5 million bales of cotton. But the Union countered by sending confiscated cotton to

Liverpool, and in 1862 British manufacturers bought enough from Egypt and India to tide them through most of the year.

The Confederacy's chances, however, seemed good in another realm of foreign affairs: Its agents contracted the building of ships in England that could run the Union blockade and deliver war materiel from Europe. Steamers had repeatedly made it through Union patrols during the first year of the war, but their effectiveness declined with the tightening blockade. Besides, those vessels that made it past Union cruisers often carried luxury goods rather than war materiel, which drained money from the South without filling military needs. But British shipbuilders were favorable to the Confederacy's requests. Although they faced a legal obstacle—the British Foreign Enlistment Act of 1819 made it unlawful to "equip, fit out, or arm in British jurisdiction a ship whose intent is to cruise against the commerce of a friendly power"—they found it easy to circumvent the law by not arming the vessels in England. The ship-building firm simply classified vessels under construction as cargo carriers, and upon departure from British waters they entered either the Bahamas or the Azores, where other steamers waited with guns, crews, and officers.

The Lincoln administration regarded the British stance on Confederate ship-building activities as a violation of neutrality. International law contained no provisions governing a neutral's building of ships and what happened to them, but the United States's experiences during the Canadian rebellions of the 1830s and its interactions with Spain and Mexico during the border problems of the first half of the nineteenth century caused the Washington government to set high standards for Britain's behavior. In London, Adams vigorously protested the masquerade by which British firms supplied the South with warships, but Russell insisted that he was powerless because the businesses involved were not breaking the law. Should the government seize the vessels, he declared, the courts would uphold the companies.

Confederate agent James G. Bulloch contracted for the building of two ships listed as the *Oreto* and *Enrica,* which later became famous under their Confederate names of *Florida* and *Alabama.* Adams had hotly protested the *Florida*'s departure from Britain, and he was likewise unsuccessful in urging Russell to hold the *Alabama,* then under construction. Adams had gathered strong testimony that the ship-building firm involved in the enterprise, Laird Brothers of Birkenhead near Liverpool, was under Confederate contract. No one could doubt the *Alabama*'s destination: Work crews had cut placements in the sides for cannon. But by the time Adams convinced Russell that the vessel was to be a Confederate raider, it was too late. In the latter part of July Bulloch and others involved in the *Alabama*'s construction staged a well-executed ruse: They announced that they were taking the ship with its passengers on a test run down the river. But when the ship reached the Atlantic, the passengers were removed to a tugboat just before the *Alabama* slipped out to sea and on to Portugal's Azores Islands. There, under Bulloch's arrangements, it was fitted with guns and war materiel, along with a crew and officers recruited from England, who arrived on board two other ships.

These and other vessels built in Britain wreaked havoc on Union ships. The *Florida,* equipped and armed in the Bahamas, took more than forty ships before being sunk off the Brazilian coast by a Union warship in October 1864. The *Alabama* began its deadly operations in August 1862, and before its sinking two years later by a Union ship-of-war near France, it inflicted more damage on the North than did any other vessel. The *Alabama* sent nineteen Union merchantmen to the bottom within three months, took fifty-seven prizes, and allowed many others to go only on bond. In addition to the work of the *Florida* and the *Alabama,* the *Shenandoah* took forty prizes in the Pacific after its purchase from British owners and damaged numerous whalers from New England—even after the war was over. (News of the Confederate defeat had not reached the

C.S.S. Alabama
Sinking of the *Alabama* by the U.S.S. *Kearsarge* off Cherbourg, France, in the English Channel on June 19, 1864. *Library of Congress.*

ship's officers before these encounters.) Adams objected to the hospitality shown in British ports toward these vessels, but the *Shenandoah* received repairs, supplies, and crew members in Melbourne, Australia, despite vehement complaints from the U.S. consul.

All told, English-built Confederate ships damaged or destroyed nearly 250 Union vessels and were responsible for soaring insurance rates that drove many merchants out of business. Enormous pressure from the Union ultimately caused the Palmerston ministry to change its policy—but not until the spring of 1863. At that time the British government seized the *Alexandra,* another warship headed for the Confederacy. The government failed to

prove its case in court and had to pay damages, but the length of the proceedings prevented the South from using the ship to advantage when it did arrive.

Meanwhile, the fighting in America seemed to be tipping in the South's favor. In early March 1862, the Union's *Monitor* fought the South's *Merrimack* to a standstill in the "battle of the ironclads" at Hampton Roads, Virginia, but McClellan's drive toward Richmond sputtered to a halt in July. Confederate General Robert E. Lee followed with a second victory for the South at Bull Run and by autumn had prepared to invade the North.

In these circumstances many Britons concluded that the war had become a blood bath

General George B. McClellan
According to Lincoln, McClellan had "the slows."
National Archives.

lar pressure grew in Britain for diplomatic recognition. The *Times* of London declared that "the time is approaching when Europe will have to think seriously of its relations to the two belligerents. . . . That North and South must now choose between separation and ruin, material and political, is the opinion of nearly everyone who, looking impartially and from a distance on the conflict, sees what is hidden from the frenzied eyes of the Northern politicians." The British were also beginning to need cotton, and threats of violence by unemployed textile workers in Lancashire drove the ministry into action. Russell agreed with the move for mediation and recommended that "in the case of failure, we ought ourselves to recognize the Southern States as an independent State."

But difficulties developed that temporarily derailed the mediation effort. Napoleon III could not join the venture because of internal problems caused by his recent military intervention in Mexico and by his emerging troubles in Italy. Russia was not a possible alternative partner in the mediation move. Bitterness lingered over its recent defeat at the hands of Britain and France during the Crimean War. Besides, Czar Alexander II admired Lincoln and openly supported the Union, a stand that resulted in part from the United States's support during the Crimean War.

The final consideration in the British ministry's thinking was the news that reached London in late September of Lee's bold raid into Maryland. Palmerston recommended waiting for the outcome: "It is evident," he wrote Russell, "that a great conflict is taking place to the north-west of Washington, and its issue must have a great effect on the state of affairs." If the Union suffered "a great defeat they may be at once ready for mediation, and the Iron should be struck while it is hot. If, on the other hand, they should have the best of it, we may wait awhile and see what may follow."

Palmerston's caution proved well-founded. At Antietam Creek near Sharpsburg, Maryland, McClellan's Union forces drove back the Confederate army in the war's bloodiest day of fighting. The South's stock seemed to

and that it was time to intervene to stop the fighting and persuade the Union to accept the existence of a southern nation. The London *Morning Herald* launched a broad appeal to its readers: "Let us do something, as we are Christian men." To "stop this carnage," some action was needed, whether it be "arbitration, intervention, diplomatic action, recognition of the South, remonstrance with the North, friendly interference or forcible pressure of some sort." In mid-September 1862 Palmerston concluded that the Union had experienced "a very complete smashing" at Second Bull Run and suggested to Russell that Britain and France offer to mediate "on the basis of a separation." If the offer were refused, the prime minister insisted, the two nations should "acknowledge the independence of the South as an established fact."

Second Bull Run seemed to confirm the South's ability to stand on its own, and popu-

plummet, but the truth was otherwise. Whereas Lee's retreat into Virginia convinced many in Britain that recognition of the Confederacy would be ill-advised, the massive bloodbath at Antietam actually *strengthened* the call among numerous other Britons who demanded an intervention that would simply bring an end to what many regarded as a stalemated war of atrocity. Contrary to traditional belief, the narrow Union victory at Antietam did not quiet the move for foreign intervention. Rather, the horrors of the battle had combined with the unending nature of the war to *heighten* the push for British mediation— preferably in the form of an armistice followed by a negotiated peace.

In Washington, President Lincoln could not have known of the surging call in England for mediation, and he followed the Union victory at Antietam with what he thought (erroneously) would be the final blow to any further thoughts of foreign intervention in the war: the Emancipation Proclamation. He had been wrestling with the dilemma of how much longer he could ignore the slaves in the border states while fighting the slave-owning Confederacy. In the summer of 1862 word arrived that slave holders in these states did not favor his suggestion of compensated liberation, and he decided to go before his cabinet in July with the draft of a proclamation of emancipation. Most members supported the idea, but Seward, known for his antislavery views before the war, argued that its announcement would have greater impact if the administration awaited a more propitious time. Such a proclamation should be "borne on the bayonets of an advancing army, not dragged in the dust behind a retreating one." Seward did not want to leave the appearance that the Union supported emancipation only as a last-ditch effort to win the war by instigating a slave uprising that would destroy the South from within. The president agreed to wait for a northern victory.

In September 1862 the outcome at Antietam provided Lincoln with what he labeled a Union triumph. It is debatable whether either

General Robert E. Lee
Lee's victory at Second Bull Run (or Manassas) in late August 1862 provided a great impetus to British recognition of southern independence. *Library of Congress.*

side actually emerged victorious, except that Lee's retreat into Virginia left the Union in control of the field and gave the impression of Confederate defeat. This was enough for the president. Within a week he released a preliminary proclamation of emancipation declaring that on January 1, 1863, all slaves in areas still in rebellion against the United States were "forever free." Thus, he skirted a clash with the border states by exempting them from the proclamation. What is more, the proclamation did not apply to the areas in the Confederacy already brought under Union control. Emancipation, he insisted, was a "military necessity" that fell under the auspices of his powers as commander in chief to adopt whatever measures were necessary to win the war.

Initially, the measure satisfied hardly anyone. Southerners denounced it as a desperate

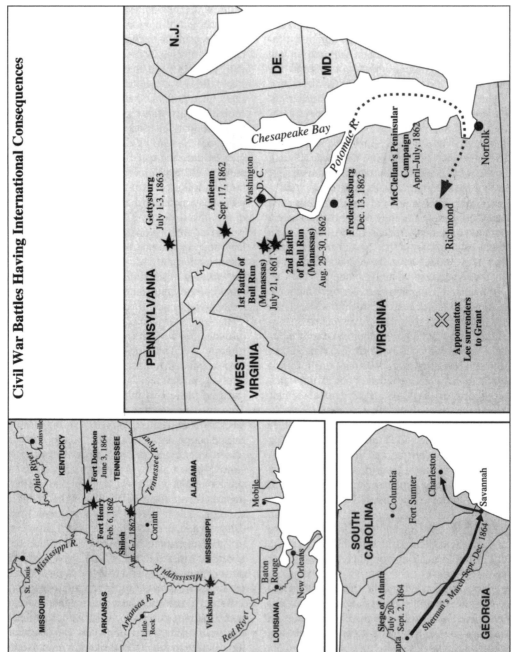

Civil War Battles Having International Consequences

Virginia/Maryland area map

N.J.

DE.

MD.

Chesapeake Bay

Potomac R.

PENNSYLVANIA

Gettysburg
July 1-3, 1863

Antietam
Sept. 17, 1862

Washington
D. C.

1st Battle of
Bull Run
(Manassas)
July 21, 1861

2nd Battle
of Bull Run
(Manassas)
Aug. 29–30, 1862

Fredericksburg
Dec. 13, 1862

McClellan's Peninsular
Campaign
April–July, 1862

Richmond

Norfolk

WEST
VIRGINIA

VIRGINIA

Appomattox
Lee surrenders
to Grant

Mississippi/Tennessee area map

St. Louis

Ohio River

Louisville

Mississippi R.

KENTUCKY

Fort Donelson
June 3, 1864

TENNESSEE

Tennessee River

MISSOURI

ARKANSAS

Fort Henry
Feb. 6, 1862

Shiloh
Apr. 6-7, 1862

Corinth

ALABAMA

Mobile

Arkansas R.

Little
Rock

Mississippi R.

MISSISSIPPI

Vicksburg

Red River

Baton
Rouge

New Orleans

LOUISIANA

South Carolina/Georgia map

Columbia

Charleston

Fort Sumter

SOUTH
CAROLINA

Savannah

Siege of Atlanta
July 20
Sept. 2, 1864

Atlanta

Sherman's March–Sept.–Dec. 1864

GEORGIA

Map 16

208

effort to foment slave uprisings and stiffened their determination to outlast the Union. Abolitionists criticized the proclamation as failing to go far enough; others decried it as an expedient of war that had no constitutional basis and could not last in the period afterward. Overseas reaction especially disappointed Lincoln, suggesting that he had miscalculated the effects of this dramatic move. Those who favored the Confederacy regarded the proclamation as the Union's last gasp, whereas those who opposed slavery noted the lack of principle in a measure that wavered over which slaves would go free. Most important, however, was the growing suspicion among many Britons, regardless of their sympathies toward the war: Emancipation, they charged, would stir up the slaves in rebellion and ultimately lead to a race war of national proportions. Lincoln's move, according to the British chargé in Washing-

ton, demonstrated no "pretext of humanity" and was "cold, vindictive, and entirely political." It offered "direct encouragement to servile Insurrections." Did not this destructive American war have any bounds?

The British press uniformly denounced the president's proclamation. The *Times* of London blasted Lincoln as "a sort of moral American Pope" who wanted to incite a "servile war" by urging the blacks to "murder the families of their masters" while they were on the battlefield. A *Times* editorial asked whether "the reign of the last PRESIDENT [was] to go out amid horrible massacres of white women and children, to be followed by the extermination of the black race in the South?" Lincoln had played "his last card," according to the *Times*. "He will appeal to the black blood of the African; he will whisper of the pleasures of spoil and of the gratification of yet fiercer

First Reading of the Emancipation Proclamation, July 22, 1862
Francis B. Carpenter's painting presented to Congress in 1878. Cabinet members, left to right: Secretary of War Edwin M. Stanton, Secretary of the Treasury Salmon P. Chase, President Lincoln, Secretary of the Navy Gideon Welles, Secretary of the Interior Caleb B. Smith, Secretary of State William H. Seward, Postmaster General Montgomery Blair, and Attorney General Edward Bates (out of picture). *National Archives.*

PUNCH, OR THE LONDON CHARIVARI.— Octobrn 18, 1862.

ABE LINCOLN'S LAST CARD; OR, ROUGE-ET-NOIR.

London Punch, *October 18, 1862*
Lincoln plays his last card—the Ace of Spades—in emancipating the slaves
in a desperate effort to prevent British intervention in the Civil War.

instincts; and when blood begins to flow and shrieks come piercing through the darkness, Mr. LINCOLN will wait till the rising flames tell that all is consummated, and then he will rub his hands and think that revenge is sweet." *Blackwood's Edinburgh Magazine* denounced the proclamation as "monstrous, reckless, devilish." To win the war "the North would league itself with Beelzebub, and seek to make a hell of half a continent."

Thus had the battle of Antietam combined with Lincoln's preliminary proclamation of emancipation to *encourage* British intervention in the war. In the most bitter of ironies, the president's announcement threatened to bring about the very calamity he had sought the most to avoid. "We are now passing through the very crisis of our fate," Charles Francis Adams anxiously and correctly observed in early October 1862. British involvement seemed certain, necessitated by

humanitarian and economic concerns that were now made even more urgent by Lincoln's apparent attempt to incite slave rebellions and ultimate race war.

Chancellor of the Exchequer William E. Gladstone joined a host of Britons in believing that the South had already demonstrated its right to independence. Gladstone had long considered southern separation irrevocable and favored some form of intervention as "an act of charity" designed to bring that monstrous war to a close. Although accused of sympathizing with the South, the truth is that he believed the war enormously destructive both in a humanitarian and an economic sense. Its prolongation, he feared, would drive economically distressed British mill workers into riots and eventually drag other nations into the fighting—including his own. Before a large and cheering audience in Newcastle he expressed a common English conviction in a stirring speech in early October: "Jefferson Davis and other leaders of the South," Gladstone proclaimed, "have made an army; they are making, it appears, a navy; and they have made what is more than either—they have made a nation." He concluded, dramatically: "We may anticipate with certainty the success of the Southern States so far as regards their separation from the North."

Gladstone's speech greatly encouraged the South by leaving the erroneous impression that recognition was at hand; the fact is that the Palmerston ministry was divided over what to do. Gladstone had only wanted to emphasize that the South had proved itself and, in the interests of peace, deserved independence. But his words in Newcastle incited an uproar that forced the Palmerston ministry to come to grips with the obstacles contained in any form of intervention. The chief problem was how to intervene without becoming involved in the war. Two other considerations were how to offer a practical solution to the fighting while persuading Russia to participate in the peace-making process. Thus, the imminence

William E. Gladstone
The British chancellor of the exchequer sought to end the American Civil War before it dragged in other nations. *H. C. G. Matthew, ed.,* The Gladstone Diaries, *9 vols., Oxford: Clarendon, 1978, 6: frontispiece.*

Union and Emancipation Meeting in Exeter Hall, London
One of numerous demonstrations in England for the American Union and emancipation. Harper's Weekly, *March 14, 1863.*

of recognition was illusory: On examining the issues, increasing numbers of Britons came to realize both the futility and the danger of intervention. Palmerston still preferred to wait until the fortunes of battle had convinced both North and South to lay down their arms. In this argument he won the enthusiastic support of his secretary for war, George Cornewall Lewis, who insisted that the South had not yet substantiated its claim to independence and that the British had no satisfactory peace terms to offer as mediator. Intervention, Lewis darkly warned, would mean war with the Union.

Russell, however, was not prepared to exercise such caution. Convinced of the rightness of his position, he soon emerged as the major proponent of intervention. A mediation based on an armistice, the foreign secretary realized, would undoubtedly culminate in recognition. But rather than regard this approach as a stimulant to a third Anglo-American war, he seemed to believe that a pause in the fighting would allow time for both sides to reflect upon the desirability of returning to the battlefield. Seeing that the only rational alternative was peace, they would finally bring "this horrible war" to a close.

In November Russell's effort to intervene was foundering when it suddenly received a boost from France. Napoleon III proposed to join Britain and Russia in arranging a six-month halt in the fighting and a suspension of the blockade for the same period. "This would put a stop to the effusion of blood," he assured Confederate Minister Slidell in Paris, "and hostilities would probably never be resumed." Unification problems in Italy had eased, and the emperor now confronted growing economic problems at home and increasing public sympathy for what his people considered to be a southern attempt to end northern oppression. He saw great advantages in promoting the South's quest for nationhood, not the least of which would be his attempt to establish a puppet emperor in Mexico. With the slavery issue seemingly resolved by the Emancipation Proclamation, Napoleon

Napoleon III
French emperor who considered the use of force in calling for foreign intervention in the Civil War. *A. R. Tyrner-Tyrnauer,* Lincoln and the Emperors, *New York: Harcourt Brace, 1962, opposite p. 96.*

felt free from moral or political constraints to pursue his imperialist objectives in the Western Hemisphere. His so-called Grand Scheme for the Americas called for recognition of the Confederacy and the formation of an alliance with the new southern nation, the establishment of monarchical rule throughout Latin America, the regeneration of French commerce in the Atlantic, the acquisition of Mexican grain and gold, and the creation of a giant buffer state against the United States that stretched from the Rio Grande River at the Gulf of Mexico to the southern tip of Baja California at the Pacific Ocean. In the meantime, French influence would convince the South to free its slaves by a program of gradual emancipation. Driven by this ambitious plan, Napoleon remarked to Slidell that a Union refusal to accept the mediation offer would provide "good reason for recognition" and, in an implicit but ominous reference to the use of force, "perhaps for more active intervention."

Although Napoleon's interventionist proposal carried certain risks of war, Russell was not aware of the implicit proposal of force made to Slidell and immediately supported the measure. In the cause of peace, the foreign secretary was willing to entertain a dangerous proposition from a person who had no reputation for restraint. He should have seen the warning signs. As explained later, Russell had in 1861 cooperated with Britain and Spain in attempting to collect debts from Mexico, only to enlarge his actions into an all-out military interventionist project that his two European cohorts had ultimately deserted. But Russell wanted to take that chance. International law

George Cornewall Lewis
British secretary for war who led the move against foreign intervention in the Civil War. *Gilbert F. Lewis, ed.,* Letters of the Right Hon. Sir George Cornewall Lewis, *London: Longmans, Green, 1870, frontispiece.*

Lord John Russell
British foreign secretary who led the move for foreign intervention in the Civil War. *Massachusetts Historical Society.*

justified an outside intervention in any war that endangered the welfare of neutrals. In addition, French involvement might encourage Russian participation. Although the Union would undoubtedly refuse to abandon one of its most effective weapons in the war—the blockade—Russell simply could not sit and do nothing. To a colleague he had earlier argued, "If a friend were to cut his throat, you would hardly like to confess, 'he told me he was going to do it, but I said nothing as I thought he would not take my advice.'" Out of a blind faith that Napoleon's plan might work, Russell deluded himself into believing that intervention could reconcile the irreconcilable: the North's refusal to accept a southern separation and the South's insistence on nothing less than independence.

Before a stormy two-day cabinet meeting in early November, Russell argued for the French proposal and encountered fierce opposition from nearly all his colleagues, including Lewis and, at the end, Palmerston himself. Lewis had led the attack with a lengthy memorandum (actually written by his stepson-in-law, William Vernon Harcourt, who was a specialist in international law and who reiterated these ideas in letters that appeared in the *Times* of London under the pseudonym "Historicus") repeating many of the arguments against intervention that he had made earlier. Lewis's most telling argument focused on the problems in determining exactly when a rebellious people had achieved nationhood. "Rebellion, until it has succeeded, is Treason; when it is successful, it becomes independence. And thus the only real test of independence is final success." Intervention before the South had established independence would subject Britain to the charge of violating international law by interfering in a war whose outcome remained uncertain; intervention afterward would put the British on the side of the slave-holding Confederacy. Furthermore, Lewis suspected that Napoleon wanted an "armed mediation" to support his own nefarious designs. As Lewis and Harcourt both warned, no one in Britain had a remedy for the American war and intervention in another people's affairs most often resulted in war. Palmerston closed the issue by declaring that continued neutrality was the wisest policy.

Napoleon's proposal had failed, both in Britain and, finally, in Russia. The British had found themselves in an impossible situation. Every kind of vital interest was at stake in the American war, and yet the Palmerston ministry could devise no resolution of the problem and could therefore take no action without itself becoming involved in the fighting. Russia simply rejected the offer as a measure opposed by its friend, the Union.

Napoleon's ill-fated scheme was the last major attempt at joint intervention in the war. Three months later, after the Confederacy won the battle of Fredericksburg, he proposed mediation directly to the Lincoln administration, but again with no success. Congress meanwhile passed a resolution denouncing all attempts at foreign intervention in U.S. affairs. After November 1862 the British never again seriously considered mediation and recognition, costing the South its best hope for victory. Seward's requiem for the intervention crisis was appropriate: "We are no longer to be disturbed by Secession intrigues in Europe. They have had their day. We propose to forget them."

Meanwhile in Britain the reaction to the proclamation of emancipation ultimately developed into what Lincoln had hoped. At first Palmerston and Russell were skeptical of its real purposes, and the restless, unemployed laborers in the country had no reason to give it much attention. But slowly the realization sank in among antislavery groups that the president had converted the war into a crusade against slavery. The Confederate argument of independence against empire lost its persuasiveness in light of the higher purpose of humanitarian reform. John Bright expressed the feelings of England's liberals: "I wish the 1st of January to be here, and the freedom of the Slaves declared from Washington," he declared to a group at Rochdale. "This will make it impossible for England to interfere for the South, for we are not, I hope, degraded enough to undertake to restore three and one half millions of Negroes to slavery." British recognition of the Confederacy now would have a deep and symbolic negative meaning; as one British writer declared, it would be "immoral." If any question remained in the Palmerston ministry about recognizing the South, the surging popular outcry in England in favor of Lincoln and his Emancipation Proclamation helped to remove it.

The Decisive Year of the War: 1863

In North America during 1863, important Union military triumphs came in two places almost simultaneously: in the woods near Gettysburg, Pennsylvania, and along the waters of the Mississippi River at Vicksburg in upper Mississippi. In July Union armies under General George G. Meade held off Lee's second and last foray into the North, and Grant won control of the Mississippi River after a successful siege of the Confederate fortress at Vicksburg, which overlooked the great waterway. The battles at Gettysburg and Vicksburg ended the South's already waning hopes for diplomatic recognition. Britain had dropped the matter, and Napoleon, who had allowed Confederate agents to contract for the purchase or construction of four war vessels in France, decided by early 1864 to withhold delivery. One of the vessels ultimately made it through Denmark and into Confederate hands, but it arrived too late to have effect.

But even the demise of the recognition issue did not repair Anglo-American relations: News of Gettysburg and Vicksburg had not yet reached London when Adams faced still another crisis over ships constructed in England for the Confederacy. He exerted pressure on Russell to order the seizure of two five-inch-thick ironclad steamers called "rams," then under construction by the Laird Company. These fast-moving, highly maneuverable ships had four nine-inch guns mounted on revolving turrets and were nearly invulnerable to enemy shells; but their most dangerous weapon, many believed, was a seven-foot iron rod resting three feet below water on the foreside, which could sink Union ships blockading the southern coast by piercing their wooden hulls.

Adams argued that even though the vessels' papers showed that a private French company had contracted them for Egypt, the rams were actually for the Confederacy. Yet the British government had no legal justification for confiscating the vessels: They carried no weapons and no irrefutable evidence proved that they belonged to the Confederacy. Russell offered assurances that his government would not permit the construction of ships for the Confederacy, but Adams was skeptical. He worried that the rams, like the *Alabama,* might also escape from England despite the government's best intentions.

Adams's fears seemed substantiated when Russell informed him on September 1, 1863, that his government had no legal grounds for detaining the rams. Yet Russell realized the war was turning in the Union's favor and that the U.S. Congress had empowered the president to license privateers that could prey on British shipping. Two days later, Russell notified Palmerston that for the public good he had privately ordered the seizure of the rams. Should there be an effort to seek reparations in the courts, Russell informed Palmerston, "we have satisfied the opinion which prevails here as well as in America that that kind of neutral hostility should not be allowed to go on without some attempt to stop it." The following day, September 4, Russell wrote Adams a second note informing him that the matter was under advisement, but it did not reach the U.S. minister until the afternoon of the next day. In the meantime Adams had only Russell's first note and sent an angry reply on the morning of September 5, which warned that "it would be superfluous in me to point out to your lordship that this is war!" Matters seemed to have gotten completely out of hand when Palmerston bristled at these "insolent threats of war" and suggested that Russell reply "in civil terms, 'You be damned.'"

Cooler heads prevailed, however, and three days later Russell notified Adams of his government's decision to seize the rams. In a thinly veiled effort to circumvent the law, the government bought the vessels at a higher price than the private contractors had offered. Britain's decision on the rams calmed Adams, whereas distraught Confederate leaders were angry and disappointed with Britain's failure to extend aid and called their diplomats home.

It is doubtful that the Laird rams could have done much damage, for they became obsolete almost as soon as their purpose was known. The rams were probably not seaworthy and clearly ineffective against a moving ship, and their advent encouraged the faster development of ironclads. The use of the rams also presented practical problems. In March 1862 the Confederate *Virginia* (previously the U.S.S. *Merrimack*) had rammed the *Cumberland* while it sat motionless in Hampton

Roads. But when the Confederate captain tried to withdraw the pike from the sinking ship, the force of the engines yanked it off and left it like a broken screwdriver embedded in the wooden hull. Even Adams later had doubts about the rams' effectiveness, but given the emotional atmosphere in the United States during the summer of 1863, no one had time for careful thought.

The year 1863 proved pivotal to the outcome of the war. The South's chances for diplomatic recognition were all but dead, primarily because it could not convince the British that their best interests lay in intervening in the war. Had Confederate military forces proved themselves on the battlefield, some form of British intervention might have taken place. But even more important to the London ministry, it had no solution to the bitter animosities that had taken North and South to war. To intervene in any form would win southern support; and for that very reason the British would be inviting a war with the Union. Britain's only course was the one it took: neutrality.

France, Mexico, and the End of the Civil War

As noted earlier, the Civil War had exposed the United States to still another danger: It provided Napoleon III an opportunity to regain a French foothold in the New World—this time in Mexico. This development, in turn, gave the South one more card to play in winning recognition. Even before Napoleon's joint interventionist proposal of late 1863, he had sought to take advantage of the widespread political disorder in Mexico that furnished an atmosphere conducive to European involvement. In January 1861 a Zapotec Indian, Benito Juárez, became constitutional president of the Mexican republic over the wishes of conservative landowners and church groups and in mid-July announced a two-year suspension of the country's foreign obligations. That same month Congress in Washington enacted a face-saving two-year mora-

torium on the Mexican government's foreign debt payments. But protests against Juárez's action came from Paris, London, and Madrid, because Mexico was heavily in debt to all three governments. In October, while Americans were at war, Napoleon devised a scheme for collecting the money from Mexico through a cooperative military expedition composed of French, British, and Spanish forces. European intervention on this scale clearly challenged Mexico's sovereignty; what is more, it presented the South with a means toward winning diplomatic recognition.

Russell tried to soften the impact of this interventionist move by asking the Lincoln administration to join the European powers in Mexico. Yet he warned that his invitation did not constitute recognition of the "extravagant pretensions" of the Monroe Doctrine. Seward, faced with the civil war at home, turned down Russell's offer but admitted to these nations' right to use force in collecting debts—as long as they did not engage in territorial or political aggrandizement in Mexico. His suspicions were well founded. Early the following year Palmerston asserted that "the monarchy scheme" would "stop the North Americans . . . in their absorption of Mexico." Britain was determined to prevent postwar U.S. or Confederate expansion into Mexico, even to the extent of engaging in this provocative move with the venturesome Napoleon. Another consideration also weighed heavily on Palmerston's mind: If Napoleon got deeply involved in Mexico, Britain's chances would increase for establishing a balance of power in Europe.

In December 1861 Spanish soldiers took Veracruz, but soon thereafter Spain and Britain decided to drop the costly enterprise. Napoleon, for his part, had already considered establishing a puppet government in Mexico under the Archduke Ferdinand Maximilian, younger brother of Emperor Francis Joseph of Austria. If Napoleon could bolster the Catholic Church in Mexico and build a nation strong enough to withstand U.S. expansion, he would regain popularity among French Catholics and revive his country's long-standing dream of a New

World empire. A monarchy in Mexico under his direction, he believed, could block the Americans' expansion south and provide enough commerce and troops to tip the European balance in his favor.

After working out a means for receiving their money, Britain and Spain pulled out of Mexico in April 1862, leaving France on its own. Napoleon's soldiers moved west toward Mexico City, where Juárez's forces held off their advance until 30,000 French reinforcements arrived and seized the capital in June 1863. While Juárez continued guerrilla resistance, Napoleon implemented the first step in his Grand Design for the Americas. The thirty-one-year-old Maximilian, accompanied by his youthful wife Carlotta, daughter of the king of Belgium, arrived in Veracruz to head the country in May of 1864. The archduke had agreed, as a condition of French aid, to assume the costs of French intervention as well as the debts Mexico owed France.

The South had already moved to take advantage of the crumbling situation in Mexico. Confederate emissaries negotiated agreements with Juárez's opposition that aimed at facilitating the contraband traffic across the Rio Grande. Once Maximilian was in power, the Confederacy offered to recognize his government in exchange for his help in persuading France to recognize the South. The new emperor of Mexico was willing, but Napoleon had altered his plans. He was more concerned about European affairs at this time and could not risk a confrontation with the Union.

The Lincoln administration could do nothing about French involvement in Mexico until the Civil War was over. A prematurely aggressive stand, Seward knew, could drive Napoleon into Confederate hands, so he appealed to historical U.S. claims against foreign intervention in this hemisphere, although never referring directly to the Monroe Doctrine. The secretary of state realized the futility in threatening the French while Union forces were locked in mortal combat with the Confederacy.

Yet the American public harbored a deep and open bitterness toward France that called

for U.S. military correctives once the Civil War had ended. In early 1864 the *New York Herald* warned, "As for Mexico, we will, at the close of the rebellion, if the French have not left there before, send 50,000 Northern and 50,000 Southern troops, forming together a grand army to drive the invaders into the Gulf." The House of Representatives unanimously passed a resolution in April, a week before Maximilian took the throne, that condemned France's violation of U.S. policy. Seward meanwhile recalled his minister to Mexico and refused to extend recognition to the new monarch. A sign of the impending Union victory in the war came from the recent nominee for the vice presidency, Andrew Johnson, who in the waning days of the Confederacy declared to a crowd in Nashville that "the day of reckoning is approaching. It will not be long before the Rebellion is put down. . . . And then we will attend to this Mexican affair, and say to Louis Napoleon, 'You cannot found a monarchy on the Continent.'" Johnson boasted that "an expedition into Mexico would be a sort of recreation to the brave soldiers who are now fighting the battles of the Union, and the French concern would be quickly wiped out."

The outcome of the Civil War was also becoming clear to Napoleon, who began to reassess the wisdom of his rash move into Mexico. Union forces under General William T. Sherman were cutting a wide swath of destruction through Georgia, and Grant was methodically and brutally trudging through southern armies in his push toward Richmond. Napoleon realized he had made a mistake: The Mexican venture was enormously expensive, his allies had left him, his French people opposed the New World involvement, and troubles were deepening in Europe. Moreover, Maximilian was unpopular and inept, meaning that his weak government could not survive against a reunited America. Napoleon suddenly became more amenable to Union wishes. He instructed Maximilian not to receive Confederate diplomats and ordered the confiscation of two Confederate rams under construction in France. Finally, he directed a step-by-step withdrawal from Mexico that was under way as the Civil War ended in 1865. Within two years, the French soldiers were gone, but Maximilian stubbornly remained, staunchly proclaiming his right to the throne as a Mexican citizen. In June 1867 Juárez's forces, back in control, executed the archduke by a firing squad.

Without the Civil War, it seems inconceivable that Napoleon III would have taken such a brash and reckless move into Mexico. But the domestic tragedy tearing apart the North American midsection afforded him an opportunity not available to his forefathers. With North and South at war, he embarked upon an aggressive policy that blatantly violated the principles of the Monroe Doctrine and, in so doing, endangered the security not only of the United States but of the entire hemisphere. The Lincoln administration recognized that it was powerless to challenge France's meddlesome behavior until the Civil War was over. Seward realistically acceded to Napoleon's actions as long as they did not lead to political gains or territorial acquisition. But once the Civil War ground to an end, so did Napoleon's fumbling enterprise have to come to a close. No longer could the Confederacy exploit France's interest in Mexico to achieve recognition. Thus did the United States survive the most serious domestic threat in its history, along with the most direct foreign challenge to its security since the War of 1812.

Concluding Observations

The South's failure to secure British recognition of its independence foreshadowed its inability to win the war. Britain's abundant cotton reserves and its capacity to buy elsewhere demonstrated the South's mistaken reliance on King Cotton Diplomacy. British purchases of northern wheat also gave the Union an advantage, although it is debatable whether this factor was integral to Britain's decision to maintain neutrality. When economic pressure failed, the Confederacy had to secure a decisive vic-

tory on the battlefield. But at two critical junctures—Antietam in 1862 and Gettysburg the following year—Lee suffered reverses that had drastic reverberations in London.

Initially, the battle of Antietam followed by Lincoln's Emancipation Proclamation increased British interest in intervention out of revulsion for the war's atrocities and the suspicion that the president was attempting to stir up slave rebellions; but the ultimate and certain impact of the document on ending slavery slowly undermined both anti-North and pro-South sentiment inside Britain. The needs of the war had moved Lincoln from his primary objective of preserving the Union of 1861 to seeking a more perfect Union that was devoid of slavery. With the wedding of liberty *and* Union, he had given the nation a new birth of freedom that cleansed the republic of slavery and dampened the ardor of British interventionists. Failure to secure diplomatic recognition undercut southern hopes that Britain and other nations would defy the blockade, further adding to the South's bankrupt position. Another vital factor was the Confederacy's inability to secure enough armed shipping to break the Union blockade and allow the purchase of war materiel from Europe. Finally, and most important, Lewis's warnings that any form of British intervention in the war would lead to war with the Union put an end to Russell's schemes, thereby ensuring the continuation of neutrality and closing the door to significant outside help for the southern cause. In large measure the South's failure to win British recognition helped to determine the outcome of the war.

Selected Readings

Adams, Ephraim D. *Great Britain and the American Civil War.* 2 vols., 1925.

Anastaplo, George. *Abraham Lincoln: A Constitutional Biography.* 1999.

Ball, Douglas B. *Financial Failure and Confederate Defeat.* 1991.

Bauer, Craig A. "The Last Effort: The Secret Mission of the Confederate Diplomat, Duncan F. Kenner," *Louisiana History* 22 (1981): 67–95.

Bellows, Donald. "A Study of British Conservative Reaction to the American Civil War," *Journal of Southern History* 51 (1985): 505–26.

Bennett, Lerone, Jr. *Forced into Glory: Abraham Lincoln's White Dream.* 1999.

Bernath, Stuart L. *Squall Across the Atlantic: American Civil War Prize Cases and Diplomacy.* 1970.

Berwanger, Eugene H. *The British Foreign Service and the American Civil War.* 1994.

Blackett, R. J. M. *Divided Hearts: Britain and the American Civil War.* 2001.

Blumenthal, Henry. *A Reappraisal of Franco-American Relations, 1830–1871.* 1959.

———. "Confederate Diplomacy: Popular Notions and International Realities," *Journal of Southern History* 32 (1966): 151–71.

Boaz, Thomas M. *Guns for Cotton: England Arms the Confederacy.* 1996.

Boritt, Gabor S., ed. *Lincoln the War President: The Gettysburg Lectures.* 1992.

———. *War Comes Again: Comparative Vistas on the Civil War and World War II.* 1995.

———. *Why the Confederacy Lost.*

Bourne, Kenneth. *Britain and the Balance of Power in North America, 1815–1908.* 1967.

———. "British Preparations for War with the North, 1861–1862," *English Historical Review* 76 (1961): 600–32.

———. *The Foreign Policy of Victorian England, 1830–1902.* 1970.

Brauer, Kinley J. "British Mediation and the American Civil War: A Reconsideration," *Journal of Southern History* 38 (1972): 49–64.

———. "Seward's 'Foreign War Panacea': An Interpretation," *New York History* 55 (1974): 133–57.

———. "The Slavery Problem in the Diplomacy of the American Civil War," *Pacific Historical Review* 46 (1977): 439–69.

Campbell, Charles S. *From Revolution to Rapprochement: The United States and Great Britain, 1783–1900.* 1974.

Carroll, Daniel B. *Henri Mercier and the American Civil War.* 1971.

Case, Lynn M., and Spencer, Warren F. *The United States and France: Civil War Diplomacy.* 1970.

Cox, LaWanda. *Lincoln and Black Freedom: A Study in Presidential Leadership.* 1981.

Crawford, Martin. *The Anglo-American Crisis of the Mid-Nineteenth Century: The Times and America, 1850–1862.* 1987.

———, ed. *William Howard Russell's Civil War: Private Diary and Letters, 1861–1862.* 1992.

Crook, David P. *Diplomacy during the American Civil War.* 1975.

———. *The North, the South, and the Powers, 1861–1865.* 1974.

Cullop, Charles C. *Confederate Propaganda in Europe, 1861–1865.* 1969.

Diggins, John P. *On Hallowed Ground: Abraham Lincoln and the Foundations of American History.* 2000.

Donald, David H. *Lincoln.* 1995.

Duberman, Martin. *Charles F. Adams: 1807–1886.* 1961.

Ellison, Mary. *Support for Secession: Lancashire and the American Civil War.* 1972.

Ferris, Norman B. *Desperate Diplomacy: William H. Seward's Foreign Policy, 1861.* 1976.

———. *The* Trent *Affair: A Diplomatic Crisis.* 1977.

Foner, Philip S. *British Labor and the American Civil War.* 1981.

Franklin, John Hope. *The Emancipation Proclamation.* 1963.

Gaddis, John L. *Russia, the Soviet Union, and the United States: An Interpretive History.* 2nd ed., 1990.

Graebner, Norman A. "Northern Diplomacy and European Neutrality," in Donald, David H., ed., *Why the North Won the Civil War,* 55–78. 1960.

Guelzo, Allen C. *Abraham Lincoln: Redeemer President.* 1999.

Hagan, Kenneth J. *This People's Navy: The Making of American Sea Power.* 1991.

Hanna, Alfred J., and Hanna, Kathryn A. *Napoleon III and Mexico: American Triumph over Monarchy.* 1971.

Hernon, Joseph M., Jr. "British Sympathies in the American Civil War: A Reconsideration," *Journal of Southern History* 33 (1969): 308–19.

Hollett, David. *The* Alabama *Affair: The British Shipyards Conspiracy in the American Civil War.* 1993.

Holzer, Harold. *Lincoln Seen and Heard.* 2000.

Hubbard, Charles M. *The Burden of Confederate Diplomacy.* 1998.

Jaffa, Harry V. *A New Birth of Freedom: Abraham Lincoln and the Coming of the Civil War.* 2000.

Jenkins, Brian. *Britain and the War for the Union.* 2 vols., 1974, 1980.

Johannsen, Robert W. *Lincoln, the South, and Slavery: The Political Dimension.* 1991.

Jones, Howard. *Abraham Lincoln and a New Birth of Freedom: The Union and Slavery in the Diplomacy of the Civil War.* 1999.

———. *Union in Peril: The Crisis over British Intervention in the Civil War.* 1992.

Jones, Wilbur D. "The British Conservatives and the American Civil War," *American Historical Review* 58 (1953): 527–43.

———. *The Confederate Rams at Birkenhead.* 1961.

Jordan, Donaldson, and Pratt, Edwin J. *Europe and the American Civil War.* 1931.

Lester, Richard I. *Confederate Finance and Purchasing in Great Britain.* 1975.

Mahin, Dean B. *One War at a Time: The International Dimensions of the American Civil War.* 1999.

Marvel, William. *The* Alabama *and the* Kearsarge: *The Sailor's Civil War.* 1996.

May, Robert E., ed. *The Union, the Confederacy, and the Atlantic Rim.* 1995.

McPherson, James M. *Abraham Lincoln and the Second American Revolution.* 1990.

———. *Battle Cry of Freedom: The Civil War Era.* 1988.

———. *Drawn with the Sword: Reflections on the American Civil War.* 1996.

———. *For Cause and Comrades: Why Men Fought in the Civil War.* 1997.

———. *Ordeal by Fire: The Civil War and Reconstruction.* 2nd ed., 1992.

———. *What They Fought For, 1861–1865.* 1994.

Merli, Frank J. *Great Britain and the Confederate Navy: 1861–1865.* 1970.

Monaghan, Jay. *Diplomat in Carpet Slippers: Abraham Lincoln Deals with Foreign Affairs.* 1945.

Musicant, Ivan. *Divided Waters: The Naval History of the Civil War.* 1995.

Neely, Mark E., Jr. *The Last Best Hope of Earth: Abraham Lincoln and the Promise of America.* 1993.

Niven, John. *Gideon Welles, Lincoln's Secretary of the Navy.* 1973.

Owsley, Frank L. and Owsley, Harriet. *King Cotton Diplomacy: Foreign Relations of the Confederate States of America.* Rev. ed. 1959.

Paludan, Philip S. *"A People's Contest": The Union and Civil War, 1861–1865.* 1988.

———. *The Presidency of Abraham Lincoln.* 1994.

Paolino, Ernest N. *The Foundations of the American Empire: William Henry Seward and U.S. Foreign Policy.* 1973.

Perkins, Bradford. *The Creation of a Republican Empire, 1776–1865.* 1993. The Cambridge History of American Foreign Relations, vol. 1. Cohen, Warren I., ed.

Perkins, Dexter. *The Monroe Doctrine, 1826–1867.* 1933.

Raat, W. Dirk. *Mexico and the United States: Ambivalent Vistas.* 1992.

Robinson, Charles M. *Shark of the Confederacy: The Story of the C.S.S.* Alabama. 1995.

Saul, Norman E. *Distant Friends: The United States and Russia, 1763–1867.* 1991.

Schoonover, Thomas D. *The United States in Central America, 1860–1911: Episodes of Social Imperialism and Imperial Rivalry in the World System.* 1991.

Spencer, Warren F. *The Confederate Navy in Europe.* 1983.

Stuart, Reginald C. *United States Expansionism and British North America, 1775–1871.* 1988.

Taylor, John M. *Confederate Raider: Raphael Semmes of the* Alabama. 1994.

Thomas, Emory M. *The Confederate Nation, 1861–1865.* 1979.

Tyrner-Tyrnauer, A. R. *Lincoln and the Emperors.* 1962.

Warren, Gordon H. *Fountain of Discontent: The* Trent *Affair and Freedom of the Seas.* 1981.

Winks, Robin. *Canada and the United States: The Civil War Years.* 1960.

Wise, Stephen R. *Lifeline of the Confederacy: Blockade Running during the Civil War.* 1988.

Woldman, Albert A. *Lincoln and the Russians.* 1952.

Young, Robert W. *Senator James Murray Mason: Defender of the Old South.* 1998.

CHAPTER 10

Prelude to American Imperialism, 1865–1897

Overview

For three decades following the Civil War, U.S. foreign policy seemed to lack direction, primarily because of the cataclysmic effects of the war and Reconstruction on domestic politics but also because of the focus on settling the vast areas west of the Mississippi River, the scarcity of visionary leaders after Secretary of State William H. Seward, and the limited power the nation could exert outside the Western Hemisphere. The dominant Republican party, concentrated in the Northeast and Midwest, was committed to protectionism at home and to a non-imperialist, New England style of expansionism. Rather than seek territorial empire, one group of Republicans emphasized the U.S. missionary role, another called for foreign markets, and a third, the Liberal wing, was split between imperialists and anti-imperialists. The Democratic party, based in the South and in the cities with the heavy Irish vote, favored low tariffs on all goods *except* sugar (because of the influence of Louisiana producers) and was anti-imperialist because many of its constituents were anti-black and anti-British. The precarious political balance in Washington obstructed the formation of an active foreign policy. Although Republicans occupied the White House for most of the last half of the century, their presidencies were only a single term and were usually hamstrung by a Congress continually shifting in party control and often challenging the power of the executive office. Before turning outward, the country had to undergo a time of internal preparation.

Despite the lack of pattern or thematic unity in foreign policy during the thirty years after the Civil War, the United States sought two basic objectives. The first was to promote trade and security through the acquisition of commercial outlets, coaling stations, and naval bases in the Caribbean, Pacific, and East Asia. The second was to construct an isthmian canal that would permit the establishment of a two-ocean navy and help ensure the safety of the Western Hemisphere. But attention turned from one matter to another almost haphazardly and negotiations often failed as domestic politics wheeled presidents in and out with such rapidity that they seldom had time to develop a consistent foreign policy. In fact, the *New York Sun* expressed a widespread feeling that "the diplomatic service has outgrown its usefulness," whereas Senator Henry Cabot Lodge of Massachusetts, soon to become a leading imperialist, sorrowfully asserted that foreign affairs occupied "but a slight place in American politics, and [exerted] generally only a languid interest." Completion of the transcontinental railroad in 1869 temporarily eased pressure for an isthmian canal, and the danger of European involvement in the Caribbean lessened when Spain pulled out of Santo Domingo in 1865 and France completed its withdrawal from Mexico two years later.

During the two decades of the 1870s and 1880s, the United States waged a series of vicious "Plains Wars" against the American Indians, or Native Americans, who had been forced west onto the Great Plains from their homes east of the Mississippi River. Leaders in Washington had regarded the Indians as obstructions to American settlements and business enterprise east and now saw them as obstacles to the movement west. The passageway for the new transcontinental railroad ran through many acres of Indian settlements, leading the Washington government to concentrate the Indians in remote reservations while trying to "Americanize" them. No longer did it make any effort to deal with the Indians as individual nations: They were totally dependent on the federal government in Washington.

The Indians resisted the hordes of white and black settlers who came in ceaseless streams, but the outcome was certain. Although outnumbered in warriors and outmatched in weaponry and technology, the Indians nonetheless won some pitched battles, such as the annihilation of Colonel George Custer and 260 soldiers by Sitting Bull, Crazy Horse, and a mixture of nearly 2000 Sioux and others at the Little Bighorn River in Montana in 1876. The Indians lost most of their encounters with the U.S. Army, however, climaxed by their last major clash—at Wounded Knee Creek in South Dakota in 1890. A Sioux fired into the soldiers who had just captured the Indians, and the soldiers responded with a ghastly slaughter that took the lives of Big Foot and nearly half of the 350 Sioux men, women, and children with him.

The series of Indian wars during the post–Civil War period had important ramifications

for U.S. policy overseas. The opening of the west provided a vital step in the nation's continuing commercial penetration into the waters beyond the North American rim. Many of the same legal justifications for the nation's treatment of the Indians would appear again in the 1890s, when the United States had to decide how to deal with various non-Americans about to come under its sovereignty. The U.S. government's conquest of the Indians proved a brutal but integral cog in facilitating the nation's movement west and then into the Pacific and East Asia.

Thus, in the thirty years following the Civil War the United States engaged in an important period of transformation from an agricultural to an industrial nation, of education to international needs and interests, and of domestic preparation for a deeper involvement in foreign affairs.

Renewed U.S. Expansion in the Western Hemisphere

As secretary of state, Seward had recognized the vital international dimension of the Civil War, and he now attempted to lead a resurgence of U.S. foreign concern after the war that would help to mend sectional division and continue to restore national security. A long-time expansionist and ardent advocate of commercial enlargement, he outlined plans for a U.S. empire that would encompass Canada, Latin America, the Pacific, and Asia. To a crowd in Boston in June 1867, Seward dramatically called for "the possession of the American continent and the control of the world." Canada remained of prime interest to many Americans. In fact, the Parliament in London, partly because of apprehension over U.S. expansionist designs, passed the British North America Act in 1867, which unified the colonies under the Dominion of Canada and hopefully warded off any thoughts of their leaving the empire. Another potential threat to Canada came from the Fenians, a secret Irish Republican Brotherhood established in New York in 1858 to secure the independence of their homeland from Britain. By the end of the American Civil War, this 10,000-member organization planned to embroil Britain and the United States in war and seize Canada as hostage in exchange for Ireland's freedom. Meanwhile Seward had other interests in the hemisphere: Caribbean bases in Haiti, Cuba, the Dominican Republic, and the Danish West Indies (Virgin Islands); Tigre Island, which belonged to Honduras; and Alaska, Iceland, and Greenland.

Despite Seward's high ambitions, he succeeded in making only one territorial acquisition—Alaska in 1867—and even that was the result of fortuitous circumstances. Seven years earlier, Russia's veteran minister in Washington, Baron Edouard de Stoeckl, had learned of U.S. interest in establishing telegraph connections across Alaska (then called Russian America) and Siberia to Europe. The Civil War intervened, but afterward, when he hinted to Seward in the spring of 1867 that his government was ready to part with Alaska, he found a willing recipient. The acquisition of Alaska would extend the northwest corner of the United States to the Bering Straits, which, though seemingly located in a lonely and nearly forgotten part of the world, actually offered the possibility of securing the strategically important Aleutian Islands and various outposts in the western Pacific, along with the vast commercial opportunities afforded by Asia. Russia decided to sell for several reasons: It needed money, and Alaska had become a liability; the area had proved difficult to colonize partly because of its great distance from home; the Russian-American Company was failing in the fur-trading industry because a vast array of hunters had rapidly diminished the number of sea otters; and Alaska's defense costs were prohibitive. Seward could have Alaska; he now had to convince Americans that they needed it.

Secret negotiations began with Stoeckl in Washington after Seward persuaded the chair of the Senate Foreign Relations Committee, Charles Sumner, that the acquisition of Alaska was in the U.S. interest. Late in the evening of March 29, 1867, Stoeckl appeared on Seward's doorstep in Washington and indicated his willingness to sell Alaska. Instead of offering to wait until morning, Seward surprised Stoeckl by opening the state department for immediate negotiations. Indeed, at 4 A.M. on March 30 the two men signed a treaty that awarded Alaska to the United States for $7.2 million, considerably more than the $5 million that the Russian government had privately authorized its minister to accept. At first glance the secretary of state's almost single-handed success appeared to be a diplomatic coup that no one could reject; but the laws of politics dictated otherwise. Seward had failed to keep Congress informed. In fact, he did not even tell the president and his cabinet of the negotiations until the treaty went up the hill to Congress.

A stormy political battle broke out as soon as the deal became public. On April 8, 1867, Sumner defended the treaty in a three-and-a-half-hour speech before the Senate that affixed the name *Alaska* to the area and probably had considerable effect on promoting support for the pact by reviving the old sense of manifest destiny in the United States. His strategy seemed to work. The initial excitement over renewed continental expansion encouraged the Senate's approval by an overwhelming margin. The House, however, divided sharply over political considerations and stalled over appropriations. Some members had legitimate concerns. Critics of the pact were worried about the cost of defense, the lack of crop yield, and the likelihood of alienating the British by acquiring an area that appeared to be the prelude to the annexation of Canada. Others simply denounced Alaska as "Seward's Folly," a "Polar Bear Garden," "Frigidia," "Seward's Icebox," "Walrussia," and the land of "walrus-covered icebergs" and of cows that gave ice cream. Seward's treaty, some skeptics somberly concluded, constituted "a dark deed done in the night."

The expansionist spirit ultimately prevailed, however, and the House finally passed the agreement on July 14, 1868. Political wrangling contributed to the long delay, but even more important was congressional preoccupation with the impeachment of President Andrew Johnson. In the meantime Stoeckl had considered offering the area as a gift in an effort to shame the United States into paying for it, but the czar turned down his suggestion for fear that the United States would accept. Rumors circulated that Stoeckl had bribed members of Congress, reporters, and other influential Americans to get the bill through, although Seward told Congress under oath that "I know of no payment to anybody, by him or of any application of the funds which he received." Whatever the truth, Seward was largely responsible for the treaty because of his campaign to educate Americans concerning the value of Alaska. His supporters had another decisive advantage: The United States had already occupied Alaska and raised the flag over the capital at Sitka. With this fait accompli in mind, the House approved the treaty, authorizing the United States to purchase 591,000 square miles of territory for a bargain price of less than two cents an acre.

The Alaska Treaty contained no assurance of statehood. It stipulated only that civilized peoples of the area would "be admitted to the enjoyment of all the rights, advantages and immunities of citizens of the United States." The principle of citizenship without statehood marked an important alteration in the pattern of American territorial acquisition. Yet as the U.S. Supreme Court made evident in *Rassmussen* v. *U.S.* in 1905, the treaty and later laws extended American customs and legislation to Alaska, and for practical purposes *did* incorporate the area into the United States.

Attention had meanwhile turned to Cuba, where an insurrection that erupted against Spain in 1868 convinced many Americans of the necessity of intervening on behalf of the islanders. The Cubans seemed to have democratic aspirations, a belief encouraged by exiles in the United States who spread propaganda to that effect, bribed reporters and legislators, and organized filibustering expeditions to further their cause. Pressure mounted on the new

Hamilton Fish
Secretary of state who staunchly opposed U.S. intervention in Cuba's insurgency against Spain. *Allan Nevins,* Hamilton Fish: The Inner History of the Grant Administration, *New York: Dodd, Mead, 1936, frontispiece.*

presidential administration of Ulysses S. Grant to extend recognition to the Cuban rebels. Although Grant appeared interested, his secretary of state, Hamilton Fish, was not. Such action, he warned the president, could provoke a war with Spain that the United States could ill afford and could well lose. Reconstruction at home was the national priority, and war would hurt domestic progress as well as rupture an already struggling commercial system. Fish also cited another compelling reason for holding back: the need to resolve the bitter *Alabama* claims issue with Britain and improve relations with that country. He had to convince the president that recognition of Cuban belligerency would be a mistake. The task would be difficult. Not only was Grant headstrong, but he had a concurrent (though ultimately abortive) interest in annexing the Dominican Republic as a refuge for U.S. blacks.

In August 1869 Grant directed Fish to extend recognition to the Cuban rebels. The secretary ignored the instruction, allowing the president's ardor to cool. But in the summer of the following year Congress called for recognition, and Fish felt so strongly about the matter that he threatened to resign if the president did not ask the legislature to drop the matter. Grant did so. Many newsmen praised his congressional message as a wise move to keep the United States out of the affair, and popular enthusiasm dissipated enough that in June 1870 Congress narrowly voted down a resolution calling for recognition.

As the war in Cuba continued, private U.S. citizens became involved and soon fomented a crisis between the United States and Spain. In November 1873 reports reached Washington that a Spanish warship had stopped the *Virginius,* flying U.S. colors, between Cuba and Jamaica. According to accounts, Spanish officials had escorted the vessel into Santiago harbor, where after a hurried court martial they shot fifty-three crew members and passengers— including Americans and Britons—as "pirates." Had a British warship not prepared to level the Cuban city, more executions could have followed. Americans from the Gulf of Mexico to New England hotly talked of war.

Fish preferred a settlement short of war, but the angry popular mood forced him to react strongly. He gave the Spanish twelve days to apologize and make reparations. In the meantime U.S. military and naval forces prepared for combat. "If Spain cannot redress the outrages perpetrated in her name on Cuba," Fish defiantly proclaimed, "the United States will."

Then news arrived that took some of the fire out of the administration's threats. Fish learned that the *Virginius* was a Cuban gunrunner illegally flying the U.S. flag and carrying fraudulent papers along with munitions and rebels. Spain nonetheless had had no legal grounds for seizing the vessel: No state of war

existed, and the Cubans were therefore not belligerents. The Madrid government apologized for the episode and awarded an indemnity. It also promised numerous reforms short of permitting self-government on the island. The United States could doubtless have had war over the *Virginius* affair; but Fish and others chose to follow the admonition expressed during the crisis by a former Confederate general: "Surely we have had war enough for one generation."

The *Alabama* Claims Dispute with Britain

Pressures continued for intervention in Cuba, but Fish managed to turn the administration's attention to the ongoing *Alabama* claims controversy with Britain. The British had rejected several U.S. recommendations for arbitration over the *Alabama*'s wartime damages to Union shipping. Even when they finally accepted one proposal, the Johnson-Clarendon Convention of 1869, the U.S. Senate voted against the measure because it contained no apology for the *Alabama* and no provision for indemnifying what some Americans termed the *indirect* costs of the war caused by British policies. Charles Sumner, the leading proponent of British reparations, had shocked and infuriated the London government by demanding both direct and indirect damages that someone later calculated at more than $2 billion. *Canada,* Sumner believed, would provide suitable recompense. British spokespersons angrily complained that Sumner sought war reparations without the existence of war.

Sumner would not relent. Destruction of Union war materiel by the *Alabama* alone amounted to $15 million, he declared, but British interference in the war had created the unforeseen costs of soaring insurance rates, forced American merchants to change their registry of vessels to neutral nations, and caused the loss of many more American lives by extending the war. Indeed, Sumner charged, fighting went on for two years after

Gettysburg because of British neutrality policies that permitted such ship-building activities and offered the hope of recognition to the Confederacy followed by enhanced material assistance.

Informal negotiations on the claims issue began in Washington during the summer of 1869 and soon grew into a treaty settlement. With the outbreak of the Franco-Prussian War the following year, the London government became concerned that in this alarming international atmosphere its own problems with Russia could lead to war and drive that regime into contracting for the building of ships in America. The British were suddenly ready for a general arbitration agreement, and in January 1871 the Foreign Office authorized a private citizen, Sir John Rose, to begin formal talks with Fish. From February through May, a Joint High Commission of ten members met in Washington to work out a treaty.

The ensuing Treaty of Washington of May 8, 1871, was of major importance in promoting better Anglo-American relations. It provided for arbitration of the *Alabama* issues, resolved British claims of nearly $2 million for property taken during the American Civil War, approved reciprocal use of canals in the Great Lakes–St. Lawrence River network, and settled numerous long-standing fishing questions recently exacerbated by U.S. abrogation of the Marcy-Elgin Reciprocity Treaty of the 1850s. The Washington Treaty also called for arbitration to determine the ownership of the San Juan Islands lying between Vancouver Island (British Columbia) and the Territory of Washington in the far northwest. The matter of ownership had grown out of the vague boundary terms of the Oregon Treaty of 1846 and had drawn greater attention after the discovery of gold in British Columbia during the late 1850s.

Perhaps the key to the diplomatic success was the U.S. decision to give up the demand for indirect damages attributable to the war. Indeed, the matter did not arise during the talks because the administration realized that failure to secure that concession would have

antagonized the Senate and ended hopes for the treaty. With that hot issue removed, the British expressed "regret" on the *Alabama* matter and agreed that a five-member panel would meet in Geneva, Switzerland, to resolve the compensation issue. The treaty established the principles that a neutral must use "due diligence" in preventing the departure of any ship suspected of engaging in war against a friendly power and that it could not allow its ports or waterways to become sources of assistance to belligerents. A little over two weeks later, on May 24, 1871, the Senate approved the pact.

The arbitration tribunal established under the Treaty of Washington convened at Lake Geneva the following December but despite high hopes, it immediately ran into trouble on the unexpected reappearance of the indirect claims issue. Charles Francis Adams, Union minister to London during the Civil War, represented the United States, and his counterpart was the lord chief justice of England, Sir Alexander Cockburn. Adams, acting under Fish's instructions, shocked the British by introducing Sumner's indirect claims proposal and almost aborted the talks at the start. Since the matter had not risen during the Washington negotiations of 1871, the British assumed that the White House had dropped this claim. Its sudden revival in Geneva caused a storm of protest in Britain. The "war prolongation claim" could lead to a British payment of $8 billion, Prime Minister William E. Gladstone estimated—*eight times* the amount exacted by Germany from France at the end of their war earlier that year.

Fish had pursued a highly dangerous diplomatic strategy in calling for indirect claims, because in reality he entertained no hopes for succeeding. But he feared that Congress might reject the treaty if he did not raise the issue, and he sought to kill the matter once and for all by having it thrown out in these high-level international proceedings. To a confidant Fish wrote, "I never believed that the Tribunal would award a cent for the 'indirect claims.'" It was not in the U.S. interest to hold neutrals "liable for the indirect injuries consequent upon an act of negligence." Recognizing that the United States would be the chief neutral nation in any European wars, he declared that "we have too large an extent of coast and too small a police, and too much of the spirit of bold speculation and adventure, to make the doctrine a safe one for our future." Fish had brought up the issue so that the tribunal might reject it and thereby eliminate the possibility of someone ever using it against the United States.

Adams devised a solution. He convinced the other members of the tribunal to give an "advisory" opinion based on accepted principles of international law. Without the British delegate present, the tribunal ruled in June 1872 against the admission of indirect claims. Both the United States and Britain accepted this decision, and the matter was closed.

On the claims matter, the arbitration court decided against the British and announced its decisions in September 1872. Its members unanimously ruled that the London government had not exercised "due diligence" in pursuing neutrality during the Civil War and was therefore responsible for $15.5 million of destruction caused by the *Alabama,* the *Florida,* and the *Shenandoah.* In the last two cases Cockburn angrily voted against paying the claims and stalked out of the room. His government had to comply with the court's decision, however—a move that the *Times* of London approved. British officials eventually attached the canceled draft of the award sum on the Foreign Office wall as a reminder of the danger of indiscreet action.

The remaining issues dealt with under the Treaty of Washington were eventually resolved, with the British winning the larger share. An arbitral commission met for two years in Washington before rejecting all other war claims and awarding Britain nearly $2 million in damages stemming primarily from what the commission considered to be an illegal U.S. blockade. In the meantime the German emperor, acting as arbiter, awarded the San Juan Islands to the United States. On the fisheries question, an arbitral commission granted $5.5 million to the British as an equivalent for allowing fishing privileges to the Americans as part of the Washington negotiations of 1871. The U.S. delegate was upset and refused to sign the agreement, but the United States honored its financial obligation.

Overall, the United States fared well from the Treaty of Washington. The monetary awards tipped in the country's favor by more than $8 million, and the treaty established a precedent for arbitration and marked a major victory for the principles of neutrality. Most important, by resolving the long-standing *Alabama* claims dispute, the settlement prevented a rupture in Anglo-American relations that would have had far-reaching ramifications.

Latin America

The opening of the Suez Canal in northeast Africa in 1869 rekindled U.S. interest in building a canal across the isthmus of Central America. The Clayton-Bulwer Treaty of 1850 remained a major obstacle because it had stipulated joint Anglo-American control over any projected isthmian route. In 1869, however, President Grant took an aggressive stance indicative of a changing national mood. He became the first chief executive to insist that the United States should have exclusive control over any canal through the isthmus. In a move that actually violated the Clayton-Bulwer Treaty, he established an Interoceanic Canal Commission that authorized surveys of possible canal routes. In 1876 the commission concluded that Nicaragua offered the most feasible site.

Canal interest dramatically grew in 1879, when the architect of the Suez Canal, seventy-five-year-old Ferdinand de Lesseps, secured a concession from the Colombian government and with private support prepared to engineer a canal through its territorial possession of Panama. His actions aroused U.S. fears of outside interference in the hemisphere. Early the following year de Lesseps arrived in the United States to promote the project and attempt to relieve American anxieties. He traveled across the country, hoping to befriend Americans by his charismatic personality and liberal dispensations of money. He was not successful.

In March of that same year, 1880, President Rutherford B. Hayes, Grant's successor, sent a ringing message to the Senate that denounced the de Lesseps project as an effort to build a canal on "virtually a part of the coastline of the United States." It was "the right and duty of the United States to assert and maintain such supervision and authority over any interoceanic canal . . . as will protect our national interests." The U.S. objective was a canal under its own control. Hayes was worried that the French government would gradually take over a canal through Panama just as the British had done in acquiring a controlling ownership interest in the Suez Canal in 1875. The House joined the Senate in criticizing the plan. To underline the point, President Hayes ordered two warships to Panama.

Washington's warnings had little effect on de Lesseps, and when he proceeded with his plans to build the canal, the United States tried to reopen the issue with Britain in 1881. Secretary of State James G. Blaine attempted to persuade the British to accept abrogation or modification of the Clayton-Bulwer Treaty on the ground that his nation could not "perpetuate any treaty that impeaches our right and long-established claim to priority on the American continent." Conditions had changed since the agreement of 1850, he asserted: Its terms condoning joint control now violated the Monroe Doctrine by challenging U.S. supremacy in the hemisphere. An Anglophobe, Blaine regarded the British as his country's chief commercial and imperial competitor in the Caribbean Basin and Latin America. British Foreign Secretary Lord Granville pointedly reminded Blaine that the stipulations contained in the Clayton-Bulwer Treaty were still in effect. The United States could take no action against the de Lesseps project, either with or without the British.

That same year of 1881, after de Lesseps's French company had begun work on the canal, the United States again pushed for a route through Nicaragua. Congress permitted the establishment of the Maritime Canal Company to open negotiations, and the Department of State again tried to persuade London to cancel the joint-control provisions of the Clayton-Bulwer Treaty. After this effort failed, the United States simply ignored the pact. It signed an agreement negotiated by Secretary of State Frederick Frelinghuysen with General Joaquín Zavala of Nicaragua in December 1884 that secured transit rights, in exchange for a permanent alliance and protection of Nicaragua's possessions. The Senate, however, rejected the treaty by a narrow vote the next month, although holding it for further consideration. Many Americans were worried about allying with Nicaragua, a country continually besieged by boundary squabbles. Others were more concerned about the impact of such an agreement on Britain. Satisfaction came from flaunting London; so also did danger.

The new president after the election of 1884, Democrat Grover Cleveland, insisted that the canal must be open to all nations and followed the state department's advice to withdraw the Frelinghuysen-Zavala Treaty from the Senate. Cleveland opposed foreign involvement anyway and warned that this measure violated the Clayton-Bulwer Treaty and would cause problems for the United States in Central America. By the 1890s the canal problem had quieted when America's Maritime Company failed to raise enough money for a Nicaraguan canal and de Lesseps's project, with less than half the digging finished, fell victim to bankruptcy, mudslides, corruption, yellow fever, and malaria.

U.S. interest in a canal in the early 1880s had been indicative of the growing interest in Latin America, which in turn soon involved the United States in the Pan-American movement. Pan-Americanism was a multilateral doctrine calling for hemispheric cooperation based on the principle of peace through trade.

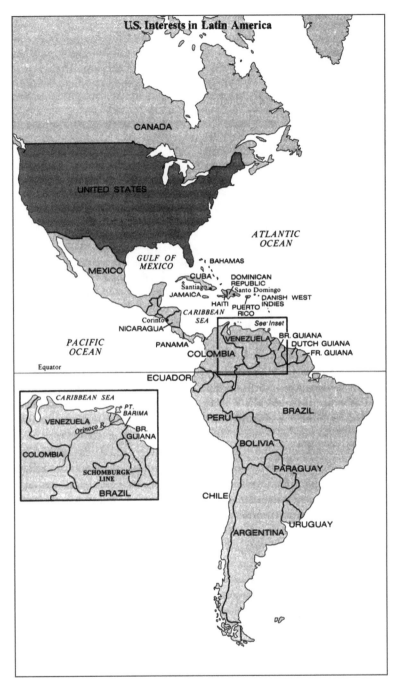

Map 17
Despite major domestic problems in the post–Civil War and Reconstruction
Era, the United States slowly expanded its involvement in the Caribbean.

Secretary of State Blaine had been uneasy that the United States had an unfavorable balance of trade with the Latin American republics, and he had wanted to tighten interhemispheric relations through commercial agreements. But his central concern had been to regain prestige that he and the United States had lost after a series of failed mediations. Blaine had therefore called for an International American Conference to meet in Washington in 1881 to discuss the establishment of close trade relations as a means of preventing war among the American nations. But Blaine had soon resigned as secretary of state because of political differences within the Republican party, and his successor called off the conference on the ground that Europe might consider it an affront.

In 1889 Blaine returned to the position of secretary of state, and under his leadership the United States sponsored the First International American Conference (or Pan-American Conference) in Washington. The eighteen delegations in attendance rejected his call for lower tariffs and mandatory arbitration of disputes, but they did create the forerunner of the Pan-American Union, the International Bureau of American Republics, which became a central information agency. The conferees also approved individual reciprocity treaties and called for improved communication and transportation facilities throughout the hemisphere. But the Latin Americans voted down arbitration primarily because they distrusted the United States. Also, the Republican party refused to support the reciprocity treaties because it favored protectionism. A further blow to Pan-Americanism came in 1891–1892, when a crisis developed between Chile and the United States over U.S. interference in that country's civil war. Still, the meeting in Washington set a precedent for other inter-American conferences.

The Pacific and East Asia

For various reasons Americans were receptive to involvement in the Pacific and East Asia.

Trade was a factor, as were U.S. military and strategic concerns. Perhaps the U.S. attitude was also attributable to the belief that the people of East Asia were backward and thus susceptible to U.S. economic and cultural influences. Whatever the reasons, the United States wanted to establish coaling stations across the Pacific at Midway Island (occupied by the navy in 1867), Samoa, and Hawaii, and it sought to broaden its economic penetration of China and Japan. Even Korea offered commercial possibilities. Completion of the transcontinental railroad in 1869 further heightened U.S. interest in the Orient. The main prize was the famed though elusive market of China, and U.S. stepping-stones across the Pacific provided the vital prerequisites to success.

The Samoan archipelago, a large group of fourteen islands lying nearly 4000 miles from San Francisco and en route to Australia, became a point of contention among the United States, Britain, and Germany by the 1870s. American whaling interests had used the islands in the pre–Civil War period, and afterward the United States had competed for the harbors at Apia and Pago Pago. An American steamship company operating out of San Francisco convinced the White House of the value of Pago Pago, and a U.S. Navy officer soon negotiated a treaty gaining harbor rights in exchange for a U.S. protectorate. The treaty never came to a vote in the Senate, but in 1878 Samoan representatives came to the United States and asked for annexation or the establishment of a protectorate. The Washington government refused the offer but negotiated a treaty that awarded the United States a coaling station at Pago Pago and gave Samoans the right to use its "good offices" in settling disputes between Samoa and any government "in amity with the United States." The Senate approved, largely because the agreement contained no political pledges to the islands.

In 1879 Britain and Germany likewise secured naval stations in Samoa. Germany had arrived late on the colonial scene: Britain and France already had claims to Africa and Asia when Prince Otto von Bismarck became interested in colonial expansion during the mid-1880s and soon posed a major challenge to British and French global interests. The British and Germans tacitly agreed to British control over Egypt in exchange for recognition of German interests in Africa and the South Pacific. By January 1886 the United States felt challenged when Germany raised its flag over Samoa and established virtual control over the government. A confrontation developed in the midst of heightening tension when the U.S. consul, allegedly acting under the good offices provision of the 1878 treaty, implanted the Stars and Stripes and tried to restore the Samoan king. The United States called for a conference that met the following year. Although the U.S. delegation insisted on Samoa's integrity, the conference ended in failure because Britain's interests elsewhere in the South Pacific compelled it to recognize German priorities in the islands.

Suspicion persisted among the three powers, but they finally achieved a Samoan settlement that was largely attributable to other factors. Late in 1888 Germany declared war on Samoa when a group of rebels tried to overthrow the German puppet government. Both Britain and the United States refused to support Germany, and in view of other growing international troubles Bismarck decided on a peaceful resolution of the problem. Another factor contributed to the easing of tensions. A tropical storm in 1889 sobered the antagonists by devastating Apia and destroying German and U.S. ships. Bismarck called a conference of all three powers in Berlin, where they drew up a tripartite protectorate over Samoa that restored the monarch and allowed the United States to retain Pago Pago. Ten years later, after a civil war had erupted in Samoa, the three governments again met in Berlin and arranged a partition of the islands between Germany and the United States. Britain gave up its Samoan claims for concessions elsewhere, but the United States maintained control over several of the islands along with the harbor at Pago Pago.

Much like Samoa, Hawaii, then called the Sandwich Islands, had attracted increased U.S. interest since the Civil War. Americans wanted Hawaii as a mission field, a boon to the sugar and whaling industries, and a strategic outpost en route to Asia. The major U.S. aim before the 1890s was not annexation, despite Secretary of State Seward's statement that "a lawful and peaceful annexation of the islands to the United States, with the consent of the people ... is deemed desirable by this government." He had made the statement to his minister in Hawaii during talks regarding a commercial reciprocity treaty, but the Senate had voted against the treaty in 1870, partly out of fear that such a measure would stir up the anti-imperialists and obstruct eventual annexation.

The chief U.S. concern at this time was to prevent other nations from seizing control of Hawaii. By 1875 the islands' sugar plantation owners, dependent on U.S. markets, warned that unless the United States allowed tariff-free entry of their product, they would establish closer ties with Britain. That same year Hawaii's sugar producers received a tremendous boost by the Treaty of Reciprocity, which allowed their goods to enter the U.S. market duty free for seven years (then terminable by either side after a one-year notice of abrogation) in exchange for their agreement not to transfer economic or territorial rights to any other country.

The great need for cheap labor in Hawaii unsettled many Americans in the United States because it attracted thousands of Chinese and Japanese workers who might strengthen the islands' ties to the Orient. Of 80,000 inhabitants by the end of the century, only about one-half were natives. Through reciprocity arrangements, Hawaii was becoming a virtual colony of the United States, and if annexation took place, the growing Asian population on the islands would lead to a tense racial situation. In 1881 the Department of State informed the British that Hawaii was "essentially a part of the American system of states, and a key to the North Pacific trade." Six years later the United States and Hawaii agreed to the Reciprocity Convention, which renewed the Reciprocity Treaty of 1875 for seven years (again terminable with a one-year notice) and included an amendment granting U.S. naval privileges in Pearl Harbor.

The same year of the renewed Reciprocity Treaty, 1887, a bloodless coup took place in Hawaii during which the white planters on the islands persuaded the king to approve a new constitution authorizing only property owners to sit in the legislature. Four years later the king died and his sister, Liliuokalani, became monarch. A strong nationalist, the new queen tried to restore the power of the throne and in so doing alarmed white business leaders, causing them to push for Hawaii's annexation by the United States. Business interests on the islands were already hurting from the McKinley Tariff of 1890, which removed Hawaiian sugar from its favored position on the American market and caused economic problems that precipitated a political crisis. Hawaiian sugar planters regarded annexation as the only path to stability, because their product would come under the protection of the high tariff. In the spring of 1892 a spokesperson for the islands' sugar interests arrived in Washington for private talks about annexation.

The following January of 1893 Queen Liliuokalani provided the spark that set off a revolution when she announced a royal decree intended to implement a new constitution based on autocratic principles and a restoration of power to the native islanders. Less than a week later white planters led an overthrow of the monarchy, and nearly all 3000 Americans on the islands requested annexation by the United States. The U.S. minister to Hawaii, John Stevens, had long favored annexation and immediately secured assistance for the revolution from U.S. marines and sailors on a nearby cruiser. Only one shot was fired and a single person injured in a revolution that brought down a monarchy and pointed toward annexation. Liliuokalani capitulated to what she called "the superior force of the United States of America," but only until Washington could "undo the action of its representative" and restore her "as the constitutional sovereign of the Hawaiian Islands." Stevens meanwhile extended recognition to the new provisional government, raised the American flag, and declared the islands a protectorate of the United States. To the state department he wrote, "The Hawaiian pear is now fully ripe, and this is the golden hour for the United States to pluck it."

The provisional government in Hawaii sent a commission to Washington to draft an annexation treaty, and in rapid time the document went to the Senate. By the proposed agreement of February, the islands were to become U.S. territory in exchange for a lifetime annual pension of $20,000 awarded to the former queen. In the meantime a public debate began over acquiring the islands. Pro-annexationists cited humanitarian, commercial, and strategic reasons and warned that if the United States did not take the islands, the British or Japanese would. Democrats and anti-imperialists charged that the entire affair was ugly and insisted that imperialist ventures led to colonial burdens. Some declared that the presence of a large non-white population in Hawaii raised questions about statehood. Before the Senate could vote, President Cleveland, recently returned to office after his re-election defeat in 1888, abruptly withdrew the treaty from consideration.

The new president thought the Hawaiian affair seemed orchestrated and wanted an investigation. Cleveland wondered also whether the southern wing of his Democratic party would support the acquisition of a non-white population and whether Americans would allow a noncontiguous territory to become a state. Also, he had little hope that the Hawaiians would subject themselves to the islands' white minority. Finally, with farmers and laborers in the United States currently restless over other matters, the president was hesitant to have his already troubled administration take on another problem. Support for his position came from Secretary of State Walter

Grover Cleveland
As president, he opposed U.S. imperialist ventures in Hawaii and Cuba. *Photo by Pach; Collection of the New York Historical Society.*

Gresham, who, although an expansionist, declared that he was "unalterably opposed to stealing territory, or of annexing a people against their consent." A former Democratic congressman, James Blount, meanwhile accepted the president's request to head an inquiry into the Hawaiian situation. The group concluded that Stevens had been integral to the success of the revolution and that the vast majority of islanders actually favored the queen.

Cleveland faced a nearly impossible situation. He had already outraged expansionists by ordering the lowering of the American flag in Hawaii, and because he had arranged the inquiry into the revolution he now seemed bound to restore the throne to the queen. Yet to do so would require the use of military force against the provisional government—which was comprised of Americans. Such a reckless venture would entail Americans fight-

ing Americans, with the unhappy prospect of the Cleveland administration squelching a republic and restoring a monarchy.

The president made a wise political decision: He turned the matter over to Congress, which did nothing. A heated debate gave the appearance of action and in fact resulted in two resolutions against interference in Hawaii. In 1894 a convention in Hawaii led to the drafting of a constitution, and on July 4 the "missionary group" in control established the Republic of Hawaii. Cleveland extended recognition, and the U.S. Congress eased problems on the islands that same year by passing a new tariff that reestablished Hawaii's favored position in the sugar market.

While the Hawaiian issue simmered, U.S. interest in East Asia had focused on China and the possibility of enlarging commercial and religious influences. The United States's East Asia policy was hesitant more than purposeful, primarily because the region's potential was not clear and the United States lacked the power to support an active stance. Yet the idea of a boundless China market persisted. Interest in cheap labor for building a transcontinental railroad had led to the Burlingame Treaty of 1868, which guaranteed Americans most-favored-nation status in China and facilitated Chinese emigration to the United States. But the need for Chinese labor had dropped with completion of the railroad in 1869, and four years later, when the United States underwent a financial panic that developed into a major depression, the Chinese people's cultural differences and willingness to work for low wages made them a convenient scapegoat for the nation's economic ills.

Violence soon broke out against the Chinese in America's far west, the area of their highest concentration, and by the 1870s many Americans wanted to bar any more from entering the country. The anti-Chinese attitude continued to grow throughout the late nineteenth century as stories came back to the United States of the harsh treatment accorded to its missionaries and other nationals in China. A revision in the Burlingame

Treaty seemed essential, and in 1882 Congress responded with the Chinese Exclusion Act, which suspended the entry of Chinese immigrants into the United States for ten years and was renewed periodically up to the 1920s.

Korea also attracted U.S. attention. Called the "Hermit Kingdom" because of its isolation, Korea was tied to a China so weak that foreign intervention in that small country went virtually unimpeded. The United States sent an expedition to Korea in 1871 to seek a treaty protecting shipwrecked sailors, but when the Koreans opened fire the U.S. ships destroyed several forts and killed more than 300 natives before leaving without a treaty. In 1876 Japan forced Korea to declare independence from China, and four years afterward a U.S. mission arrived to seek the same commercial favors Japan received. Commodore Robert Shufeldt of the U.S. Navy secured the first Korean agreement with the West—the Treaty of Peace, Amity, Commerce and Navigation in 1882. It permitted most-favored-nation privileges to Americans, authorized diplomatic and consular representatives, provided for temporary extraterritorial rights, and contained a mutual assurance of good offices (which the United States later ignored). The Senate approved the treaty the following year. Despite high hopes, U.S. influence in Korea remained negligible during the ensuing period of intense rivalry over the peninsula among Japan, China, and, eventually, Russia.

Increasing competition for Korea led Japan to declare war on China in August 1894. The reverberations of the Sino-Japanese War suggested that the Japanese, Russians, French, Germans, and perhaps the British intended to partition China permanently. Equality of commercial opportunity, forerunner of the Open Door of the 1890s, was in jeopardy. The possibility of big power cooperation against American commercial interests raised questions in the United States about whether it might soon have to take some action to keep China open.

The Great Anglo-American Rapprochement

Despite the United States's expansionist activity during the latter half of the nineteenth century, perhaps the most profound and long-lasting development of those years was its eventual rapprochement with Britain. This gradual change in relations resulted from social, economic, political, and cultural similarities as well as from mutual need. Anglo-Saxon ties pulled the Atlantic nations together, particularly as they encountered challenges from Germany and Russia. But the trans-Atlantic friendship did not come easily. Four Anglo-American controversies by the 1890s—about fisheries, the 1888 election, seal hunting, and Venezuela—initially undermined hope for improved relations after the hard feelings stemming from British neutrality during the Civil War. The fisheries question, a recurring issue since 1783, again caused problems. Americans were also upset because they suspected British interference in the presidential election of 1888, and both Canadians and Americans became incensed over seal hunting practices off Alaska. Finally, a boundary dispute between Britain and Venezuela raised questions about the status of the Monroe Doctrine. Yet a major balancing factor was the growing world tensions that made Americans and Britons realize they needed each other.

The fisheries issue threatened Anglo-American relations again when, in the mid-1880s, the United States terminated rights granted Canada by the Treaty of Washington of 1871. Canadians retaliated by seizing Americans for violating fishing privileges allowed under the Convention of 1818. The House of Representatives in 1887 empowered the president to bar Canadians from U.S. ports. President Cleveland signed the measure, but only to place pressure on Canada to change its policy. A joint Anglo-American commission met in Washington that November and in the following February of 1888 reached a compromise; but the U.S. Senate hesitated to approve the pact. Republicans were afraid of a Democratic success so near a presidential election, and Democrats worried that a settlement with Britain would cost them the Irish-American vote. The Senate rejected the treaty.

Cleveland attempted to arouse popular support for the treaty by pursuing a usually profitable game of denouncing the British. Two days after the Senate's negative vote, he sent a fiery message to Congress calling on that body to authorize him to cut off all exports to Canada. While Anglophobes and Irish-Americans applauded this jab at Britain, Republican businessmen opposed commercial restrictions and sought to wriggle out of the partisan situation they had helped create. With an election imminent, the verdict rested with the American people.

Anglophobia permeated the campaign of 1888 as Cleveland lost ground in a bizarre episode during his bid for reelection. In an effort to determine the incumbent's real feelings toward England, a Californian wrote a letter of inquiry to the British minister in Washington, Sir Lionel Sackville-West, who violated diplomatic protocol by assuring the correspondent in a letter marked "private" that Cleveland was pro-English. A month later, the reply from Sackville-West appeared in the Republican *Los Angeles Times*. A New York paper trumpeted headlines that constituted a monument to Sackville-West's indiscretion as well as an epitaph to Cleveland's presidency: "THE BRITISH LION'S PAW THRUST INTO AMERICAN POLITICS TO HELP CLEVELAND."

Reaction was hot and heavy on both sides of the Atlantic. British Foreign Secretary Lord Salisbury sought an investigation, and the president helplessly watched the Irish-American vote slip from his grasp. Cleveland further escalated embittered relations with Britain when he sent Sackville-West home. The British press denounced the president, and Salisbury delayed sending a replacement until the following March, when Cleveland surrendered his office to the newly elected president, Republican Benjamin Harrison. Domestic political interests in the United States had created

the atmosphere for the shoddy affair, but peaceful foreign relations could be the chief casualty.

While this issue smoldered, the Harrison administration soon became locked in an emotional controversy with Britain over the fur-bearing seals of the Bering Sea. The Alaska Treaty of 1867 had included U.S. control over the Pribilof Islands in those waters, the habitat of nearly 4 million seals. As prices steadily rose for sealskins, hunters engaged in a mass slaughter of the animals drew such an angry cry of protest that the Washington government felt obligated to intervene. It first tried to restrict the killing to males since females were polygamous and could continue to replenish the supply. But it proved virtually impossible to distinguish male from female in the water, and increasing demands for the skins drove hunters into illegal pelagic, or open sea, sealing. Because the U.S. jurisdiction encompassed only the islands and territorial waters, hunting expeditions led primarily by Canadians simply hovered outside the three-mile zone and killed the seals, male and female.

President Harrison cautioned Canadians that anyone engaged in pelagic sealing was subject to capture, and he drew protests from both the British and Canadian governments when he authorized U.S. vessels to patrol the Bering Sea as a *mare clausum,* or closed sea, *not* as international waters. In early 1890 the state department warned the British that pelagic sealing created a state of "lawlessness" on the seas and that the next step would be a charge of piracy. Russia, the Harrison administration insisted, had long controlled the waters beyond the three-mile limit, and the acquisition of Alaska in 1867 had passed this "prescriptive right" to the United States. In mid-June the London government rejected these arguments and ominously proclaimed the United States "responsible for the consequences."

After another year of bitter disagreement, the United States and Britain submitted the seals dispute to arbitration. In the autumn of 1893 a tribunal meeting in Paris ruled against the United States on every count. The Bering Sea was international water, meaning that the Americans had no exclusive property rights over the seas. The United States eventually reimbursed Britain for damages, although by the early 1900s the two nations resolved the matter by joining other interested governments in placing regulations on the hunting of seals.

The seals controversy provided further evidence of the deep distrust between the Anglo-American peoples. If hard feelings developed over such a localized matter, even more serious trouble could erupt should problems arise over vital interests or national honor. Such an event developed in 1895, when Britain became embroiled in a boundary dispute with Venezuela.

The Venezuelan boundary problem had its roots in the early nineteenth century. In 1840 a British explorer and engineer, Robert Schomburgk, drew a border between Venezuela and British Guiana that the former refused to accept. The region in question affected control of the Orinoco River, which in turn determined the commerce of upper South America. During the 1880s gold was discovered in the disputed area, and Venezuela severed relations with Britain. The Venezuelans called for arbitration of the boundary issue, and the British agreed—but only in regions *west* of the Schomburgk line and *not* in lands inhabited by their nationals. Venezuela turned to Washington for arbitration of the disputed area, but the London government repeatedly rejected the U.S. proposals. By the 1890s the diplomatic situation had deteriorated enough to foment a crisis over the boundary.

Several reasons explain the stiffening mood in the United States. The depression of the 1890s had encouraged a search for foreign markets, and both President Cleveland and his secretary of state, Richard Olney, became concerned about Europe's deepening commercial penetration of South America. In 1894 William Scruggs, a former U.S. minister to Venezuela who now worked as special

agent for that government, wrote a widely read pamphlet that influenced Olney. Entitled *British Aggressions in Venezuela, or the Monroe Doctrine on Trial,* it warned that a British victory in the boundary dispute would give them control over a vital part of South America. Early the following year Congress unanimously approved a joint resolution instructing the president to recommend that Britain and Venezuela submit the matter to arbitration.

But before the resolution of the Venezuelan problem, Britain aroused fears about intervention in Nicaragua that in turn cast another shadow over the boundary issue. In April 1895 domestic unrest in that Central American country had led to property damage and expulsion of the British consul, and the London ministry retaliated by ordering the seizure of the port and customs house at Corinto. Although the Nicaraguan government made reparations the following month and British forces withdrew, the Cleveland administration remained concerned. It had not initially regarded the British action in Corinto as a violation of the Monroe Doctrine, but complaints had arisen from Americans over a British admiral's alleged dismissal of the Monroe Doctrine as meaningless. The president was already under attack for his stand on the Hawaiian matter, and the impression seemed to be growing that he was weak on Nicaragua. He *had* to move with dispatch on Venezuela.

An article by Republican Senator Henry Cabot Lodge had challenged the administration to assert "the supremacy of the Monroe Doctrine . . . peaceably if we can, forcibly if we must," and Olney prepared to do just that. In his proposed note to Britain, he focused on the Monroe Doctrine as his major argument. After Cleveland read the note, he responded that "your deliverance on Venezuelan affairs" was "the best thing of the kind I have ever read and it leads to a conclusion that one cannot escape if he tries—that is, if there's anything in the Monroe Doctrine at all."

Olney's note insisted on the right of the United States to step into any argument affecting Latin America and the Monroe Doctrine. He referred to the victory of the doctrine in the Maximilian affair of the 1860s and then quoted from it in denouncing Britain's actions in Venezuela. British use of force would violate the noninterference principle of the Monroe Doctrine and place Venezuela under "virtual duress." Their acquisition of land in Venezuela would encourage other European nations to seek permanent territorial gains out of "American soil." The United States was "practically sovereign on this continent, and its fiat is law." Its "infinite resources combined with its isolated position render it master of the situation and practically invulnerable as against any or all other powers." Olney then gave the note the air of an ultimatum by calling for arbitration and asking for a reply that the president could send Congress when it convened in early December.

Cleveland recognized the political capital accruing from the note, which he referred to as the "twenty-inch gun," but, to his credit, he also wanted the United States to use the Monroe Doctrine as justification for protecting a small *American* country being bullied by the British. A fellow Democrat assured him, "Turn this Venezuela question up or down, North, South, East or West, and it is a 'winner.'" The European powers, Cleveland believed, had staked out areas in Asia, Africa, and Latin America and needed a stern warning from the United States that it would not condone any threats to its economic and strategic interests in the hemisphere. Olney had stretched the meaning of Monroe's original declaration to encompass an alleged U.S. right to arbitrate any disagreement in the Western Hemisphere capable of attracting Old World intervention; yet the president complimented

Richard Olney
Secretary of state who used the Monroe Doctrine to protect U.S. interests in Latin America against believed British intrusions. *Henry James,* Richard Olney and His Public Service, *Boston: Houghton Mifflin Co., 1923, between pp. 78 and 79.*

him for placing the Monroe Doctrine "on better and more defensible ground than any of your predecessors—*or mine*." Britain's threat to Venezuela seemed providential—*if* the United States could resolve the issue short of war and with national honor intact.

British Foreign Secretary Salisbury failed to recognize the gravity of the situation and did not send a reply to the United States before Congress assembled in December. Indeed, he dismissed Olney's note as a simple outburst of Anglophobia designed for domestic political consumption. The U.S. ambassador to England, Thomas Bayard, had been unable to deliver the note to Salisbury until early August and had then failed to convince the foreign secretary of the seriousness of the matter. Bayard later recorded that Salisbury "expressed regret and surprise" that the United States had found it necessary "to present so far-reaching and important a principle and such wide and profound policies of international action in relation to a subject so comparatively small." Salisbury, preoccupied with other pressing issues, finally sent his reply in late November—by mail (not cable), and after going through the U.S. ambassador's office. The missive arrived in the United States on December 6, with Congress already in session.

Salisbury's note bore a near casual tone, but it left no doubt that he had rejected Olney's argument concerning the Monroe Doctrine. "I must not . . . be understood as expressing any acceptance of [the Monroe Doctrine] on the part of Her Majesty's Government," Salisbury emphasized. "The United States have a right, like any other nation, to interpose in any controversy by which their own interests are affected," he admitted, but "their rights are in no way strengthened or extended by the fact that the controversy affects some territory which is called American." The Monroe Doctrine, he said, bore no relevance to the Venezuelan boundary matter. The issue was neither European colonization nor an attempt by a European state to impose its government onto an American nation. The only matter at hand,

Salisbury concluded, was "the determination of the frontier of a British possession which belonged to the Throne of England long before the Republic of Venezuela came into existence."

President Cleveland hotly declared that Salisbury's note made him "mad clean through" and prepared to settle the boundary matter by a commission of Americans. In a special congressional message of December 17, 1895, he again highlighted the Monroe Doctrine: "If the balance of power is justly a cause for jealous anxiety among the Governments of the Old World and a subject for our absolute noninterference, none the less is an observance of the Monroe Doctrine of vital concern to our people and their government." Since the British had refused arbitration, he recommended that Congress empower him to appoint a commission to locate the boundary and the United States stand ready to enforce that commission's findings. It was, he admitted, "a grievous thing to contemplate the two great English-speaking peoples of the world as being otherwise than friendly competitors in the onward march of civilization." And yet the United States could never submit to "wrong and injustice, and the consequent loss of national self-respect and honor." Although it seemed that Cleveland's anger had taken control of his senses, he had actually provided an escape from war through a time-consuming boundary commission.

Congress voted $100,000 for the commission amid a wave of acclaim in Venezuela and the United States. The U.S. minister in Venezuela reported that thousands of people had gathered outside the legation to praise President Cleveland and that parades and demonstrations were widespread. Irish-Americans in the United States prepared for war, and New York City Police Commissioner Theodore Roosevelt bombastically proclaimed, "Let the fight come if it must; I don't care whether our sea coast cities are bombarded or not; we would take Canada." The editor of the *New York Tribune,* Whitelaw Reid, chimed in with the call for aggressive action by exalting the great opportunity afforded American merchants to expand trade into Central and South America. Although a host of influential Americans denounced the possibility of war over such a small issue, their protests rang hollow before the gathering storm.

What few observers seemed to realize (and what Cleveland and Olney doubtless foresaw) was that the long and tedious work of a boundary commission would permit the diplomats to take over. European events worked in the United States's favor. The British had problems in South Africa that would result in the disastrous Boer War, and they faced threats to world peace in Turkey and China. Finally, they were worried about their growing German rival. Salisbury recognized the absurdity in going to war over Venezuela's boundary, and he also understood the need for U.S. friendship. Public figures in Britain further defused the controversy when they joined the press in recalling good relations with the United States. The major concern of both the United States and Britain was to settle the matter by arbitration, but without loss of prestige.

By early 1897 the two nations were beginning to work their way out of the Venezuelan crisis. The solution did not come easily. They first negotiated the Olney-Pauncefote Treaty in January, which provided for general arbitration of disputes. The Senate, however, added several amendments before narrowly rejecting the package in May. The senators were concerned that an arbitration panel would take away their control over foreign affairs, whereas Irish-Americans feared that an arbitration treaty could lead to an Anglo-American alliance. The British found a face-saving way out of the imbroglio when they proposed that areas occupied by British subjects for fifty years or more could not pass to Venezuela or any other country.

In February 1897 Britain and Venezuela signed a treaty settling the boundary issue, but only after Olney exerted great pressure on the latter to come to the negotiating table. According to the agreement, arbitration would resolve the boundaries of all areas except those inhabited by subjects of either party for fifty years or more. This marked a British victory, because the approach removed from consideration the region east of the Schomburgk line of 1840, which British subjects had long inhabited. In October 1899 an arbitral court awarded Britain nearly 90 percent of the disputed territory, leaving Venezuela a small inland strip along the headwaters of the Orinoco River as well as Point Barima, which controlled its mouth. These were the only alterations in the original Schomburgk line. The results did not differ greatly from what Britain had tried to secure from Venezuela numerous times in the past.

The United States aroused the anger of many European nations and Latin American republics during the Venezuelan boundary dispute. Several Old World powers—including Germany, France, and Russia—resented the United States's claims of domination in the hemisphere, and in the New World Argentina, Chile, and Mexico expressed serious misgivings. Three years before the arbitral awards, a group of Latin American states had gathered in Mexico City, where several denounced the expansionist policies of the United States. Venezuelans remained unhappy because they had not participated in all of the negotiations and then had undergone U.S. pressure to sign a pact favorable to the British.

Yet the most far-reaching results of the Venezuelan boundary controversy were its impetus to Anglo-American rapprochement and to U.S. expansionist feeling. The appearance was that the British had retreated and that the Monroe Doctrine stood confirmed, but the truth is that the Cleveland administration had distorted the meaning of the Monroe Doctrine in a matter that the United States considered important to its interests. Both nations, however, had sensed the irrationality of an Anglo-American war and realized their mutual need for friendship. The ensuing rapprochement proved crucial to Britain's welfare and to the United States's continued rise to world power. The Venezuelan crisis fueled a wave of patriotism in the United States that would emerge in the imperialist and warlike "jingoist" spirit of the late 1890s.

Prognosis

By the end of the nineteenth century Americans had gone a long way toward recovering from the Civil War and appeared ready to focus again on a purposeful foreign policy that rested on a mix of strategic and commercial objectives. In retrospect, it seems clear that U.S. flirtations in the Caribbean, Pacific, and East Asia by the mid-1890s were signals of an imminent and deepening involvement once the embattled republic had healed its psyche and completed its time of preparation for overseas ventures. As if orchestrated by some higher hand, the United States now stood ready to take the first real steps toward becoming a world power.

Selected Readings

Allen, Helena G. *The Betrayal of Queen Liliuokalani, Last Queen of Hawaii, 1838–1917.* 1982.

Anderson, David L. *Imperialism and Idealism: American Diplomats in China, 1861–1898.* 1985.

Armstrong, William M. *E. L. Godkin and American Foreign Policy, 1865–1900.* 1957.

Barth, Gunther P. *Bitter Strength: A History of the Chinese in the United States, 1850–1870.* 1964.

Becker, William H. *The Dynamics of Business-Government Relations: Industry and Exports, 1893–1921.* 1982.

Beisner, Robert L. *From the Old Diplomacy to the New, 1865–1900.* 2nd ed., 1986.

Bourne, Kenneth. *Britain and the Balance of Power in North America, 1815–1908.* 1967.

Boyd, Nancy. *Emissaries: The Overseas Work of the American YWCA, 1895–1970.* 1987.

Bradford, Richard H. *The Virginius Affair.* 1980.

Brown, Dee. *Bury My Heart at Wounded Knee: An Indian History of the American West.* 1970.

Brown, Robert C. *Canada's National Policy, 1883–1900: A Study in Canadian-American Relations.* 1964.

Calhoun, Charles W. *Gilded Age Cato: The Life of Walter Q. Gresham.* 1988.

Campbell, Alexander E. *Great Britain and the United States, 1895–1903.* 1960.

Campbell, Charles S. *From Revolution to Rapprochement: The United States and Great Britain, 1783–1900.* 1974.

——. *The Transformation of American Foreign Relations, 1865–1900.* 1976.

Carosso, Vincent P. *The Morgans: Private International Bankers, 1854–1913.* 1987.

Carstensen, Fred V. *American Enterprise in Foreign Markets: Studies of Singer and International Harvester in Imperial Russia.* 1984.

Chay, Jongsuk. *Diplomacy of Asymmetry: Korean-American Relations to 1910.* 1990.

Chên, Jerome. *China and the West: Society and Culture, 1815–1937.* 1979.

Chester, Edward W. *Clash of Titans: Africa and U.S. Foreign Policy.* 1974.

Clendenen, Clarence, Collins, Robert, and Duignan, Peter. *Americans in Africa, 1865–1900.* 1966.

Cohen, Warren I. *America's Response to China: An Interpretive History of Sino-American Relations.* 2000.

Cook, Adrian. *The* Alabama *Claims: American Politics and Anglo-American Relations, 1865–1900.* 1975.

Cooling, Benjamin F. *Gray Steel and Blue Water Navy: The Formative Years of America's Military-Industrial Complex, 1881–1917.* 1979.

Crapol, Edward P. *America for Americans: Economic Nationalism and Anglophobia in the Late Nineteenth Century.* 1973.

——. *James G. Blaine: Architect of Empire.* 2000.

Crowe, Sybil E. *The Berlin West African Conference, 1884–1885.* 1942.

Darby, Phillip. *Three Faces of Imperialism: British and American Approaches to Asia and Africa, 1870–1970.* 1987.

Davids, Jules. *American Political and Economic Penetration of Mexico, 1877–1920.* 1976.

Davies, Robert B. *Peacefully Working to Conquer the World: Singer Sewing Machines in Foreign Markets, 1854–1920.* 1976.

DeConde, Alexander. *Ethnicity, Race, and American Foreign Policy: A History.* 1992.

Debo, Angie. *A History of the Indians in the United States.* 1970.

Devine, Michael J. *John W. Foster: Politics and Diplomacy in the Imperial Era, 1873–1917.* 1981.

Doenecke, Justus D. *The Presidencies of James A. Garfield and Chester A. Arthur.* 1981.

Donald, David H. *Charles Sumner and the Rights of Man.* 1970.

Drake, Frederick C. *The Empire of the Seas: A Biography of Rear Admiral Robert Wilson Shufeldt, USN.* 1984.

Duignan, Peter, and Gann, L. H. *The United States and Africa: A History.* 1984.

Dulles, Foster Rhea. *Prelude to World Power: 1860–1900.* 1965.

Eggert, Gerald G. *Richard Olney: Evolution of a Statesman.* 1974.

Faulkner, Harold U. *Politics, Reform and Expansion, 1890–1900.* 1959.

Flynt, Wayne, and Berkley, Gerald W. *Taking Christianity to China: Alabama Missionaries in the Middle Kingdom, 1850–1950.* 1997.

Friedberg, Aaron L. *The Weary Titan: Britain and the Experience of Relative Decline, 1865–1905.* 1988.

Fritz, Henry E. *The Movement for Indian Assimilation, 1860–1890.* 1963.

Fry, Joseph A. *Henry S. Sanford: Diplomacy and Business in Nineteenth-Century America.* 1982.

———. *John Tyler Morgan and the Search for Southern Autonomy.* 1992.

Garraty, John A. *The New Commonwealth, 1877–1890.* 1968.

Gay, James T. *American Fur Seal Diplomacy: The Alaska Fur Seal Controversy.* 1987.

Goldberg, Joyce S. *The* Baltimore *Affair.* 1986.

Graham, Gael. *Gender, Culture, and Christianity: American Protestant Schools in China, 1880–1930.* 1995.

Grenville, John A. S., and Young, George B. *Politics, Strategy, and American Diplomacy: Studies in Foreign Policy, 1873–1917.* 1966.

Hagan, Kenneth J. *American Gunboat Diplomacy and the Old Navy, 1877–1889.* 1973.

———. *This People's Navy: The Making of American Sea Power.* 1991.

Hanna, Alfred J., and Hanna, Kathryn A. *Napoleon III and Mexico: American Triumph over Monarchy.* 1971.

Harrington, Fred H. *God, Mammon, and the Japanese: Horace N. Allen and Korean-American Relations, 1884–1905.* 1944.

Headrick, Daniel R. *The Invisible Weapon: Telecommunications and International Politics, 1851–1945.* 1991.

Healy, David. *U.S. Expansionism: The Imperialist Urge in the 1890s.* 1970.

Hernández, José M. *Cuba and the United States: Intervention and Militarism, 1868–1933.* 1993.

Hill, Patricia R. *The World Their Household: The American Woman's Foreign Mission Movement and Cultural Transformation, 1870–1920.* 1985.

Hofstadter, Richard. *Social Darwinism in American Thought, 1860–1915.* 1944.

Holbo, Paul S. *Tarnished Expansion: The Alaska Scandal, the Press, and Congress, 1867–1871.* 1983.

Hoogenboom, Ari A. *Rutherford B. Hayes: Warrior and President.* 1995.

———. *The Presidency of Rutherford B. Hayes.* 1988.

Hunt, Michael H. *Ideology and U.S. Foreign Policy.* 1987.

———. *The Making of a Special Relationship: The United States and China to 1914.* 1997.

Iriye, Akira. *Across the Pacific: An Inner History of American-East Asian Relations.* 1967.

Jenkins, Brian. *Fenians and Anglo-American Relations during Reconstruction.* 1969.

Jensen, Ronald J. *The Alaska Purchase and Russian-American Relations.* 1975.

Johnson, Robert E. *Far China Station: The U.S. Navy in Asian Waters, 1800–1898.* 1979.

Kennedy, Paul M. *The Samoan Tangle: A Study in Anglo-German-American Relations, 1878–1900.* 1974.

Koistinen, Paul A. *Mobilizing for Modern War: The Political Economy of American Warfare, 1865–1919.* 1997.

Kushner, Howard I. *Conflict on the Northwest Coast: American-Russian Rivalry in the Pacific Northwest, 1790–1867.* 1975.

Kuykendall, Ralph S. *The Hawaiian Kingdom: The KalaKaua Dynasty, 1874–1893,* vol. 1, 1967.

LaFeber, Walter. *The American Search for Opportunity, 1865–1913.* 1993. The Cambridge History of American Foreign Relations, vol. 2. Cohen, Warren I. ed.

———. *The New Empire: An Interpretation of American Expansion, 1860–1898.* 1963, 1998.

Lake, David A. *Power, Protection, and Free Trade: International Sources of U.S. Commercial Strategy, 1887–1939.* 1988.

Langley, Lester D. *The Cuban Policy of the United States: A Brief History.* 1968.

———. *Struggle for the American Mediterranean: United States–European Rivalry in the Gulf-Caribbean, 1776–1904.* 1976.

Lee, Yur-Bok. *Diplomatic Relations Between the United States and Korea, 1866–1887.* 1970.

Long, David F. *Gold Braid and Foreign Relations: Diplomatic Activities of U.S. Naval Officers, 1798–1883.* 1988.

Martin, Lawrence. *The Presidents and the Prime Ministers: Washington and Ottawa Face to Face: The Myth of Bilateral Bliss, 1867–1982.* 1982.

Martinez-Fernández, Luis. *Torn Between Empires: Economy, Society, and Patterns of Political Thought in the Hispanic Caribbean, 1840–1878.* 1994.

Masterman, Sylvia. *The Origins of International Rivalry in Samoa, 1845–1884.* 1934.

Mattox, Henry E. *The Twilight of Amateur Diplomacy: The American Foreign Service and Its Senior Officers in the 1890s.* 1989.

May, Ernest R. *Imperial Democracy: The Emergence of America as a Great Power.* 1961.

McCabe, James O. *The San Juan Water Boundary Question.* 1965.

McClain, Charles J. *In Search of Equality: The Chinese Struggle Against Discrimination in Nineteenth-Century America.* 1994.

McClellan, Robert. *The Heathen Chinee: A Study of American Attitudes Toward China, 1890–1905.* 1971.

McFeely, William S. *Grant: A Biography.* 1981.

McWilliams, Tennant S. *The New South Faces the World: Foreign Affairs and the Southern Sense of Self, 1877–1950.* 1988.

Miller, Stuart C. *The Unwelcome Immigrant: The American Image of the Chinese, 1785–1882.* 1969.

Morgan, H. Wayne. *From Hayes to McKinley: National Party Politics, 1877–1896.* 1969.

Neidhardt, Wilfried. *Fenianism in North America.* 1975.

Nevins, Allan. *Hamilton Fish: The Inner History of the Grant Administration.* 1936.

Orde, Anne. *The Eclipse of Great Britain: The United States and British Imperial Decline, 1895–1956.* 1996.

Osborne, Thomas J. *"Empire Can Wait": American Opposition to Hawaiian Annexation, 1893–1898.* 1981.

Pakenham, Thomas. *The Scramble for Africa, 1876–1912.* 1991.

Paolino, Ernest N. *The Foundations of the American Empire: William Henry Seward and U.S. Foreign Policy.* 1973.

Pérez, Louis A. *Cuba and the United States: Ties of Singular Intimacy.* 1997.

———. *Cuba Between Empires, 1878–1902.* 1982.

Perkins, Bradford. *The Great Rapprochement: England and the United States, 1895–1914.* 1968.

Perkins, Dexter. *The Monroe Doctrine, 1867–1907.* 1937.

Pike, Frederick B. *Chile and the United States, 1880–1962: The Emergence of Chile's Social Crisis and the Challenge to United States Diplomacy.* 1963.

Plesur, Milton. *America's Outward Thrust: Approaches to Foreign Affairs, 1865–1890.* 1971.

Pletcher, David M. *The Awkward Years: American Foreign Relations under Garfield and Arthur.* 1961.

———. *The Diplomacy of Trade and Investment: American Economic Expansion in the Hemisphere, 1865–1900.* 1998.

———. *Rails, Mines, and Progress: Seven American Promoters in Mexico, 1867–1911.* 1958.

———. "Rhetoric and Results: A Pragmatic View of American Economic Expansionism, 1865–98," *Diplomatic History* 5 (1981): 93–105.

Preston, Richard A. *The Defence of the Undefended Border: Planning for War in North America, 1867–1939.* 1977.

Priest, Loring B. *Uncle Sam's Stepchildren: The Reformation of United States Indian Policy, 1865–1887.* 1969.

Raat, W. Dirk. *Mexico and the United States: Ambivalent Vistas.* 1992.

Redkey, Edwin S. *Black Exodus: Black Nationalist and Back-to-Africa Movements, 1890–1910.* 1969.

Rosenberg, Emily S. *Spreading the American Dream: American Economic and Cultural Expansion, 1890–1945.* 1982.

Ruiz, Ramón E. *Cuba: The Making of a Revolution.* 1968.

———. *The People of Sonora and Yankee Capitalists.* 1988.

Russ, W. A., Jr. *The Hawaiian Republic, 1894–98.* 1961.

———. *The Hawaiian Revolution, 1893–94.* 1959.

Rydell, Robert W. *All the World's a Fair: Visions of Empire at American International Expositions, 1876–1916.* 1984.

———. *World of Fairs: The Century-of-Progress Expositions.* 1993.

Sater, William F. *Chile and the United States: Empires in Conflict.* 1990.

Saul, Norman E. *Concord and Conflict: The United States and Russia, 1867–1914.* 1996.

———. *Distant Friends: The United States and Russia, 1763–1867.* 1991.

Schmitt, Karl M. *Mexico and the United States, 1821–1973: Conflict and Coexistence.* 1974.

Schonberger, Howard B. *Transportation to the Seaboard: The Communication Revolution and American Foreign Policy, 1860–1900.* 1971.

Schoonover, Thomas. *Dollars over Dominion: The Triumph of Liberalism in Mexican–United States Relations, 1861–1867.* 1978.

———. *The United States in Central America, 1860–1911: Episodes of Social Imperialism and Imperial Rivalry in the World System.* 1991.

Schoultz, Lars. *Beneath the United States: A History of U.S. Policy Toward Latin America.* 1998.

Seager II, Robert. *Alfred Thayer Mahan.* 1977.

Shippee, Lester B. *Canadian-American Relations, 1849–1874.* 1939.

Shulman, Mark R. *Navalism and the Emergence of American Sea Power, 1882–1893.* 1995.

Skinner, Elliott P. *African Americans and U.S. Policy Toward Africa, 1850–1924: In Defense of Black Nationality.* 1992.

Smith, Goldwin. *The Treaty of Washington, 1871.* 1941.

Smith, Joseph. *Illusions of Conflict: Anglo-American Diplomacy Toward Latin America, 1865–1896.* 1979.

Socolofsky, Homer E., and Spetter, Allan B. *The Presidency of Benjamin Harrison.* 1987.

Sprout, Harold and Margaret. *The Rise of American Naval Power, 1776–1918.* 1944.

Spurr, David. *The Rhetoric of Empire: Colonial Discourse in Journalism, Travel Writing, and Imperial Administration.* 1993.

Stephanson, Anders. *Manifest Destiny: American Expansionism and the Empire of Right.* 1995.

Stevens, S. K. *American Expansion in Hawaii, 1842–1898.* 1945.

Still, William N., Jr. *American Sea Power in the Old World: The United States Navy in European and Near Eastern Waters, 1865–1917.* 1980.

Storti, Craig. *Incident at Bitter Creek: The Story of the Rock Springs Chinese Massacre.*

Stuart, Reginald C. *United States Expansionism and British North America, 1775–1871.* 1988.

Tansill, Charles C. *The United States and Santo Domingo, 1798–1873: A Chapter in Caribbean Diplomacy.* 1938.

Tate, Merze. *Hawaii: Reciprocity or Annexation.* 1968.

———. *The United States and the Hawaiian Kingdom: A Political History.* 1965.

Terrill, Tom. *The Tariff, Politics, and American Foreign Policy, 1874–1901.* 1973.

Topik, Steven C. *Trade and Gunboats: The United States and Brazil in the Age of Empire.* 1996.

Travis, Frederick F. *George Kennan and the American-Russian Relationship, 1865–1924.* 1990.

Trefousse, Hans L. *Carl Schurz: A Biography.* 1982.

Trennert, Robert A., Jr. *Alternatives to Extinction: Federal Indian Policy and the Beginnings of the Reservation System, 1846–51.* 1975.

Tsai, Shih-shan Henry. *China and the Overseas Chinese in the United States, 1868–1911.* 1983.

Tweed, Thomas A. *The American Encounter with Buddhism, 1844–1912: Victorian Culture and the Limits of Dissent.* 1992.

Tyrrell, Ian R. *Women's World/Women's Empire: The Woman's Christian Temperance Union in International Perspective, 1800–1930.* 1991.

Utley, Robert M. *The Indian Frontier of the American West, 1846–1890.* 1984.

———. *The Lance and the Shield: The Life and Times of Sitting Bull.* 1993.

Van Deusen, Glyndon G. *William Henry Seward.* 1967.

Vestal, Stanley. *War-Path and Council Fire.* 1948.

Walker, Mabel G. *The Fenian Movement.* 1969.

Warner, Donald F. *The Idea of Continental Union: Agitation for the Annexation of Canada to the United States, 1849–1893.* 1960.

Washburn, Wilcomb E. *The Indian in America.* 1975.

Weeks, Philip. *Farewell, My Nation: The American Indian and the United States, 1820–1890.* 1990.

Welch, Richard E., Jr. *The Presidencies of Grover Cleveland.* 1988.

Weston, Rubin F. *Racism in U.S. Imperialism: The Influence of Racial Assumptions on American Foreign Policy, 1893–1946.* 1972.

Wiebe, Robert H. *The Search for Order, 1877–1920.* 1967.

Wilkins, Mira. *The Emergence of Multinational Enterprise: American Business Abroad from the Colonial Era to 1914.* 1970.

Williams, Walter L. *Black Americans and the Evangelization of Africa, 1877–1900.* 1982.

Williams, William A. *The Roots of the Modern American Empire.* 1969.

———. *The Tragedy of American Diplomacy.* 1959, 1962.

CHAPTER 11

U.S. Imperialism and the New Manifest Destiny, 1897–1900

Background

During the late 1890s the entire demeanor of the United States dramatically changed as it became deeply involved in the Caribbean, Pacific, and Asia in a surge of national feeling that became known as the "new manifest destiny." Whereas the expansionist drive of the 1840s had spent itself within the continental United States, the great industrial, technological, and commercial advances of the post–Civil War era turned U.S. interests toward distant shores. Expansion was inevitable and relentless, according to Secretary of State John Hay. "No man, no party, can fight with any chance of final success against a cosmic tendency; no cleverness, no popularity avails against the spirit of the age."

By the 1890s any U.S. interest in the actual annexation of territory had given way to "informal empire," or commercial penetration that led either to economic dominance without direct political controls or to the acquisition of colonies having no prospect of statehood. The expansionist mood was not national, partly because of the lack of cohesion in the political parties, and partly because of the general fragmentation still evident from the Civil War. Anti-imperialist feelings ran strong, especially among Americans who rec-

ognized their nation's limitations outside the hemisphere, but also among those who feared the incorporation of nonwhite peoples and worried about the negative effects of imperialism on democratic institutions. But the economic hard times of the decade dictated a search for new commercial outlets, not so much for acquiring sources of raw materials as for securing markets capable of absorbing the United States's excess stock of manufactured goods. Although business and government did not jointly orchestrate a push toward expansion, commercial interests often had the Washington government's tacit support in searching for investment fields and foreign markets that would promote the good of the economy and hence safeguard the national interest.

During the last third of the nineteenth century some Americans had already taken the lead in trying to revive the spirit of expansion. Church groups called for increased missionary work among the primitive areas of the world and soon found themselves with unnatural allies. The English philosopher Herbert Spencer and the Yale sociologist William Graham Sumner, both using Charles Darwin's ideas of evolution, advocated the theories of Social Darwinism and Anglo-Saxon superiority in encouraging Americans to believe that the strong would survive and that the only limitations on growth were self-imposed. Darwin wrote that "there is apparently much truth in the belief that the wonderful progress of the United States as well as the character of the people are the results of natural selection" and that the American nation was "the heir of all ages."

A number of Americans helped to popularize these ideas, including historian John Fiske, Reverend Josiah Strong, intellectual Brooks Adams, political scientist John Burgess, and public figures such as William H. Seward, Ulysses S. Grant, James G. Blaine, and, the most outspoken of all, the wealthy and flamboyant New Yorker Theodore Roosevelt. Brooks Adams and Roosevelt often gathered at Henry Adams's (Brooks's brother) house in Washington, discussing these ideas and developing into a tightly knit group that advocated commercial and territorial expansion as the chief means toward building a stronger nation and guaranteeing national security. Historian Frederick Jackson Turner suggested the imminence of increased international involvement in 1893 when he declared before the American Historical Association that the American frontier was closed; the end of free land, he seemed to assert, portended expansion abroad. Philosophers, missionaries, naval officers, business leaders, farmers—all warned that U.S. hesitation on the international front would concede Africa, Asia, and the Pacific to European powers.

The United States's growing export trade necessitated a larger navy to defend projected sea lanes. During the Civil War, Union naval commanders had become aware of the need for coaling stations in the Caribbean and Pacific. Afterward, many Americans supported the ideas of Captain Alfred T. Mahan of the navy, who in his seminal work, *The Influence of Seapower upon History, 1660–1783* (1890), called for overseas bases, expanded commerce, and an isthmian canal—but only after the United States had built a navy strong enough to protect its possessions. Ironically, Mahan's initial influence was greatest in Great Britain, Germany, and Japan. But even before his great work appeared, his ideas had attracted con-

Alfred T. Mahan
His writings on seapower influenced the thinking of the Germans, Japanese, and Americans— in particular, Theodore Roosevelt. *Contact print from Frances Benjamin Johnson negative; Library of Congress.*

siderable interest. One of the founders of the Naval War College in the United States, Rear Admiral Stephen B. Luce, was a major advocate of Mahan's ideas and helped establish the modern U.S. Navy. Mahan soon became an instructor among the first faculty at the War College and continued to spread his ideas in the years afterward, with notable impact on Theodore Roosevelt. Congressional and popular support for a navy had been negligible before the mid-1880s, primarily because relative peace in Europe had allowed security to develop in the Western Hemisphere through only minimal effort. Thus, while other nations built steel ships, the United States continued to repair sails, replace rotted wooden hulls, and deploy ironclads for inland duties. But growing international rivalries in Europe forced a change in America's world outlook. Interest in steel battleships soon grew so rapidly in the United States that within a decade its fleet ranked seventh in the world.

U.S. expansionists encountered many obstacles. Anti-imperialist groups, led by Senator Carl Schurz, writer Mark Twain, and newspaper editor E. L. Godkin, were more interested in bettering America's domestic institutions than in acquiring territories. Despite a growing race for European partition of Africa by the last years of the century, Americans lacked the naval power to show anything more than mild interest in that continent as a potential trade outlet or source of private adventure. Some Americans simply opposed the addition of dark-skinned peoples to the United States. Godkin fought against the acquisition of Santo Domingo because, he declared, that country had 200,000 "ignorant Catholic Spanish negroes" who might expect U.S. citizenship. Others argued that the establishment of colonies necessarily ruled out self-government and often led to competition that caused wars.

Political considerations had also blocked any interest in expansion. The United States could not make any firm moves toward world involvement until 1896, when the Republicans won the White House and both houses of Congress and soon banded together behind a new kind of foreign expansion built upon a two-headed missionary and commercial impulse. The expansionist Democratic party had been able to gain control of the presidency on only two occasions between 1865 and the first part of the new century. Even then, its standard bearer both times, Grover Cleveland, opposed imperialism. By 1897, however, the United States was ready to assume a global role under Republican leadership.

Several factors combined to push U.S. interests beyond its present borders. One catalyst was the desire to act before European powers incorporated everything of value. Expansionist Senator Henry Cabot Lodge of Massachusetts exuberantly declared in 1895 that "the great nations are rapidly absorbing for their future expansion and their present defense all the waste places of the earth. It

is a movement which makes for civilization and the advancement of the race. As one of the great nations of the world," he warned, "the United States must not fall out of the line of march." Another impetus to U.S. expansion was commercial—encouraged by the Panic of 1893 and the ensuing economic depression. Still another was the adventuresome feeling of seeing the American flag flying over some foreign shore. Perhaps most important, however, was the growing understanding among Americans that their security was integrally related to events beyond their continental borders.

As in the 1840s the United States sought to harmonize realistic expansionist aims based on commercial and security considerations with idealistic goals focusing on the exportation of democracy and humanitarianism. And, as in the earlier period, Americans colored their realistic drive for imperialism—or empire—with idealistic labels emphasizing "destiny," "progress," and the spread of "civilization." Encouraged by the warlike jingoes and the sensationalist news stories carried by the burgeoning "yellow press," the United States entered a war with Spain in 1898 that resulted in the republic's first acquisition of an overseas colony and helped to end the divisive legacy of the Civil War. The war with Spain also furthered the decline of American isolationism and, because the British found themselves without an ally in this period and tended to take the side of the Americans against Spain, tightened the growing Anglo-American rapprochement. At virtually the same time—and not by sheer coincidence—Americans turned greater attention toward Asia for both realistic and idealistic reasons. The overseas expansion of the late 1890s alerted the world that the United States was about to become a great power.

Final Overture to Imperialism: Cuba and the Yellow Press

The renewed insurrection in Cuba in February 1895 led the United States into the imperialist age. Three years earlier, a Cuban exile in the United States had established the Cuban Revolutionary Party, whose goal was to overthrow Spanish rule on the island. The United States's official concern over Cuba had meanwhile declined when Spain abolished slavery and promised other reforms after the Ten Years' War had ended in 1878. In 1890 the U.S. Congress passed the McKinley Tariff, which stimulated the island's sugar industry, and the following year the United States agreed to permit tariff-free entry of the Cuban product. But the economic boom proved temporary, because the Panic of 1893 and Democratic control of Congress led to a new tariff setting high duties and virtually slamming the door on Cuban sugar imports. The ensuing depression in Cuba plus accumulated political and economic grievances set off the insurrection in 1895.

Led by General Máximo Gómez, the Cuban rebels proclaimed a republic on the eastern end of the island and proceeded to extend control over most of the surrounding region. The war was actually a resumption of the Ten Years' War, because the Spanish peace had promised much and delivered little. The Cubans had supposedly won amnesty and certain governmental rights, but the changes proved to be only a façade and the problems that had caused the long conflict persisted. Spain had not fulfilled its assurances of relief, and the bulk of the island's revenues went either toward paying Cuba's debt or directly into Spain's coffers. Cuba's complaints went unheeded by Spanish officials on the island, and Gómez, a hardened veteran of the Ten Years' War, retaliated with a "scorched-earth" policy, which entailed dynamiting passenger trains and burning the Spanish loyalists' property and sugar plantations—including many owned by Americans. Gómez intended to make the island a liability for the Spanish and force its independence or to bring about U.S. intervention in its behalf. By late 1896 the guerrilla forces controlled nearly two-thirds of the island, with the Spanish hovering along the coast and in the cities.

The Cuban war took an even uglier twist in February 1896, when Spain's new captain general on the island, Valeriano Weyler, sought to destroy the rebels' rural quarters by dividing the island into districts and establishing reconcentration centers. His directives herded all inhabitants of central and western Cuba into the towns, which Weyler barricaded with trenches rimmed by barbed wire and reinforced with soldiers in guardhouses overlooking the encampments. Nearly half a million Cubans, young and old, male and female, were quartered in hot, unsanitary, and sparsely provisioned barbed wire enclosures; anyone refusing to go along was shot. By the spring of 1898 the reconcentrado policies of "Butcher" Weyler, as he was soon called, led to widespread hunger and disease that took the lives of thousands of the captives (mostly women and children), a large proportion of the Cuban population.

The realities of the reconcentration camps were harsh enough, but the sordid episode soon fell prey to a major development in U.S. news reporting known as "yellow journalism." William Randolph Hearst had bought the struggling *New York Journal* in late 1895 and prepared to challenge Joseph Pulitzer's *New York World* for top circulation in the country. Dramatic headlines, lurid and exaggerated stories, creative writing, graphic detail, suggestions of sexual misconduct by Spanish officials—all ploys became acceptable means for selling newspapers. Hearst hired the famous portrait artist of the Indian and American West, Frederic Remington, to visit Cuba and bring back drawings illustrating the fighting. When Remington soon notified Hearst of his inability to locate the war, the newspaper owner shot back: "You furnish the pictures and I'll furnish the war." Spain emerged in the yellow press as the sole perpetrator of atrocity in Cuba, arousing strong sentiment for U.S. intervention to ensure the island's independence.

Day after day the *Journal* and *World* competed with each other for the most spectacular coverage. Hearst's paper set the tone by describing "Weyler the soldier[,] ... Weyler the brute, the devastator of haciendas, the destroyer of families, and the outrager of women. . . . Pitiless, cold, an exterminator of men." The *Journal* saw no way "to prevent his carnal, animal brain from running riot with itself in inventing tortures and infamies of bloody debauchery." Pulitzer's *World* retaliated in kind, writing of "blood on the roadsides, blood in the fields, blood on the doorsteps, blood, blood, blood! The old, the young, the weak, the crippled—all are butchered without mercy." It finally asked, "Is there no nation wise enough, brave enough, and strong enough to restore peace in this bloodsmitten land?"

Not to be outdone, Hearst's *Journal* exploited sex to sell copy. His press picked up the story of a young Cuban girl named Evangelina Cisneros, who was thrown into prison, allegedly after fending off the advances of her male Spanish captors. Thousands of American women responded to Hearst's appeal for help by signing petitions in her behalf and dismissing the Spanish minister's claim that Hearst had fabricated the story. Shortly afterward, a reporter for Hearst's paper made his way to Havana, freed Evangelina by sawing through the jail bars, and, after disguising her as a boy, brought her to the United States. The *Journal* proudly sported the headline: "An American Newspaper Accomplishes in a Single Stroke What the Best Efforts of Diplomacy Failed Utterly to Bring about in Many Months." Washington, D.C., and New York City's Madison Square Garden hosted great receptions in her honor, and the governor of Missouri mockingly suggested that Hearst send 500 reporters to liberate the entire island of Cuba.

In the same vein, another headline event drew attention to a group of females removed from a U.S. vessel. Spanish officers had boarded the ship as it prepared to leave Havana, allegedly to search three young Cuban women suspected of carrying rebel mail packets. Highlighting the inflammatory story was Remington's fabricated sketch of a nude female suspect standing before leering Spanish officers. The

Journal indignantly asked: "Does Our Flag Protect Women?"

The yellow press deepened U.S. concern for Cuba. The United States already had economic interests in the war's outcome. Investors had sunk nearly $50 million in sugar and tobacco production and in iron and manganese mines and other enterprises, and trade between the countries had reached as high as $100 million in an exceptional year. These businesses drastically declined during the revolution. In the meantime, the Cuban war became a heavy expense for the U.S. government. Spanish officials on the island arrested Americans who had become naturalized Cubans, and the United States felt bound to secure their freedom. U.S. naval vessels meanwhile patrolled the Atlantic coast to halt illegal arms shipments to the Cuban rebels. In an attempt to end the hostilities, humanitarians, religious leaders, Americans with economic stakes in Cuba, and a large number of daily newspapers from both political camps became allies in denouncing Spanish oppression and urging reform. Few considered annexation of the island as a solution. Interventionists wanted an independent Cuba, not a transfer of title to Washington.

The Cleveland administration resisted the growing popular clamor for intervention in Cuba. Yet it could not ignore the pressure from a Republican Congress to recognize Cuban belligerency. The White House had several options. It could recognize the Cuban belligerents, although Secretary of State Richard Olney warned that such a policy would prevent Americans from securing damage claims from Spain after the war. Recognition of Cuban independence posed another possibility. Both the president and Olney feared that the Cubans were unfit to govern themselves, however, and that the ensuing anarchy would invite Old World intervention. Besides, Spain might declare war and force U.S. involvement on the ground that a Spanish effort to defeat a newly independent Cuba would constitute an infraction of the Monroe Doctrine. The third possibility was the only feasible choice: Exert pressure on the Madrid government to permit the Cubans a degree of autonomy within the empire that would undermine native resistance. In April 1896 Olney sent a note to Spain urging reforms on the island.

But popular sentiment for the rebels continued to grow in the United States, forcing Congress to pass a resolution extending recognition to Cuban belligerency. The resulting anti-American demonstrations in Spain exploded in violence when 15,000 people stoned the U.S. consulate in Barcelona and destroyed the American flag. Despite widespread support for Cuba in the United States, Cleveland warned that should Congress declare war on Spain, he as commander in chief of the armed forces would refuse to send Americans to fight. Spain did not implement Washington's reform recommendations, and the administration did not want war. Yet the president had to protect U.S. interests in Cuba. While Congress called for stronger measures, the U.S. consul general in Havana repeatedly urged annexation. With Cleveland's Democratic party disintegrating on the eve of the presidential election of 1896, his administration could do little about the Cuban problem. The situation on the island had to await a new president.

The Cuban Prologue to War

In November 1896 the Republican party, led by William McKinley of Ohio, won the White House on a platform stressing expansion. Four years earlier the Republicans had resurrected the term "manifest destiny" and incorporated it into their campaign. Although the presidential race of 1896 had centered on currency and tariff issues, the Republicans called for a strong foreign policy that rested on an expanded naval power. Their platform advocated the acquisition of Hawaii, the use of U.S. influence to bring peace and independence to Cuba, the construction of a Nicaraguan canal under U.S. ownership and control, and the establishment of a naval base in the West Indies. Although McKinley agreed

with Alfred T. Mahan's ideas about the need for a stronger navy, he was not an imperialist. He assured anti-imperialist Carl Schurz that his administration would permit "no jingo nonsense." McKinley's first secretary of state, John Sherman, declared his opposition "to all acquisitions of territory not on the mainland."

The new administration, however, quickly realized that the Cuban issue was again approaching crisis intensity and could force U.S. intervention in the name of humanity. Spain had not implemented needed reforms, and in June 1897 the Washington government sent a note to Madrid protesting Weyler's tactics. The following month the administration instructed the new U.S. minister in Spain, Stewart Woodford, to demand Spanish withdrawal from Cuba. By the autumn, prospects for reform looked brighter when a liberal government took over in Madrid after a shocking incident—the assassination of the prime minister. The new ministry called Weyler home, assured Washington of an end to reconcentration policies, and guaranteed more autonomy to the islanders through the popular election of legislatures. President McKinley told Congress in his annual message in December that the United States should give the reforms a chance. Yet if they yielded no results, he warned, intervention might take place because of "our obligations to ourselves, to civilization and humanity."

By early 1898 Spain's promised political reforms had still not materialized, and in January the United States sent the battleship *Maine* to Cuba as a show of force to persuade the Spanish to grant the changes necessary to end the war. The Cuban rebels had elevated their demands for autonomy to independence, putting Madrid's ministry in an uneasy position between them and Spanish loyalists in Cuba who rioted that same month over the question of autonomy. Such a concession, the loyalists feared, would promote the election of a legislature injurious to their interests on the island. Besides, the granting of Cuban independence could bring down the ministry at home. Meanwhile the *Maine,* anchored in

Havana harbor, became a symbol of U.S. imperialism and a veritable announcement of deepening intervention by Washington. A close adviser to the president prophetically warned that sending the vessel to Cuba was like "waving a match in an oil well for fun."

While tensions grew over the *Maine,* a crisis developed when the Department of State in Washington received a copy of a private letter written in late 1897 from the Spanish minister in the United States, Enrique Dupuy de Lôme, to a friend in Cuba. De Lôme opposed war with the United States and had become frustrated over the events that seemed to be leading irrevocably to conflict. Already reputed to be arrogant and cynical, he confirmed these observations by indiscreetly describing McKinley as "weak and a bidder for the admiration of the crowd, . . . a would-be politician who tries to leave a door open behind himself while keeping on good terms with the jingoes of his party." Worse, de Lôme suggested that his government simply reject the Cuban demand for autonomy and consider economic reprisals, which, to many Americans, proved Spain's lack of sincerity about seeking peace.

By the time the de Lôme letter reached Washington, it had become a *cause célèbre* because a rebel partisan had somehow gotten hold of it and shared it with a number of Americans, including William Randolph Hearst. The same day the state department received the missive, February 9, the letter appeared in the *New York Journal* under the carefully crafted headline, "Worst Insult to the United States in Its History." Madrid's unavoidable decision to recall de Lôme, who had already packed his bags, further exacerbated the dangerous situation by removing Spain's chief spokesman for peace in the United States. During the next critical weeks Spain had no minister in Washington to vent Americans' anger.

Less than a week later, on the night of February 15, the *Maine* blew up in Havana harbor, sending more than 260 U.S. officers and men to their watery graves as the 7000-ton battleship crumpled and sank. Americans blamed Spain. In their anger, they failed to consider that such an act meant certain war with the United States—a calamity the Spanish could *not* have wanted. But emotions swept aside reason as the *New York Journal* trumpeted these headlines: "The Warship Maine Was Split In Two By An Enemy's Infernal Machine"; "The Whole Country Thrills With War Fever"; "The Maine Was Destroyed By Treachery." Two days after the incident, the *Journal* included a diagram on the front page allegedly showing the placement of a mine that sank the ship. To right this great wrong, the paper offered $50,000 for information on the assailants.

President McKinley agreed with his secretary of the navy, John D. Long, that the explosion was an accident and hoped to calm Americans by arranging an immediate inquiry into the tragedy. But the idea persisted that a mine had blown up the magazines on the *Maine.* On March 6, 1898, the president asked Congress for $50 million in arms appropriations and just as quickly received approval. The Madrid government, according to Woodford, found this measure difficult to believe. On March 28 the U.S. court of inquiry, comprised of American naval officers, published its findings on the explosion: Although it now seems likely that an overheated boiler blew up the ship, the court in 1898 concluded that an external mine had destroyed the *Maine* but left the door open for speculation by declaring its inability to determine the guilty party. Americans did not need to know any more. The duplicity and animosity seemingly exhibited in the de Lôme letter had taken material form in this naval disaster. Theodore Roosevelt privately wrote that "the *Maine* was sunk by an act of dirty treachery on the part of the Spaniards," while Americans already were chanting:

Remember the *Maine*
To hell with Spain!

In the midst of the excitement over the *Maine,* a Republican senator, Redfield Proctor

The U.S.S. Maine—*Before and After*
An explosion sank the *Maine* in Havana Harbor on February 15, 1898, making
"Remember the *Maine*!" the rallying cry for the Spanish-American War. *National
Archives.*

New York Journal

An example of the yellow press. No one ever claimed the $50,000 reward. *American Heritage Library.*

of Vermont, reported to his colleagues about his recent private tour of Cuba. With notable absence of passion, which paradoxically made his speech in the Senate more effective, he solemnly declared that in the outskirts of Havana, the situation "is not peace nor is it war. It is desolation and distress, misery and starvation." Thousands of Cubans lived in reconcentration camps, and "one-half have died and one-quarter of the living are so diseased that they cannot be saved." Weyler had left the island, but his replacement did not know what to do. Proctor's graphic description of the camps gave credence to the stories in the U.S. press, because he was a known opponent of war. The children wander around with "arms and chest terribly emaciated, eyes swollen, and abdomen bloated to three times the natural size. . . . I was told by one of our consuls," he continued, "that they have been found dead about the markets in the morning, where they had crawled, hoping to get some stray bits of food from the early hucksters." The greatest atrocity was "the entire native population of Cuba, struggling for freedom and deliverance from the worst misgovernment of which I ever had knowledge."

Proctor's vivid account had a major impact on Americans concerned about both humanitarian and property interests on the island. Action on behalf of Cuba's independence seemed justified as a crusade, and even U.S. business owners previously opposed to involvement recognized that the United States had to do something before the entire Cuban economy collapsed and took their investments with it. The usually unflappable *Wall Street Journal* declared that Proctor's speech had "made the blood boil." Intervention in Cuba, according to the equally cautious *Literary Digest,* was "the plain duty of the United States on the simple ground of humanity."

The Spanish-American War

President McKinley's role in these events was greater than once thought. Some contemporary observers argued that he was a gentle and

Judge
Many Americans had this image of Spain as they called for war after the sinking of the *Maine.*
Library of Congress.

unassuming man caught up in forces beyond his control. By the spring of 1898 he could not sleep without sedatives. His mood grew irascible as his invalid wife failed in health, and he continually had to grapple with the jingoes demanding war. A friend claimed that in late March the president broke under the strain and wept over recent events. Congress, McKinley charged, was pushing the nation into war. But this was not the entire story. Nor did the full truth lay in the view of the president's harshest critics who accused him of pursuing a cold and calculating expansionist policy that included war as the final solution. The real McKinley lay somewhere between the two extremes. He sought to expand his nation's commercial boundaries; but he was not a single-minded imperialist willing to do anything to achieve this objective. He was a devout Methodist, extremely sensitive to what was going on around him; but he also believed in the use of power to spread U.S. influence as an impetus to bettering mankind. McKinley wanted the spoils but preferably not at the cost of war. When war came, however, he took command, even establishing a war room in the White House from which he helped to plan strategy and maintain control of events by keeping close contact with U.S. forces both in the Caribbean and Asia. But these behind-the-scenes activities remained hidden from public view, leaving the impression of inaction. Theodore Roosevelt and other jingoes denounced the president as weak and indecisive and regarded the Cuban conflict as a God-given opportunity to enlarge the American interest.

Political pressures and the desire for reelection in 1900 helped push McKinley toward war. Members of his party demanded war, and rival Democrats led by the outspoken and histrionic William Jennings Bryan dramatically called for an independent Cuba. Pressure in the United States for war was enormous. Secretary of War Russell Alger warned that "Congress will declare war in spite of him. He'll get run over and the party with him." A Protestant journal self-righteously declared that "if it be the will of Almighty God, that by war the last trace of this inhumanity of man to man shall be swept away from this Western Hemisphere, let it come!" When business leaders emphasized a peaceful recovery from the depression rather than a war that would bring expansion abroad, Roosevelt snorted at Ohio Senator Mark Hanna, one of their biggest spokesmen: "We will have this war for the freedom of Cuba, in spite of the timidity of the commercial interests." Exasperated with the president's apparent indecision, Roosevelt allegedly proclaimed that "McKinley has no more backbone than a chocolate eclair!"

The president staunchly searched for a way out of war and finally emerged with a policy that left room for an eleventh-hour peace. On March 27 the United States notified Spain that the president would arbitrate a settlement unless it agreed to an immediate armistice and

peace by October 1. McKinley also called for a relief program for the Cuban victims and urged the government to fulfill its assurance of ending the reconcentration camps. Though making no demand for the island's independence, the Washington administration sent a telegram to Madrid the next day referring to Cuba's freedom as the natural outcome of negotiations. The Spanish government was already tottering in early 1898 and could not risk total concession without promoting its own downfall. On March 31 it ordered the end of the reconcentration policy, promised immediate reforms in Cuba, agreed to an armistice if the rebels made the request, and offered to submit the *Maine* issue to international arbitration. But the Spanish could not condone McKinley's intervention and, all importantly, would *not* grant Cuban independence.

The same day of the Spanish reply, however, Woodford offered encouraging news by notifying McKinley that Spain's stern attitude was softening as fast as was politically possible. "I am told confidentially," Woodford wrote, "that the offer of armistice by the Spanish Government would cause revolution here." Madrid's leaders "are ready to go as far and as fast as they can and still save the dynasty here in Spain. They know that Cuba is lost." He emphasized that "no Spanish ministry would have dared to do one month ago what this ministry has proposed today." Three days later Woodford informed Washington that the pope had persuaded the Madrid government to accept an armistice. "I know that the Queen and her present ministry sincerely desire peace and that the Spanish people desire peace," Woodford declared. "If you can still give me time and reasonable liberty of action I will get for you the peace you desire so much and for which you have labored so hard."

But the counsels of war in the United States were stronger than the plaintiffs for peace, and Spain's only way out seemed to be to secure European assistance in preventing U.S. intervention in Cuba. Failure to satisfy the Washington government's expectation of

Cuban independence would lead to war with the United States; compliance meant upheaval at home. All Old World powers except Britain, which needed the United States as an ally to counter the growing German threat in the Pacific and elsewhere, expressed sympathy with Spain and accused the McKinley administration of intending to seize Spanish holdings in the Western Hemisphere. But the German foreign minister offered the Spanish ambassador a bluntly realistic appraisal of the situation that precluded European involvement. "You are isolated," he declared, "because everybody wants to be pleasant to the United States, or, at any rate, nobody wants to arouse America's anger; the United States is a rich country, against which you simply cannot sustain a war." Finally, on April 6, the ambassadors of six European governments called on McKinley and urged him to stay out of Cuba. Two days afterward the *New York World* characterized the conversation between the president and his guests in these words: "The six ambassadors remarked: 'We hope for humanity's sake you will not go to war.' McKinley replied: 'We hope if we do go to war, you will understand that it is for humanity's sake.'"

Spain's reply to the president's note of late March was unsatisfactory because it did not concede Cuban independence, and on April 11, 1898, McKinley sent Congress a message asking authorization to use force if necessary to stop the war on the island. Two days earlier the Madrid government had granted a further concession by directing the Spanish troop commander in Cuba to permit a unilateral armistice designed to bring peace. Yet such an armistice seemed hardly enough to the White House, which now considered Cuba's freedom a prerequisite to negotiations. Besides, the armistice was conditional on a Spanish decision to resume the war, and the Cuban rebels had not complied with the offer because they considered their demand for independence to be nonnegotiable. McKinley emphasized to Congress that "in the name of humanity, in the name of civilization, in behalf of endangered American interests which give us the right and the duty to speak and to act, the war in Cuba must stop."

To counteract the "very serious injury to the commerce, trade, and business of our people, and the wanton destruction of property," McKinley asked Congress for authority "to secure a full and final termination of hostilities between the Government of Spain and the people of Cuba." Although he reminded the lawmakers to give "just and careful attention" to Spain's last-hour armistice offer, this lame plea came in the message *after* his request for arms. Given the heated atmosphere in the United States, along with Spain's past performance in failing to deliver promised reforms, most Americans regarded the armistice as another delay tactic while trying to show that they were not warmongers. McKinley had *not* asked Congress to declare war on Spain, they pointed out in drawing a distinction that in practical terms did not exist; he wanted the United States to act "as an *impartial neutral*" in ending the war in Cuba.

Congress soon approved a joint resolution in support of McKinley's request, but not until after a floor debate that took on the air of a circus. A resurgent martial spirit became conspicuously obvious in the great hall when northern congressmen sang "The Battle Hymn of the Republic" and southerners countered with "Dixie." On April 19 Congress passed a joint resolution (requiring a simple majority in each House) by the margins of 42 to 35 in the Senate and 311 to 6 in the House. The measure *directed* (not authorized) the president to use military force in securing Spain's withdrawal from Cuba and guaranteeing the island's independence. Even though no support was evident for recognition of Cuba as a republic, Congress pledged that the United States would not seek its annexation.

The last part of the joint resolution—the promise against annexing Cuba—came through the efforts of Senator Henry Teller of Colorado and seems to have passed unanimously by voice vote. The Teller Amendment proclaimed that "the United States hereby disclaims any disposition or intention to exercise sovereignty, jurisdiction, or control over said Island except for the pacification thereof, and asserts its determination, when that is accomplished, to leave the government and control of the Island to its people." Teller defended his amendment as an effort to ward off expected European charges that the United States had intervened in Cuba "for the purpose of aggrandizement." Yet he carefully added that this restriction relating to Cuba had no bearing on what the United States "may do as to some other islands," which was a thinly veiled reference to its interests in Puerto Rico and the Philippines.

Although the Teller Amendment had the appearance of altruism on the part of the United States, the realization that its sponsor was a well-known expansionist raises serious questions about motive. American sugar growers (primarily Louisiana Democrats) were among the strongest advocates of the measure, because they wanted Cuba to remain outside U.S. tariff walls and thus subject to regulation. Politics was a prime concern, because Teller was a supporter of Bryan, and Bryan's Populist and Democratic followers suspected the McKinley administration of wanting to acquire the island in an effort to protect American investments. Some legislators worried that if the United States took the island, Americans would become responsible for Cuba's debts. Finally, the promise not to annex Cuba had great appeal to racist Americans who opposed the incorporation of nonwhites into their nation. William Graham Sumner of Yale sarcastically pointed out that "the prospect of adding to the present Senate a number of Cuban senators, either native or carpetbag, is one whose terrors it is not necessary to unfold." The Teller Amendment became a convenient shield for numerous groups who opposed Cuba's annexation.

The seemingly narrow support for intervention in the upper chamber was misleading. Many of the thirty-five senators who voted in opposition actually favored intervention:

They did not like the wording of the resolution that supported the independence of Cuba without including recognition of the rebels' republican government. The McKinley administration had insisted, however, that recognition of the rebel regime would severely hamper U.S. military efforts should war develop with Spain. By 3 A.M. of April 20 (the official date remaining the 19th), Congress sent the joint resolution to the White House for the president's signature.

Events now passed quickly toward a declaration of war on Spain. That same day, April 20, 1898, the president approved the congressional resolution and insisted that "the people of Cuba are, and of right ought to be, free and independent." He then issued an ultimatum giving Spain three days to withdraw from the island. The following day word reached Washington that the Spanish government had severed diplomatic relations with the United States. On April 23 President McKinley called for 125,000 volunteers, and two days later he signed the joint resolution. The United States and Spain were at war, effective April 21.

Ideals and reality had again come together in the U.S. decision for war. For many Americans the war with Spain constituted a crusade to free Cuba from Old World oppression; for others the reasons for war were mixed. More than a few agreed with Senator George Hoar of Massachusetts, who later opposed imperialism but in 1898 wrote that "we cannot look idly on while hundreds of thousands of innocent human beings . . . die of hunger close to our door. If there is ever to be a war it should be to prevent such things as that." Protestant religious leaders prepared to convert the island's Catholic population, imperialists dreamed of empire, politicians looked forward to reelection, and business leaders formerly opposed to war now considered the commercial possibilities opened by the imminent end of Spain's colonial system. Whether or not Americans were for empire, they liked the prospect of seeing their flag waving over some tropical shore. Expansionist Senator Albert

Beveridge of Indiana rejoiced that "at last, God's hour has struck. The American people go forth in a warfare holier than liberty—holy as humanity." Irish satirist Finley Peter Dunne used his famous fictional news character Mr. Hennessy to beam forth in Irish brogue: "We're a gr-reat people." To which a fictitious Mr. Dooley agreed: "We ar-re . . . We ar-re that. An' the best iv it is, we know we ar-re."

The Spanish-American War "wasn't much of a war," Roosevelt admitted afterward, "but it was the best war we had." The Spanish were almost as sure they would lose as the Americans were certain they would win. U.S. author Sherwood Anderson remarked that going to war with Spain was "like robbing an old gypsy woman in a vacant lot at night after a fair." Ambassador to England John Hay, soon to become secretary of state, christened it "a splendid little war." Indeed it was—for the United States. Three months of uninterrupted

Map 18
Despite the prevalence of Cuba in America's explanation for war with Spain in 1898, the first battle occurred in the Philippines.

naval and land victories followed as U.S. battleships easily outmatched the antiquated vessels of the Spanish navy. Spanish officers and crew were situated far from their home base and in a state of declining morale, whereas the U.S. Navy was ready and eager, largely due to the determined efforts of Assistant Secretary of the Navy Theodore Roosevelt. The Spanish army in Cuba was larger than the U.S. force, but it was poorly provisioned, exhausted from the long guerrilla war, and cut off from Madrid by the U.S. naval blockade of the island. "We may and must expect a disaster," the Spanish naval commander wrote privately. "But . . . I hold my tongue and go forth resignedly to face the trials which God may be pleased to send me."

The first conflict in the Spanish-American War ironically occurred many miles from Cuba, when Commodore George Dewey engaged a Spanish squadron in the Philippines. The battle's location was a surprise to many, but it is clear now that the navy had earlier made secret contingency plans calling for the United States, in the event of war with Spain, to attack its fleet in Manila Bay. The moment arrived when Roosevelt became acting secretary of the navy during the hectic afternoon of February 25, 1898. He instructed Dewey to move the Asiatic Squadron from Hong Kong to Manila Bay and, when sure war was under way, to launch an offensive in the Philippines. Roosevelt immediately resigned his position to accept a commission in the army and make his mark as a "Rough Rider" at the battle of San Juan Hill, leaving the erroneous impression that he alone had engineered the Manila affair.

Near dawn of May 1, 1898, Dewey's cruisers steamed into Manila Bay and prepared for a battle that quickly took its place in mythology as well as history. His ships merely stayed out of the Spaniards' firing range, methodically and repeatedly circling past the enemy while raking its vessels, until by noon they had destroyed the entire squadron. At little cost Dewey had seized the naval station at Cavite along with Manila Bay, and the war department prepared to send an occupation force to the city of Manila. Dewey eventually encountered difficulties with German warships (more powerful than his) over blockade procedures in the Philippines, but that problem passed when it became evident that the German commander wished not to fight the Americans but to take any spoils upon their withdrawal from the islands. Indeed, the German presence permitted the British commander in those same waters to cultivate, however inadvertently, the Anglo-American rapprochement. In seeking to view the U.S. assault, he had moved his vessels in such a position that they were stationed between those of Germany and those of the United States, thereby giving rise to the legend that the British had warded off a German attack on the U.S. fleet. Dewey could remark after his triumph in Manila: "If I were a religious man, and I hope I am, I should say that the hand of God was in it."

Dewey's victory at Manila Bay revived the expansionists' arguments for Hawaii, which the Senate had shelved the previous March in light of the approaching war with Spain. On June 16, 1897, President McKinley had agreed to a treaty of annexation, and sent it to the Senate that same day. In the meantime the proposal aroused opposition again. Democrats and sugar interests aligned in denouncing the treaty, as did the Japanese government, which argued that U.S. annexation would endanger the rights of Japan's 25,000 nationals on the islands and disrupt Pacific affairs. Roosevelt would not have hesitated. He told Mahan that "if I had my way we would annex those islands tomorrow [and] . . . hoist our flag over the island leaving all details for after action." The Department of State assured Japan that annexation would not infringe upon its rights, but it also informed the U.S. naval commander in Honolulu that if he detected any evidence of Japanese aggression, he was to raise the U.S. flag and proclaim Hawaii a protectorate. Japan withdrew its protest in December 1897. Troubles with Spain again delayed action, leading the Senate to adjourn before deciding on the annexation treaty.

Now, in May 1898, the United States seemed determined to hold the Philippines as the gateway to China, which, in turn, thrust Hawaii into the fore as a vital naval and coaling station en route to Asia. Hawaii would serve as a defensive outpost for the American mainland and as a guardian of U.S. interests in the Pacific and Asia. On May 4, three days after Dewey's triumph, the annexationists introduced a joint resolution in the House that soon received overwhelming approval there and in the Senate. The president signed the bill on July 7, and Hawaii became U.S. territory.

In the meantime U.S. forces had landed on Cuban shores, where they encountered no Spanish opposition and quickly collaborated with the island's insurgents. Their objective was Santiago, where demoralized Spanish forces had prepared to defend themselves against superior firepower. On July 1, about 7000 U.S. troops seized El Caney, garrisoned by 600 Spaniards. That same day, Roosevelt's Rough Riders joined the Ninth Cavalry's black soldiers in outnumbering the Spanish about seven to one and taking San Juan Hill. U.S. casualties resulting from the two battles stood at more than 1500, but they had won control of the high bluffs east and north of Santiago and were in place to begin an artillery barrage on both the city and the Spanish fleet. Santiago and 24,000 Spanish troops surrendered on July 17, 1898.

Treaty of Paris

After U.S. victories at Santiago in Cuba and in Guam, the Philippines, and Puerto Rico, the Spanish ambassador in Paris asked the French Foreign Office to intervene and arrange a peace. Instructions immediately went to the French ambassador in Washington, who signed an armistice for Spain, effective August 12.

The joy of victory was tempered by the perplexing question of what to do with the Philippines. President McKinley recognized Manila's strategic and commercial importance

Theodore Roosevelt and the "Rough Riders"
TR and his companions pose shortly after their victory at San Juan Hill in Cuba. *Library of Congress.*

Commodore George Dewey
Dewey on the bridge of the U.S.S. *Olympia* during the Battle of Manila Bay on May 1, 1898. *Naval Historical Center, Washington, D.C.*

and at first had seemed willing to allow Spain to keep all of the Philippines except for the city. But these intentions had changed during the war. The acquisitions of Hawaii and Guam provided stepping-stones to China, and the Philippines suddenly stood as the doorway into Asia. *All* areas seemed vital to trade. Assistant Secretary of the Treasury Frank Vanderlip voiced the sentiments of Asia enthusiasts when he called the Philippines the "pickets of the Pacific, standing guard at the entrances to trade with the millions of China and Korea, French Indo-China, the Malay Peninsula, and the islands of Indonesia." U.S. business leaders recognized that colonial acquisitions might safeguard economic interests in China, continually threatened by foreign powers. The *New York Journal of Commerce* warned that returning the Philippines "would be an act of inconceivable folly in the face of our imperative future necessities for a basis of naval and military force on the Western shores of the Pacific." McKinley feared that the Filipinos were unfit to govern themselves and that France or Germany would eventually subjugate them. Some time after the war he explained to a group of Methodist clergymen visiting the White House that the Philippines were "a gift from the gods" and that "there was nothing left for us to do but to take them all, and to educate the Filipinos, and uplift and civilize and Christianize them."

When the U.S. peace delegation arrived in Paris for the first session at the Quai D'Orsay Palace on September 29, its membership revealed its purpose: Four of the five men chosen by McKinley were expansionists, and the fifth ultimately became a convert. Three of them were ranking members of the Senate Foreign Relations Committee, which meant that they would also vote on the treaty when it came before the Senate. The delegation was to seek the independence of Cuba, the acquisition of Puerto Rico, and at least the island of Luzon in the Philippines, which was the site of Manila. For almost a month the Spanish and U.S. delegates discussed Cuba's fate. The Spanish actually preferred that it come

Map 19
The realities of war in Cuba were considerably different from the implications contained in Secretary of State Hay's calling it a "splendid little war."

under U.S. ownership because of the likelihood of greater protection for their subjects and property. Although the Americans appeared to stand behind the Teller Amendment for selfless reasons, they also realized that the country owning the island would inherit a debt of $400 million that Spanish officials in Cuba had run up in trying to put down the rebellion.

By late October the United States had decided to take all of the Philippines. Americans on the islands warned that separating Manila from the Philippines was ill-advised and that the islands comprised an integrated economic whole. McKinley had recently returned from the midwestern sector of the United States, where he sensed widespread support for holding on to them. Despite demands for independence made by Filipinos under insurgent leader Emilio Aguinaldo, the United States decided that the rebel government near

Manila was unstable and that continued disorder could attract German involvement. A protectorate was out of the question in view of the difficulties experienced in Samoa with the islands' regime. The war with Spain, McKinley explained, had thrust new responsibilities on the United States, and the Philippines offered a "commercial opportunity to which American statesmanship cannot be indifferent." Through his fictitious Mr. Dooley, Finley Peter Dunne questioned the wisdom of taking the islands, which "not more thin two months since ye learned whether they were islands or canned goods." But Mr. Hennessy expressed growing American sentiment in declaring: "Hang on to thim. What we've got we must hold." Dooley agreed but remarked prophetically: "We've got the Ph'lippeens, Hinnisy; we've got thim the way Casey got the bulldog—be th' teeth."

After more than two months of negotiations, the United States and Spain emerged with the Treaty of Paris in December 1898. The Spanish agreed to assume Cuba's debt and accepted $20 million from the United States for relinquishing "all claim of sovereignty over and title to Cuba," along with the Philippines, Guam, Puerto Rico, "and other islands now under Spanish sovereignty in the West Indies" (Culebra and a few small islands near Puerto Rico plus the Isle of Pines below Cuba). Inhabitants of the transferred areas were assured religious freedom, but the U.S. Congress was to determine their "civil rights and political status." The United States had not guaranteed citizenship; nor had it promised statehood. As a Puerto Rican newspaper later complained, "We are and we are not a foreign country. We are and we are not citizens of the United States.... The Constitution ...

Treaty of Paris of 1899
Secretary of State John Hay signs the ratification of the peace treaty with Spain, while President William McKinley (standing beneath the clock) and others observe. *Library of Congress.*

applies to us and does not apply to us." For the first time in its history, the United States had become a colonial power when it acquired the Philippines and Puerto Rico.

Arguments against the treaty began early in 1899. Anti-imperialists in the United States were both angered and saddened by what they regarded as a breakdown of American idealism. The Anti-Imperialist League in Boston considered the acquisition of the Philippines a contradiction in policy because the United States had turned down the annexation of Cuba for humanitarian reasons. Furthermore, Hawaii, Puerto Rico, and Guam seemed acceptable additions because white people on the islands formed a potential political base, whereas the darker skinned Filipinos were primarily Malays whose incorporation begged lasting trouble. New Hampshire's outspoken peace advocate Lucia Mead declared that the American presence did not automatically elevate the status of native inhabitants and therefore remove the stain of imperialism. Any nation that conquers other peoples without assuring their independence was imperialist. The anti-imperialists insisted that Aguinaldo's demands for independence ensured bitter resistance to U.S. rule that would culminate in a jungle war 6000 miles from the United States.

Many opponents of the treaty insisted that absorption of peoples without their consent was a violation of the Declaration of Independence, the U.S. Constitution, and other great republican pronouncements in America's history. Senator George Vest of Missouri sponsored a resolution (which never came to a vote) "that under the Constitution of the United States, no power is given to the Federal Government to acquire territory to be held and governed permanently as colonies." Senator Hoar of the Republican party joined Democrats in proclaiming the unconstitutionality of Old World colonialism "built upon the fundamental idea that the people of immense areas of territory can be held as subjects, never to become citizens." Expansion had turned America into "a cheapjack country, raking after the cart for the leavings of European tyranny." According to another anti-imperialist, "Dewey took Manila with the loss of one man—and all our institutions." And that was not all: U.S. involvement in the Philippines was costly and would lead to international rivalries over Asia. But despite the support of William Jennings Bryan (who had soured on expansionism, even for humanitarian reasons), Andrew Carnegie, Mark Twain, and other notables, the anti-imperialists were unable to muster enough support to reverse recent events.

The imperialists' counterarguments in favor of the treaty were difficult to refute. The McKinley administration received valuable assistance from Roosevelt, Lodge, and numerous businessmen in defending the treaty as a boon to trade and the natural outcome of U.S. superiority. British poet Rudyard Kipling expressed a strong argument for expansion when he penned these lines for *McClure's Magazine* in February 1899:

> Take up the White Man's burden—
>   Ye dare not stoop to less—
> Nor call too loud on Freedom
>   To cloke your weariness.

The United States had seemingly assumed the responsibility of spreading civilization into the "backward" areas of the World. Social Darwinists hailed the fulfillment of their teachings, missionaries planned their strategy for saving the many lost souls, commercial groups looked forward to exploiting the potentially vast China market, and proponents of a larger navy at last saw their aims become possible. The United States, many Americans argued, had to redeem the sacrifice of its soldiers by keeping all the lands their blood had bought. Lest doubt remain, expansionists warned that if the United States did not take the areas, Germany, Japan, or some other power would do so. As for the danger in acquiring distant areas, Senator Beveridge of Indiana dramatically declared that "the ocean does not separate us from the lands of our duty and desire—the ocean joins us, a river never to be dredged, a canal never to be repaired." He concluded that "steam joins us, electricity joins us—the very elements are in league with our destiny."

As for the constitutionality of territorial acquisitions, Connecticut Senator Orville Platt advocated a position that later became the essence of U.S. Supreme Court decisions on the matter: In the spirit of Albert Gallatin during the debate over the Louisiana Purchase, Platt declared that the United States as a sovereign nation could incorporate territory and institute the type of government it believed best suited for the people involved. But unlike Madison and Jefferson with their call for an empire of liberty, Platt insisted that the United States had no duties to ensure either citizenship or statehood. Like other imperial nations, it could add dependencies or colonies. The Supreme Court affirmed these principles in a series of *Insular* cases beginning in 1901, when it declared that the Constitution did not necessarily follow the flag—that U.S. citizenship rights did not automatically extend to territorial inhabitants.

After a bitter fight in the Senate, the Treaty of Paris won approval on February 6, 1899, by a scant single vote more than the required two-thirds majority. Just two days before the vote, conflict broke out in the Philippines between Aguinaldo's partisans and U.S. troops, and news of this development probably encouraged support for the treaty as the only alternative to seeing some other power take the islands. Several anti-imperialists became converts at the last moment, perhaps in part because of William Jennings Bryan's argument that prolongation of the war with Spain was out of the question and that the United States could grant independence to the Philippines when emotions cooled.

The Spanish-American War, though short and inexpensive compared to other conflicts, had far-reaching consequences. It climaxed the long, steady decline of Spain's empire and at the same time initiated world recognition of the United States's newly acquired power status. The war's realities became clear in pro-portion to the growing casualty lists. More than 5000 Americans died—fewer than 400 directly attributable to battle. Most deaths resulted from malaria and yellow fever. Yet the war had redeeming features. Some Americans believed the conflict with Spain laid their Civil War to rest. Massachusetts soldiers en route to Cuba met a joyous reception in Baltimore, which sharply contrasted with the treatment accorded the state's forces in 1861 when they marched through the same city to defend Washington and a mob pelted them with stones. With "Dixie" ringing from the band in 1898, Massachusetts Senator Henry Cabot Lodge wistfully recalled years later that "it was 'roses, roses all the way'—flags, cheers, excited crowds. Tears were in my eyes. I never felt so moved in my life. The war of 1861 was over at last and the great country for which so many died was one again."

War's Aftermath: Implications for Asia

Americans could not enjoy their conquest for long; Filipino rebels and U.S. forces on the islands soon became locked in a vicious jungle combat that lasted three years. The roots of the insurrection actually wound back to the period before the U.S. war with Spain. By the time the Spanish lost Manila to U.S. soldiers in August 1898, the city stood as the only major spot in the islands not yet under rebel control. Aguinaldo, who had led an uprising in 1895 that the Spanish crushed, had believed that his homeland would receive freedom when the United States defeated Spain. His confidence seemed justified. He had returned from exile on board a U.S. ship, and Dewey had urged him to renew the struggle against the Spanish. Indeed, after the revolution had begun anew in February 1899, Congress in Washington presented a resolution for independence that failed by only a slender margin. Aguinaldo and his cohort responded by establishing a government, drawing up a constitution, and proclaiming the new Philippine Republic. Such high expectations met a cold reception in Washington. The McKinley administration's decision to retain the islands had not only strapped them around the U.S. flag, but it left their inhabitants with no rights of citizenship. To put down the ensuing Filipino insurrection, the United States dispatched 70,000 troops to the islands, a force four times larger than that used in Cuba.

The end of the guerrilla war in the Philippines came in July 1902, but only after 200,000 Filipinos and 5000 Americans had died. The United States had sent 175,000 men to the islands and expended $160 million. More than that, both sides had committed atrocities, leaving a bitter taste among Americans that doubtless contributed to the rapid demise of the expansionist spirit. The philosopher William James declared: "Here were the precious beginnings of an indigenous national life, with which . . . it was our first duty to have squared ourselves. . . . We are destroying the lives of these islanders by the thousands, their villages and their cities," he charged. "Could there be a more damning indictment of that whole bloated ideal termed 'modern civilization' than this amounts to?"

The war in the Philippines heightened the ongoing debate over the United States's increasing foreign involvement. Writer Mark Twain cynically suggested that the United States paint black over the white stripes in the American flag and replace the stars with a skull and cross bones. Yale sociologist William Graham Sumner declared with disgust, "We talk of civilizing lower races, but we have never done it yet. We have exterminated them." Perhaps the most biting indictment came from Senator Benjamin Tillman, a South Carolina Democrat, who delighted in seeing northern Republicans squirm over the Philippines: "No Republican leader will now dare to wave the bloody shirt and preach a crusade against the South's treatment of the negro. The North has a bloody shirt of its own. Many thousands of them have been made into shrouds for murdered Filipinos, done to death because they were fighting for liberty." Yet the civil gover-

Philippine Insurrection
U.S. soldiers occupying native huts during the Filipino insurrection of 1899–1902. *Library of Congress.*

nor of the Philippines and later president of the United States, William Howard Taft, urged Americans to focus on long-range objectives. The United States's goal, he insisted, was to "teach those people individual liberty, which shall lift them up to a point of civilization . . . and which shall make them rise to call the name of the United States blessed." The *New York World* moaned over the difficulties in administering "uncivilized" peoples when it addressed these lines to Rudyard Kipling:

> We've taken up the white man's burden
>   Of ebony and brown;
> Now will you kindly tell us, Rudyard,
>   How we may put it down?

The United States found that the acceptance of international responsibilities made it nearly impossible to lay them down. During the war it had established control over Hawaii, Guam, the Philippines, and Puerto Rico, and in mid-January of 1899 the U.S. Navy occupied Wake Island in the Pacific and proclaimed it U.S. territory. In December of that year Britain and Germany signed a treaty in Washington conceding to the United States the

Samoan island of Tutuila—home of the valuable harbor of Pago Pago—along with nearby islands known as American Samoa. The following year the native chiefs on Tutuila formally ceded their island to the United States, and four years later, in 1904, the string of small Manua Islands did the same. Expansion seemed to breed expansion, the anti-imperialists heatedly charged.

In retrospect most of the areas acquired by the United States took on the shape of a crudely shaped arrow pointing to China. The opportunities for trade with that massive land of countless peoples, according to numerous observers, were virtually endless. But Americans had long exaggerated the commercial importance of the Celestial Kingdom: By the late 1890s the China market consumed only about 1 percent of their total exports. Determined Americans believed, however, that the volume of exchange would grow in an atmosphere of equal opportunity encouraged by their own paternal interest in the Chinese people. Japan's victory in the Sino-Japanese War of 1894–1895 had demonstrated the weakness of China's Manchu dynasty, which in turn led to further outside encroachments upon its sovereignty. Spheres of influence, long-term leases, tariff controls, transportation and communication rights—all were poorly disguised imperialist measures by European nations that permitted inroads into the Chinese mainland and caused deep concern among U.S. commercial and missionary groups. Shortly after the Sino-Japanese War, Russia, Germany, Britain, France, and Japan exacted railroad and commercial concessions in China. For good reason, Americans worried that their path to the Orient lay cluttered with other countries' entrenched interests.

The United States's active involvement in China largely originated in Britain's efforts to establish an Open Door policy. Twice in less than a year's time the British had recommended a joint venture aimed at guaranteeing equal trade opportunities in China, only to have the United States turn down both proposals as a violation of its traditional isola-

tionism. But in 1899 a British visitor to Asia and member of Parliament, Lord Charles Beresford, aroused even greater U.S. interest in China through his book *The Breakup of China* and his speeches in the United States, which warned of Russian encroachments and called for the Open Door. In the meantime U.S. merchants and missionaries put pressure on the state department to adopt an active China policy. Then, during the summer of that year, a private British citizen working for China's Customs Service, Alfred Hippisley, discussed the matter with his long-time friend in the United States, William Rockhill, who was an adviser on Asia and himself a friend of Secretary of State John Hay. Hippisley did not speak in any official capacity for his government in London, but he knew of its continued interest in China. Hippisley emphasized the commercial importance of the Open Door to *both* Britain and the United States, and he warned that continued outside penetration of China would undermine the Customs Service and lead to the partitioning of the huge country. The United States should take the initiative in establishing international respect for the Open Door. Anti-British sentiment in the United States, Hippisley realized, was still too strong to permit the London government to lead the way.

Hippisley and Rockhill worked with Hay in composing a memorandum that expressed the London government's wishes, and that document became the basis of U.S. policy toward China. On September 6, 1899, Hay sent the statement in the form of a diplomatic note to the governments in Berlin, London, and St. Petersburg, and in November he sent it to Paris, Rome, and Tokyo. Patterned after the most-favored-nation principles of the earlier part of the century, Hay's circular note called for equal commercial opportunity within the various powers' spheres of influence and took a stand against outside interference with China's tariff controls. Hay did not condemn spheres of influence, nor did he attempt to safeguard China's territorial integrity. The success of his Open Door efforts depended on whether the

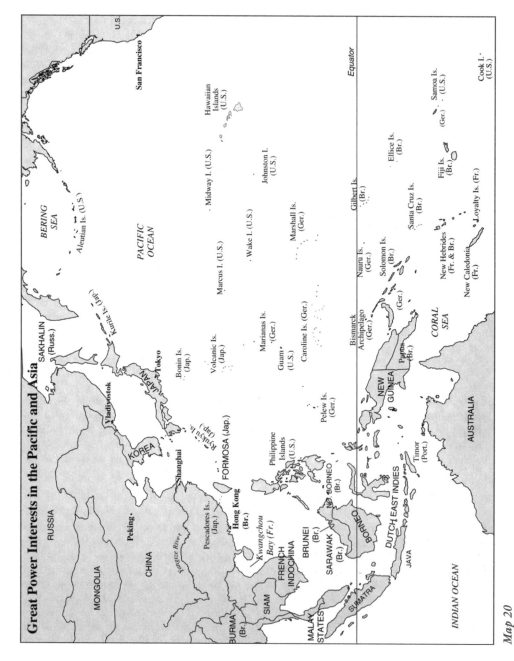

Great Power Interests in the Pacific and Asia

Map 20

By the end of the nineteenth century, numerous countries (including the United States) had made claims to parts of Asia and the Pacific.

interested powers would either publicly deny imperialist designs in China or admit to them by remaining silent. All governments sent replies to Washington, but most of them were noncommittal: They conditioned their adherence to the Open Door on the acceptance of its principles by the other parties. When Russia eventually indicated unwillingness to comply, its stand released the others from the pledge. Hay, however, simply ignored the Russian response and announced in March 1900 that the powers' *unanimous* decision to respect the Open Door had made the policy statement "final and definitive."

It would be erroneous to dismiss the United States's Open Door policy as ineffective. Admittedly, the United States lacked the military or naval might to enforce equal commercial opportunity in China, but it also recognized that the balance of power in that section of the world was so tenuous that the mere involvement of another country in Asian affairs could turn that balance either way. No one wanted war; yet no one could be sure of the other's intentions. As with the most-favored-nation approach, the United States gained equal commercial privileges in China without having to resort to military measures.

China's problems did not end with Hay's Open Door pronouncements: Continued and deepening foreign involvement ultimately led to an outbreak of fierce nationalist resistance against outsiders that became known as the Boxer Rebellion. The fast-declining Manchu dynasty, which had been in power since the mid-1600s and would finally collapse in 1911, was incapable of defending its homeland. In 1900 a secret society known as *I-ho-ch'üan* ("Righteous and Harmonious Fists"), or the Boxers, armed themselves with spears and swords and led an insurrection against foreigners in China. Hundreds of missionaries and Christian converts fell in the bloody rebellion, as the Boxers, allied with imperial soldiers and apparently encouraged by the Manchu government, laid siege on the foreigners now isolated in the legation section of Peking.

The United States decided to act when the other powers prepared to send a punitive force that would likely culminate in the permanent partition of China. To save Peking the McKinley administration in August 1900 directed 2500 soldiers from the Philippines to China, where they joined 15,000 troops from Britain, France, Germany, Japan, and Russia. Meanwhile, Hay circulated a second note affirming the Open Door policy, but with a different emphasis. Whereas the first note of September 1899 had advocated only equal commercial opportunity, the second in July 1900 urged respect for that nation's "territorial and administrative entity" and called on the interested powers to "safeguard for the world the principle of equal and impartial trade with all parts of the Chinese Empire." Hay thus widened the parameters of the Open Door to include more than trade and more than the areas in China that had come under outside control: His policy now incorporated respect for China's national independence. He did not seek a reply this time; this was to be *America's* policy—with or without the other countries' acquiescence.

Paradoxically, each foreign government deepened its involvement in China while affirming agreement with Hay's proclamation—largely to deter the others from expanding their holdings. The Open Door pronouncement of 1900 did not save China: The essential restraint was mutual distrust among the interested powers that held them all at bay. Professed adherence to the Open Door seemed wiser than to risk a world war brought on by its rivals' expansionist activities.

The U.S. policy toward China perhaps lightened the impact of the Boxer Rebellion on the growth of foreign influence in the country, but serious doubt persists about Hay's philanthropic claim that the United States sought only an "abstention from plunder" through the Open Door statement. The international expeditionary force put down the insurrection at the cost of numerous lives, and China received a huge reparations bill of about $333 million. But China had been wracked with outside intervention and internal disorder for so long that it could not pay that exorbitant amount. The United States was to receive $25 million, although it kept only $7 million to cover private damage claims and canceled the remainder. This decision bought considerable favor among the Chinese because their government used the unexpended fund to facilitate the education of their students in the United States. Meanwhile, outside intervention continued in China. In fact, in late 1900 Hay acceded to the U.S. Navy's wishes and requested a piece of territory and a naval base at Samsah Bay, located within the Japanese sphere of influence. Peking's leaders were in no position to refuse, but the Japanese government quietly yet firmly called Hay's attention to the Open Door principles. The United States dropped its request.

The United States's Open Door policy went through several shades of meaning in succeeding years, but it was above all an extension of the most-favored-nation approach of the early 1800s: a guarantee of equal commercial opportunity in China. Despite the apparently selfless aims of the first Open Door declaration of 1899, the truth is that it was largely an effort to preserve U.S. commercial interests in China. The military weakness of the United States prohibited any consideration of a stronger stand. The following year Hay's second note announced opposition to violations of China's territorial integrity, but a *statement* of policy was again the most the United States could offer. Unable to enforce the Open Door, the Washington government issued idealistic pronouncements that nonetheless affirmed its deepening realistic interests in China and the rest of Asia.

Expansion in Perspective

The United States had become an integral part of the world community by the turn of the twentieth century. Though not yet a first-rate power, it had made great strides toward that status because of the international events

of the latter 1890s. The war with Spain and the liberation of Cuba, the annexation of Caribbean and Pacific islands, the colonization of the Philippines, the growing rapprochement with Britain, the Open Door in China—all entailed foreign involvements that would doubtless expand in scope. In 1899 the United States took another step toward deeper foreign involvement by participating in the First International Peace Conference at The Hague in the Netherlands. Called by the Russian czar to encourage disarmament, the meeting brought together twenty-six nations. The goal was to draw up rules of war and devise steps toward peaceful settlement of international disputes through the newly established Permanent Court of Arbitration.

European powers meanwhile worried that the United States might ally with Britain. Anglo-American rapprochement had become more of a reality after the Venezuelan episode and the rise of Germany. In addition, the British had been partial to the United States during its war with Spain, and the Americans had reciprocated by favoring Britain in its ongoing war with the Boers of South Africa. Social, political, and economic similarities underscored the growing Atlantic understanding, as did personal familial ties between the countries and shared racial views. The *Times* of London proclaimed that blood ties held the nations together, while a leading British journalist declared that his compatriots "should never stand idly by and see a hundred millions of people who speak English trampled on by people who speak Russian or French or German."

McKinley's solid reelection victory in 1900, with war hero Theodore Roosevelt at his side as vice president, assured the world that Americans were beginning to realize that their security rested, at least in part, on international events. Furthermore, victory over Spain had given Americans their first taste of empire, and the sample proved highly pleasant to their senses. They did not yet understand that following the initial thrust of power came the aftermath of responsibility.

Selected Readings

Anderson, Stuart. *Race and Rapprochement: Anglo-Saxonism and Anglo-American Relations, 1895–1904.* 1981.

Beale, Howard K. *Theodore Roosevelt and the Rise of America to World Power.* 1956.

Beisner, Robert L. *From the Old Diplomacy to the New, 1865–1900.* 2nd ed., 1986.

———. *Twelve against Empire: The Anti-Imperialists, 1898–1900.* 1968.

Braeman, John. *Albert J. Beveridge: American Nationalist.* 1971.

Brands, H. W. *Bound to Empire: The United States and the Philippines.* 1992.

———. *T.R. The Last Romantic.* 1997.

Campbell, Alexander E. *Great Britain and the United States, 1895–1903.* 1960.

Campbell, Charles S. *From Revolution to Rapprochement: The United States and Great Britain, 1783–1900.* 1974.

———. *Special Business Interests and the Open Door Policy.* 1951.

———. *The Transformation of American Foreign Relations, 1865–1900.* 1976.

Clymer, Kenton J. *Protestant Missionaries in the Philippines, 1898–1916: An Inquiry into the American Colonial Mentality.* 1986.

Cooper, John M., Jr. *The Warrior and the Priest: Woodrow Wilson and Theodore Roosevelt.* 1983.

Cosmas, Graham A. *An Army for Empire: The United States Army in the Spanish-American War.* 1971.

Craig, John M. "Lucia True Ames Mead: American Publicist for Peace and Internationalism." In Edward P. Crapol, ed., *Women and American Foreign Policy: Lobbyists, Critics, and Insiders,* 67–90. 2nd ed., 1992.

Davis, Calvin D. *The United States and the First Hague Peace Conference.* 1962.

Dulles, Foster Rhea. *Prelude to World Power: 1860–1900.* 1965.

Dunne, Finley Peter. *Mr. Dooley in Peace and War.* 1899.

Faulkner, Harold U. *Politics, Reform and Expansion, 1890–1900.* 1959.

Freidel, Frank. *The Splendid Little War.* 1958.

Fry, Joseph A. *John Tyler Morgan and the Search for Southern Autonomy.* 1992.

Gould, Lewis L. *The Presidency of William McKinley.* 1980.

———. *The Spanish-American War and President McKinley.* 1982.

Grenville, John A. S., and Young, George B. *Politics, Strategy, and American Diplomacy.* 1966.

Healy, David F. *Drive to Hegemony: The United States in the Caribbean, 1898–1917.* 1988.

———. *U.S. Expansionism: The Imperialist Urge in the 1890s.* 1970.

Hofstadter, Richard. "Manifest Destiny and the Philippines," in Daniel Aaron, ed., *America in Crisis,* 173–200. 1952.

Hoganson, Kristin L. *Fighting for American Manhood: How Gender Politics Provoked the Spanish-American and Philippine-American Wars.* 1998.

Hunt, Michael H. *The Making of a Special Relationship: The U.S. and China to 1914.* 1983.

Johnson, Robert E. *Far China Station: The U.S. Navy in Asian Waters, 1800–1898.* 1979.

Karnow, Stanley. *In Our Image: America's Empire in the Philippines.* 1989.

Kennan, George F. *American Diplomacy.* Expanded ed., 1984. Originally published as *American Diplomacy, 1900–1950.* 1951.

LaFeber, Walter. *The New Empire: An Interpretation of American Expansion, 1860–1898.* 1963.

Langley, Lester D. *The Cuban Policy of the United States: A Brief History.* 1968.

Leech, Margaret. *In the Days of McKinley.* 1959.

Linderman, Gerald F. *The Mirror of War: American Society and the Spanish-American War.* 1974.

Linn, Brian M. *The U.S. Army and Counterinsurgency in the Philippine War. 1899–1902.* 1989.

May, Ernest R. *Imperial Democracy: The Emergence of America as a Great Power.* 1961.

McCormick, Thomas J. *China Market: America's Quest for Informal Empire, 1893–1901.* 1967.

Miller, Stuart C. *"Benevolent Assimilation": The American Conquest of the Philippines, 1899–1903.* 1982.

Morgan, H. Wayne. *America's Road to Empire: The War with Spain and Overseas Expansion.* 1965.

———. *From Hayes to McKinley: National Party Politics, 1877–1896.* 1969.

———. *William McKinley and His America.* 1963.

Morris, Edmund. *The Rise of Theodore Roosevelt.* 1979.

Offner, John L. *An Unwanted War: The Diplomacy of the United States and Spain Over Cuba, 1895–1898.* 1992.

Papachristou, Judith. "American Women and Foreign Policy, 1898–1905: Exploring Gender in

Diplomatic History," *Diplomatic History* 14 (1990): 493–509.

Pérez, Louis A., Jr. *Cuba and the United States.* 1997.

———. *The War of 1898: The United States and Cuba in History and Historiography.* 1998.

Perkins, Bradford. *The Great Rapprochement: England and the United States, 1895–1914.* 1968.

Perkins, Dexter. *The Monroe Doctrine, 1867–1907.* 1937.

Pratt, Julius W. *Expansionists of 1898.* 1936.

Rickover, Hyman G. *How the Battleship* Maine *Was Destroyed.* 1976.

Ruiz, Ramón. *Cuba: The Making of a Revolution.* 1968.

Schirmer, Daniel B. *Republic or Empire: American Resistance to the Philippine War.* 1972.

Seager, Robert, II. *Alfred Thayer Mahan.* 1977.

Smith, Ephraim K. " 'A Question from Which We Could Not Escape': William McKinley and the Decision to Acquire the Philippine Islands," *Diplomatic History* 9 (1985): 363–75.

Spector, Ronald. *Admiral of the New Empire: The Life and Career of George Dewey.* 1974.

Sprout, Harold, and Sprout, Margaret. *The Rise of American Naval Power, 1776–1918.* 1944.

Tompkins, E. Berkeley. *Anti-Imperialism in the United States.* 1970.

Trask, David F. *The War with Spain in 1898.* 1981.

Weems, John E. *The Fate of the* Maine. 1992.

Welch, Richard. *Response to Imperialism: The United States and the Philippine-American War, 1899–1902.* 1979.

Williams, William A. *The Roots of the Modern American Empire.* 1969.

———. *The Tragedy of American Diplomacy.* 1959, 1962.

Young, Marilyn B. *The Rhetoric of Empire.* 1968.

CHAPTER 12

Theodore Roosevelt and the Search for World Order, 1900–1913

The United States at the Threshold of World Power

The United States and Theodore Roosevelt arrived on the international stage at the same time, a development that was not entirely coincidental. The United States was not a world power by the opening of the twentieth century, but with Roosevelt's lead it soon became the leading determinant in Caribbean matters, a force worth considering in East Asia, and more than an idle observer of European events. Meanwhile, Roosevelt promoted the growing public interest in foreign affairs by using the White House as a "bully pulpit" to dominate the U.S. scene as few leaders have done in the nation's history. He realized that world events were inseparable from the country's security. He also knew that the reform spirit of the early 1900s—Progressivism—had permeated foreign as well as domestic affairs. In foreign policy, Roosevelt first sought stability in the Western Hemisphere before working toward a world order that rested on a balance of power.

Roosevelt's background was rich and cosmopolitan. A Harvard graduate, he became police commissioner of New York City, assistant secretary of the navy, hero of the Spanish-American War, governor of New York, vice

president, and, upon the assassination of McKinley in the autumn of 1901, president—an office to which he was elected in his own right three years later. Despite his active public career he found time for world travel, big game hunting in Africa, the life of a cowboy in the rugged Black Hills of South Dakota, and a continuing interest in scholarship that found him reading extensively and writing a dozen books. Roosevelt moved easily among wealthy families and intellectuals on both sides of the Atlantic, which facilitated the informal and personal brand of diplomacy he practiced while in the White House. A man of forceful personality, he relished any form of competition that resulted in efficiency and progress. Roosevelt was "pure act," Henry Adams once remarked. "Teddy," as Ohio Republican Mark Hanna sarcastically called him (behind his back), excitedly pounded his fist into his cupped left hand for emphasis and regularly appeared in cartoons highlighting his round wire-rimmed glasses, full-bristled mustache, and ever-prominent teeth. Roosevelt was a master of the strenuous life. When not behind his desk, he could be in the boxing ring, on the tennis court, demonstrating jujitsu, or on his way to Rock Creek Park, followed by panting and stiffly dressed foreign dignitaries whom he had invited for a hike.

Theodore Roosevelt
An ideal candidate for caricature. *Library of Congress.*

Roosevelt urged Americans to support their country's involvement in international affairs. The world, he believed, was divided between the civilized states and the uncivilized or backward peoples. Before becoming president, he had made his message clear to a large and cheering audience: "Exactly as it is the duty of a civilized power scrupulously to respect the rights of weaker civilized powers . . . so it is its duty to put down savagery and barbarism." As president, he emphasized to Congress in 1902 that "the increasing interdependence and complexity of international political and economic relations render it incumbent on all civilized and orderly powers to insist on the proper policing of the world." The United States, he declared through a West African proverb, needed to "speak softly and carry a big stick." An advocate of Darwinian principles, he adopted a patrician attitude toward the world's unfortunate people and in the spirit of *noblesse oblige* called on

Americans to join other Anglo-Saxons in taking up the "white man's burden" and spreading enlightenment, culture, liberty, and order.

In truth, the first decade or so of the new century stands as the era of Theodore Roosevelt. His realistic diplomacy was not new to the republic, but his verve and vitality surely marked a welcome change from the generally tired presidential administrations of the past four decades. Rarely has a White House occupant displayed such flair, exuberance, knowledge, and wit. At the heart of his spirited showmanship lay a primary concern for U.S. interests that comprised a blend of economic and strategic considerations. While president, he used almost any method short of war as an instrument of policy aimed at guaranteeing national security. "When I left the presidency," Roosevelt proudly recorded in his *Autobiography*, "I finished seven and a half years of administration, during which not one shot had been fired against a foreign foe. We were at absolute peace, and there was no nation in the world . . . whom we had wronged, or from whom we had anything to fear."

A blatant embellishment perhaps, but Roosevelt did pursue certain principles that kept the nation out of foreign entanglements conducive to war. He never pushed beyond his country's capabilities in attempting to safeguard his country's prestige. He did not believe in idle threats, because failure to deliver when challenged would destroy America's effectiveness abroad. He perceived that the United States had to adopt a foreign policy that extended only as far as the nation's military arm would permit. He wrote his close friend William Howard Taft in 1910, "I utterly disbelieve in the policy of bluff, in national and international no less than in private affairs, or in any violation of the old frontier maxim, 'Never draw unless you mean to shoot.'" To implant U.S. power and prestige throughout the world, Roosevelt sought to expand the navy. When he became president, the navy numbered less than twenty major ships, some still under construction. By 1907 it had grown to rank second in the world to

Theodore Roosevelt Wielding the "Big Stick"
All over the world, the president attempted to "speak softly and carry a big stick." *Tyler Dennett,* John Hay: From Poetry to Politics, *New York: Dodd, Mead, 1933, between pp. 394 and 395.*

Britain, and despite Germany's rapidly escalating program of naval expansion, the U.S. Navy remained in the top three (with Germany as third ranking power) on the eve of the Great War in 1914.

The United States was fortunate during the first decade of the twentieth century in that while growing in strength, it was partly isolated and largely unthreatened by outside forces. Both inside and outside the Western Hemisphere, Americans could indulge in an active foreign policy through the show of force rather than the use of force. And Roosevelt could rightfully boast afterward that during his administration the United States mediated to end one war and helped to prevent another while itself remaining at peace.

Panama Canal

Building an isthmian canal occupied much of Roosevelt's attention during his first years in office, because the Spanish-American War had revealed a security problem by demonstrating the difficulty of moving naval vessels between the Atlantic and the Pacific. The U.S. battleship *Oregon,* for example, had hurriedly left San Francisco for the Caribbean during the first

signs of trouble in 1898, but it had to steam around South America and through the treacherous Strait of Magellan before completing the arduous 14,000-mile, sixty-eight-day voyage. President McKinley reiterated the importance of a canal in his annual message to Congress in December of that year. With the annexation of Hawaii, he declared, the building of such a waterway under U.S. control had become vital to the national interest. A French corporation, the New Panama Canal Company, had taken over the bankrupted de Lesseps business along with its equipment and its Panama concessions granted by Colombia, and it now sought to sell them to the United States—for the exorbitant price of $109 million.

Immediately after the negotiations ending the Spanish-American War, McKinley instructed Secretary of State John Hay to talk with the British ambassador in Washington, Sir Julian Pauncefote, about revising the prohibitive joint construction and control provisions of the Clayton-Bulwer Treaty of 1850. The two men reached an agreement in February 1900 that allowed the United States to build and administer a canal but not to fortify it. The Hay-Pauncefote Treaty then fell into the political swirls of that year's presidential campaign. Democrats denounced the pact as a capitulation to the British, and Irish-Americans opposed it as part of the detested rapprochement with Britain. Roosevelt, at that time the highly influential governor of New York, emphasized that U.S. control of the canal was vital to the Monroe Doctrine and to the nation's security. He told the well-known naval theorist Alfred T. Mahan, "I do not see why we should dig the canal if we are not to fortify it." It was better "to have no canal at all than not give us the power to control it in time of war." Roosevelt urged his friend Senator Henry Cabot Lodge and other Republicans to insist on full U.S. control. The treaty proceedings collapsed when the London government rejected Senate amendments that would have achieved this objective for the United States.

Shortly after Roosevelt became president in September 1901, he called for new negotiations with Britain on the subject. Hay, invited to remain as secretary of state, worked closely with Lodge, and President Roosevelt publicly emphasized the necessity of establishing U.S. control of the canal. The strategy worked. In November Hay signed a second agreement with Pauncefote that permitted the United States to build the canal and, by tacit understanding, to fortify it as well. The only stipulation in the second Hay-Pauncefote Treaty was that the United States had to grant equal access to any other nation's commercial or war vessels. The British actually had little choice in signing the agreement. The outbreak of the Boer War in South Africa the previous month had found them without an ally and in need of better relations with the United States. Indeed, the United States had purposely observed a benevolent neutrality toward Britain during the war (despite the U.S. public's support for the Boers) that reciprocated its neutrality during the United States's war with Spain. The result was this important Anglo-American pact, which the Senate overwhelmingly approved in December. The second Hay-Pauncefote Treaty released the United States from the Clayton-Bulwer

agreement and further stimulated the Anglo-American rapprochement.

While Hay and Pauncefote were negotiating their treaty, the Walker Isthmian Canal Commission, established during the McKinley administration, completed its two-year study of the most feasible canal route through Central America. The commission concluded, albeit with reservations, that the best route lay through Nicaragua. Engineers on the commission thought Nicaragua's rivers too shallow for a major canal, and yet that route was less expensive than one through Panama, partly because it could be a sea-level canal (whereas Panama's could not) but primarily because the New Panama Canal Company was asking too much money for the transit rights acquired from Colombia.

The Walker Commission's findings convinced the House of Representatives, making the Senate the focal point of the debate. In January 1902 the House overwhelmingly approved the Hepburn bill, which stipulated that the projected isthmian canal cut through Nicaragua. Yet final approval depended on the Senate, and there the New Panama Canal Company tried to counter the House decision by lowering its demands to $40 million, the estimated value of the company's holdings. This change, urged by Philippe Bunau-Varilla, former chief mining engineer for de Lesseps's operation and now a major stockholder in the New Panama Canal Company, would make the total expenditure for the Panama project considerably less than that required for Nicaragua. In an effort to induce the Senate to reject the House decision, the French company hired the prestigious New York attorney William Nelson Cromwell to begin a lobbying campaign in that body for Panama. Meanwhile, Bunau-Varilla worked to persuade Roosevelt, members of the Walker Commission, and leading Republican senators to change the route from Nicaragua to Panama.

As if by design, factors beyond human control also played a part in the Senate's deliberations. A volcano on the Caribbean island of Martinique had erupted, destroying a city and killing 30,000 people. Less than two weeks later Mt. Momotombo in Nicaragua rumbled menacingly and threatened to do the same. Bunau-Varilla explained how he seized the moment by hurriedly visiting stamp dealers in Washington:

> I was lucky enough to find there ninety stamps, that is, one for every Senator, showing a beautiful volcano belching forth in magnificent eruption. . . .
> I hastened to paste my precious postage stamps on sheets of paper. . . . Below the stamps were written the following words, which told the whole story: "An official witness of the volcanic activity of Nicaragua."

Bunau-Varilla then placed one stamp showing Mt. Momotombo on each senator's desk in the chamber.

Thus, for several reasons Congress switched its favor to Panama. Indeed, Roosevelt and Hay believed that they had an arrangement with Colombia's octogenarian scholar and dictator, José Marroquín, by which his government approved U.S. acquisition of the rights and property holdings from the New Panama Canal Company—a considerable portion of whose stock belonged to Colombia itself. The White House had therefore exerted great pressure on Congress to change the canal site to Panama. The Senate relented. It cast support for Panama in the form of an amendment to the Hepburn bill, and when the lower chamber agreed to accept the change, the bill became law with Roosevelt's signature in June 1902. Under the Spooner Amendment the president was to negotiate with Colombia for transit rights through Panama; if unable to secure an arrangement "within a reasonable time and upon reasonable terms," he could turn to Nicaragua.

Once Panama became the designated route, the last obstacle was Colombia. Hay opened negotiations with the Colombian chargé d'affaires in Washington, Tomás Herrán, who unexpectedly demanded higher yearly lease rates than those offered by the United States. When Hay irately warned that the United States

would deal with Nicaragua, Herrán capitulated. In January 1903 he signed a treaty awarding the United States control of a six-mile-wide strip of land connecting the two oceans, for one hundred years, which actually was in perpetuity (forever) because it was renewable solely by the United States. For these concessions Colombia was to receive $10 million at the outset and annual payments of $250,000 to begin in nine years, the time calculated for building the canal. Less than a week after Herrán signed the treaty, he received a telegram from Bogotá directing him to delay treaty talks until new instructions arrived. But Herrán made no effort to cancel the treaty he had signed; nor did he inform Hay of the importance of the new instructions. The U.S. Senate acted quickly, approving the Hay-Herrán Treaty in March.

Colombia, however, rejected the pact. The Bogotá government, as legal sovereign over Panama, denounced the lease in perpetuity as unconstitutional and disapproved of other provisions affecting the canal zone as a violation of Colombian sovereignty. The prime reason was financial, however: Marroquín wanted more money to replenish a treasury depleted by a lengthy civil war. Colombia sought $10 million from the New Panama Canal Company's passing its concessions to the United States and eventually demanded that the United States raise the initial payment to $15 million.

The president would have none of this. Colombia's abrupt reversal of policy drew a furious reaction from Roosevelt, who thought Marroquín honor bound to comply. The president angrily told Hay that "those contemptible little creatures in Bogotá ought to understand how much they are jeopardizing things and imperilling their own future." Negotiating with Colombia was like trying to "nail currant jelly to the wall." Marroquín and his cohort were "greedy little anthropoids" who stood before the world as guilty of blackmail and robbery.

And yet, despite Roosevelt's tirade over Marroquín's behavior, Colombia had a legitimate case. Panama was a Colombian colony, and Bogotá's leaders were particularly irritated that the Hay-Herrán Treaty barred them from future negotiations over their own territory. Furthermore, the money securing the concessions could pass to the French firm without giving Colombia a share. And, as was the case with the United States, no treaty became official until ratified by the home government. Stall tactics seemed the only way out. The concessions to the French company were due to expire in October 1904, and the Bogotá government could then sell them directly to the United States—perhaps for $40 million. The congress in Bogotá, called together for the first time in years by a regime that needed popular support, denounced the Hay-Herrán Treaty, and in August 1903 the Colombian senate unanimously turned it down.

The Colombian action did not derail the effort of leaders in Washington; they became convinced that the Panamanians themselves might resolve the question by winning their independence. The decision in Bogotá had not surprised Roosevelt; Cromwell had talked with him the previous June and then followed the meeting with an assertion in the *New York World* that if Colombia rejected the pact, Panama would move for independence and grant canal rights to the United States. Roosevelt, the story claimed, supported this approach. Since becoming Colombia's possession, the Panamanians had had a long history of insurrections—over fifty of them, Roosevelt calculated—about one a year. "You don't have to foment a revolution," he flippantly remarked. "All you have to do is take your foot off and one will occur." If questions lingered over the justification for earlier revolts, none could arise now. The Hay-Herrán Treaty had conjured up the economic benefits of a canal through Panama, denied only because of Colombia's greed. After Colombia voted down the Hay-Herrán Treaty, Panamanian and U.S. inhabitants of the small province gathered privately in August. They must gain independence and negotiate another canal treaty—*before* the United States turned to Nicaragua.

Although many details remain unknown, the ensuing Panama revolution was clearly the result of a conspiracy. Numerous private discussions involving Bunau-Varilla and others took place at the Waldorf-Astoria Hotel in New York City. Bunau-Varilla, in fact, referred to room 1162 as "the cradle of the Panama Republic," because while his wife listened and sewed a flag for the new country, he pledged $100,000 for the revolution and worked with its eventual leader, Dr. Manuel Amador Guerrero, who had arrived on the scene to help formulate plans for a declaration of independence and a constitution. Though a physician, Guerrero fitted his new position well: He had interests in the Panama Railroad, which belonged to the New Panama Canal Company. The conspirators soon organized a small "patriot" force in Panama that even included 500 members of the Colombian occupation army—all suitably bribed to join the revolution.

Still, however, Colombian loyalists could easily crush the revolt unless the United States acted quickly and favorably toward the rebels. The key to U.S. policy was the Treaty of 1846 with Colombia (then New Granada), because by it the United States had guaranteed Panama's neutrality. Six times before 1903 U.S. soldiers had entered the isthmian area to restore order during insurrections—four times at Colombia's request. Now, in a strange twist that could develop only in truth rather than fiction, the Americans could argue that the threat to Panama came from *Colombia*. No one during the 1840s could have envisioned the United States protecting Panama from its proprietor; but the treaty, strictly speaking, did not prohibit such an act.

Suspicions linger over the question of U.S. complicity in the shadowy events leading to the revolution in early November 1903. One fact seems certain, however: Bunau-Varilla, in talking with Roosevelt, Hay, and other notables in Washington, could not have expected an *unfavorable* reaction to news of an impending insurrection. In October Bunau-Varilla asked the president whether he would act on

Colombia's behalf when the revolution began. "I cannot say that," Roosevelt cagily replied. "All I can say is that Colombia by her action has forfeited any claim upon the U.S. and I have no use for a government that would do what that government has done." At that, the Frenchman arose, thanked Roosevelt for his time, and left the White House, clearly satisfied that the United States would not interfere. A week after this meeting, Bunau-Varilla learned from Hay that U.S. warships were en route to Central America. Estimating their time of arrival in the city of Colón on the Caribbean side of Panama, he cabled his contacts there that the first ship, the U.S.S. *Nashville,* should be in those waters on November 2.

Thus, it was not by coincidence that the revolt took place in the early evening of the following day, November 3. When the Colombian government sent 400 additional soldiers to Colón on the Atlantic side of the isthmus, the New Panama Canal Company, whose railroad was necessary for transporting the men to Panama City, managed not to have any cars available. Commander John Hubbard of the *Nashville* then dispatched U.S. sailors to the scene, and the Colombian officer in charge, tricked into separating from his troops, accepted a bribe from the rebels' leaders and withdrew from the isthmus. Orders had reached Hubbard that day from the state department in Washington: "In the interests of peace, make every effort to prevent [Colombian] Government troops at Colón from proceeding to Panama."

The Panamanian revolution was a huge success. At the cost of only two lives (an innocent bystander and a donkey), the rebels that same day placed the Colombian general under arrest, paid the bribed Colombian officials and soldiers in a formal ceremony in Panama City, and established a provisional government. "Quiet prevails," the U.S. consul assured Washington. Manuel Amador, as planned in the New York hotel room, became president of the new republic and in a roaring speech attributed his people's freedom to the White House. "President Roosevelt has made good. . . . Long live the Republic of Panama! Long live President Roosevelt!"

The president, however, repeatedly denied complicity and, strictly speaking, was probably telling the truth. In diplomacy, however, the line between appearances and truth is often so thin as to be indistinguishable. On several counts, the U.S. role *appeared* vital to Panama's move for independence. Three days after the revolution Roosevelt extended *de facto* recognition to Panama upon learning of the overthrow of Colombian rule only an hour before. The Washington government immediately stationed U.S. soldiers in Panama City to prevent attempts by Colombia to regain control. It seems indisputable that the Roosevelt administration was aware of the imminence of revolution and skillfully took advantage of a propitious situation. Bunau-Varilla assured suspicious inquirers that through the newspapers he had followed the *Nashville*'s route and correctly predicted its arrival time in Colón. Bunau-Varilla is "a very able fellow," Roosevelt asserted, "and it was his business to find out what he thought our Government would do. I have no doubt that he was able to make a very accurate guess, and to advise his people accordingly. In fact," the president added, "he would have been a very dull man had he been unable to make such a guess."

Questions also remain about the negotiations following the revolution. After the new republic received U.S. recognition, it appointed Bunau-Varilla as "Envoy Extraordinary and Minister Plenipotentiary" to initiate treaty discussions aimed at granting rights to build, fortify, and operate a transoceanic canal. In the meantime, the Panama government sent three emissaries—Amador and two others—to join him in Washington to complete the treaty arrangements. It also forwarded instructions forbidding Bunau-Varilla from agreeing to any terms that endangered Panama's sovereignty. Bunau-Varilla was *not* to draft any treaty without the assistance of the three emissaries: "You will proceed in everything strictly in agreement with them."

But neither the instructions nor the three Panamanians arrived in time. After Hay presented a treaty proposal much like the Hay-Herrán Treaty, Bunau-Varilla took it to his hotel room, where he worked feverishly all night and day in revising the terms to make them more attractive to the U.S. Senate. Amador and his two companions had arrived in New York City and would be in Washington the next day. Just hours before their arrival in the capital, Bunau-Varilla and Hay signed the treaty.

The Hay–Bunau-Varilla Treaty of November 18, 1903, was far more generous than the Hay-Herrán pact. The new agreement guaranteed the United States a ten-mile-wide strip of land through Panama, which became the canal zone. Although Panama retained civil control over Colón and Panama City, the United States received extremely broad powers in the zone connecting the two cities. As would have been the case with Colombia, Panama was to receive $10 million outright and $250,000 a year beginning nine years after the exchange of ratifications. Then, in the most important alterations that Bunau-Varilla inserted, the U.S. government secured *in perpetuity* "all the rights, power and authority within the Zone . . . which the United States would possess and exercise if it were the sovereign of the territory." Article I of the treaty stipulated that "the United States guarantees and will maintain the independence of the Republic of Panama." In a move strikingly similar to the status accorded Cuba under the Platt Amendment of 1901 (discussed later), the United States established a protectorate over Panama.

Six hours after Bunau-Varilla signed the treaty, he excitedly greeted the Panamanians at the train station in Washington with what he termed "the happy news": "The Republic of Panama is henceforth under the protection of the United States. I have just signed the Canal Treaty." Amador nearly fainted, and one of his companions angrily socked Bunau-Varilla in the nose.

Hay brought great pressure on the Senate for hurried approval: The Panamanian representatives, he feared, might bear treaty stipulations less favorable than those allowed by Bunau-Varilla. Senate Democrats wanted to know more about suspected White House involvement in the Panamanian uprising, but the president, despite the suspicions aroused by the *Nashville*'s convenient actions, staunchly proclaimed that "no one connected with this Government had any part in preparing, inciting, or encouraging the late revolution." It was difficult to counter this statement without documentation, and on February 23, 1904, the Senate easily approved the treaty.

Bunau-Varilla also proved instrumental in closing the deal. To ensure the treaty's passage in Panama, he sent a 370-word cable warning its new leaders that failure to approve the pact would cause Roosevelt to put an end to U.S. protection and either seize the canal zone or sign a canal treaty with Nicaragua. The Panama government immediately approved the Hay–Bunau-Varilla Treaty. What happened to the $40 million in U.S. money? The banking magnate J. P. Morgan had become financial agent for the company's holdings, which meant that he engineered the transfer of the entire treasury of the New Panama Canal Company to a list of stockholders never made public. Bunau-Varilla, however, held a large share of that stock and received an undetermined but assuredly fair share of that sum.

The United States's behavior during the Panamanian affair drew a mixed public reaction. Democrats and many others in the country denounced the president, Europeans self-righteously complained of the United States's notable lack of morality, and in succeeding years Latin Americans intensified their opposition to the Panamanian episode as the United States deepened its Caribbean involvement. If Roosevelt's supporters acted for partisan reasons, they defended their policies on a realistic ground: For security's sake, the United States *needed* a canal.

Roosevelt never shied away from upholding his actions during the Panama manipulations. To Congress in December 1903, he declared that the United States had a "mandate from

Elihu Root
Secretary of war and later secretary of state who played an integral role in Theodore Roosevelt's foreign policy. *Oscar King Davis,* William Howard Taft: The Man of the Hour, *Philadelphia: P. W. Ziegler Co., 1908, p. 20.*

civilization" to build an isthmian canal. In his *Autobiography,* he boasted that building the Panama Canal was "by far the most important action I took in foreign affairs." All of his administration's policies, he asserted, had been "carried out in accordance with the highest, finest and nicest standards of public and governmental ethics." Yet skepticism existed even among his cabinet members. In one heated meeting the president turned to Attorney General Philander C. Knox and declared that "it will be just as well for you to give us a formal legal opinion sustaining my action in this whole matter." Knox shrewdly replied: "No, Mr. President, if I were you I would not have any taint of legality about it." On another occasion Roosevelt plodded through an elaborate defense of his behavior and then turned sharply to Secretary of War Elihu Root for his reaction. The elderly man wryly commented:

"You have shown that you were accused of seduction and you have conclusively proved that you were guilty of rape."

The Panama Canal story was still not complete. Several years after ratification of the Hay–Bunau-Varilla Treaty, as the passageway neared the last stages of construction, Roosevelt gave an intriguing speech to a stadium audience in 1911 at the University of California: "I am interested in the Panama Canal because I started it," he proudly asserted. "If I had followed traditional conservative methods I would have submitted a dignified State paper of probably 200 pages to Congress and the debates on it would have been going on yet; but I took the Canal Zone and let Congress debate; and while the debate goes on the Canal does also." The stupendous engineering feat, led by George Goethals, became possible only after Dr. William Gorgas brought under control the two greatest obstacles to de Lesseps's effort: yellow fever and malaria. The Panama Canal, fifty miles long and consisting of a series of locks, opened for use in August 1914—on the eve of the Great War. It came into existence at a cost since 1904 of $352 million (four times that of the Suez Canal) and over 5600 deaths. Seven years later, after Roosevelt had died (ironically, having never seen the completed project), the United States, partly out of guilt but also because of the discovery of oil in Colombia, sent that government an additional $25 million ("canalimony," according to one critic) as recompense for its loss of Panama. In the meantime the United States expanded its involvement in Caribbean affairs in an effort to safeguard the canal from foreign encroachments.

Roosevelt Corollary

As U.S. interest in an isthmian canal had heightened after the Spanish-American War, so did the very thought of its construction underline Cuba's importance by the turn of the twentieth century. The Teller Amendment of 1898 had prohibited its annexation, but the island's location made its independence

Panama Canal under Construction
This picture demonstrates the intricate and complex process required to link the
Atlantic and Pacific Oceans. *Library of Congress.*

Panama Canal after Completion
U.S.S. *Ohio* passing Cucaracha Slide in 1915, shortly after the opening of the
Panama Canal in August 1914. *Library of Congress.*

dangerous because of possible absorption by some other power. President McKinley had warned Congress in December 1899 that Americans had "a grave responsibility for the future good government of Cuba" and that the island had to "be bound to us." The Filipino insurrection raised fears in Washington that the same could happen in Cuba. To prevent this unhappy situation, Secretary of War Root appointed General Leonard Wood as military governor of Cuba. Wood was to rid the island of yellow fever and to institute an educational program, a public works system, and an orderly government. His efforts were largely unsuccessful, but they led to a more direct U.S. involvement in Cuban affairs.

By early 1901 Root had worked with the chair of the Senate Foreign Relations Committee, Orville Platt, in drafting a congressional bill establishing a U.S. protectorate over Cuba until that island's government drew up a constitution containing certain stipulations. According to the Platt Amendment, Cuba was nominally free but could not sign a treaty or borrow money without approval from Washington. In the event of internal disorder, the United States could intervene. Finally, Cuba granted the United States "lands necessary for coaling or naval stations." The Platt Amendment became an annex to the new Cuban constitution of 1901 only under Wood's pressure and after Root's assurances that the United States would not intervene unless the Cuban government was in danger. U.S. insistence on incorporating the amendment into the Cuban constitution was attributable to Washington's concern that the Cubans could amend their constitution unilaterally; the amendment required U.S. approval before they could make changes. In May 1903 the United States and Cuba formalized the amendment into a treaty, and later that year the U.S. Navy built a base at Guantánamo Bay, located near Santiago on the southeastern side of the island. The United States was to hold this base in perpetuity.

The Platt Amendment aroused bitter opposition both inside and outside the United States. While U.S. anti-imperialists resurrected their arguments against foreign involvement, many Cubans complained that the United States had merely taken the place of their former Spanish oppressor. President Roosevelt characterized the opposition groups in the United States as "unhung traitors[,] . . . liars, slanderers and scandal mongers," and Root unconvincingly tried to establish a difference between "interventionism" and "interference" with the island's domestic affairs. U.S. intervention, he argued, would occur only to safeguard Cuba's government and preserve the island's independence—*not* to permit interference in internal matters. The United States meanwhile signed the Reciprocity Treaty with Cuba in 1902, which further tied the two peoples together by lowering duties on the island's exports to America.

In the aftermath of the Platt Amendment the United States confirmed the Cuban leaders' fears by expanding its economic and military involvement on the island. U.S. investments and trade more than quadrupled from the mid-1890s to 1913. Meanwhile, U.S. Marines repeatedly intervened because of the island's internal troubles, and in one period, from 1906 to 1909, they actually assumed control of the government. Roosevelt rigidly opposed annexation but feared that continued domestic unrest would force the United States into such a step. He could not understand why the Cubans were unable to "behave themselves." He finally turned to his friend and now secretary of war, William Howard Taft, to resolve the island's problems. As former civil governor of the Philippines, Taft recognized the importance of settling Cuba's troubles before a full-scale insurrection broke out. He served as Cuba's provisional governor for a month and upon his return home in October 1906, he left behind more than 5000 U.S. soldiers who were prepared to implement the reforms called for earlier by General Wood.

The Platt Amendment established a precedent for similar U.S. actions in other parts of the hemisphere and appears to have become

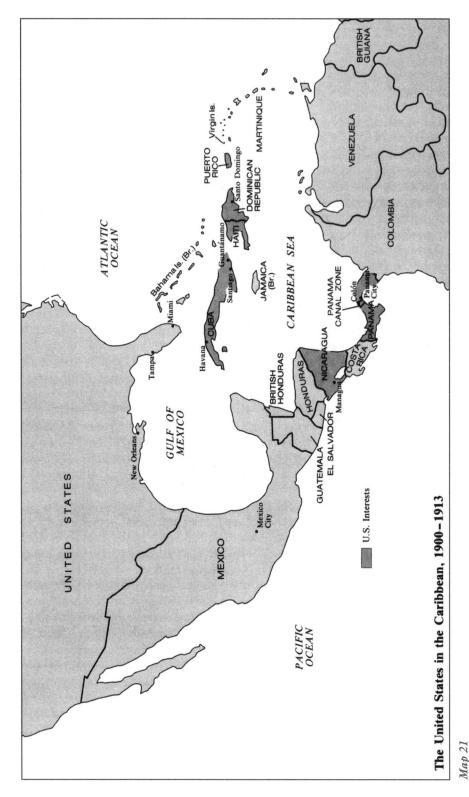

The United States in the Caribbean, 1900–1913

Map 21

In the early twentieth century, the United States announced the Roosevelt Corollary of the Monroe Doctrine and sought to "police" Central America and the Caribbean.

the basis of a new Latin American policy by the United States. As early as Roosevelt's first months in office, he seemed to be moving toward a major pronouncement on Latin American affairs intended to discourage Old World involvement. Negotiations over Panama and Cuba weighed heavily on his mind when, in his first annual message to Congress in December 1901, he termed the Monroe Doctrine "a guarantee of the commercial independence of the Americas." On another occasion he declared that as Voltaire had said of God, "if the Monroe Doctrine did not already exist, it would be necessary forthwith to create it." Yet Roosevelt admitted to limitations on U.S. actions. After Germany gave notice in 1901 of its intent to dispatch a punitive expedition to Venezuela, he took a stand similar to that of Secretary of State Seward during the European intervention in Mexico of the 1860s. Roosevelt asserted that the United States would not guarantee any hemispheric nation against punitive action by a non-American power unless that action involved the acquisition of territory. Roosevelt appeared to be searching for a middle ground between U.S. intervention and outright annexation. Like a watchdog, he explained, the United States would oversee Latin America's relations with the Old World.

The first test of Roosevelt's Latin American policy came in Venezuela, where Germany and Britain sought reimbursement of debts long overdue. German intentions in the hemisphere worried Americans more than did those of the British, largely because of the recent Anglo-American rapprochement but also because of recent instances of German expansionism. Kaiser Wilhelm II had tried to improve relations with the United States, but with little success. The Germans called for arbitration of the debt question by The Hague Court, but Venezuelan dictator Cipriano Castro refused the proposal. Germany and Britain then notified Washington that they were preparing to use force to collect their money, but at the same time they assured the president of having no territorial aims. Meeting no

opposition from the Roosevelt administration, they issued an ultimatum to Venezuela in December 1902 and proceeded to set up a "pacific blockade" of its main ports. But as tensions mounted, the British shelled two forts and landed troops, and the Germans sank two of Venezuela's gunboats. When U.S. popular reaction stiffened with Germany's additional bombardment of Venezuelan territory, Roosevelt insisted on arbitration. Germany and Britain agreed to his proposal but maintained the blockade. Castro, called by Roosevelt an "unspeakable villainous little monkey," had brought on a deeper European involvement in the hemisphere, provoked a challenge to the credibility of the Monroe Doctrine, and forced the United States to intervene.

British interest in maintaining the rapprochement explains that nation's retreat, but the reasons for Germany's sudden change of policy were not clear in 1902. Part of the explanation lies in the kaiser's decision to send a new ambassador to Washington. This ambassador, Hermann Speck von Sternburg, had befriended Roosevelt sometime before and now worked to defuse the dangerous situation. But there is more to the story.

In a 1916 reprinting of William R. Thayer's biography of John Hay, the author included a copy of a letter he had recently received from Roosevelt asserting that he had played a major but hidden role in resolving the Venezuelan crisis. As president in 1902, Roosevelt explained in the letter to Thayer, he became alarmed that Germany might establish a base in Venezuela that would endanger an isthmian canal and other U.S. interests. The Berlin government had at first refused the call for arbitration, according to Roosevelt, and its assurances were not convincing that any seizures of territory would be temporary. Roosevelt thereupon ordered Admiral George Dewey moved near Puerto Rico and readied for action. If Germany did not agree to arbitration within ten days, Roosevelt pointedly told von Sternburg, Dewey would go to Venezuela. The German ambassador expressed "very grave concern," Roosevelt recalled, and warned that such U.S. action would have "serious consequences." When a week passed with no reply from Berlin, Roosevelt informed the ambassador of a change in plans: Dewey would leave twenty-four hours earlier than previously announced. Germany agreed to arbitration.

Controversy exists over Roosevelt's account of his actions during the Venezuelan crisis of 1902–1903. Critics have argued that he either fabricated or embellished the story, and yet no one can deny that the actions outlined in the letter were well within Roosevelt's character and temperament. The nation's interests in the hemisphere were involved: Roosevelt recognized that a European power entrenched so close to Panama posed a potential threat to the canal as well as to the entire Caribbean. Germany did not want a confrontation with the United States, and chances are that Roosevelt may have hurried the kaiser into a decision he would have made anyway. But there is little reason to doubt the essence of Roosevelt's testimony.

In February 1903 Germany and Britain lifted the Venezuelan blockade and turned over the claims issue to the Permanent Court of Arbitration at The Hague. The British government had recognized its lack of wisdom in following Germany's lead in Venezuela, and Prime Minister Arthur Balfour had attempted to calm Anglophobes in the United States by renouncing territorial aims in the New World and recognizing the Monroe Doctrine as part of international law. The Hague Court meanwhile decided in favor of Germany and Britain, which drew a concerned reaction in the Western Hemisphere. The Department of State feared that the decision would encourage the use of force in international disputes and increase the likelihood of further European intervention in Latin America.

Seeing the danger, the Argentine minister of foreign affairs, Luis Drago, tried to reduce the chances of foreign intervention in the hemisphere. He had opposed the use of force in collecting debts from Venezuela, and in 1902 he notified the Roosevelt administration that the loss of investments was a risk business leaders took in any transactions, including those outside their country. The Drago Doctrine, as his argument became known, was incorporated into international law at the Second Hague Conference of 1907. The United States approved but added the stipulation that intervention was acceptable only if the debtor nation either rejected arbitration or refused to abide by the arbitrator's decision.

A second debt problem in the hemisphere, this one in the Dominican Republic, led the Roosevelt administration to issue a formal statement on its Latin American policy. The Dominican government owed nearly $32 million to a host of countries, including Germany and the United States (a company in New York holding U.S. and British funds). Over the years the Dominicans had repeatedly assured creditors of remuneration from customs collections, but with no results. Internal disorder had rocked the Dominican Republic since the 1890s, and though some Americans pondered annexation, Roosevelt privately declared, "I have about the same desire to annex it as a gorged boa constrictor might have to swallow a porcupine wrong-end to." Both American and European business leaders exerted pressure on the U.S. government to act, and although Roosevelt hesitated, he recognized that the Venezuelan arbitration award had established a precedent for the forceful collection of debts.

Roosevelt prepared to deal with the Dominican situation through a policy later known as the Roosevelt Corollary of the Monroe Doctrine. In May 1904 he indicated the direction of his thinking in a letter to Secretary of War Root, when he pledged U.S. friendship to any nation that acted responsibly in international affairs. He went on to advise Congress in December that the United States had to keep order in the hemisphere. "Chronic wrongdoing may in America, as elsewhere, ultimately require intervention by some civilized nation, and in the Western Hemisphere the adherence of the United

States to the Monroe Doctrine may force the United States, however reluctantly, in flagrant cases of such wrongdoing or impotence, to the exercise of an international police power."

Later, to the Senate, Roosevelt elaborated on his congressional message. Under the Monroe Doctrine, the United States could not allow any European country to "seize and permanently occupy the territory of one of these republics; and yet such seizure of territory, disguised or undisguised, may eventually offer the only way in which the power in question can collect any debts, unless there is interference on the part of the United States." The president used the situation in the Dominican Republic as the occasion to announce the Roosevelt Corollary, a unilateral statement asserting U.S. police control over the hemisphere.

In December 1904 the United States opened negotiations with the Dominican Republic to resolve the debts controversy. The resulting agreement authorized the New York company to administer the country's customs offices at two ports until the claimants received monetary satisfaction. European creditors immediately objected, arousing concern in the Roosevelt administration that its action would set off a race for the remainder of the offices. The Dominican government, as a result of the urgings of the U.S. minister in that country, asked the United States to take over all customs offices and allocate the funds in such a way as to meet the republic's financial obligations at home and abroad. Democrats and others in the United States questioned the constitutionality of such a measure, but Roosevelt sent the proposed agreement to the Senate in January 1905. Under the arrangement, he was to appoint an American to handle receivership duties. Whereas 45 percent of collected funds would go to the Dominicans, most of the remainder would go into a trust fund in a New York bank, reserved for the republic's creditors. Should the Senate oppose the agreement, the balance of the customs revenues would go to the Dominican government as well. The

Senate, however, adjourned in March without approving the pact.

Roosevelt was furious and in April 1905 negotiated an executive agreement with the Dominicans that did not require Senate approval and rested on a *modus vivendi* (temporary arrangement pending final settlement). Although the Democrats denounced his action as unconstitutional, the executive agreement remained in effect until February 1907, when the Senate finally caved in and approved a treaty granting legal standing to the American whom Roosevelt had already sent as customs collector. The Dominicans' creditors scaled down their demands, and the government secured a new bond in the United States to cover the debt and establish a public works program on the island. Root, by that time secretary of state, defended the pact in the Senate by declaring that the Panama Canal, then under construction, placed Latin American countries "in the front yard of the United States" and forced it "to police the surrounding premises" in the interest of hemispheric stability and trade.

The Dominican Republic approached economic and political soundness during the following years, but renewed insurrections soon forced the United States to broaden its involvement in the island's affairs. In late 1911 the president of the Dominican Republic was assassinated, and the next year rebels from neighboring Haiti raided and pillaged at will. Customs offices under U.S. control had to shut their doors, and in September 1912 a U.S. commission and several hundred marines arrived to restore order. By December the U.S. force had achieved some stability, but sporadic outbreaks of violence caused the Washington government to continue military occupation of the island into the early 1920s.

President Taft followed Roosevelt's example in using the Monroe Doctrine as the basis of his Latin American policy when during his administration of 1909 through 1913 the United States deepened its economic influence in Nicaragua through "dollar diplomacy." Defined by Taft as "substituting dollars for bullets," the term was new, but the idea behind it was not. Foreign policy and commercial interests had long been supportive of each other, but in this period the Washington government worked ever more closely with the nation's financial and industrial concerns in seeking out new foreign markets. Taft expressed dissatisfaction with the military thrust of Roosevelt's Caribbean policy, recognizing that such a stance would hurt the U.S. reputation throughout Latin America and provide substance for his administration's critics. He insisted that dollar diplomacy "appeals alike . . . to idealistic humanitarian sentiments, to the dictates of sound policy and strategy, and to legitimate commercial aims." During his presidency, U.S. investments and foreign policy became virtually inseparable as the economic and strategic objectives of business and government leaders often ran parallel.

When in late 1911 the Nicaraguan government threatened to cancel mine concessions to the United States and executed two Americans for aiding an ongoing revolution, the Taft administration sent marines to help bring about a new regime. The Senate in Washington opposed a treaty with Nicaragua that, like a pact negotiated with Honduras that same year (also defeated by the Senate), would have authorized a U.S. loan and placed the United States in charge of customs. Such a treaty, Democratic senators argued, would lead to an unwarrantable and dangerous extension of U.S. power. In addition, many senators feared that the president had assumed excessive authority in making treaties. But the state department became party to an agreement involving Nicaragua and various New York banks, which established a receivership similar to that set up for the Dominican Republic. Another revolution in Nicaragua in late 1912 prompted the Washington government to send out more than 2000 marines, who put down the insurrection, forced the rebel leaders out of the country, and stationed a small legation guard in the capital of Managua that remained off and on until 1933.

Although the United States had intended its Nicaraguan involvement to safeguard the areas surrounding the Panama Canal, its policies left a long-standing feeling of distrust throughout Latin America.

The Alaskan Boundary Dispute

U.S. diplomatic activities were not confined to the southern half of the hemisphere: The discovery of gold in the Klondike River area of northwest Canada in 1896 set off a boundary dispute between Alaska and British Columbia that reached dangerous proportions during Roosevelt's presidency. The best route into the area lay through the panhandle of southern Alaska, and the Canadians found a way to claim that narrow strip of territory. They suddenly argued that the original line in the Anglo-Russian Treaty of 1825, which ran thirty miles inland from the Pacific and became the basis of the U.S. purchase of Alaska more than forty years later, did not follow the twisting contours of the coast but moved due south. If that claim were correct, the United States would lose commercial control over the Alaskan interior, because Canada would own the headwaters of the larger coves and harbors cutting into North America.

Controversy intensified during the summer of 1898. In June the Canadians claimed the largest bay in the region, the Lynn Canal, which flowed by three settlements and connected with harbors (Pyramid, Dyea, and Skagway) providing access to the gold fields and the sea. The Canadian government was willing to negotiate, but only if the Americans first accepted its claim to Pyramid Harbor. Secretary of State Hay bitterly condemned the claim: "It is as if a kidnapper, stealing one of your children, should say that his conduct was more than fair, it was even generous, because he left you two."

Hay proposed the establishment of a joint commission to settle the Alaskan boundary dispute, but both nations soon became preoccupied with other more pressing matters: the United States with its war with Spain, and

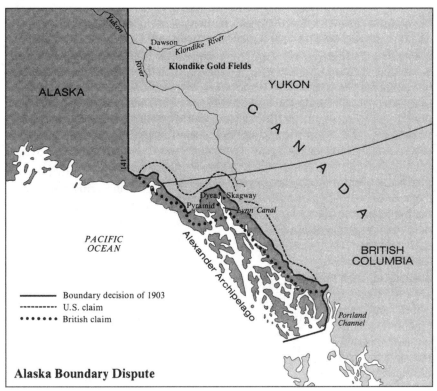

Map 22
President Theodore Roosevelt resorted to a joint commission in settling the dispute, but only after he had used various pressures to ensure a favorable outcome.

Britain with its growing problems with the Boers in South Africa. In the meantime the McKinley administration quieted the Alaskan situation by agreeing to Canada's temporary use of the land at the opening of the Lynn Canal. When Hay recommended the commission approach to Roosevelt shortly after his arrival in the White House, the new president expressed concern. He feared that arbitration would lead to a compromise whereby the United States lost territory that the Canadians had no right to have. In March 1902, however, Roosevelt felt compelled to act because rumors had spread that gold might also be discovered in the disputed territory and force another crisis. To Hay in July, he termed the Canadians' claim "an outrage pure and simple. . . . To pay them anything where they are entitled to nothing would in a case

like this come dangerously near blackmail." As tensions mounted in the disputed area, Roosevelt dispatched 800 additional troops to keep order.

Late that same year the Canadians saw no support coming from England and retreated from their demands, indicating that their only concern now was to save face. If the United States agreed to arbitration, they would accept a decision roughly corresponding with the U.S. position. Canada had no choice. British leaders in London were worried that the Alaskan issue might endanger the Anglo-American rapprochement. British foreign secretary Lord Henry Lansdowne expressed the general feeling among his countrymen: "America seems to be our only friend just now, and it would be unfortunate to quarrel with her."

In late January 1903 Britain agreed to Hay's joint-commission proposal. The resulting Convention of 1903 called for "six impartial jurists," three American and three British to comprise an Alaskan Boundary Tribunal that would gather in London and settle the matter by majority vote. Little imagination was needed to predict the outcome. "In this case," Hay confidently remarked, "it is impossible that we should lose, and not at all impossible that a majority should give a verdict in our favor." To the commission Roosevelt appointed his friend Senator Henry Cabot Lodge of Massachusetts, Elihu Root, then the president's secretary of war, and a former senator from Washington, George Turner. None of the men fitted the category of "impartial jurists," but appointing them was politically important because their support for the U.S. boundary claims was well known. The British king appointed a commission consisting of two Canadians and the lord chief justice of England, Richard E. W. Alverstone. Both Alverstone and his Canadian companions understood that the maintenance of good relations with the United States was more important than a breakdown over Alaska's boundary. But they also knew that failure to gain something in the proceedings would pit them against an angry populace at home.

In late 1903 the Alaskan Boundary Tribunal met in London. After weeks of bitter discussions the two Canadians refused to compromise, as did the three Americans, and the outcome rested with England's Lord Alverstone. Roosevelt meanwhile exerted pressure by letting it be known that a decision against the United States would lead to U.S. military occupation of the disputed territory while the army itself drew the boundary. The London government decided to accept the U.S. interpretation of the line. Despite Canada's threats of secession, Alverstone voted with the three Americans in October 1903. Although he succeeded in reducing the width of the coastal award, he secured for Canada only two of four small islands in dispute. The United States had a clear victory. Alverstone insisted that he had

decided solely on the basis of "the law and the evidence," and yet if so, the law and the evidence conveniently fitted a decision dictated by his country's need to maintain the rapprochement with the United States.

East Asia

U.S. attention had in the meantime turned toward East Asia, where growing problems would lead to the Russo-Japanese War of 1904–1905. China remained a major concern, because outside powers had expanded their claims in defiance of the Open Door declarations of 1899 and 1900. Russia had joined European powers in obstructing Japan's attempt in 1895 to secure a lease on the Liaotung Peninsula in southern Manchuria and had refused to withdraw its soldiers from Manchuria after the Boxer Rebellion of 1900. Indeed, the Russians were now building a railway through northern Manchuria and into Vladivostok, which was their major port in north Pacific waters. They had also won the right to construct and control another railroad connecting Harbin with Port Arthur in the south, where they would soon have a naval base. These advances into Manchuria threatened Japan's interests both there and in Korea, the latter traditionally regarded as "a dagger pointed at the heart of Japan." The Japanese had gradually extended control over Korea since the end of the Sino-Japanese War in 1895, and they had negotiated an alliance with Britain in 1902 admitting to each party's special interests in China. What was more important, in exchange for Japan's support of Britain in Europe, the British recognized Japan's political, commercial, and industrial concerns in Korea. The Anglo-Japanese Alliance offered Japan some guarantee that war with Russia would not necessarily lead to French intervention on behalf of their Russian ally. After Japan failed to negotiate a favorable settlement with Russia over Manchuria and Korea, the Japanese navy launched a surprise attack on Port Arthur in February 1904 that wiped out Russia's Pacific fleet. Two days later Japan declared war.

Americans initially joined the Roosevelt administration in praising the Japanese in their war with Russia. "Was not the way the Japs began the fight bully?" remarked Root. Roosevelt wrote his son less than a week after the Port Arthur attack that "I was thoroughly pleased with the Japanese victory for Japan is playing our game" in trying to halt the Russians. The Washington government of course maintained official neutrality, but it favored Japan out of expectations that its leaders would respect the Open Door in China. The president's distaste for Russian leadership and supposed backwardness was as well known as his favor for Japan's industriousness and efficiency. He was determined that France, Russia's ally, and Germany, which supported Russia in Asia, would not deny Japan the spoils of war. Roosevelt realized that the outcome of the Russo-Japanese War would determine the balance of power in that part of the world and hence affect U.S. interests—particularly in China and the Philippines.

Russia was irate over the U.S. reaction to the war. The Russians were unaware of the change in attitude in the United States brought by their expansionist policies in East Asia and by their harsh treatment of Jews and political opponents at home. Roosevelt privately considered Czar Nicholas II "a preposterous little creature," yet dangerous because he could close Manchuria to the outside world. Japan, Roosevelt believed, might preserve the Open Door and safeguard U.S. interests both in China and the Philippines. Gradually, however, this hope disappeared as Japan unexpectedly and overwhelmingly won the war by 1905 and soon posed a new danger on the Pacific horizon.

The Russo-Japanese War of 1904–1905 proved enormously expensive, even to the victorious Japanese—so costly that the Japanese minister in Washington, Kogoro Takahira, privately asked Roosevelt in the spring of 1905 to intervene and bring the warring powers to the peace table. Russia could not sustain the war because of growing internal problems that would culminate in revolution during the au-tumn of that same year and because of pressure from France. The Paris government was more concerned about a concurrent crisis with Germany over Morocco than about Russia's plight in East Asia. Roosevelt's condition for intervention was a guarantee for the Open Door policy, which Japan gave but Russia did not. Roosevelt recognized the important role thrust upon him: If he played the balance-of-power game adeptly, he might keep the advantage from shifting too far toward Tokyo and thereby preserve U.S. interests in that part of the world.

Peace talks began on a U.S. naval base in Portsmouth, New Hampshire, during August 1905, and only after considerable difficulty did the peace-making teams manage a settlement. Japan demanded that Russia pull out of Manchuria, give up the Liaotung Peninsula and the South Manchurian Railroad from Harbin to Port Arthur, recognize Japanese hegemony in Korea and on Sakhalin Island off the north Chinese mainland, and pay $600 million in reparations. The discussions stalemated when Russia refused to relinquish Sakhalin and turned down the reparations demand. Fearing that Nicholas would rather resume the war than yield to Japan, Roosevelt sought a compromise calling for Russia to receive the northern half of Sakhalin and Japan the rest and for the two powers to agree "in principle" to a reparations bill. After a carefully crafted discussion led by the U.S. ambassador to St. Petersburg, George Meyer, the czar accepted the first part of the plan, but he still refused to pay war damages. Japan eventually gave up that demand. Resumption of the war to obtain reparations, it realized, would cancel their worth, cause permanent injury at home, and therefore cost more than peace. Japan also discerned a change in U.S. public opinion. Whether owing to the demands and seeming arrogance of the Japanese delegates at Portsmouth or to the Russians' repeated warnings that Japan was the real threat to peace, the Americans' ardor for the Japanese had noticeably cooled.

The antagonists finally came to terms with the Treaty of Portsmouth on September 5, 1905. Japan regained what it had lost in the war with China in 1894–1895: the Liaotung Peninsula, which was the site of Port Arthur, Dairen, and the South Manchurian Railroad. Russia also recognized Japan's special interests in Korea and south Sakhalin. Manchuria returned to China's civil jurisdiction, and all Japanese and Russian soldiers were to withdraw except those needed to guard the railroad. Russia remained a prominent force in the region by retaining the northern half of Sakhalin and the Chinese Eastern Railway in upper Manchuria, but Japan emerged from the Russo-Japanese War as the dominant power in East Asia.

The results of the Portsmouth Conference were mixed. U.S. relations hardened with both Russia and Japan as those countries searched for a scapegoat to explain their failures in the war. Whereas the Russians claimed they could have won the war had the Americans not intervened, the Japanese people, heavily burdened by taxation, blamed their leaders in Tokyo along with the U.S. government for failing to win an indemnity and other concessions. Violent antigovernment and anti-American demonstrations broke out in Tokyo and other cities. In February 1906 the United States protested commercial discrimination in Japanese-controlled areas in Manchuria; the Japanese, it became clear, had no intentions of respecting the Open Door. While Japanese-American relations rapidly deteriorated, Roosevelt accepted the Nobel Peace Prize in 1906 for his efforts at Portsmouth (and in settling the Moroccan dispute, as discussed later).

Not all results of the Russo-Japanese War were self-evident: Another outgrowth of the conflict was the Taft-Katsura "agreed memorandum" of late July 1905. This secret document tied the United States to Japan (and with Britain too, because of its alignment with Japan in 1902). A year earlier Roosevelt had agreed to recognize Japan's special interests in Korea, and in midsummer of the following year Secretary of War Taft, en route to the Philippines, repeated the assurance in a conversation in Tokyo with Prime Minister Taro Katsura. Japan's ongoing conquests in the war with Russia during the spring of 1905 had caused concern in Washington over the Philippines, and through this informal understanding the United States agreed to drop claims to Korea in exchange for Japan's renunciation of "any aggressive designs whatever" on the islands. Roosevelt approved the memorandum, and within a year the United States closed its legation at Seoul and conducted Korean business through the government in Tokyo.

The Taft-Katsura understanding signaled a retreat on the Open Door, but the United States had no choice. Root explained years afterward that "all we might have done was to make threats which we could not carry out." Such a move would have violated one of Roosevelt's maxims: "I never take a step in foreign policy unless I am assured that I shall be able eventually to carry out my will by force."

Americans were soon to perceive Japan as a threat to their interests at home and abroad. By 1905 about 100,000 Japanese were in the United States. They settled mostly along the west coast, where their presence reminded Californians of recent troubles with Chinese coolies who had flocked into the United States to work as cheap labor on the transcontinental railroad completed in 1869. But the Japanese soon totaled almost a tenth of the state's population and aroused deep racial animosities. Congress barred further Chinese immigration into the United States during the 1880s but did not extend the measure to include the Japanese. In 1900 the Tokyo government had prohibited its laborers from entering the United States, but this ruling proved easy to circumvent as Japanese immigrants continued in through Hawaii, Mexico, and Canada. California became the focal point of Japanese immigration, and whether for racial or economic reasons (or both), the state's inhabitants protested that Orientals were undermining the economy by working for lower wages than whites would accept. Japan's recent victory over Russia and the inflammatory articles in the U.S. press stirred up a hotbed of emotions over an alleged "yellow peril" that needed only a catalyst to set off trouble.

That catalyst came in October 1906, when the San Francisco school board acted on the separate-but-equal principle of the *Plessy v. Ferguson* Supreme Court case of 1896 in restricting the city's ninety-three Japanese children to an Oriental Public School already attended by Chinese and Korean youths. This school board decision, weakly based on the arguments that the Japanese youths were overaged and overcrowding the classrooms, drew strong complaints locally and in Japan from the Japanese press and public, who felt humiliated at seeing the United States treat their people as racial inferiors.

Roosevelt immediately detected a threat to his foreign policy. Though also concerned about the vast influx of Japanese into the United States, he feared that ill feeling over the school situation might hurt relations with Japan and thus endanger U.S. interests in the Philippines and Hawaii. Roosevelt publicly denounced the school board's decision as a "wicked absurdity" while exerting pressure on what he called the "idiots of the California legislature" to halt their racially discriminatory policies. He also recommended that the U.S. Congress enact laws naturalizing those Japanese who had made the United States their permanent home. But when he waved the big stick, he succeeded only in fanning the wrath of Californians.

The president lacked the constitutional power to act in this state matter, and he again resorted to personal diplomacy. He arranged for the transportation of San Francisco's mayor and entire school board to Washington, where he discussed the matter with them in the Oval Office. There, in February 1907, the president convinced the school board to withdraw the segregation order in exchange for his promise to halt the flow of Japanese into the United States. Through a series of diplomatic notes in late 1907 and early 1908, he secured an informal "gentlemen's agreement" with Japan whereby its government voluntarily restricted the immigration of laborers into the continental United States, and then he approved a U.S. policy prohibit-ing their indirect entrance through Hawaii, Mexico, and Canada. Again, to avoid political wrangling in the Senate, the president implemented the arrangement through executive agreement.

Roosevelt recognized the possibility of future problems with Japan in the Pacific and decided to send the U.S. fleet on a world cruise to demonstrate its strength, allow crew members to gain firsthand experience at sea, and encourage Congress to appropriate money for a larger navy. In July 1907 the administration announced that the "Great White Fleet"—sixteen battleships and their escorts—would leave the Atlantic for a practice cruise around the world. East Coast Americans complained about being left defenseless, and the chair of the Senate Committee on Naval Affairs piously notified Roosevelt that no funds for the enterprise were available. The president crisply replied that he had enough finances on hand to move the navy to the Pacific, and that if Congress wanted to leave the ships there, that was its decision. Congress allotted the money.

In December 1907 the Great White Fleet steamed out of Hampton Roads and eventually around Cape Horn, arriving in Lower California and preparing to cross the Pacific and honor invitations from Japan, Australia, and other countries. The Japanese, perhaps wanting a closer view of U.S. naval power, welcomed the men from the ships with throngs of youths along the roadsides waving small U.S. flags and singing the National Anthem in English. After a three-day visit in Japan, the fleet departed, making its way through the Suez Canal, European waters, and the Atlantic before returning home safely and without incident in February 1909.

The cruise drew a mixed assessment. The president proclaimed it "the most important service that I rendered to peace." And evidence does suggest that the Tokyo visit cleared the air between the nations. Yet a rise in naval armaments programs took place in Japan, Germany, and other countries—perhaps partly in response to the cruise. In the spring of

1908 the U.S. Congress approved the construction of additional battleships. The cruise also demonstrated the nation's need for Pacific naval bases near East Asia, especially to enhance the security of the Philippines.

The visit of the U.S. fleet to Tokyo probably stimulated the Root-Takahira agreement of November 1908. On the day of the fleet's departure from Japan, the Tokyo government reversed a previous stance and instructed its new ambassador in Washington, Kogoro Takahira, to propose an arrangement with Secretary of State Root that would recognize both the status quo in the Pacific and the Open Door in China. The Root-Takahira agreement thus guaranteed U.S. interests in the Philippines, but it constituted a tacit admission to Japan's dominance in Korea and Manchuria and hence a violation of the Open Door. In a weak effort to safeguard the Open Door, the agreement also called on each signatory to preserve "by all pacific means" the "independence and integrity of China and the principle of equal opportunity for commerce and industry of all nations in that Empire."

Controversy developed over the measure shortly after Roosevelt likewise enacted it through executive agreement. China was irritated at not having participated in the negotiations. The interested European powers approved the agreement only because East Asia seemed left open for exploitation. Americans praised it for safeguarding the Open Door in China and their own control over the Philippines, however, and the Japanese were pleased because respect for the status quo meant their continued economic control over Manchuria. Yet many Americans were concerned that the agreement only implicitly won Japan's assurances against interfering with U.S. interests in the Philippines and Hawaii— and at the huge cost of accepting Japan's deepening entrenchment in Manchuria.

If Root allowed questions to remain about the sanctity of the Open Door, it was a result of Roosevelt's guidance. The president realized that the United States lacked the military strength to stop Japanese expansion in China.

He later explained to Taft, himself then president, that "if the Japanese choose to follow a course of conduct [in Manchuria] to which we are adverse, we cannot stop it unless we are prepared to go to war, and a successful war about Manchuria would require a fleet as good as that of England, plus an army as good as that of Germany." The Open Door "completely disappears as soon as a powerful nation determines to disregard it."

Taft did not fare as well as his predecessor did in East Asian affairs. He followed dollar diplomacy in China as he had done in Latin America, but before his presidency was over, his East Asian policies proved disillusioning to the Chinese and threatening to Japan. Whereas Roosevelt had recognized power realities and tried to mollify the Japanese through concessions disguised as treaties, Taft sought a stronger policy based on economic means. To strengthen U.S. interests and promote orderly development overseas, Taft and his secretary of state, Philander C. Knox, attempted to use U.S. investments as a mechanism for undercutting outside influence in China. Shortly after Taft's arrival in the White House, he demanded that the Chinese government permit U.S. banking interests to participate in a consortium (international association of banking interests) with England, France, and Germany. This consortium would arrange a loan enabling China either to buy the Manchurian railroads from Russia and Japan or to build competing railways and drive the others into bankruptcy. Such a so-called neutralization scheme posed a direct challenge to Japan's interests. But continued unrest in China made the Manchurian venture too risky for U.S. bankers. Taft's East Asian policies succeeded only in driving Russia and Japan closer together, and by the time he left office four years later, the Open Door in China, both in the commercial and territorial sense, was nearly shut.

The Algeciras Conference

One last matter further illustrated Roosevelt's belief that U.S. interests reached beyond the

Western Hemisphere: his decision to mediate the 1905 Franco-German crisis over Morocco. The year before, France had approved British claims in Egypt for reciprocal recognition of its rights in the North African country of Morocco. The Germans decided to test the Anglo-French Entente, or understanding. With France's ally Russia at war with Japan, Kaiser Wilhelm II arrived in the Moroccan capital of Tangier in March 1905 and delivered a belligerent speech praising the sultan as "an absolutely independent sovereign" and demanding German rights in that country. The French turned him down, and war seemed imminent. Although the British prepared to support the French, the premier in Paris declared that his country was not ready for war and could not depend on Russian assistance along with British support. The cabinet forced a change in the foreign ministry, and France moved to conciliate the Germans.

The Berlin government asked Roosevelt to call a meeting with Russia and Germany to resolve the Moroccan question. Roosevelt agreed, though reluctantly, because he recognized that a European war would affect everyone, including the United States. The French were also wary about a conference in which they could gain nothing and probably would *lose* territory in a predictable compromise solution. Roosevelt finally convinced them to attend. In the meantime, according to contemporary U.S. accounts that their German colleagues disputed, Wilhelm offered assurances that in case of serious disagreements at the conference, he would accept whatever decision Roosevelt considered fair. Roosevelt justified his decision to intervene on three bases: (1) a commercial convention in 1880 that the United States had signed in Madrid affecting Morocco, (2) his desire to prevent the country's partition, and (3) his wish to preserve the principle of the Open Door. Realizing the opportunity to reset the European balance of power, Roosevelt agreed to send representatives to a conference in the small Spanish coastal town of Algeciras, located near Gibraltar.

The Algeciras Conference opened in January 1906 and closed with a treaty in April. Henry White, ambassador to Italy and the ranking member of the U.S. delegation, managed to reconcile the disagreements between the opposing parties without capitulating to Germany's demand for Morocco's partition. By the General Act of Algeciras, Morocco's territorial integrity remained intact, although France and Spain won the right to establish controls over that country's police force. Germany had suffered a severe defeat—and not only at the treaty table. The crisis drove France and England closer together and convinced many Americans that the Berlin government wanted war.

Roosevelt later claimed to have been highly instrumental in resolving the crisis. When the Germans opposed French and Spanish control over the Moroccan police force, Wilhelm gave in only after being warned of the publication of his alleged promise to abide by the president's decisions. To soothe the German emperor, Roosevelt asserted that he had flattered him with the "sincerest felicitation" on his policy that had been "masterly from beginning to end." Yet to a friend Roosevelt boasted, "You will notice that while I was most suave and pleasant with the Emperor, . . . when it became necessary at the end I stood him on his head with great decision." As mentioned earlier, Roosevelt soon received the Nobel Peace Prize for his roles in the Algeciras and Portsmouth settlements.

Americans generally praised Roosevelt's efforts in the success of the Algeciras Conference, although they warned that the U.S. involvement did not signal a break with traditional isolationism from European political or military affairs. The Senate approved the pact in December 1906, but only after attaching an amendment reiterating opposition to Old World entanglements. A number of Americans insisted that their country's security was too much to risk for guaranteeing the sanctity of a North African state neither commercially nor strategically important to the United States. Yet Roosevelt's participation in the Algeciras proceedings constituted a warning to the Old World that the United States was prepared to make decisions affecting the balance of power outside the Western Hemisphere.

A Final Analysis

Theodore Roosevelt sought to promote the national interest by leading the United States in a new and more assertive style of foreign policy. In the Western Hemisphere, he worked to safeguard U.S. military and economic interests by building the Panama Canal and by claiming the right of intervention in Latin American affairs through the Roosevelt Corollary. Outside the hemisphere, he strengthened the Anglo-American rapprochement, mediated the Russo-Japanese War, facilitated a resolution of the Moroccan crisis at the Algeciras Conference, helped engineer a Second Peace Conference at The Hague in 1907, and enhanced the stature of the U.S. Navy by sending a fleet around the world. Not all his moves were popular. Three times he bypassed the Senate in negotiating treaties through controversial executive agreements, and critics would denounce his rough-riding arrogance toward those peoples who did not fit his definition of "civilized." And yet no one could deny that the president, for good or ill, had moved the United States into the same international arena occupied by imperial powers more accustomed to such status.

Roosevelt had demonstrated an understanding of the intricacies of balance-of-power relationships, both on the continent of Europe and in regard to the way European matters affected East Asia and hence the world power system. Americans remained reluctant to become involved in international politics, but Roosevelt had made great advances in shaping a national mood more receptive to major-power status. By the time he left the political scene, the United States had solidified its security in the Western Hemisphere and set the path toward a deepening involvement in international affairs.

Selected Readings

Anderson, Stuart. *Race and Rapprochement: Anglo-Saxonism and Anglo-American Relations, 1895–1904.* 1981.

Beale, Howard K. *Theodore Roosevelt and the Rise of America to World Power.* 1956.

Blum, John M. *The Republican Roosevelt.* 1954.

Brands, H. W. *T.R. The Last Romantic.* 1997.

Burton, David H. *Theodore Roosevelt: Confident Imperialist.* 1968.

Campbell, Alexander E. *Great Britain and the United States, 1895–1903.* 1960.

Campbell, Charles S. *Anglo-American Understanding, 1898–1903.* 1957.

Chessman, G. Wallace. *Theodore Roosevelt and the Politics of Power.* 1969.

Coletta, Paolo E. *The Presidency of William Howard Taft.* 1973.

Collin, Richard H. *Theodore Roosevelt, Culture, Diplomacy, and Expansion: A New View of American Imperialism.* 1985.

———. *Theodore Roosevelt's Caribbean: The Panama Canal, the Monroe Doctrine, and the Latin American Context.* 1990.

Conniff, Michael L. *Panama and the United States.* 1992.

Cooper, John M., Jr. *The Warrior and the Priest: Woodrow Wilson and Theodore Roosevelt.* 1983.

Daniels, Roger. *The Politics of Prejudice: The Anti-Japanese Movement in California and the Struggle for Japanese Exclusion.* 1962.

Davis, Calvin D. *The United States and the First Hague Peace Conference.* 1962.

———. *The United States and the Second Hague Peace Conference: American Diplomacy and International Organization, 1899–1914.* 1976.

Dennett, Tyler. *John Hay.* 1933.

Dyer, Thomas G. *Theodore Roosevelt and the Idea of Race.* 1980.

Esthus, Raymond A. *Double Eagle and Rising Sun: The Russians and Japanese at Portsmouth in 1905.* 1988.

———. *Theodore Roosevelt and Japan.* 1966.

———. *Theodore Roosevelt and the International Rivalries.* 1970.

Gould, Lewis L. *The Presidency of Theodore Roosevelt.* 1991.

Graham, Terence. *The "Interests of Civilization": Reaction in the United States against the Seizure of the Panama Canal Zone, 1903–1904.* 1983.

Griswold, A. Whitney. *The Far Eastern Policy of the United States.* 1938.

Harbaugh, William H. *The Life and Times of Theodore Roosevelt.* 1975 ed.

Hart, Robert A. *The Great White Fleet: Its Voyage around the World, 1907–1909.* 1965.

Healy, David F. *Drive to Hegemony: The United States in the Caribbean, 1898–1917.* 1988.

———. *The United States in Cuba, 1898–1902.* 1963.

Hogan, J. Michael. *The Panama Canal in American Politics.* 1986.

Hunt, Michael H. *The Making of a Special Relationship: The United States and China to 1914.* 1983.

Iriye, Akira. *Across the Pacific.* 1967.

———. *Pacific Estrangement: Japanese and American Expansion, 1897–1911.* 1972.

LaFeber, Walter. *The Clash: A History of U.S.-Japanese Relations.* 1997.

———. *Inevitable Revolutions: The United States in Central America.* 1993 ed.

———. *The Panama Canal: The Crisis in Historical Perspective.* 1989 ed.

Langley, Lester. *The Banana Wars: An Inner History of American Empire, 1900–1934.* 1983.

Leopold, Richard W. *Elihu Root and the Conservative Tradition.* 1954.

Major, John. "Who Wrote the Hay–Bunau-Varilla Convention?", *Diplomatic History* 8 (1984): 115–23.

Marks, Frederick W., III. "Morality as a Drive Wheel in the Diplomacy of Theodore Roosevelt," *Diplomatic History* 2 (1978): 43–62.

———. *Velvet on Iron: The Diplomacy of Theodore Roosevelt.* 1979.

McCullough, David G. *The Path Between the Seas: The Creation of the Panama Canal, 1870–1914.* 1977.

McKee, Delber L. *Chinese Exclusion versus the Open Door Policy, 1900–1906.* 1976.

Miller, Edward S. *War Plan Orange: The U.S. Strategy to Defeat Japan, 1897–1945.* 1991.

Millett, Allan R. *The Politics of Intervention: The Military Occupation of Cuba, 1906–1909.* 1968.

Miner, Dwight C. *The Fight for the Panama Route.* 1940.

Mitchell, Nancy. "The Height of the German Challenge: The Venezuela Blockade, 1902–3," *Diplomatic History* 20 (1996): 185–209.

Morris, Edmund. *Theodore Rex.* 2001.

Munro, Dana G. *Intervention and Dollar Diplomacy in the Caribbean, 1900–1921.* 1964.

Neu, Charles E. *An Uncertain Friendship: Theodore Roosevelt and Japan, 1906–1909.* 1967.

———. *The Troubled Encounter: The United States and Japan.* 1975.

Ninkovich, Frank. "Theodore Roosevelt: Civilization as Ideology," *Diplomatic History* 10 (1986): 221–45.

O'Brien, Thomas F. *The Revolutionary Mission: American Business in Latin America.* 1996.

Papachristou, Judith. "American Women and Foreign Policy, 1898–1905: Exploring Gender in Diplomatic History," *Diplomatic History* 14 (1990): 493–509.

Penlington, Norman. *The Alaska Boundary Dispute: A Critical Reappraisal.* 1973.

Pérez, Louis A., Jr. *Cuba and the United States.* 1997.

———. *Cuba under the Platt Amendment, 1902–1934.* 1986.

Perkins, Bradford. *The Great Rapprochement: England and the United States, 1895–1914.* 1968.

Perkins, Dexter. *The Monroe Doctrine, 1867–1907.* 1937.

Pratt, Julius W. *America's Colonial Experiment.* 1950.

———. *America and World Leadership, 1900–1921.* 1967. Originally published as *Challenge and Rejection.* 1967.

Pringle, Henry F. *Theodore Roosevelt.* 1931.

Randall, Stephen J. *Colombia and the United States: Hegemony and Interdependence.* 1992.

Scholes, Walter V., and Scholes, Marie V. *The Foreign Policies of the Taft Administration.* 1970.

Schoonover, Thomas. "Max Farrand's Memorandum on the U.S. Role in the Panamanian Revolution of 1903," *Diplomatic History* 12 (1988): 501–6.

———. *The United States in Central America, 1860–1911.* 1991.

———, and Langley, Lester D. *The Banana Men: American Mercenaries and Entrepreneurs in Central America, 1880–1930.* 1995.

Tilchin, William N. *Theodore Roosevelt and the British Empire.* 1997.

Tompkins, E. Berkeley. *Anti-Imperialism in the United States: The Great Debate, 1890–1920.* 1970.

Trani, Eugene P. *The Treaty of Portsmouth.* 1969.

Varg, Paul A. *The Making of a Myth: The United States and China, 1897–1912.* 1968.

Vevier, Charles. *The United States and China, 1906–1913.* 1955.

INDEX

Note: Page numbers in *italics* indicate illustrations. Page numbers followed by letter *m* indicate maps.